T0210582

Communications
in Computer and Information Science   1321

More information about this series at http://www.springer.com/series/7899

Zhanjun Hao · Xiaochao Dang ·
Honghong Chen · Fenfang Li (Eds.)

Wireless Sensor Networks

14th China Conference, CWSN 2020
Dunhuang, China, September 18–21, 2020
Revised Selected Papers

Springer

Editors
Zhanjun Hao
Computer Science
and Engineering Department
Northwest Normal University
Lanzhou, China

Xiaochao Dang
Computer Science
and Engineering Department
Northwest Normal University
Lanzhou, China

Honghong Chen
Computer Science
and Engineering Department
Northwest Normal University
Lanzhou, China

Fenfang Li
Computer Science
and Engineering Department
Northwest Normal University
Lanzhou, China

ISSN 1865-0929   ISSN 1865-0937 (electronic)
Communications in Computer and Information Science
ISBN 978-981-33-4213-2   ISBN 978-981-33-4214-9 (eBook)
https://doi.org/10.1007/978-981-33-4214-9

This Springer imprint is published by the registered company Springer Nature Singapore Pte Ltd.
The registered company address is: 152 Beach Road, #21-01/04 Gateway East, Singapore 189721, Singapore

Preface

The China Conference on Wireless Sensor Networks (CWSN) is the annual conference on Internet of Things (IoT) which is sponsored by the China Computer Federation (CCF). The 14th CWSN was took place in Dunhuang, China. As a leading conference in the field of IoT, CWSN is the premier forum for IoT researchers and practitioners from academia, industry, and government in China to share their ideas, research results, and experiences, which highly promotes research and technical innovation in these fields domestically and internationally.

The conference provided an academic exchange of research and a development forum for IoT researchers, developers, enterprises, and users. Exchanging results and experience of research and application on the IoT, and discussing the key challenges and research hotspots faced is the main goal of the forum. As a high-level forum for the design, implementation, and application of IoT, the conference promoted the exchange and application of theories and technologies of on IoT-related topics.

This year, CWSN received 185 submissions, including 85 English papers and 100 Chinese papers. After a careful two-way anonymous review, 20 revised and completed papers were selected. The high-quality program would not have been possible without the authors who chose CWSN 2020 as a venue for their publications. We are also very grateful to the members of the Program Committee and Organizing Committee, who put a tremendous amount of effort into soliciting and selecting research papers with a balance of high quality, new ideas, and new applications. We hope that you enjoy reading and benefit from the proceedings of CWSN 2020.

November 2020

Xiaochao Dang
Zhanjun Hao

Organization

Conference Chairs

HuaDong Ma   Director of CCF Internet of Things Special Committee, China

ZhongKui Liu   Northwest Normal University, China

HaiFeng Wang   Deputy Director of Gansu Provincial Department of Industry and Information Technology, China

Honorary Chair

Hao Dai   Chinese Academy of Engineering, China

Steering Committee Chair

JianZhong Li   Harbin Institute of Technology, China

Program Committee Chairs

LiMin Sun   Institute of Information Engineering, Chinese Academy of Sciences, China

XiaoChao Dang   Northwest Normal University, China

Program Committee Co-chairs

Liang Liu   Beijing University of Posts and Telecommunications, China

ZhanJun Hao   Northwest Normal University, China

XiangHong Lin   Northwest Normal University, China

ZhiChang Zhang   Northwest Normal University, China

Outstanding Paper Award Chair

Xue Wang   Tsinghua University, China

Enterprise Forum Chair

Li Cui   Institute of Computing Technology, Chinese Academy of Sciences, China

Outstanding Young Scholars Forum Chair

Zheng Yang   Tsinghua University, China

Organization Committee Chair

XinBing Wang   Shanghai Jiao Tong University, China
ZhanJun Hao   Northwest Normal University, China

Organization Committee Co-chair

HaiMing Jin   Shanghai Jiao Tong University, China
XiangHong Lin   Northwest Normal University, China

Organization Committee

HuiFang Ma   Northwest Normal University, China
Yong Li   Northwest Normal University, China
GuiPing Niu   Northwest Normal University, China
GuoZhi Zhang   Northwest Normal University, China
HongHong Chen   Northwest Normal University, China
YanXing Liu   Northwest Normal University, China
WeiYi Wei   Northwest Normal University, China
FenFang Li   Northwest Normal University, China

Program Committee

GuangWei Bai   Nanjing Tech University, China
Ming Bao   Institute of Acoustics, Chinese Academy of Sciences,
                                 China
QingSong Cai   Beijing Technology and Business University, China
ShaoBin Cai   Huaqiao University, China
Bin Cao   Harbin Institute of Technology, China
DeZe Zeng   China University of Geosciences, China
FanZai Zeng   Hunan University, China
Hong Chen   Renmin University of China, China
Wei Chen   Beijing Jiaotong University, China
Xi Chen   State Grid Information & Telecommunication Co.,
                                 Ltd., China
Xu Chen   School of Data and Computer Science, SYSU, China
GuiHai Chen   Nanjing University, China
HaiMing Chen   Ningbo University, China
HongLong Chen   China University of Petroleum, China
JiaXing Chen   Hebei Normal University, China
LiangYin Chen   Sichuan University, China
XiaoJiang Chen   Northwestern University, China

ZhouFang Kuang	Central South University of Forestry and Technology, China
Chao Li	Institute of Computing Technology, Chinese Academy of Sciences, China
Fan Li	Beijing Institute of Technology, China
Feng Li	Shandong University, China
Jie Li	Northeastern University, China
Zhuo Li	Beijing Information Science and Technology University, China
DeYing Li	Renmin University of China, China
FangMin Li	Wuhan University of Technology, China
GuangHui Li	Jiangnan University, China
GuoRui Li	Northeastern University, China
HongWei Li	University of Electronic Science and Technology of China, China
JianQiang Li	Shenzhen University, China
JianBo Li	Qingdao University, China
JianZhong Li	Harbin Institute of Technology, China
JinBao Li	Heilongjiang University, China
MingLu Li	Shanghai Jiao Tong University, China
RenFa Li	Hunan University, China
XiangYang Li	University of Science and Technology of China, China
YanTao Li	Chongqing University, China
YanJun Li	Zhejiang University of Technology, China
ZheTao Li	Xiangtan University, China
Wei Liang	Shenyang Institute of Automation, Chinese Academy of Sciences, China
HongBin Liang	Southwest Jiaotong University, China
JiuZhen Liang	Changzhou University, China
Chi Liu	Beijing Institute of Technology, China
Kai Liu	Chongqing University, China
Liang Liu	Beijing University of Posts and Telecommunications, China
Min Liu	Institute of Computing Technology, Chinese Academy of Sciences, China
Peng Liu	Hangzhou Dianzi University, China
JiaJia Liu	Xidian University, China
XingCheng Liu	Sun Yat-sen University, China
ZhouZhou Liu	Xi'an Aeronautical University, China
Xiang Liu	Peking University, China
Juan Luo	Hunan University, China
ChengWen Luo	Shenzhen University, China
HanJiang Luo	Shandong University of Science and Technology, China
JunZhou Luo	Southeast University, China
ZiCheng Lv	The Chinese University of Hong Kong, China

Li Ma	North China University of Technology, China
HuaDong Ma	Beijing University of Posts and Telecommunications, China
LianBo Ma	Northeastern University, China
JianWei Niu	Beihang University, China
XiaoGuang Niu	Wuhan University, China
Hao Peng	Zhejiang Normal University, China
Jian Peng	Sichuan University, China
Li Peng	Jiangnan University, China
ShaoLiang Peng	National University of Defense Technology, China
XiaoHui Peng	Institute of Computing Technology, Chinese Academy of Sciences, China
YuanYuan Pu	Yunnan University, China
WangDong Qi	PLA University of Science and Technology, China
Kaiguo Qian	Kunming University, China
Tie Qiu	Tianjin University, China
JieFan Qiu	Zhejiang University of Technology, China
Ju Ren	Central South University, China
FengYuan Ren	Tsinghua University, China
ShiKai Shen	Kunming University, China
YiRan Shen	Harbin Engineering University, China
YuLong Shen	Xidian University, China
Jian Shu	Nanchang Hangkong University, China
XiaoXia Song	Shanxi Datong University, China
Geng Sun	Jilin University, China
LiJuan Sun	Nanjing University of Posts and Telecommunications, China
LiMin Sun	Institute of Information Engineering, Chinese Academy of Sciences, China
HaiSheng Tan	University of Science and Technology of China, China
Dan Tao	Beijing Jiaotong University, China
Ming Tao	Dongguan University of Technology, China
Ye Tian	Computer Network Information Center, China
XiaoHua Tian	Shanghai Jiao Tong University, China
ShaoHua Wan	Zhongnan University of Economics and Law, China
Yang Wang	University of Science and Technology of China, China
Jin Wang	Changsha University of Science & Technology, China
Kun Wang	Nanjing University of Posts and Telecommunications, China
Lei Wang	Dalian University of Technology, China
Ping Wang	Chongqing University of Posts and Telecommunications, China
Tian Wang	Huaqiao University, China
Xue Wang	Tsinghua University, China
Zhi Wang	Zhejiang University, China
Zhu Wang	Harbin Institute of Technology, China

LiangMin Wang	Jiangsu University, China
QingShan Wang	Hefei University of Technology, China
RuChuan Wang	Nanjing University of Posts and Telecommunications, China
XiaoMing Wang	Shaanxi Normal University, China
XiaoDong Wang	National University of Defense Technology, China
XiaoLiang Wang	Hunan University of Science and Technology, China
XinBing Wang	Shanghai Jiao Tong University, China
YiDing Wang	North China University of Technology, China
YueXuan Wang	Tsinghua University, China
ZhiBo Wang	Wuhan University, China
Wei Wei	Xi'an University of Technology, China
LianSuo Wei	Qiqihar University, China
Hui Wen	Institute of Information Engineering, Chinese Academy of Sciences, China
ZhongMing Weng	Tianjin University, China
XingJun Wu	Beijing Tsinghua Tongfang Microelectronics Co., Ltd., China
HeJun Wu	Sun Yat-sen University, China
XiaoJun Wu	Shaanxi Normal University, China
ChaoCan Xiang	PLA Army Service Academy, China
Fu Xiao	Nanjing University of Posts and Telecommunications, China
Liang Xiao	Xiamen University, China
Ling Xiao	Hunan University, China
DeQin Xiao	South China Agricultural University, China
Kun Xie	Hunan University, China
Lei Xie	Nanjing University, China
ManDe Xie	Zhejiang Gongshang University, China
XiaoLan Xie	Guilin University of Technology, China
YongPing Xiong	Beijing University of Posts and Telecommunications, China
Jia Xu	Nanjing University of Posts and Telecommunications, China
ChenRen Xu	Peking University, China
GuangTao Xue	Shanghai Jiao Tong University, China
Zhan Huan	Changzhou University, China
Geng Yang	Nanjing University of Posts and Telecommunications, China
Zheng Yang	Tsinghua University, China
GuiSong Yang	University of Shanghai for Science and Technology, China
WeiDong Yang	Henan University of Technology, China
WeiDong Yi	University of Chinese Academy of Sciences, China
ZuWei Yin	Information Engineering University, China
Wei Yu	Rizhao Hi-Tech Industrial Development Zone, China

RuiYun Yu	Northeastern University, China
JiGuo Yu	Qufu Normal University, China
PeiYan Yuan	Henan Normal University, China
Ju Zhang	Information Engineering University, China
Lei Zhang	Tianjin University, China
LiChen Zhang	Shaanxi Normal University, China
LianMing Zhang	Hunan Normal University, China
ShiGeng Zhang	Central South University, China
ShuQin Zhang	Zhongyuan University of Technology, China
YanYong Zhang	University of Science and Technology of China, China
YunZhou Zhang	Northeastern University, China
JuMin Zhao	Taiyuan University of Technology, China
JunHui Zhao	East China Jiaotong University, China
ZengHua Zhao	Tianjin University, China
JiPing Zheng	Nanjing University of Aeronautics and Astronautics, China
Ping Zhong	Central South University, China
Huan Zhou	China Three Gorges University, China
AnFu Zhou	Beijing University of Posts and Telecommunications, China
RuiTing Zhou	Wuhan University, China
XiaoBo Zhou	Tianjin University, China
ChangBing Zhou	China University of Geosciences, China
HongZi Zhu	Shanghai Jiao Tong University, China
HongSong Zhu	Institute of Information Engineering, Chinese Academy of Sciences, China
PeiDong Zhu	Changsha University, China
YiHua Zhu	Zhejiang University of Technology, China
LieHuang Zhou	Beijing Institute of Technology, China
ShiHong Zou	Beijing University of Posts and Telecommunications, China

Organizers

Organized by

China Computer Federation, China

Hosted by

Northwest Normal University, China

Corporate Sponsors

Xiaomi Technology

Zhong Tian Yi Technology

Tridium Company

Lanzhou Qidu Data Technology

H3C Company

Alibaba Local Life

Contents

Internet of Things Security and Privacy Protection

Perception and Positioning

Wireless Sensor Network Theory and Technology

An Improved Topology Control Algorithm for Wireless Sensor Networks Based on Energy Saving

Baofeng Duan[1], Cuiran Li[1], Ling Yang[2(✉)], and Jianli Xie[1]

[1] School of Electronic and Information Engineering, Lanzhou Jiaotong University, Lanzhou 730070, China
[2] School of Information Science and Engineering, Lanzhou University, Lanzhou 730000, China
lingyang@lzu.edu.cn

Abstract. For wireless sensor networks (WSNs) with limited energy, topology control aiming at saving energy is a hot topic. Based on the research of developing a hierarchical topology control algorithm, we have proposed an improved algorithm, which is implemented by selecting cluster-head nodes, by dividing the cluster areas and by ensuring the communication stability. When selecting cluster-head nodes, the weight calculation is comprehensively considered by taking into consideration the remaining energy, the distance from base station (BS) and the connectivity of the nodes. When 100 sensor nodes are randomly deployed, the experimental results indicate that the numbers of cluster-head nodes with the lowest energy consumption during network cluster reconstruction are five and six respectively based on two different methods. The clustering process of the improved algorithm is more reasonable than that of the low energy adaptive clustering hierarchy (LEACH) algorithm. Furthermore, the proposed approach can still extend the network lifetime by 3.49% when the volume of data transmitted is increased by 10.59%.

Keywords: Wireless sensor networks · Clusters reconstruction · Survival nodes · Energy conservation

1 Introduction

Wireless sensor networks (WSNs) are essential components of the Internet of Things (IoT). The main purpose of studying topology control is to extend the lifetime of WSNs. The topology of a network considerably influences its overall performance, and thus, more attention should be paid to developing a topology control algorithm. From the perspective of network architecture, WSNs are simple and flexible [1]. Because of their low carrying capacity, low processing speed and small storage space of nodes, WSNs with low power consumption and low cost have been developed [2, 3]. They can acquire, process and transmit target information in the monitoring area. Due to the limitation of requiring a specific-application environment, sensor nodes powered by batteries cannot be supplemented after the energy is exhausted. Therefore, it has become an important

Z. Hao et al. (Eds.): CWSN 2020, CCIS 1321, pp. 3–15, 2020.
https://doi.org/10.1007/978-981-33-4214-9_1

research topic to utilize the optimized topology control algorithm to extend the network lifetime [4].

As for topology control algorithm, scholars have done some research. As suitable topology can boost the performance of a network, several protocols have been proposed to adjust the transmission ranges of sensor nodes [5–7], but there is no significant improvement in prolonging the network lifetime. In [8], a degree constrained minimum-weight version of the connected dominating set problem, seeking for the load-balanced network topology with the maximum energy, is presented to model the energy efficient topology control problem in WSNs. However, this method can only achieve better performance when the density of sensor nodes is large and the overlapping coverage area is wide. The reliable topology control in WSNs has been studied in [9], whose authors proposed an evolutionary multi-objective-based protocol with the goal of maximizing energy efficiency and probabilistic reliability of a WSN, but the impact of varying sink location and applying another communication model has not been analysed. In [10], authors transformed topology control into a model of multi-criteria degree constrained minimum spanning tree and designed a non-dominated discrete particle swarm optimization to deal with this problem, but the simplicity and convergence efficiency need to be further improved. Lu et al. have developed the simulation environment to examine various aspects of WSNs [11]. LEACH [12] is the most classical method towards cluster-based routing. In the setup phase, cluster-head nodes are selected using a dynamic, distributed and randomized algorithm. Provided the random number of the node is less than the threshold by the algorithm, it will become the cluster-head. Although the network is stratified quickly, the generation of cluster-head nodes is a random process. This leads to the following negative factors. If there are too many cluster-head nodes, the network will consume more energy to aggregate data; if the selected cluster-head node has less energy, there is a risk that it cannot complete the monitoring task of its cluster area; some nodes remote from base station (BS) are randomly selected as cluster-head, and the monitoring efficiency of the whole network will be reduced instead; nodes with more neighbours have no greater chance of being selected as cluster-head nodes than isolated nodes.

A novel improved algorithm is proposed to make the distribution of cluster-head nodes even and to realize the stability of communication. The performance of the network needs to be improved to achieve the purpose of extending the network lifetime. As the experimental results show, the improved topology control algorithm for WSNs has more living nodes, consumes less energy and receives more effective data. The rest of this paper is organized as follows. In Sect. 2, the structure of WSNs topology control is presented and the energy consumption of each component module is obtained through the measured data. Section 3 elaborates the improved algorithm of topology control. The experimental results are presented to verify the effectiveness of the proposed algorithm in Sect. 4. Finally, Sect. 5 summarizes the whole article.

2   Structure of Topology Control of WSNs

A schematic diagram of the BS and the monitoring area is shown in Fig. 1. Sensor nodes within the data source scope of the monitoring targets send the collected information to BS through the transmission path formed by topology control. Through the Internet, remote users can complete the monitoring tasks in real time on the visual interface. The purpose of network design is to collect information through sensor nodes scattered in the monitoring area, and then selectively remove and fuse the data according to the monitoring tasks to provide users with the data. BS powered by electricity has a relatively robust capability of processing, storage and communication.

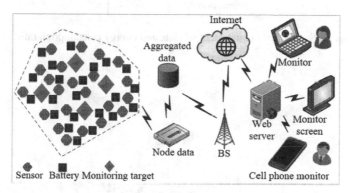

Fig. 1. Architecture of WSNs.

As shown in Fig. 2, the processor module is responsible for controlling the operation of the entire sensor node, storing and processing the data collected by itself and the data sent by other nodes. The wireless communication module, which takes the most energy, is responsible for wirelessly communicating with other sensor nodes. The sensor module consumes the least amount of energy. Since the energy consumed by each module is not equal in the same time, the energy distribution can be coordinated uniformly in topology control design so that the network can achieve the purpose of energy saving. Finally, the survival time of the network can be extended.

The two-layer structure of topology control simplifies the routing of WSNs. As shown in Fig. 3, if the network is not hierarchical, the shortest transmission path for node 16 to complete communication with node 2 is 16-13-12-9-3-1-2, with a total of 6 hops. In the case of network stratification, the shortest path of this communication is 16-13-5-1-2, which requires a total of 4 hops.

3   Improved Topology Control Algorithm

3.1   Analysis of Energy Consumption

A simple communication system consists of transmitting circuit, amplifying circuit and receiving circuit. The energy consumption by sending k bit and distance d is

$$E_{Tx}(k, d) = E_{Tx-elec}(k) + \varepsilon(k, d) = \begin{cases} k \times E_{elec} + k \times \varepsilon_{fs} \times d^2 & d < d_0 \\ k \times E_{elec} + k \times \varepsilon_{amp} \times d^4 & d \geq d_0 \end{cases} \quad (1)$$

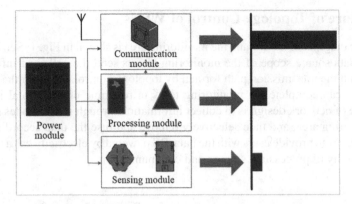

Fig. 2. Sensor node component module and energy consumption ratio.

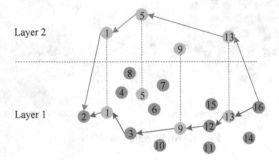

Fig. 3. Two-layer structure of topological control.

Where, d_0 represents the critical distance. Accordingly, the energy consumption of receiving this message is

$$E_{Rx}(k, d) = E_{Rx-elec}(k) = k \times E_{elec} \qquad (2)$$

The relationship between wireless communication energy consumption and distance is

$$E = \eta d^n \qquad (3)$$

Where, η represents the coefficient of energy consumption, and n represents the loss index of communication path, $2 \leq n \leq 4$. When $d < d_0$, it is the free-space channel model, $n = 2$, and amplifier coefficient is ε_{fs}; when $d \geq d_0$, it is the multipath fading channel model, $n = 4$, and amplifier coefficient is ε_{amp}. In the two channel models, the parameters of wireless communication are shown in Table 1. The value of average energy consumption (AEC) is obtained from a large amount of test data of sensor terminals.

Table 1. Parameters of wireless communication.

Parameters	AEC
$E_{Tx\text{-}elec}$	50 nJ/bit
$E_{Rx\text{-}elec}$	50 nJ/bit
E_{elec}	50 nJ/bit
ε_{fs}	10 pJ/bit/m^2
ε_{amp}	0.0013 pJ/bit/m^4

3.2 Algorithm Designs

In a monitoring area there is only one BS, which is installed in a fixed position. Each node in the network has the same physical properties, carries the same energy, and its communication radius is r. Sensor nodes with different transmitting power can be selected according to the density of objects monitored in the monitoring area. Assume the following conditions:

(1) The communication between sensor nodes is symmetric, that is, if node i can receive the message sent by node j, then node j can also receive the message sent by node i;

(2) To complete the communication task with distance d, the average routing is $d/0.75r$ hops.

The proof of condition (2) is as follows. In Fig. 4, the shortest distance of the two-hop route is $r + \Delta$, and the shortest distance of the triple hop route is $r + 2\Delta$, where, Δ is any small value. A to B can be extended to n to $n + 1$. The shortest distance between them is $n(r + \Delta)/2$. Similarly, the shortest of $n + 1$ hop is $n(r + \Delta)/2 + \Delta$, which has a limit of $nr/2$. The maximum distance of n tops is nr. Then, the average distance is $3nr/4$. Therefore, the communication between two sensor nodes with distance d goes through an average of two-hop.

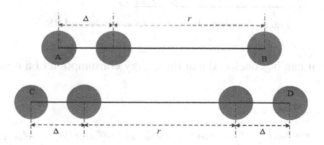

Fig. 4. Shortest route distance of two-hop and three-hop.

Cluster reconstruction energy consumption refers to the energy consumed by WSNs considering the number of nodes, the average distance between nodes and BS, the size of each packet sent by nodes and other factors in the process of re-dividing cluster area. As shown in Fig. 5, N nodes are randomly deployed in the $M \times M$ square monitoring area. In the process of dividing clusters, the monitoring area is divided into several clusters of equal area, and the number of nodes in each cluster is equal. Each cluster has one cluster-head node and $n/a - 1$ intra-cluster nodes. Since BS is at the edge of the monitoring area, or even outside the monitoring area, the communication between the cluster-head node and BS chooses the multi-path fading channel model, that is, the path loss index is 4. Assuming the energy consumed by a node to fuse packet of one bit is E_{DA}, it can be concluded that the energy consumed by one cluster-head node to complete the process of receiving, fusing and sending k bit packets to BS is

$$E_C = k \times \left[E_{elec} \left(\frac{N}{a} - 1 \right) + E_{DA} \frac{N}{a} + \left(E_{elec} + \varepsilon_{amp} d_{ave-BS}^4 \right) \right] \tag{4}$$

Where, d_{ave-BS} is the average distance between cluster-head nodes and BS. In one cluster area, the distance between the cluster-head node and the other nodes is relatively close, so the communication between them is a free-space channel model, that is, the path loss index is 2. The energy consumed by one cluster node sending k bit packet to the cluster-head node is

$$E_{non-C} = k \times \left(E_{elec} + \varepsilon_{fs} d_{ave-C}^2 \right) \tag{5}$$

Where, d_{ave-C} is the average distance between cluster-head nodes and the other nodes.

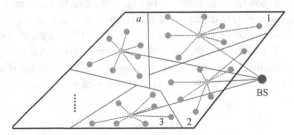

Fig. 5. Topology diagram of sensor nodes and BS.

To sum up, it can be concluded that the energy consumption of a round of cluster reconstruction is

$$E_{cycle} = aE_C + (N - a)E_{non-C}$$
$$= akE_{elec} \left(\frac{N}{a} - 1 \right) + kNE_{DA} + ak\varepsilon_{amp} d_{ave-BS}^4 + kNE_{elec} + k(N - a)\varepsilon_{fs} d_{ave-C}^2 \tag{6}$$

$N/a - 1$ can be approximated to N/a. Therefore, Eq. (6) is simplified to

$$E_{cycle} = 2kNE_{elec} + kNE_{DA} + ak\varepsilon_{amp} d_{ave-BS}^4 + k(N - a)\varepsilon_{fs} d_{ave-C}^2 \tag{7}$$

The value of a that is too large or too small will affect the lifetime of WSNs. When E_{cycel} reaches the minimum value, the value of a is the optimal number of cluster-head nodes. In the case of cluster head nodes selection, the residual energy, distance from BS and connectivity of nodes are considered based on weight calculation. Each sensor node i for becoming cluster-head node is assigned a weight to measure its fitness, which is represented as

$$W_i = p \times \left(\frac{E_i^f}{\overline{E^f}} \right) + \frac{1-p}{2} \times \frac{d_{\max} - d_{BS}^i}{d_{\max} - \overline{d_{ave-BS}}} + \frac{1-p}{2} \times \frac{C_i}{N/k} \tag{8}$$

Where,E_i^f is the residual energy of node i in the round f of cluster reconstruction. $\overline{E^f}$ represents the average residual energy of all nodes in the sensor network at round f, and $d_{\max}$ is the maximum distance of nodes to BS. The distance from the node i to BS is d_{BS}^i, and $\overline{d_{ave-BS}}$ refers to the average distance of all sensor network nodes to BS. C_i is the connectivity of the nodes, that is, the number of neighbours. The weighting factor is p, which is increasing in range $[1/3, 1/2]$. As for the value of p, it is mainly considered that the residual energy of nodes gradually decreases with the extension of working time of WSNs, so the weight of residual energy is gradually enhanced when choosing cluster-head nodes. Accordingly, the weight of the distance from the node to BS and the connectivity of the node is gradually reduced. Based on W_i from high to low, optimal a are selected as cluster-head nodes, which broadcast the "join cluster" message separately. And the non-cluster-head nodes receiving the message only feeds back the "request join cluster" message to the first node of "join cluster" message. In this way, cluster division is completed. The specific process of energy saving topology control algorithm is shown in Table 2.

4 Experimental Results and Analysis

4.1 Experimental Environments and Parameters

With the simulation platform (NS2), 100 sensor nodes are randomly deployed in the 100 m × 100 m monitoring area, as shown in Fig. 6. Each packet k sent or received is 2000 bit. The energy consumption of data packet fusion of one bit is 5 pJ. Each sensor node carries energy of 2 J during network initialization. When either of the following conditions is reached, the experiment is over.

4.2 Optimal Number of Cluster-Head Nodes

The positions of sensor nodes and BS in the monitoring area with length and width M respectively are shown in Fig. 7. Too few or too many cluster-head nodes are the disadvantageous factors to save the energy consumption and prolong the lifetime of the network. The relationship between the optimal number of cluster-head nodes and the energy consumption of cluster reconstruction can be obtained by calculating the value of E_{cycel}. According to Eq. (7), values of d_{ave-BS} and d_{ave-C} must be known to calculate the energy consumption of cluster reconstruction. It is assumed that the position of any node is (x, y). The expression of d_{ave-BS}^4 is as

Table 2. Algorithm process.

Input: BS broadcasts the message of "campaign cluster head" to all sensor nodes in the monitoring area.

Process:
1: All sensor nodes have received broadcast message;
2:   for $i=1,2,...,m$ do;
3:     if $E_i^f \geq E^f$ then;
4:       Sensor nodes reply the message of "to run for cluster-head nodes";
5:       Sensor nodes replying this message perform a weight calculation;
6:       W_i from high to low count optimal a;
7:       if the sensor node is the cluster-head node **then**;
8:         Broadcast "join cluster" message;
9:       **else**;
10:        Receive "join cluster" the message;
11:        Feedback "request to join cluster" to the first one;
12:      **end if**;
13:    **else**;
14:    **Repeat** 10-13
15:    **end if**;
16: **end for**;
Output: Cluster division and the stage of communication stabilization.

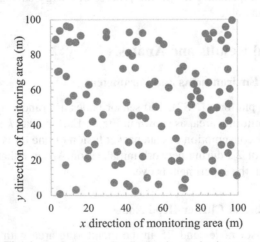

Fig. 6. Sensor nodes distribution in monitoring area.

$$d_{ave-BS}^4 = \left(\frac{\iint (x^2 + y^2)\rho dxdy}{a} \right)^2 = \left(\frac{1}{M^2} \int_0^M \int_0^M (x^2 + y^2)dxdy \right)^2$$

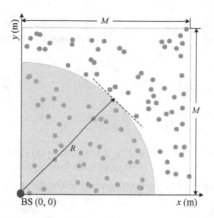

Fig. 7. Average distance from sensors node to BS

$$= \left(\frac{1}{M^2}\int_0^M\left[\int_0^M (x^2+y^2)dy\right]dx\right)^2 = \left(\frac{1}{M^2}\int_0^M\left(Mx^2 + \frac{M^3}{3}\right)dx\right)^2 = \frac{4M^4}{9} \quad (9)$$

There is an easier way to calculate the value of d_{ave-BS}^4. Taking the coordinate $(0, 0)$ as the center of the circle and R as the radius to draw a circle, forming a sector with the area of $M^2/2$ in the monitoring area. The expression is as

$$d_{ave-BS}^4 \approx R^4 = \frac{4M^4}{\pi^2} \quad (10)$$

The square of the average distance from nodes to cluster-head nodes is

$$d_{ave-C}^2 = \iint (x^2+y^2)\rho dxdy = \iint r^2\rho(r,\theta)drd\theta \quad (11)$$

Since the area of clusters is divided by equal area, the area of each cluster in the monitoring area is M^2/a. If each cluster area is approximated as a circle, its radius

$$r = \frac{M}{\sqrt{\pi a}} \quad (12)$$

At this point, Eq. (11) can be reduced to

$$d_{ave-C}^2 = \rho \int_{\theta=0}^{2\pi} \int_{r=0}^{\frac{M}{\sqrt{\pi a}}} r^3 drd\theta = \frac{\rho M^4}{2\pi a^2} = \frac{M^2}{2\pi a} \quad (13)$$

In a WSN with 100 nodes, the numbers of cluster-head nodes with the lowest energy consumption during network cluster reconstruction are five and six respectively based on Eqs. (9) and (10). With the increase of cluster-head nodes, the energy consumption of cluster reconstruction decreases first and then increases as shown in Fig. 8.

The comparison of cluster partition between the improved algorithm and LEACH algorithm is shown in Fig. 9. The number of cluster-head nodes is 5 and 6 respectively, and the result of cluster division is the topological structure formed after the first round of

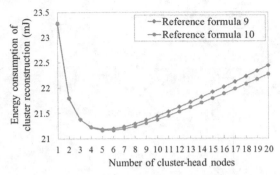

Fig. 8. Relationship between the energy consumption of cluster reconstruction and the number of cluster-head nodes

cluster reconstruction. Obviously, the LEACH algorithm does not divide cluster region as reasonably as the proposed algorithm. The reason for the uneven distribution of cluster regions is that LEACH algorithm randomly selects cluster head nodes. The improved algorithm takes into consideration other factors, such as residual energy and connectivity of nodes.

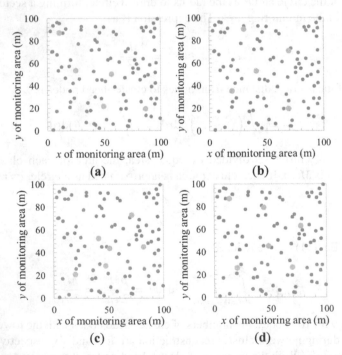

Fig. 9. Comparison of cluster-head nodes distribution in monitoring area: (a) LEACH algorithm with five cluster-head nodes; (b) Improved algorithm with five cluster-head nodes; (c) LEACH algorithm with six cluster-head nodes; (d) Improved algorithm with six cluster-head nodes.

The curve of the number of surviving nodes of the improved algorithm and LEACH algorithm over time is shown in Fig. 10. When it is five cluster-head nodes, the improved algorithm increased the network survival time from 890 s to 900 s. When it is six cluster-head nodes, the improved algorithm increases network survival time from 860 s to 890 s. The time of death node appears in the improved algorithm is tens of seconds earlier than the traditional algorithm. In each round of cluster reconstruction, because sensor nodes send information such as residual energy and connectivity to cluster-head nodes, so they consume more energy than LEACH algorithm, which randomly generates cluster-head nodes in the initial stage.

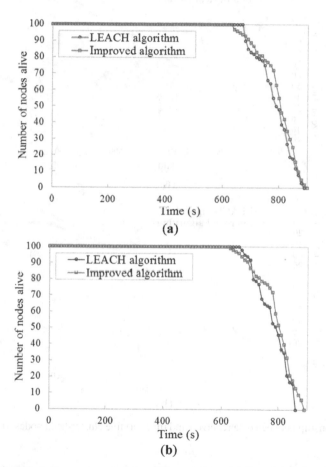

Fig. 10. Relationship between sensor nodes alive and time. (a) five cluster-head nodes; (b) six cluster-head nodes.

The curve of the size of data received of the improved algorithm and LEACH algorithm over time is shown in Fig. 11. When it is five cluster-head nodes, the improved algorithm increased network data received from 132 kbit to 144 kbit. When it is six cluster-head nodes, the improved algorithm increased network data received from 128 kbit to

142 kbit. The above two experimental results show that the improved algorithm not only receives more data than LEACH algorithm, but also extend the lifetime of WSNs. The main reason is that the cluster-head nodes selected in each round have the characteristics of higher residual energy, shorter distance and greater connectivity. Different number of cluster-head nodes results in different cluster division structure, which also affects the lifetime of WSNs and the efficiency of data transmission.

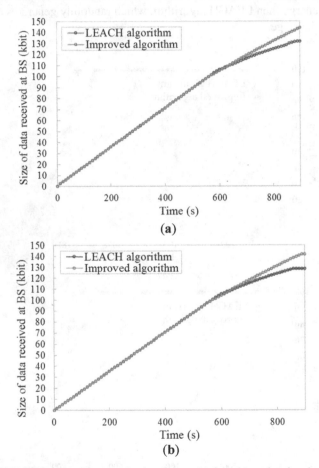

Fig. 11. Relationship between data received and time. (a) five cluster-head nodes; (b) six cluster-head nodes.

5   Discussion

This paper systematically studies and summarizes the existing topology control algorithms, and proposes an improved topology control algorithm. By selecting cluster head nodes, dividing the cluster area, improving the communication stability, and improving the algorithm, the cluster-head nodes have the characteristics of high residual energy, short distance, and high connectivity. Simulation results show that the algorithm is superior to LEACH algorithm and can extend the lifetime of WSNs.

Although the improved algorithm is implemented theoretically and simulated, how to extend the network survival time maximized by remedial measures after partial nodes failure is still the direction of future research. With the development of sensor technology, topology control algorithm still has more room for optimization because sensor nodes will have higher communication efficiency, faster calculation rate and more powerful capacity of energy storage.

References

1. Wang, X., Zhang, H., Fan, S., Gu, H.: Coverage control of sensor networks in IoT based on RPSO. IEEE Internet Things J. **5**(5), 3521–3532 (2018)
2. Soni, V., Mallick, D.K.: Fuzzy logic based multihop topology control routing protocol in wireless sensor networks. Microsyst. Technol. **24**(5), 2357–2369 (2018)
3. Wei, W., Xia, X., Wozniak, M., Fan, X., Damaševičius, R., Li, Y.: Multi-sink distributed power control algorithm for cyber-physical-systems in coal mine tunnels. Comput. Netw. **161**, 210–219 (2019)
4. Samanta, A., Misra, S.: Energy-efficient and distributed network management cost minimization in opportunistic wireless body area networks. IEEE Trans. Mob. Comput. **17**(2), 376–389 (2018)
5. Zhang, X., Zhang, Y., Yan, F., Vasilakos, A.: Interference-based topology control algorithm for delay-constrained mobile ad hoc networks. IEEE Trans. Mob. Comput. **14**(4), 742–754 (2015)
6. Lin, S., et al.: ATPC: adaptive transmission power control for wireless sensor networks. ACM Trans. Sens. Netw. **12**(1), 1–31 (2016)
7. Li, M., Li, Z., Yu, Y., Vasilakos, A.: A survey on topology control in wireless sensor networks: taxonomy, comparative study, and open issues. Proc. IEEE **101**(12), 2538–2557 (2013)
8. Torkestani, J.: An energy-efficient topology construction algorithm for wireless sensor networks. Comput. Netw. **57**(7), 1714–1725 (2013)
9. Khalil, E., Ozdemir, S.: Reliable and energy efficient topology control in probabilistic wireless sensor networks via multi-objective optimization. J. Supercomput. **73**(6), 2632–2656 (2017)
10. Guo, W., Zhang, B., Chen, G., Wang, X., Xiong, N.: A PSO-optimized minimum spanning tree-based topology control scheme for wireless sensor networks. Int. J. Distrib. Sens. Netw. **2013**, 1–14 (2013)
11. Lu, T., Liu, G., Chang, S.: Energy-efficient data sensing and routing in unreliable energy-harvesting wireless sensor network. Wirel. Netw. **24**(2), 611–625 (2016)
12. Heinzelman, W.B., Chandrakasan, A.P., Balakrishnan, H.: An application-specific protocol architecture for wireless microsensor networks. IEEE Trans. Wirel. Commun. **1**(4), 660–670 (2002)

Research on Efficient Data Collection Strategy of Wireless Sensor Network

Gaocun Lv[1], Hui Wang[1(✉)], Yuchen Shan[1], and Lingguo Zeng[2]

[1] School of Mathematics and Computer Science, Zhejiang Normal University,
Jinhua 321004, China
hwang@zjnu.cn
[2] College of Physics and Electronic Information Engineering, Zhejiang Normal University,
Jinhua 321004, China

Abstract. Recently, compressed sensing (CS) has been widely studied to collect data in wireless sensor network (WSN), which usually adopts greedy algorithm or convex optimization method to reconstruct the original signal, but noise and data packet loss are not considered in the compressed sensing (CS) model. Therefore, this paper proposes an efficient data collection strategy based on Bayesian compressed sensing (BCS-DCS) to improve the performance of data acquisition performance and network lifetime. Firstly, adopt a random packet loss matrix to update the compressed sensing (CS) model and employ Bayesian method to reconstruct the original signal. Then, according to the covariance of the reconstructed signal and the energy constraint of the sensor nodes, construct the active node selection optimization framework to optimize the node selection matrix quickly and effectively. Simulation results show that the efficient data collection strategy based on Bayesian compressed sensing (BCS-DCS) proposed in this paper can improve the signal acquisition performance and lifetime of wireless sensor network (WSN).

Keywords: Wireless sensor network · Bayesian compressed sensing · Node selection optimization

1 Introduction

In recent years, with the rapid development of computing, sensing, communication, storage and other technologies, and sensors have the advantages of small size, low energy consumption, and low cost. The WSN has been applied in many fields, such as electrical automation [1], monitoring technology [2], positioning technology [3] and so on. Since the communication in WSN needs a lot of storage space and much energy consumption [4], and sensors have very limited calculation, power and storage capacity, so how to reduce the storage space and energy consumption in the transmission has become a popular research in the WSN.

Foundation Item: Natural Science Foundation of Zhejiang Province, China (No. LY16F020005).

Z. Hao et al. (Eds.): CWSN 2020, CCIS 1321, pp. 16–27, 2020.
https://doi.org/10.1007/978-981-33-4214-9_2

Compressed sensing (CS) technology can sample the signal randomly and obtain the discrete sampling when the sampling rate is far less than Nyquist, and then reconstruct the original signal perfectly through the nonlinear reconstruction algorithm [5, 6]. The most important direction of CS is the study of recovery algorithms. Traditional signal reconstruction methods are generally divided into two categories, one is convex optimization algorithms, such as: Basis Pursuit (BP) [7], Gradient Projection for Sparse Reconstruction (GPSR) [8] and so on; the other is greedy algorithms, such as : Orthogonal Matching Pursuit Algorithm (OMP) [9], Compressive Sampling Matching Pursuit (CoSaMP) [10], Sparsity Adaptive Matching Pursuit (SAMP) [11] and so on. However, traditional restoration methods do not consider the situation that the observation signal contains noise, which usually happens in the actual data collection process of WSN. The Bayesian method [12] has the function of noise reduction, and the computing speed is relatively fast, so it is a good idea to use Bayesian method to restore original signal in compressed sensing. Because most of the data collected by large-scale WSNs are sparse, only need some active nodes in the WSNs can complete to collect the data and save the communication resources of WSNs, such as researches of the compressed sleep strategy [13, 14].

Therefore, this paper designs an efficient data collection strategy based on Bayesian compressed sensing (BCS-DCS) to improve recovery performance and prolong the lifetime of the network. The main research work of this paper is as follows:

1) Update the CS model and construct the original signal. Considering the possibility of packet loss in the WSNs communication, it designs a random packet loss parameter matrix to update the CS model, and adopts Bayesian method to recover the original signal.
2) Optimize the node selection. According to the original signal recovery information and the energy limitation of sensor nodes, construct the active node selection optimization framework to optimize the node selection matrix.
3) Simulation results show that the BCS-DCS can improve the signal acquisition performance and network lifetime of WSN.

2 Background and System Model

2.1 Background

In the WSN, different from the traditional signal processing method, the CS combines the transmission and compression of the original signal, which can reduce data consumption in communication, as shown in Fig. 1.

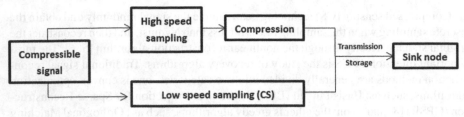

Fig. 1. WSN signal processing

The basic model of compressed sensing is as follows:

$$y = \Phi x = \Phi \Psi s = \Theta s \tag{1}$$

Where $\Phi \in R^{M \times N} (M \ll N)$ is the perception matrix, $x \in R^N$ is the original signal, and $y \in R^M$ is the measurement signal. Assume the original signal can be sparse, $\Psi = [\psi_1, \ldots, \psi_N] \in R^{N \times N}$ is the sparse basis matrix and $s \in R^N$ is the sparse signal. Update the perception matrix to Θ and the matrix must satisfy the RIP condition of order K, as follows:

$$(1 - \varepsilon)\|s\|_2 \leq \Theta \|s\|_2 \leq (1 + \varepsilon)\|s\|_2 \tag{2}$$

Where $\varepsilon \in (0, 1)$ is a constant and $\forall \|s\|_0 \leq K$. However, to recover K sparse signal, it is necessary to satisfy the 2 K order RIP conditions to ensure the uniqueness of the mapping. The sampling principle of the CS is shown in Fig. 2.

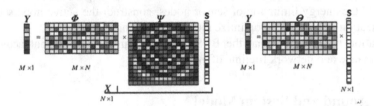

Fig. 2. CS sampling principle

2.2 System Model

The WSN architecture considered in this paper is composed of N sensor nodes (SNs) and a sink node. Suppose that the WSN is a single-hop transmission network, that is, each sensor node directly transmits its collected data to the sink node, as shown in Fig. 3. The data collected by all sensor nodes is expressed as $x \in R^N$, where $x_i \in x$ represents the data collected by the i-th sensor node.

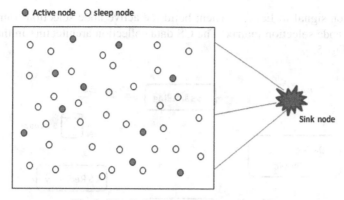

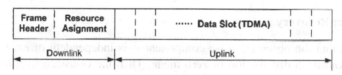

Fig. 3. Single-hope transmission network

Due to the limitation of energy, the collected data by many nodes has potential relevance, so only need some active nodes to complete the data collection in the WSN. To support this CS-based solution, we consider the usage of a time division multiplexing access (TDMA) transmission as shown in Fig. 4.

Fig. 4. Frame structure

The sink node controls the SNs to be activated to collect and transmit data, and coordinates the channel access between these active nodes through the downlink. The data of active nodes are transmitted to the sink node via uplink. By using such MAC protocol, a collision-free operation can be realized, so the energy wasted due to conflict can be eliminated. In addition, the node can be shut down in the unallocated time slot, to save the energy consumption caused by idle detection and monitoring.

Data packet loss often occurs when WSN transmits data, and the data collected by sensor nodes is also interfered by noise. Therefore, it is necessary to update the compressed sensing model as follows:

$$y = \Phi F \Psi s + v = \Theta s + v \tag{3}$$

Where $F \in R^{N \times N}$ is a random packet loss parameter matrix, $v \in R^M$ is the observation noise, and $\Phi \in R^{M \times N}$ is the node selection matrix. In each row of the Φ, there is one element is 1, which means only one node is active, and all other elements are 0, which means other sensor nodes are in a sleep state. It is assumed that the sink node knows the node selection matrix Φ, the packet loss parameter matrix F and the sparse basic matrix Ψ, and can control the operation of the sensor node through some control signal commands. The first goal is to accurately reconstruct the original signal from the observation signal in Eq. (3). Then, build the active node selection framework to optimize the node selection matrix. The CS data collection architecture in the WSN is as shown in Fig. 5.

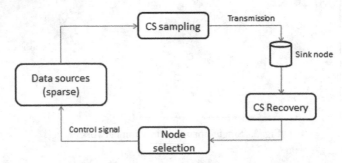

Fig. 5. CS data collection architecture in the WSN

3   Bayesian Recovery and Node Selection Optimization

3.1   Bayesian Recovery

It is assumed that the observed noise component v_i is independent of each other, and satisfies the Gaussian distribution of zero mean. Then the Gaussian likelihood model can be expressed as:

$$p(y|s, v) \sim N(\Theta s, V) \tag{4}$$

The goal is to find the rarest solution. If we directly maximize the likelihood model (4) to estimate the sparse signal s, it is likely to lead to model over learning. It can use a hierarchical prior model which has a conjugate prior with Gaussian likelihood to avoid such problems. It is assumed that the Gaussian conditional probability distribution of sparse signal subject to $s_i \sim N(0, \alpha_i^{-1})$ is expressed as

$$p(s|\alpha) \sim \prod_{i=1}^{N} N(s_i|a, b) \tag{5}$$

The hyper-parameter α determines the prior distribution of the sparse signal s. Since the inverse of Gaussian normal distribution is conjugate with gamma distribution, it is assumed that the hyper-prior probability distributions of α_i and $\sigma^2 (\beta = \sigma^{-2})$ are:

$$p(\alpha) = \prod_{i=1}^{N} \mathrm{Gamma}(\alpha_i|a, b)$$

$$p(\beta) = \mathrm{Gamma}(\beta|c, d)$$

Since there is no prior knowledge, suppose $a = b = c = d = 0$ obtains a consistent hyper-prior, so there is:

$$p(s_i) = \int N(s_i|0, \alpha_i^{-1})\text{Gamma}(s_i|a, b)ds_i \tag{6}$$

According to Bayesian inference, the posterior of the sparse signal s can be expressed as:

$$p(s|y, \alpha, \beta) = \frac{p(y|\alpha, \beta)p(s, \alpha, \beta)}{p(y|\alpha, \beta)} \tag{7}$$

According to (4) (5), the posterior distribution of the sparse signal s can be derived as follows:

$$p(s|y, \alpha, \beta) \sim N(\mu, \Sigma) \tag{8}$$

Where μ, Σ is the recovered mean and covariance of the sparse signal s:

$$\mu = \Sigma\Theta^T By \tag{9}$$

$$\Sigma = (\Theta^T B\Theta + A)^{-1} \tag{10}$$

$A = diag(\alpha_1, \ldots, \alpha_N)$, $B = diag(\beta_1, \ldots, \beta_N)$. In Bayesian inference, the denominator normalization term $p(y|\alpha, \beta)$ in Bayesian inference is called marginal likelihood, which can be written as:

$$p(y|\alpha, \beta) = \int p(y|s, \beta)p(s|\alpha)ds$$
$$= (2\pi)^M |H|^{-\frac{1}{2}} \exp\{-\frac{1}{2}y^T H^{-1}y\} \tag{11}$$

$H = B + \Theta A^{-1}\Theta^T$. Take the logarithm of (11) as follows:

$$\log p(y|\alpha, \beta) \sim M\log 2\pi + \log|H| + y^T H^{-1}y \tag{12}$$

According to Eq. (12), the updated estimation of the hyper-parameters can be obtained by deriving α_i, β and taking zero respectively, as follows:

$$\alpha_i^{new} = \frac{1}{\mu_i^2 + \Sigma_{ii}} \tag{13}$$

Let $\gamma_i = 1 - \alpha_i \Sigma_{ii}$ have a way to quickly update the hyper-parameters [15], as follows:

$$\left(\sigma^2\right)^{new} = \frac{y - \Theta\mu^2}{N - \Sigma_i \gamma_i} \tag{14}$$

3.2   Node Selection Optimization

In this section, considering the differences in the performance of sensor nodes, the quality of data collected by sensor nodes will be different, that is, each sensor node collects data with different noise interference. In order to further improve the recovery performance of Bayesian compressed sensing, establish an active node selection optimization framework, optimize the node selection matrix, and increase WSN lifetime. In order to understand the relationship between the selection criteria of active sensor nodes and the estimation error, it is assumed that the sink node provides perfect information about the hyper-parameters. Rewrite the mean and covariance in Eq. (9) (10) as follows:

$$\mu = \Sigma \Psi^T F^T \Phi^T V_F^{-1} \Phi^T y \tag{15}$$

$$\Sigma = (\Psi^T F^T \Phi^T \Phi V_F^{-1} \Phi^T \Phi F \Psi + A)^{-1}$$
$$= (\Psi^T F^T \tilde{\Phi}^T V_F^{-1} \tilde{\Phi} F \Psi + A)^{-1} \tag{16}$$

Where $\tilde{\Phi} = \Phi^T \Phi$, $\tilde{\Phi} \in R^{N \times N}, B = V^{-1}, V = \Phi V_F \Phi^T$ and V_F is the hyper-parametric matrix of all sensor nodes. The minimum covariance problem of Eq. (16) involves the inverse operation of the matrix. It can simplify the calculation by maximizing the inverse covariance of Eq. (18), as follows:

$$\max_{\hat{\Phi}} Tr(\Psi^T F^T \tilde{\Phi}^T V_F^{-1} \tilde{\Phi} F \Psi + A) \text{ s.t. } Tr(\tilde{\Phi}) = M \tag{17}$$

However, the optimization problem of Eq. (18) is an NP-hard problem. It can adopt the convex relaxation to reduce the computational complexity, as follows:

$$\max_{\tilde{\Phi}} Tr(\Psi^T F^T \tilde{\Phi}^T V_F^{-1} \tilde{\Phi} F \Psi + A) \text{ s.t. } 0 \leq \tilde{\Phi}_{i,i} \leq 1, i = 1, \ldots, N \ Tr(\tilde{\Phi}) = M \tag{18}$$

Integer to convex relaxation makes the problem easier to solve than the original integer program. By solving Eq. (18), we can select m largest $\tilde{\Phi}_{i,i}$ and associate the corresponding index with sensor nodes, that is, the nodes need to be activated. However, such an active node selection framework does not consider the energy constraint of the node itself. We need to integrate the energy constraint of the node into the active node selection framework to improve the lifetime of WSN.

4   Extend Network Lifetime

Consider the energy factor of the node itself and optimize the active node selection framework, so as to clearly solve the problem of extending network life, we proposed the following optimization problems:

$$\max_{\tilde{\Phi}} Tr(\Psi^T F^T \tilde{\Phi}^T V_F^{-1} \tilde{\Phi} F \Psi + A) + \kappa Tr(\tilde{\Phi} H)$$
$$\text{s.t. } 0 \leq \tilde{\Phi}_{i,i} \leq 1, i = 1, \ldots, N \tag{19}$$
$$Tr(\tilde{\Phi}) = M$$

Where κ is the balance factor, $H \in R^{N \times N}$ is a diagonal matrix and the penalty item $Tr(\tilde{\Phi} H)$ reflects the total energy consumed by the selected sensor node by setting $H_{i,i}$.

Inspired by Chen's study of the average network lifetime [16], the penalty $H_{i,i}$ set as follows:

$$H_{i,i} = -\frac{\varepsilon_i}{\xi_i} \tag{20}$$

Where ε_i is the storage of energy in the i-th sensor node and ξ_i is the required energy of message transmission in the i-th sensor node. This penalty term is combined with the node selection framework of Eq. (18), which aims to extend the life of the network by avoiding excessive usage of any particular sensor node.

Compare the node selection scheme proposed in this paper with the distributed random node selection scheme. Set some parameters as follows: E^c is the level of continuous energy consumption required to maintain the network in sleep mode without collecting data, E^e is the energy associated with a radio-electronic device, $\bar{E}_{\delta_1}$ is the energy consumption rate that realizes the target signal strength in unit distance between the transmission of the sink node and sensor nodes, $\hat{r}$ is the distance between the sink node and all sensor nodes, γ represents the path loss exponent. Assume the length of each sensing data packet to be δ_1 bits and the overhead to be δ_2 bits. The energy consumption of activity nodes and sleep nodes in the proposed scheme are shown as follows:

$$\begin{cases} E^a(\delta_1 + \delta_2) + \bar{E}_{\delta_1}\delta_1 r^\gamma & \text{active node} \\ E^e + E^c\delta_2 & \text{sleep node} \end{cases} \tag{21}$$

The energy consumption of activation nodes and sleep nodes in the distributed random scheme are shown as follows:

$$\begin{cases} E^e\delta_2 + \bar{E}_{\delta_1}\delta_1\hat{r}^\gamma & \text{active node} \\ E^c & \text{sleep node} \end{cases} \tag{22}$$

It is assumed that p nodes need to be activated in the proposed scheme, and q nodes need to be activated in the distributed random scheme, and downlink and uplink use the same modulation scheme. The energy consumption ratio of the proposed scheme compared with the random scheme can be expressed as:

$$ratio = \frac{p(E^e(\delta_1 + \delta_2) + \bar{E}_{\delta_1}\delta_1\hat{r}^\gamma) + (n - p)(E^e + E^c\delta_2)}{q(E^e\delta_2 + \bar{E}_{\delta_1}\delta_1\hat{r}^\gamma) + (n - q)E^c} \tag{23}$$

According to (23), compare the energy consumption performance of the proposed approach with the distributed random scheme, as shown in Fig. 6. When the node activation rate of the two schemes is 30%, the energy consumption ratio is approximately 1. However, the scheme proposed in this paper can further improve the reconstruction performance of compressed sensing, and it can extend the network lifetime when the node activation rate of the proposed scheme is less than 30%.

5   Simulation Analysis

In order to verify the effectiveness of the data collection strategy (CBS-DCS) based on Bayesian compressed sensing proposed in this paper, build a simulation environment on

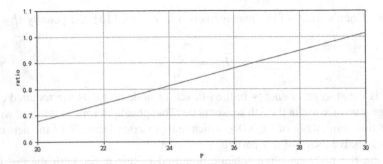

Fig. 6. Energy consumption performance of the proposed approach against the distributed random scheme ($n = 100$, $E^e = \bar{E}_{\delta_1} = 1$, $E^c = 0.1$, $\hat{r} = 10$, $\gamma = 2$, $q = 30$, $\delta_1 = \delta_2 = 100$)

the MATLAB2014a software platform, in accordance with the system model described in Sect. 2.2. In the numerical simulation, the number of sensor nodes in WSN is set as N = 100, which is uniformly deployed in the region of interest, and each node can provide the measured value of sparse vector x. For a given sparsity K = 25, M sensor nodes are selected and read their measured values. Therefore, randomly generated K-sparse vector x, support set $S(|S| = K)$ is selected uniformly and randomly in the set $\{1, 2, \ldots, N\}$. Sparse basis matrix $\Psi \in R^{N \times N}$ adopts independent identically distributed Gaussian matrix. The random packet loss rate is set to 10%. In addition, it is assumed that the measured value of the sensor is polluted by zero-mean Gaussian noise $N(0, \sigma^2)$. All simulations were repeated 10000 times to get reliable results.

Compare the performance of BCS-DCS strategy with Jeffrey, BP and OMP compressed sensing algorithms, as shown in Fig. 7. From the figure, we can find that the BCS-DCS has better recovery performance than Jeffrey, BP, and OMP compressed sensing algorithms, without noise and data packet loss. However, under the interference of data packet loss and noise, the recovery performance of Jeffrey, BP and OMP will deteriorate sharply with the increase of redundancy (M/N), while the BCS-DCS can still maintain the almost perfect reconstruction.

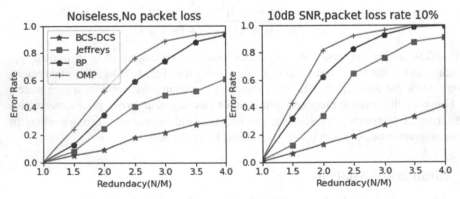

Fig. 7. Recovery performance with different redundancy

When the observation noise is introduced into the CS, the traditional CS recovery algorithms (such as: Jeffrey, BP) cannot achieve noise reduction like Bayesian method, but can reduce the influence of model overlearning by introducing the balance factor λ(λ is actually equivalent to the observation noise σ^2). Compare the performance of the BCS-DCS strategy with Jeffrey and BP algorithms under the change of balance factor, as shown in Fig. 8. It can be seen from the figure that when the balance factor is small, the BCS-DCS strategy have the best recovery performance; when the balance factor is large, all algorithms will deteriorate sharply. Fortunately, this situation rarely exists in real applications.

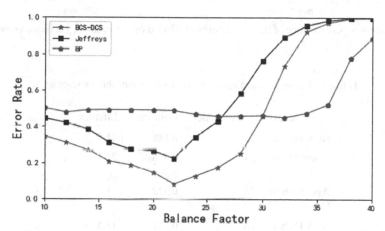

Fig. 8. Recovery performance with different balance factor (unit: 10^{-4})

According to the performance comparison in Fig. 7, with increasing the number of active nodes in the WSN, the recovery performance of the CS can be improved, but the energy consumption of the network will also increase. The purpose of designing the BCS-DCS strategy is to improve the recovery performance of the CS with less network energy consumption. Therefore, the recovery performance of the BCS-DCS strategy compared with the distributed node selection scheme in [13] and [14], in terms of activation node number and network lifetime, as shown in Fig. 9.

It can be seen from the Table 1 that compared with the approaches in [13, 14], the BCS-DCS strategy can effectively improve the recovery performance of the CS with less network cost, and the CBS-DCS strategy has a longer network life than the approaches in [13, 14] under the same CS recovery performance. However, the performance of the BCS-DCS strategy in signal acquisition precision and network lifetime decreases with the increase of time. Since the energy and spectrum resource consumption caused by each SN sending a large amount of data to FC can be ignored, this strategy is more suitable for data-intensive applications.

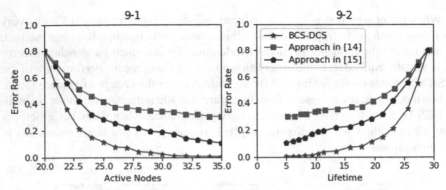

Fig. 9. Recovery performance of three strategies (9-1 based on active node, 9-2 based on network lifetime)

Table 1. Comparison of recovery performance of three strategies

Approaches	Active nodes	Error rate	Lifetime
BCS-DCSS	24	0.148	21.4
Approach in [13]	24	0.458	22.1
Approach in [14]	24	0.322	21.6
BCS-DCSS	28	0.041	13.5
Approach in [13]	28	0.357	13.9
Approach in [14]	28	0.216	13.7

6 Conclusions

This paper studies the efficient data acquisition strategy of the WSN, and designs an efficient data acquisition strategy based on Bayesian compressed sensing (BS-DCS). First, update the CS model in consideration of data packet loss and data acquisition interference in the WSN. Then, reconstruct the original signal, according to the Bayesian method. Finally, according to the posterior covariance of reconstructed signals and considering the energy constraints of sensor nodes, construct an active node selection optimization framework and optimize the node selection matrix. According to the comparison of simulation experiments, the strategy proposed in this paper can realize perfectly the signal acquisition of the WSN and extend the WSN lifetime.

References

1. Vikram, N.K., Harish, K.S., Nihaal, M.S., et al.: A low cost home automation system using wi-fi based wireless sensor network incorporating internet of things (IoT). In: IEEE International Advance Computing Conference, pp. 174–178 (2017)
2. Zakaria, S.Z., Aziz, A.A., Drieberg, M., et al.: Multi-hop wireless sensor network for remote monitoring of soil moisture. In: International Symposium on Robotics, pp. 1–5 (2017)
3. Kirichek, R., Grishin, I., Okuneva, D., et al.: Development of a node-positioning algorithm for wireless sensor networks in 3D space. In: International Conference on Advanced Communication Technology, pp. 279–282 (2016)
4. Shaok, Z.: Architecture and scheduling scheme design of TsinghuaCloud based on OpenStack. J. Comput. Appl. (2013)
5. Zhao, C., Zhang, W., Yang, Y., et al.: Treelet-based clustered compressive data aggregation for wireless sensor networks. IEEE Trans. Veh. Technol. **64**(9), 4257–4267 (2015)
6. Candes, E.J., Romberg, J., Tao, T., et al.: Stable signal recovery from incomplete and inaccurate measurements. Commun. Pure Appl. Math. **59**(8), 1207–1223 (2006)
7. Van Houwelingen, H.C.: The Elements of Statistical Learning, Data Mining, Inference, and Prediction (Ed. by, T. Hastie, R. Tibshirani, J. Friedman), pp. xvi+533. Springer, New York (2001). ISBN 0–387-95284-5. Stat. Med. **23**(3), 528–529 (2004)
8. Mallat, S., Zhang, Z.: Matching pursuits with time-frequency dictionaries. IEEE Trans. Sig. Process. **41**(12), 3397–3415 (1993)
9. Needell, D., Vershynin, R.: Uniform uncertainty principle and signal recovery via regularized orthogonal matching pursuit. Found. Comput. Math. **9**(3), 317–334 (2009)
10. Needell, D., Tropp, J.A.: CoSaMP: iterative signal recovery from incomplete and inaccurate samples. Appl. Comput. Harmonic Anal. **26**(3), 301–321 (2009)
11. Do, T.T., Gan, L., Nguyen, N., et al.: Sparsity adaptive matching pursuit algorithm for practical compressed sensing. In: ASILOMAR Conference on Signals, Systems and Computers, pp. 581–587 (2008)
12. Mohsenzadeh, Y., Sheikhzadeh, H., Reza, A.M., et al.: The relevance sample feature machine: a sparse bayesian learning approach to joint feature-sample selection. IEEE Trans. Syst. Man Cybern. **43**(6), 2241–2254 (2013)
13. Ling, Q., Tian, Z.: Decentralized sparse signal recovery for compressive sleeping wireless sensor networks. IEEE Trans. Sig. Process. **58**(7), 3816–3827 (2010)
14. Xue, T., Dong, X., Shi, Y., et al.: Multiple access and data reconstruction in wireless sensor networks based on compressed sensing. IEEE Trans. Wirel. Commun. **12**(7), 3399–3411 (2013)
15. Tipping, M.E.: Sparse bayesian learning and the relevance vector machine. J. Mach. Learn. Res. 211–244 (2001)
16. Chen, Y., Zhao, Q.: On the lifetime of wireless sensor networks. IEEE Commun. Lett. **9**(11), 976–978 (2005)

Single Beacon Rotating Based Node Localization Algorithm for Underwater Sensor Networks

Ying Guo[✉], Ping Ji, and Longsheng Niu

Qingdao University of Science and Technology, Qingdao 266061, China
guoying@qust.edu.cn

Abstract. Currently, numerous localization algorithms for underwater wireless sensor networks have been proposed without solving beacon redundancy with the expansion of the deployment area. And due to the special condition in underwater environment, beacons move with the water flow and they are difficult to deploy accurately. These factors bring great challenges to underwater node localization. To solve these problems, a novel underwater localization algorithm (Single Beacon Rotating based Node Localization Algorithm, SBR) is proposed, which based on a single rotating beacon to calculate the position of unlocated nodes. The position and angle information from beacon are used to calculate the relationship between the unlocated node and the beacon. And the relationship information can be used to obtain the exact position of the unlocated node. In the localization process, unlocated nodes do not need to send message actively, which greatly reduce the communication cost.

Keywords: Underwater wireless sensor networks · Node localization · Single Beacon Rotating

1 Introduction

As various marine-based industries are booming, the attention of the masses is gradually focused on underwater wireless sensor networks (UWSNs). UWSNs have provided adequate technical support for many applications such as marine environment monitoring, natural disaster prevention and military defense [1]. However, the sensing data without location parameters are valueless in the above application scenarios. Therefore, along with the rapid development of UWSNs, the localization for UWSNs has become a research hotspot [2].

Due to the special and complicated underwater environment, the method of ground node localization cannot be directly applied to UWSNs [3]. Therefore, many underwater localization algorithms have been proposed, such as, Hybrid Localization Scheme (HLS) [3], Mobility Constrained Beacon based Localization Algorithm (MCB) [4], Multi-hops Fitting Localization Approach [5], and so on. However, these algorithms do not solve the problem of beacon redundancy with the expansion of the deployment area, and the precise deployment difficulties of beacons following the flow of water. Beacon, also called as anchor node, is a node of which specific position is known before node localization

Z. Hao et al. (Eds.): CWSN 2020, CCIS 1321, pp. 28–41, 2020.
https://doi.org/10.1007/978-981-33-4214-9_3

[6]. The position of the beacon can be obtained by GPS or artificial designation [7]. Moreover, the ground positioning technology like GPS is not feasible under the water [8].

The movement of beacons with water flow during localization will also seriously affect the localization accuracy of underwater nodes. It is difficult to accurately deploy underwater beacons that move with the water flow due to the special condition in underwater environment. Beacons cannot use GPS to update their location information. Localization errors of beacons can cause localization errors. Algorithm proposed in this paper only requires one beacon, and the beacon can obtain the exact position from the ship. Therefore, the localization error caused by the deployment error of the underwater beacon can be reduced.

Because we plan to apply our algorithm to project OCEANSENSE deployed in Qingdao Bay [9], We have to solve the problem of beacon redundancy with the expansion of the deployment area. As shown in Fig. 1, it is the way most ocean networks work that cruising ships are dispatched periodically to collect information and maintain nodes in the deployed sea area. Based on a period of observations, we decided to take advantage of it. As a result, we fixed the beacon under the cruise ship so that ship can locate nodes while cruising such a vast coastal water, which could solve the problem of beacon redundancy with the expansion of the deployment area and could reduce deployment costs. We believe it has good practical value and wide application field, and it could be used in other similar occasions, such as using underwater sensor networks to monitor offshore environment or species, and to track underwater targets.

Fig. 1. Ship cruising and deployment area

An algorithm called Single Beacon Rotating based Node Localization Algorithm (SBR) is presented in this paper, which is a range-based localization algorithm of UWSNs. A range-based localization algorithm needs enough beacons to calculate the position information between the nodes, which consume more energy and has great requirements on the computing power of the nodes. However, SBR algorithm only needs one beacon, it measures the angle information between the beacon and the unlocated node, and then calculates the position information of the unlocated node with the angle information. Compared to other range-based algorithms, SBR algorithm enhances the positioning accuracy. Due to unlocated nodes do not need to send information actively, energy consumption will be greatly reduced.

2 Related Work

The localization algorithm in UWSNs has different requirements on the anchor (or beacon) node, such as the synchronization mechanism or the ranging factors. The types of localization algorithms are also different according to different standards. Some of them are briefly introduced below.

According to the requirements of the algorithm for the anchor node, the localization algorithm can be divided into anchor-based algorithm and anchor-free algorithm [4]. Use anchor nodes in the localization algorithm UWSNs is more common. However, anchor nodes are not required, and some researchers have proposed self-localization algorithms that do not require anchor nodes [5]. Anchor node is a node used to reference and calculate unknown nodes [10]. The location of the anchor node can be obtained by GPS or by artificial designation [11].

A Hybrid Localization Scheme (HLS) [3] is an anchor-based scheme, which consists of four types of nodes: surface buoys, Detachable Elevator Transceivers (DETs), anchor nodes and ordinary nodes. In addition, the program divides the node into two phases. First, the anchor node uses a range-based distributed approach to locate itself. Secondly, ordinary nodes use the regional positioning scheme to achieve location-free centralized approach [12]. An anchor-less location algorithm for active restricted UWSNs is proposed in Anchor-Free Localization Algorithm [13] (AFLA) which uses the relationship between adjacent nodes to turn on positioning calculations. The underwater sensor node floats in the sea and moves within the hemispherical area. Node broadcasts a message with unknown positions and simultaneously receive information from other nodes. When a node receives two messages from two different nodes, it initiates a localization calculation process [13].

According to the bearer information such as the distance and angle between the measurement nodes, the localization algorithm can be divided into range-based localization algorithm and range-free localization algorithm [14]. Range-based schemes estimate distances by various algorithms and then convert them into positional information. Range-free schemes do not require distance measurement and bearer information, but use local typologies and locations of adjacent anchor nodes to obtain position estimates. However, the range-free scheme can only obtain a rough position with low accuracy [14].

In an Area Localization Scheme [15] (ALS), the author proposes an effective localization algorithm. This scheme estimates the location of the sensor within a particular area. The anchor node broadcasts the beacon signal to the sensor node and transmits an acoustic signal having a varying power level. The sensor node passively monitors the signal and records the received information and then forwards it to the receiver. The receiver uses the information gathered from the sensor nodes to estimate the area in which the sensor is located [15].

According to different ways of processing information, it can be divided into centralized localization algorithm and distributed localization algorithm [16]. The centralized localization algorithm sends information to the central node for processing, and the central node performs a localization algorithm to obtain a positioning result [16]. The distributed localization algorithm does not need to send information to the central node, but is calculated independently by different sensor nodes.

Based on the research in recent years, many new excellent localization algorithms have appeared in UWSNs, and we have selected some comparative studies. As shown in Table 1.

Table 1. Comparison of underwater localization algorithms

Reference	Computation algorithm	Anchor requirement	Range measurement	Communication between nodes
[3]	Hybrid	Anchor-based	Hybrid	Single stage
[13]	Distributed	Anchor-free	Range-free	Single stage
[15]	Centralized	Anchor-based	Range-based	Multi-stage
[16]	Distributed	Anchor-based	Range-based	Multi-stage
[17]	Distributed	Anchor-based	Range-based	Single stage
[18]	Distributed	Anchor-based	Range-based	Single stage
[19]	Distributed	Anchor-based	Range-based	Multi-stage
[20]	Distributed	Anchor-based	Range-based	Multi-stage
[21]	Distributed	Anchor-based	Range-based	Multi-stage
[22]	Centralized	Anchor-based	Range-based	Multi-stage
[23]	Distributed	Anchor-based	Hybrid	Multi-stage

The SBR algorithm proposed in this paper is an anchor-based, range-based algorithm. Inter-node communication in the SBR algorithm is single-level. Different from above localization algorithms, SBR only needs one beacon, and makes use of angle relationship to calculate nodes position. The SBR algorithm has greatly improved localization accuracy and stability.

3 Algorithm Design

This section designs a localization algorithm based on a rotating beacon, gives the beacon rotation trajectory, and analyses the positioning error caused by rotation.

3.1 Basic Idea

A rotateable beacon is fixed under the ship on the sea surface, the beacon can obtain its own position through the GPS of the ship. It can rotate according to a predetermined trajectory and transmit its position and angle information, as shown in Fig. 2. The unlocated nodes receive this information and calculate their own locations.

In the process of rotating and transmitting information of the beacon, the unlocated node may receive the position and angle information transmitted by the beacon multiple times. Of course, the signal transmission area is a cone rather than a straight line. The unlocated node selects the intermediate information in the received information for the

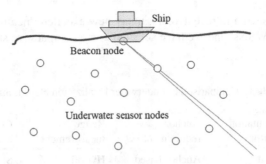

Fig. 2. Single beacon rotating based node localization

localization calculation. Because the multiple signals which unlocated node receives should be symmetrically distributed on both sides of the midpoint of the line between the beacon and the unlocated node. We select the intermediate information, which is to choose the position where the unlocated node is located exactly in the direction of the beacon's transmitting signal, so that the angular error is the minimum.

For example, in Fig. 3, the range formed by dotted lines of the same color is the range in which the signal propagates. The solid line is the direction in which the signal was emitted. The calculation error of the black propagation path (intermediate information) selected by the unlocated node is less than blue and red paths. For a specific example, if the unlocated node receives 6 times of information transmitted by the rotating beacon, it selects the average information received for the third and fourth times for the positioning calculation.

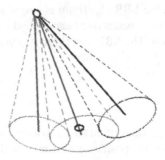

Fig. 3. Signal selection diagram (Color figure online)

Assume that the unlocated node is N and the beacon is B. The beacon transmits its position and angle information (XB, YB, ZB, α, β, γ) while rotating, where XB, YB, ZB are the coordinates of the beacon, and α, β, γ is the angle between the transmitted signal and the three planes. As shown in Fig. 4.

Make a vertical line from the node N to the plane xy where the beacon is located, the pedal is A. Make a vertical line from N to the plane xz, the pedal is E, the vertical line from A to the plane yz, and the pedal is D. The angle between the BN and the plane xy is α, which BN is the connected line between the rotating beacon and the unlocated

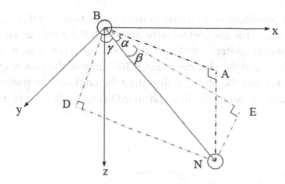

Fig. 4. Node localization calculation

node. The angle between BN and plane xz is β, the angle between BN and plane yz is γ. Plane XY represents sea level.

Since the node itself has a pressure sensor, the water depth can be measured, which is

$$AN = \Delta z = Z_N - Z_R \tag{1}$$

Then

$$NB = \frac{AN}{\sin \alpha} \tag{2}$$

The y-axis coordinate of node N is consistent with E, and the x-axis coordinate is consistent with D, could be found,

$$\begin{cases} \Delta y = NE = NB \sin \beta \\ \Delta x = ND = NB \sin \gamma \end{cases} \tag{3}$$

The coordinates of the node N can be obtained by the coordinates of the beacon.

$$\begin{cases} x_N = x_B + \Delta x \\ y_N = y_B + \Delta y \end{cases} \tag{4}$$

It is indeed complicated of underwater communication which affected by many factors. We take the approach which use the measured value of the pressure sensor to calculate the distance instead of using underwater acoustic propagation. It could avoid ranging errors caused by the non-linearity of underwater acoustic propagation and could simplify the model.

3.2 Rotation Trajectory Selection and Error Analysis

There are many path choices for rotating beacon. Regardless of which trajectory is used, it should cover all underwater areas during rotation. It can use clockwise or counter clockwise circular trajectories, or choose horizontal and vertical interlaced linear trajectories, or select random trajectories etc. Circular trajectory was selected from all the trajectories we have considered for its ease of implementation, and its trajectory is shown in the Fig. 5. The beacon rotates horizontally 360° with the z-axis as an axis, and transmits signal while rotating. After completing the 360-degree rotation, it turns away from plane xy by an angle θ. and then beacon rotates 360° around the z-axis again to transmit signal. The beacon repeats the above action until the angle of the transmitted signal is perpendicular to plane xy. Angle θ will be adjusted to ensure that the signal can be cover the entire area.

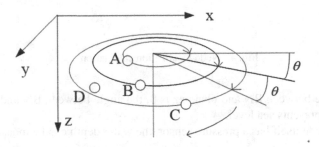

Fig. 5. Beacon rotation trajectory

Then we analyse the errors caused by the trajectory. The rotation angle of the beacon will bring errors to the positioning. Taking the rotation trajectory of Fig. 5 as an example, when the connection between the unlocated node and the beacon coincides with the direction of the information sent by the rotating beacon, no positioning error is caused, such as nodes A, B, and C in Fig. 5. However, when the connection between the unlocated node and the beacon is located between the directions of the information sent by the two positions of rotating beacon, a positioning error is caused, such as node D in Fig. 5. At this point, node D selects the information sent by its nearest rotated beacon for positioning. Since the signal strength decays as distance increases, the strongest signal received by node D is the information sent by its nearest rotating beacon. Due to factors such as environment interference, when the received signal strength is the same for several times, the intermediate value can be used for the positioning calculation. This will bring an error to the angle, and the error range is $(0, \theta/2]$.

The time interval of the beacon that sending the location information also causes positioning errors. When the connecting line of the unlocated node and the beacon is located between the directions of the two times of information sent by the rotating beacon, an error is brought to the angles β and γ. Similarly, the information sent by the nearest rotating beacon of the unlocated node can be used for the positioning calculation.

Reducing the angle θ can reduce the error of the angle α, and shortening the time interval at which the beacon position information is transmitted can reduce the error of the angle β and γ. The effect of the angle error is also discussed in detail in experiment section.

Algorithm pseudo code is as follow:

Single Beacon Rotating based Node Localization Algorithm

```
Notation:
Xnode,Ynode,Znode : They are the X-axis, Y-axis, and Z-
axis coordinates of the node, respectively.
Algorithm:
1: procedure select_msg
2: use list save message
3: for 1 to times
4:     list.add(currentMsg)
5: end for
6: selectOrderNum ← (int) ( times / 2 )
7: info ← list [ selectOrderNum ]
8: if times is odd number then
9:     msgOne ← list [ selectOrderNum ]
10:    msgTwo ← list [ selectOrderNum +1 ]
11:    info ← average location infomation of msgOne and
msgTwo
12: end if
13: select info as calculation condition information
14: end procedure
15: procedure receive_msg
16: depth ← Zn - Zb
17: Lnb ← depth / sinα
18: Lne ← Lnb * sinβ
19: Lnd ← Lnb * sinγ
20: Xn ← Xb + Lnd
21: Yn ← Yb + Lne
22: end procedure
```

---

4 Simulations

At this stage, we do not have the equipment to control the rotation accuracy of the beacons, and we cannot do experiment in the platform OCEANSENSE. Therefore, we used MATLAB R2016b to simulate the algorithm. We will conduct actual experiments if meeting experiment conditions in the future.

In our all simulation, unlocated nodes were randomly deployed in the range of 300 m in length, 300 m in width and 200 m in water depth for experimentation, and the seawater temperature was set to 15 °C. The seawater salinity is set to 35‰, which is the seawater salinity in the northern hemisphere. Since these influence parameters affect the propagation speed of the water acoustic wave, these influence parameters adopt the practical values used in real applications.

In this simulation, we separately analyze localization accuracy of the SBR algorithm, comparison between SBR and similar types of algorithms, the impacting factors in the SBR algorithm.

4.1 Analyze Localization Accuracy of the SBR Algorithm

At first, ten nodes are randomly deployed in the above simulation environment. And then SBR algorithm is used for locating them. The SBR algorithm is used to calculate the coordinates of each node. In order to conform to the real application in the simulation experiment, we add a small random error to the pressure sensor of the unlocated node. It is to simulate a real hardware problem. The errors between the calculated result and the real coordinate are shown in Fig. 6.

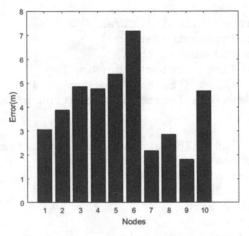

Fig. 6. Error analysis of ten random nodes

Under the impact of the error caused by the pressure sensor, the localization accuracy of SBR algorithm is accurate and the fluctuations are not obvious which indicating good stability.

4.2 Analyze Comparison of Algorithms

In order to better verify the SBR algorithm proposed in this paper, we compare the error with TP-TSFLA algorithm [23] and MNLS algorithm [24]. The TP-TSFLA algorithm first performs the particle swarm optimization algorithm to obtain the coordinates of the unlocated nodes. And then based on the range-free localization algorithm of the circle, to locate the unlocated node that was previously unable to be located. The MNLS algorithm is a localization algorithm for mobile nodes. Compared with SBR algorithm, the two algorithms have certain similarities. The comparison between them is more comparable, and the results are sufficient to prove the superiority of our proposed SBR algorithm.

The comparison results of localization error of SBR algorithm, MNLS algorithm and TP-TSFLA algorithm are shown in Fig. 7. The error of SBR algorithm can be visually observed from the figure that is significantly lower than MNLS algorithm and TP-TSFLA algorithm.

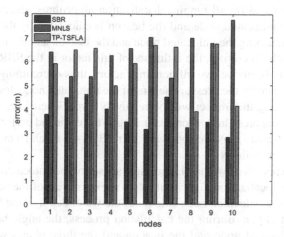

Fig. 7. Error comparison of SBR, MNLS and TP-TSFLA algorithm

Table 2 shows the average and variance value of errors of SBR algorithm, MNLS algorithm and TP-TSFLA algorithm in this simulation.

Table 2. Comparative average and variance value of errors (m)

Algorithm	Average value of errors	Variance of errors
SBR	3.7494	0.3905
MNLS	6.3684	0.6829
TP-TSFLA	5.7899	1.1508

The SBR algorithm is the best of the three algorithms in terms of accuracy. The variance of SBR algorithm is the smallest, and the error of the calculated result is relatively smooth, indicating that the algorithm has high stability. Although the mean error of TP-TSFLA algorithm is smaller than that of MNLS algorithm, the variance of the error is much larger than MNLS algorithm and SBR algorithm, which indicates that the localization error of TP-TSFLA algorithm is unstable. The average value and variance of the SBR algorithm are much lower than other algorithms. Therefore, the SBR algorithm has a significant improvement in accuracy and stability.

4.3 Analyze Impacting Factor

For SBR algorithm, there are two key factor that have a large impact on the accuracy of localization. One is the underwater depth error generated by the pressure sensor. It is an inevitable hardware factor. The other is the angle error between the straight line connecting the unlocated node and the beacon and the three planes. The distance error between the unlocated node and the beacon is difficult to control, and is currently a common difficulty faced by all ranging localization algorithms. Because the straight line connecting the unlocated node and the beacon is calculated by the angle between the straight line connecting the unlocated node and the beacon and the three planes, and the underwater depth. Therefore, the influence of this factor in the SBR algorithm will be decomposed into the above two influencing factors, thus overcoming this problem.

The error generated by the pressure sensor of the unlocated node directly affects the depth of the water, and the impact will be relatively large. Therefore, we grouped the errors generated by the pressure sensors according to the error and performed simulation experiments. The pressure sensor errors were 1.5 m, 3 m, 4.5 m, and 6 m. The simulation results obtained are as follows.

The simulation results show that the pressure sensor of the unlocated node can affect the accuracy of the localization algorithm to some extent, part of the reason is that the pressure sensor of the unlocated node calculates the water depth of the unlocated node. And the other part is that, during the calculation process, the angle between the line connecting the unlocated node and the beacon and the three planes will also change slightly due to the underwater depth error caused by the pressure sensor. It can be seen from Fig. 8 that when the water depth error difference caused by the pressure sensor is increased, the final ranging error will also increase by approximately equal difference. The error generated by the pressure sensor can be improved by selecting a high-precision pressure sensor.

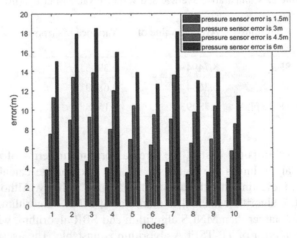

Fig. 8. Pressure sensor error factor impact comparison

The angle error between the line connecting the unlocated node and the beacon and the three planes will have a greater impact on the ranging error. The reason for this error is the position of unlocated node may not be exactly at the angle of the beacon transmits the signal in practice. As the distance increases, the impact of the angular error will also increase. We simulated the experiment by adding 0.5°, 1°, and 1.5° errors to all three angles.

As shown in Fig. 9, the increase of the error in all three angles will increase the ranging error rapidly. When the distance exceeds 1.5°, the ranging error is already very large. Since the environment set by the simulation is large, the influence of the angle on the ranging error is very large, and the larger the angle error, the larger the ranging error. When the angles of α, β, and γ have errors, the impacting effect is obviously.

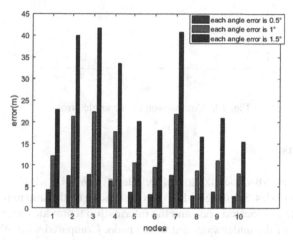

Fig. 9. Angle factor impact comparison

Then, we use the same set of unlocated nodes, and only change one of the three angles α, β, and γ: the first group only increases the error of the angle α by 1°, and the other two angles have no errors. Similarly, the second and third groups only change the two angles of β and γ, respectively. The results obtained are shown in Fig. 10.

The same group of unlocated nodes only adds an error of 1° to one angle. The error of the angle α has the greatest influence on the final ranging error, and the error of the angle γ has less influence on the ranging error. The effect of the angle α on the ranging error is greater than the angle β and γ. The main reason is that when the angle β and γ are involved in the calculation, the result of the angle α participating in the calculation is required to be calculated. The error of the angle α affects the calculation results obtained by the angle β and γ, so that the calculation results of the other two angles participating in the calculation will cause errors due to the error of the angle α, thereby greatly affecting the final ranging error. The error generated by the angle error can be improved by improving the angular control precision of the rotating beacon, and provides feedback during the calculation process. When the angle error is greater than the pre-set value, the angle correction is performed to improve the positioning accuracy.

Above all, the proposed algorithm has greatly improved in both stability and accuracy. There are fewer factors that can have a significant impact on the algorithm. This algorithm overcomes the problem that the straight-line ranging error of the unlocated node and the beacon is difficult to control. It is much better than MNLS algorithm and TP-TSFLA algorithm.

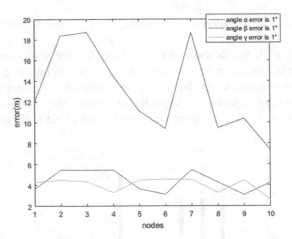

Fig. 10. Comparison of one angle error

5 Conclusions

This paper proposes SBR localization algorithm of UWSNs, which is used to locate underwater sensor nodes. SBR algorithm uses the beacon on the ship to form a geometric relationship with the unlocated node and the information it provides, thereby calculating the exact position of the underwater unlocated node. Compared with other localization algorithms, SBR algorithm has higher accuracy and stability.

In the future, we will continue our research to make the signal transmitted by the beacon on the surface accurately reach the bottom node if the network is deeper, and to find better beacon trajectories. Meanwhile, we will make rotating beacon as soon as possible in order to proposed algorithm is applied in practice, such as project Oceansense which is our primary target.

Acknowledgments. The work was supported by Natural Science Foundation of Shandong Province (No. ZR201910280170).

References

1. Han, G., Jiang, J., Shu, L., Xu, Y., Wang, F.: Localization algorithms of underwater wireless sensor networks: a survey. Sensors **12**(2), 2026–2061 (2012)
2. Das, A.P., Thampi, S.M.: Fault-resilient localization for underwater sensor networks. Ad Hoc Netw. **55**, 132–142 (2017)
3. Krishna, C.R., Yadav, P.S.: A hybrid localization scheme for Underwater Wireless Sensor Networks. In: 2014 International Conference on Issues and Challenges in Intelligent Computing Techniques (ICICT), pp. 3–5 (2014)
4. Guo, Y., Han, Q., Kang, X.: Underwater sensor networks localization based on mobility-constrained beacon. Wirel. Netw. **26**, 2585–2594 (2019)
5. Liu, L., Wu, J., Zhu, Z.: Multihops fitting approach for node localization in underwater wireless sensor networks. Int. J. Distrib. Sens. Netw. **11**(2), 11 (2015)

6. Zandi, R., Kamarei, M., Amiri, H.: Distributed estimation of sensors position in underwater wireless sensor network. Int. J. Electron. **103**(5), 1–15 (2015)
7. Luo, H., Wu, K., Ruby, R., Hong, F., Guo, Z., Ni, L.M.: Simulation and experimentation platforms for underwater acoustic sensor networks: advancements and challenges. ACM Comput. Surv. (CSUR) **50**(2), 1–44 (2017)
8. Li, J., Wang, J., Wang, X., Qiao, G., Luo, H., Gulliver, T.A.: Optimal beamforming design for underwater acoustic communication with multiple unsteady sub-Gaussian interferers. IEEE Trans. Veh. Technol. **68**, 12381–12386 (2019)
9. OCEANSENSE. http://osn.ouc.edu.cn/main.htm
10. Wang, S.L.: Research on rigid location discrimination of underwater sensor networks based on skeleton extraction. Hefei Univ. Technol. **38**(3), 589–601 (2014)
11. Luo, H., Xie, X., Han, G., Ruby, R., Feng, H., Liang, Y.: Multimodal acoustic-RF adaptive routing protocols for underwater wireless sensor networks. IEEE Access **7**(9), 134954–134967 (2019)
12. Luo, H., Wu, K., Ruby, R., Liang, Y., Guo, Z., Ni, L.M.: Software-defined architectures and technologies for underwater wireless sensor networks: a survey. IEEE Commun. Surv. Tutor. **20**(4), 2855–2888 (2018)
13. Guo, Y., Liu, Y.: Localization for anchor-free underwater sensor networks. Comput. Electr. Eng. **39**(6), 1812–1821 (2013)
14. Ismail, N.N., Hussein, L.A., Ariffin, S.H.S.: Analyzing the performance of acoustic channel in underwater wireless sensor network (UWSN). In: 2010 Fourth Asia International Conference on Mathematical/Analytical Modelling and Computer Simulation (AMS) (2010)
15. Chandrasekhar, V., Seah, W.: An area localization scheme for underwater sensor networks. In: OCEANS 2006 - Asia Pacific, pp. 1–8 (2006)
16. Cheng, W., Thaeler, A., Cheng, X., Liu, F., Lu, X., Lu, Z.: Time-synchronization free localization in large scale underwater acoustic sensor networks. In: 29th IEEE International Conference on Distributed Computing Systems Workshops, pp. 80–87 (2009)
17. Bhuvaneswari, P.T.V., Karthikeyan, S., Jeeva, B., Prasath, M.A.: An efficient mobility based localization in underwater sensor networks. In: Proceedings of the 2012 Fourth International Conference on Computational Intelligence and Communication Networks, pp. 90–94 (2012)
18. Diamant, R., Lampe, L.: Underwater localization with time-synchronization and propagation speed uncertainties. IEEE Trans. Mob. Comput. **12**(7), 1257–1269 (2013)
19. Zhou, Z., Cui, J., Bagtzoglou, A.: Scalable localization with mobility prediction for underwater sensor networks. In: The 27th Conference on Computer Communications, INFOCOM 2008. IEEE (2008)
20. Kurniawan, A., Ferng, H.W.: Projection-based localization for underwater sensor networks with consideration of layers. In: Proceedings of the IEEE 2013 Tencon-Spring, pp. 425–429 (2013)
21. Ren, Y., Yu, N., Guo, X., Wan, J.: Cube-scan-based three-dimensional localization for large-scale Underwater Wireless Sensor Networks. In: 2012 IEEE International Systems Conference SysCom 2012 (2012)
22. Bian, T., Venkatesan, R., Li, C.: Design and evaluation of a new localization scheme for underwater acoustic sensor networks. In: 2009 IEEE Global Telecommunications Conference, GLOBECOM 2009 (2009)
23. Luo, J., Fan, L.: A two-phase time synchronization-free localization algorithm for underwater sensor networks. Sensors **17**(4), 726 (2017)
24. Wang, M.L., Song, A.J.: Positioning of 3D underwater sensor network based on mobile node. Comput. Syst. Appl. **23**(10), 162–166 (2014)

A Gap Repair Algorithm Based on Clustered Barrier Coverage in 3D Environment

Xiaochao Dang[1,2], Yuexia Li[1], and Zhanjun Hao[1,2(✉)]

[1] College of Computer Science and Engineering, Northwest Normal University,
Lanzhou 730070, Gansu, China
zhanjunhao@126.com
[2] Gansu Province Internet of Things Engineering Research Center, Northwest Normal
University, Lanzhou 730070, Gansu, China

Abstract. Aiming at the repair of barrier coverage gap in wireless sensor networks in three-dimensional environment, a clustered barrier gap repair algorithm (Gap repair algorithm of clustered barrier, GRCB) is proposed in this paper. First of all, the three-dimensional environment is gridded in two dimensions, and a novel clustered barrier coverage model is proposed. Then, under the constraints of this model, the joint perception probability is introduced to find the barrier gap and construct the repair trajectory circle model. Finally, the grid gradient is introduced to construct the relationship between the mobile node and the barrier gap trajectory circle model. finally, the optimal repair position and mobile node are determined. The simulation results show that the algorithm proposed in this paper can effectively improve the node utilization, reduce the node energy consumption, and has strong self-adaptability in the barrier gap repair in 3D environment.

Keywords: Three-dimensional barrier · Clustered barrier · Gap repair · Mesh gradient · Repair trajectory circle

1 Introduction

Barrier coverage [1, 2] (Barrier Coverage, BC) is one of the widely used coverage models in wireless sensor networks (Wireless Sensor Networks, WSNs). Barrier coverage is divided into strong barrier coverage and weak barrier coverage. Strong barrier coverage is mainly used to study how to ensure that the intrusion target is monitored when the intrusion target invades and deploys the sensor node area [3–5]. With the growing demand for monitoring intrusion targets, wireless sensor network barrier coverage technology has been widely used in national defense security, forest disaster relief, environmental protection, water pollution and many other fields [6–9]. However, sensor nodes in wireless sensor networks may fail due to insufficient energy, hardware failures, environmental problems, human factors and other reasons [10, 11]. In this case, the problem of barrier gap will occur in the barrier coverage, resulting in a reduction in coverage, so that the barrier coverage can not achieve efficient monitoring of intrusion targets to the maximum

© Springer Nature Singapore Pte Ltd. 2020
Z. Hao et al. (Eds.): CWSN 2020, CCIS 1321, pp. 42–56, 2020.
https://doi.org/10.1007/978-981-33-4214-9_4

extent, which is likely to lead to the lack of some important data monitoring. Therefore, the repair of the gap between the barrier is extremely necessary.

In the related research, it is necessary to synthesize many aspects of performance indicators, as well as better barrier gap repair methods for research. In addition, nowadays, the research work on the repair of barrier gap in wireless sensor networks mostly stays on the 2D plane in the ideal environment. Therefore, on the basis of summarizing the previous work, this paper combines the advantages of static network and dynamic network to repair barrier gap, and proposes a clustering-based barrier coverage gap repair algorithm in 3D environment.

Compared with other barrier gap repair algorithms, the main contributions of the proposed algorithm are as follows:

(1) A clustered barrier coverage model is proposed, which makes up for the shortcomings of long repair distance and long repair time of mobile nodes to some extent.
(2) In this paper, a method of finding the barrier gap in the net format is proposed, and whether the grid is a barrier gap is judged by the joint probability minimum threshold and the joint perception probability of the grid.
(3) The relationship model between the mobile node and the gap to be repaired is proposed. through this model, the mobile node selects the repair position with the minimum distance on the target trajectory circle to realize the efficient repair of the barrier gap in the three-dimensional environment.

Section 1 of this paper introduces the related work, and Sect. 2 introduces the node and network model. Section 3 introduces the barrier gap repair algorithm proposed in this paper in detail. Section 4 evaluates the performance of the algorithm proposed in this paper through simulation experiments. Section 5 summarizes the full text and introduces the next step of work.

2   Related Work

With the development of science and technology, it is no longer a difficult problem to move the node to the position to be repaired. For example, the developed flying robot can fly to a fixed position and perform the corresponding work [3]. This makes moving the node to the repair position to repair the gap is an important method of repairing the gap [9]. This makes moving the node to the repair position to repair the gap is an important method to repair the gap. For example, reference [12] proposed an energy-saving barrier gap repair algorithm, when there is a barrier gap, the use of mobile nodes to redeploy to improve barrier coverage. Reference [13] proposes how to use multiple types of mobile sensor nodes to repair the gap between pre-deployed fixed sensors in heterogeneous WSN. A periodic monitoring and scheduling (PMS) algorithm is designed in reference [14]. The algorithm uses mobile sensors to periodically monitor the points along the barrier coverage line, and uses dynamic sensor patrols to achieve barrier coverage in the case of node failure. Reference [15] studies an efficient mobile sensor location algorithm based on deployment line, and discusses how to relocate the mobile sensor to repair the gap when the gap is found. A centralized barrier energy-saving relocation algorithm is proposed in reference [16], which uses fewer moving sensor nodes to repair the barrier gap. In addition to moving nodes to repair barrier gaps, there are also many studies on gap repair in hybrid sensor networks. For example, reference [17] studied the problem of barrier gap repair based on line deployment in directed network, and proposed a simple rotation algorithm and chain reaction algorithm to repair barrier gap. Literature [18] proposed the CGR algorithm, by detecting low-energy nodes in the network, moving the movable nodes around the node to repair the inter-barrier. In reference [19], SRA algorithm and CRA algorithm are proposed to repair the gap problem in directed sensor networks. In reference [20], it is proposed that in hybrid directed sensor networks, the gap is repaired by moving sensor nodes and re-forming a barrier with fixed sensors. Literature [21] proposed a centralized algorithm based on distributed learning automata. In an adjustable direction sensor network that does not move nodes, it uses non-overlapping forms to adjust the direction to repair the gap. In reference [22], an effective algorithm based on directional barrier graph is proposed to find the barrier gap, and the directed sensor node is used to repair the gap. Literature [23] proposed a new maximum fault-tolerant barrier coverage problem in hybrid sensor networks, and optimized the barrier coverage problem by relocating mobile sensor nodes. In reference [24], the coverage area is divided by divide-and-conquer strategy, and the barrier gap is repaired based on asynchronous wake-up mode.

However, The above researches on gap repair are mostly from the unilateral research of dynamic sensor networks and static sensor networks. In addition, most of the research on barrier gap repair is generally carried out in two-dimensional environment, which is not suitable for barrier gap repair in three-dimensional environment. Based on this, this paper proposes a distributed barrier gap repair algorithm suitable for 3D environment: Firstly, the 3D environment is gridded in two dimensions, and a novel clustered barrier coverage model is proposed; Then, under the constraints of this model, the joint perception probability is introduced to find the barrier gap, and the gap repair trajectory circle model is constructed. Finally, the grid gradient is introduced at the same time, and the relationship between the grid gradient and the barrier gap trajectory circle model and the mobile node is used to determine the optimal repair location and mobile node.

3 Network Model

The traditional barrier coverage is basically deployed by random sensor nodes, and the network model of the barrier is basically in the shape of a strip. However, when the barrier gap occurs, it will take a lot of time to move the node to repair the gap. At the same time, this traditional barrier has a high probability of missing some monitoring events. Therefore, a clustered strong barrier coverage model is proposed in this paper, which has the following definitions:

Definition 1 (strong barrier coverage). All traversing paths through the monitoring area in any direction can be detected by at least one sensor.

Definition 2 (clustered strong barrier coverage). A strong barrier coverage consisting of a cluster network containing several nodes, as shown in Fig. 1.

Figure 1 shows a clustered barrier coverage model with 6 nodes in the cluster. It is a network that divides the nodes into a cluster with a number of 6 ordinary nodes in

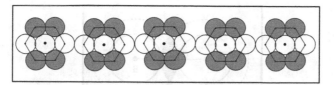

Fig. 1. Clustered barrier cover model

the network. Among them, the grey node is the dormant node, the white node is the normal working node, and the area in the circle is the maximum perception range of the node. Its central position is the cluster head node, which is responsible for the node communication in its own network. According to the different nodes in the cluster, we can be divided into different number of cluster networks.

3.1 Node Perception Model

However, in the practical application environment, the perceived quality of the node is related to the distance between the node and the monitoring target. Generally speaking, the sensing ability of sensor nodes mainly changes with the change of distance. Therefore, for the sensor node perception model, this paper uses the circular probability perception model. In addition, in the WSN, monitoring events may be jointly covered by multiple nodes, and the coverage of events is the result of joint perception of multiple nodes. Therefore, there are the following definitions:

Definition 3 (Node probability perception model). The perception model of the node is the probability perception model, that is, the probability of the node perceiving the intruder decreases with the increase of the distance between the intruder and the node. We assume that s_q is any point within the node perception range, and the probability that node s_i can perceive point s_q is P:

$$P(s_i, t) = \begin{cases} 1 & r > d(s_i, t) \\ e^{-\lambda \alpha^\beta} & r \leq d(s_i, t) \leq R_s \\ 0 & R_s < d(s_i, t) \end{cases} \tag{1}$$

Among them, $\alpha = d(s_i, s_q) - r$, λ and β are the sensing parameters of the sensor. R_s is the maximum perceptual radius of node s_i, r is the 100% perceptible radius of the node, and $d(s_i, s_q)$ is the distance from target events s_q to the node.

Definition 4 (Joint perception probability). When two or more nodes overlap, the perception probability within the overlap range is called joint perception probability.

$$P_q(s_n, q) = \prod_{i=1}^{n} (1 - P_1(s_i, q)) \tag{2}$$

Where s_n represents all nodes that can detect event q, and $P_q(s_n, q)$ is the joint perception probability of n nodes of event q. The joint probability is explained in detail below.

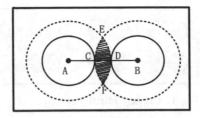

Fig. 2. Joint probabilistic perception model

As shown in Fig. 2, assume that nodes A and B are two adjacent nodes in the barrier cover. The radius of the solid circle is r, the dashed circle is the detection probability in the probabilistic perception model, and the maximum detection radius is R. Here we assume that the minimum threshold is 0.9. Under the Boolean perception model, the dotted circle is the area where the event detection rate is greater than 0.7. According to the Boolean model, in the closed area composed of arcs of CDEF, the solid circle can not be covered, and the joint perception probability of nodes is less than 0.9, which is the gap of barrier coverage. Under the probabilistic perception model, The enclosed area CDEF outside the circle with a radius of r of node A is covered by two dashed circles A and B. Due to the action of neighbor nodes, the detection probability of the area greater than r may be greater than 0.9. For the overlapping coverage area of two dotted circles, the joint perception rate obtained by formula (2) is 0.91, which is greater than the minimum threshold, so the shadow part can be monitored.

3.2 Barrier Gap Repair Model

In the 3D environment, there are often some unpredictable external factors that affect the node, so that the node can not work properly and form a barrier gap, and some monitoring events may be missed if the barrier gap is not repaired in time. If such problems occur in military applications, the losses will be inestimable. Aiming at the three-dimensional environment, a clustered barrier coverage gap repair algorithm is proposed in this paper. The algorithm first grids the 3D environment in 2D, finds out the barrier gap, then determines the optimal repair node location, and then wakes up the dormant node to move to the virtual node position. The schematic diagram of barrier gap repair is shown in Fig. 3, in which the dotted circle is with repair gap, which is likely to become the intrusion path chosen by the intrusion target.

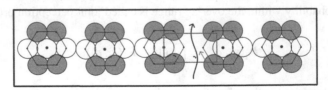

Fig. 3. Schematic diagram of barrier gap

In addition, this paper mainly considers the dynamic sensor network deployed on the three-dimensional smooth slope. The picture above shows the 2D WSN coverage network model in the three-dimensional environment. The coverage of the real three-dimensional environment is different from that of the two-dimensional environment, and the coverage area of the node on the slope is smaller. Therefore, this paper proposes a two-dimensional gridding of the 3D environment, while increasing the grid gradient, so that the node can choose a smoother path coverage, reduce the moving distance, and at the same time make the node coverage larger, and achieve more efficient repair of the barrier gap.

Definition 5 (Grid weight). Taking the starting node as the horizontal plane, the grid in the monitoring area is given different weights, which is called grid weight, which is expressed by ξ_{ij}.

$$g = \frac{\partial h(x, y)}{\partial x}|x0 \cos\psi + \frac{\partial h(x, y)}{\partial y}|y0 \cos(\frac{\pi}{2} - \psi) \tag{3}$$

$$\xi_{ij} = \frac{g_{ij}^{now} - g_{ij}^{next}}{g_{ij}^{next}} \tag{4}$$

The gradient of the grid is represented by g g_{ij}^{now} represents the mesh gradient of the current grid, and g_{ij}^{next} represents the mesh gradient of the next hop node. When the distance between node S_a and node S_b is equal to the position to be filled, if there is a grid gradient of node S_a and node S_b, there is $g_a > g_b$, then $\xi_a < \xi_b$, that is, when the node that fills the gap position is selected from node S_a and node S_b, the node S_b with a gentle slope will be selected. In this way, the node coverage is higher and the moving distance is shorter.

4 GRCB

This chapter will give a detailed introduction to the clustering barrier gap repair algorithm, which is mainly divided into the following parts: First, determine the repair gap according to the different perception range of the node, and then construct the barrier gap repair trajectory circle model according to the repair gap, finally, according to the barrier gap repair trajectory circle model, put forward the repair gap algorithm, and give the corresponding steps.

4.1 Determination of Barrier Clearance

In order to detect the barrier gap in the whole WSN more accurately, we propose a method to find the gap: Firstly, the normal working neighbor nodes between the barrier covers are marked as 1 and the dormant nodes are marked as 0; secondly, a reasonable threshold P_{min} is quantified by using the joint perception probability model, and then whether there is a gap is judged according to the comparison between P_{min} and the joint perception probability P_{min} of the node. Then, record the grid that exists in the gap between the barrier as X, and if there is no gap, do not mark it. As shown in Fig. 4, the shaded part is a circular barrier model.

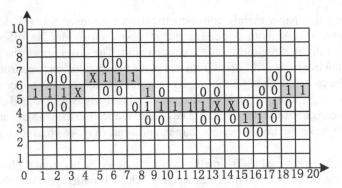

Fig. 4. Schematic diagram of gridded barrier gap

If the joint probability between the neighbor nodes on the barrier cover is greater than the threshold, then there is no barrier gap on the barrier cover, and there is no need to wake up the dormant node to move and repair. The pseudo code is given as follows (Table 1):

Table 1. Gap look up pseudo code

Output: G_{num}; $g_{star}(x_i, y_i)$, $g_{over}(x_i, y_i)$
Input: $s_i^{work}(x_i, y_i)$, $s_i^{sleep}(x_i, y_i)$, P_{now}^{work}
1. Traversing nodes, recording the coordinates of work nodes and dormant nodes
2. Traversing nodes, recording the coordinates of work nodes and dormant nodes
3. Calculate the probability of P_{all} knowledge of the sense of association between working nodes
4. The ant searches for the barrier, and the barrier increases accordingly. After there is no optional node, the ant stops searching.
5. When $P_{all}^{work} < P_{min}$ Calculation $g_{star}(x_i, y_i)$, $g_{over}(x_i, y_i)$
6. else continue traversing
7 end

G_{num} grid number, $g_{star}(x_i, y_i)$ indicates the grid gradient at the initial position of the mobile node, $g_{over}(x_i, y_i)$ indicates the grid gradient at the position to be repaired, $s_i^{work}(x_i, y_i)$, indicates the node at work, $s_i^{sleep}(x_i, y_i)$ indicates the sleeping node, and P_{now}^{work} indicates the perceived probability of the currently working node. Others have been introduced and will not be repeated here.

4.2 Determine the Location of the Patch Node

It is known that the three-dimensional environment of the target area is gridded in two dimensions, and the barrier gap is obtained by calculating the grid joint perception probability between neighbor nodes. After learning the barrier gap, determine whether the gap length is greater than the maximum perceived diameter range of the sensor node $2R$ to determine the optimal location to be repaired and the optimal mobile node.

Define 5 (Patch track Circle) Draw a circle with the point on the line between the nearest nodes on both sides of the barrier gap, which is called the repair track circle. The red dotted line in Fig. 5 shows.

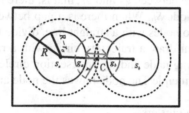

Fig. 5. Repair trajectory circle model (Color figure online)

The black dotted circle in the picture is the largest perception range of the sensing node. with the consumption of the energy of the node, when there is a barrier gap between node s_a and node s_b, the point on the connection between the neighboring nodes in the barrier gap is the center of the circle with a radius of r, of which $R = 2r$. As shown in circle C, when the node moves to the repair trajectory circle, the circle can be repaired.

The gap between the barrier may not exist, or it may exist. If there is no barrier gap, no action is required on the node. The existence of the gap may be in this cluster or between the two clusters.

(1) There is a gap in this cluster.

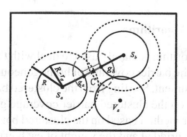

Fig. 6. Gap in this cluster

As shown in Fig. 6, it is assumed that S_a and node S_b are in the same cluster, where the dotted circle of S_a and node S_b still represents the initial perceived probability of its node, and the solid circle represents the current perceived probability range.

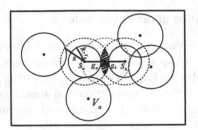

Fig. 7. Gap between clusters

It can be seen that a gap between g_a and g_b, that is, there is a gap between node S_a and another adjacent node S_b. When there is a gap between the two nodes in the cluster, connect the two nodes with a straight line, divide the straight line segment with a radius of r, then draw a trajectory circle with a radius of r, calculate the position of each sleeping node and the intersection circle, and wake up the sleep within the cluster in principle The node moves the node and moves the node to the location to be repaired.

(2)   There is a gap between clusters.

In Fig. 7, sensor node S_a and sensor node S_b are nodes in two clusters, respectively, and there is a gap $g_a g_b$. With reference to the case that the mobile nodes between clusters repair the gap, the main problem of the gap between adjacent clusters is the selection of mobile sensor nodes V_a. On the target trajectory circle between the sensor node S_a and the sensor node S_b. In the aspect of optimal mobile node selection, we first select the node from the left inter-cluster network, and then also select the right inter-cluster network dormant node. Calculate the position distance of all dormant nodes and the trajectory circle, and introduce the grid gradient, and then select the optimal mobile repair gap. At this time, the sensor node V_a should move in the direction of the line segment where S_a and S_b are located, so that it can reach the minimum grid of the gradient between node V_a and the target trajectory circle. This method of moving straight lines minimizes the moving distance of V_a and maximizes coverage.

4.3   Barrier Gap Repair Algorithm

In this paper, the GRCB algorithm is mainly used to deal with the problem of finding and repairing the barrier gap in the barrier coverage of homogeneous mobile sensor networks in three-dimensional environment. Starting from the clustered barrier structure, this paper designs an algorithm based on the clustered barrier coverage gap search and repair, and proposes a barrier gap repair method based on the clustered barrier. First of all, the three-dimensional environment is gridded and the weight of each grid is calculated; secondly, a reasonable threshold is quantified by the joint perception probability model, and then the gap between nodes is calculated by formula (2) according to this threshold; then, the gap repair trajectory circle is constructed for the gap, and the repair model between the dormant node and the trajectory circle is established. Finally, the optimal mobile node is selected to repair the barrier gap through distance and grid weight.

The GRCB algorithm is mainly divided into two stages:

The stage of barrier gap discovery: Through the two-dimensional gridding of the three-dimensional environment, the normal working nodes between the deployed clustered barrier covers are judged by the probability minimum threshold to find the barrier gap, and then draw a circle according to the length of the gap. Determine the length of the barrier gap.

Barrier gap repair stage: According to the position of the barrier gap calculated in the first stage, and by adding grid weights, the sleeping sensor nodes are sequentially moved to the optimal position to be repaired.

The main idea of a repair algorithm based on clustered barrier gap is as follows:

First of all, the 3D environment is gridded in two dimensions, and a clustered barrier is deployed to cover the wireless sensor network. After a period of time, the power of the node will be consumed, and some nodes may be exhausted or destroyed. Through the minimum probability threshold, the barrier gap between the critical neighbor nodes is calculated, and then the repair track circle of the barrier gap is determined. The circle of each target track circle to be patched in this group is the best location for mobile node patching. Record the grid weight of the grid on the circle, calculate the distance and consider the grid weight of the mobile node and the position to be repaired, iterate in turn, and the final best repair position can be found. That is, to meet the best position to maximize coverage, the goal of this article can be achieved.

GRCB algorithm is a distributed algorithm. Each cluster head node knows the location information of the nodes in the cluster and can interact with each other. The implementation steps of GRCB algorithm are as follows:

Step 1: Deploys clusters as groups in a rectangular three-dimensional space, and randomly distributes several clusters of sensors to form a barrier coverage.

Step 2: Two-dimensional gridding of three-dimensional environment. For each working sensor node, calculate the joint perception probability between neighbors, traverse the neighbor nodes through the minimum threshold, and then find the barrier gap. If there is no barrier gap, it means that there is no node to move, jump to Step6. If you find the barrier gap, then Step3.

Step 3: Connect according to the found critical neighbor nodes, and calculate whether the distance is less than or equal to $2R$. If so, draw a circle with the center of this line segment as the origin and radius of r. Both the circle and the inside are repairable positions, check whether there are sleeping nodes on the circle and inside. If they exist, directly wake up the nodes, join the cluster network, jump to Step6. If not, record the grid location information, and jump to Step5.

Step 4: If the connection of the critical neighbor node is greater than $2R$, the line segment is divided by radius r. Then take the dividing point as the center of the circle and draw a circle with a radius of r to record the grid position information on the circle. From right to left, record the dormant nodes between clusters and jump to Step5.

Step 5: According to the grid gradient position information, the grid gradient is obtained. The location information of the dormant node is traversed, from which the optimal location and mobile node with the smallest grid gradient and the nearest distance are selected to wake up the node and join the cluster network.

Step 6: Determines whether to traverse to the last node. If so, the gap between the barrier is repaired and ends. If not, continue to iterate to see if there is still a gap, and if so, jump to Step3.

5 Simulation Results

In this paper, the simulation experiment deploys a rectangular target area with a deployment area of $1000\,\text{m} \times 100\,\text{m}$, and the grid division ratio is 5:1. $N_s : N_m$ is 1:1. The number of throwing nodes increases sequentially according to the number of clusters, and the simulation experiment of clustered 1-strong barrier gap repair is carried out in $P_{\min} = 0.9$ pairs of target areas. If there is no special description, the following simulation results are taken as the average of 100 random trials, and the number of iterations is set at 100. In order to verify the performance of the algorithm in this paper, the comparison algorithm uses the traditional Greedy algorithm and the DBCR algorithm in the literature [25] for comparison.

5.1 Moving Distance Comparison

As shown in Figs. 8 and 9, the simulation result is the total moving distance of the mobile nodes repaired by GRCB algorithm under the default parameters. It can be seen that when the number of grids is fixed, with the increase of the number of clusters, the number of nodes increases, and the moving distance of the repair gap decreases gradually. When the number of clusters is 65, the moving distance is basically unchanged. This is because with the increase of the number of nodes in the cluster, there is an overlapping relationship between nodes. When a node fails, Directly awaken the node that coincides with the failed node to work without moving. In the algorithm GRCB, it is obvious that the moving distance of the node is slightly higher than that of the DBCR algorithm. This is because when the GRCB mobile node repairs the gap, the mobile node itself is farther away from the gap, so the moving distance is farther. While the Greedy algorithm repairs the barrier gap, it is easy to repair the barrier gap when choosing the nearest distance, and does not consider the problem of three-dimensional down slope, so the distance of moving nodes is larger. The GRCB algorithm can choose a smoother moving distance and select a closer mobile node to repair the barrier. As can be seen from Figs. 8 and 9, when repairing the same barrier gap, the moving distance of the repair barrier gap gradually decreases with the increase of the number of nodes, because the more the number of nodes, the more accurate the moving distance, so the smaller the total moving distance.

5.2 Mobile Energy Consumption Comparison

In the process of repairing the barrier gap, the energy consumption of the node repairing gap is an important index to evaluate the method of repairing the gap. The shorter the total moving distance, the less energy consumption, and the lower the cost of repairing the barrier. Now it is assumed that the node moves 1 m per unit distance, consuming 3.6 J energy, and the node perception probability is 7.5. The experimental results are

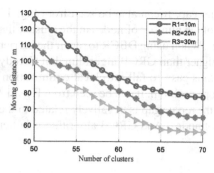

Fig. 8. Different radius comparison

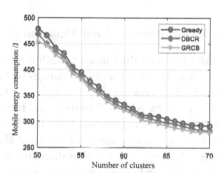

Fig. 9. Different algorithms comparison

shown in Fig. 10. It can be seen that with the increase of the number of nodes, the total energy consumption of mobile nodes to fill the gap decreases. When using DBCR to repair the barrier gap, the average energy consumption of movable nodes is slightly higher than that of GRCB. The Greedy algorithm consumes the most energy, because the Greedy algorithm always tends to choose the nearest mobile node to be filled for barrier gap repair, which often falls into the local optimization. On the other hand, the energy consumption of the repair gap of the mobile node is positively correlated with the moving distance (Fig. 11).

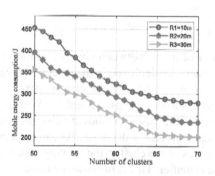

Fig. 10. Different radius comparison

Fig. 11. Different algorithms comparison

5.3 Comparison of the Number of Mobile Nodes

As shown in Fig. 12, when the number of nodes in the cluster is different, the number of mobile nodes to repair the barrier gap is different. When the radius of the nodes in the cluster is different, the number of mobile nodes to repair the gap of the barrier is also different. It can be seen that the number of mobile nodes is negatively related to the node radius and the number of nodes in the cluster. When the nodes in the cluster are fixed, the larger the radius is, the less the number of nodes moves. When the node radius is constant, with the increase of nodes in the cluster, the number of nodes moving becomes smaller and smaller. This is because both the increase of nodes and the increase of node radius will increase the overlap rate between nodes, which means that the reduction of node moving distance can also repair the barrier gap. It can also be seen from Fig. 13 that when the radius is fixed, with the increase of the number of nodes in the cluster, the number of mobile nodes filling the gap decreases. When using DBCR to repair the barrier gap, the number of movable nodes is slightly higher than GRCB algorithm, but Greedy is the highest, this is because Greedy algorithm is easy to fall into local optimization, and does not consider the three-dimensional slope problem. It can be seen from Figs. 12 and 13 that the number of removable nodes in the repair gap is negatively related to the number of nodes in the cluster and the radius of nodes. And GRCB algorithm is better than the other two algorithms.

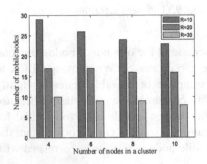

Fig. 12. Different radius comparison   **Fig. 13.** Different algorithms comparison

5.4 Comparison of Three Algorithms

In order to verify the impact of different number of nodes between clusters on mobile distance and mobile energy consumption, 60 clusters are deployed in the detection area, and the maximum sensing radius is 1. The number of nodes in the cluster increases from 4 to 10 by adding 2 in turn, and the result is shown in Figs. 12 and 13. With the increase of nodes in the cluster, the number of nodes increases, the moving distance and mobile energy consumption of the three algorithms gradually decrease. As can be seen in Fig. 12, with the increase of the number of nodes in the cluster, the moving distance of the repair gap between mobile nodes becomes smaller. This is because the number of nodes in the cluster increases and the overlap rate of the nodes in the cluster increases. When the gap exists, directly wake up the overlapping nodes to repair the gap. When the number of nodes in the cluster is 8, the moving distance and mobile energy consumption of the intra-cluster nodes are basically the same as those of the intra-cluster nodes for 10. The total mobile energy consumption is shown in Fig. 13. The same as the previous two experiments, the GRCB algorithm is the best (Figs. 14 and 15).

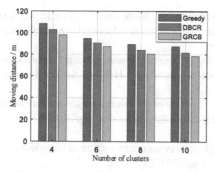

Fig. 14. Different nodes comparison   **Fig. 15.** Different nodes comparison

6 Conclusions

In order to solve the problem of barrier gap repair in 3D environment, a distributed barrier gap repair algorithm in 3D environment is proposed in this paper. First of all, the repair gap is determined according to the joint perception probability of nodes, and then the barrier gap repair trajectory circle model is constructed according to the repair gap. Finally, according to the barrier gap repair trajectory circle model, the grid weight is introduced, and the repair gap algorithm is proposed. And the corresponding steps are given. The experimental results show that when the GRCB algorithm is used to repair the 3D barrier gap, the node moving distance and energy consumption can be reduced, and the number of nodes can be used.

References

1. Kumar, S., Lai, T.H., Arora, A.: Barrier coverage with wireless sensors. Wirel. Netw. **13**(6), 817–834 (2007)
2. Chang, C.Y., Chang, C.T., Wang, C.S., et al.: A barrier coverage mechanism in wireless mobile sensor networks. J. Comput. Theor. Nanosci. **20**(20), 1881–1884(4) (2014)
3. Senouci, M.R., Assnoune, K., Mellouk, A.: Localized movement-assisted SensorDeployment algorithm for HoleDetection and healing. IEEE Trans. Parallel Distrib. Syst. **25**(5), 1267–1277 (2014)
4. Dash, D., Gupta, A., Bishnu, A., et al.: Line coverage measures in wireless sensor networks. J. Parallel Distrib. Comput. **74**(7), 2596–2614 (2014)
5. Saipulla, A.: Barrier coverage in wireless sensor networks. IEEE Trans. Mob. Comput. **9**(4), 491–504 (2010)
6. Mostafaei, H., Meybodi, M.R.: An energy efficient barrier coverage algorithm for wireless sensor networks. Wirel. Pers. Commun. **77**(3), 2099–2115 (2014)
7. Zhu, C., Zheng, C., Shu, L., Han, G.: A survey on coverage and connectivity issues in wireless sensor networks. Netw. Comput. Appl. **35**(2), 619–632 (2015)
8. Ahmed, N., Kanhere, S.S., Jha, S.: The holes problem in wireless sensor networks: a survey. ACM SIGMOBILE Mob. Comput. Commun. Rev. **9**(2), 4–18 (2016)
9. Kim, D., Wang, W., Son, J., et al.: Maximum lifetime combined barrier-coverage of weak static sensors and strong mobile sensors. IEEE Trans. Mob. Comput. **16**, 1956–1966 (2016)

10. Dai, H., Wu, X., Xu, L., et al.: Practical scheduling for stochastic event capture in wireless rechargeable sensor networks. In: Wireless Communications and Networking Conference, pp. 986–991. IEEE (2013)
11. He, L., Gu, Y., Pan, J., et al.: On-demand charging in wireless sensor networks: theories and applications. In: IEEE, International Conference on Mobile Ad-Hoc and Sensor Systems, pp. 28–36. IEEE (2013)
12. Zhao, L., Bai, G., Shen, H., et al.: Strong barrier coverage of directional sensor networks with mobile sensors. Int. J. Distrib. Sens. Netw. **14**(2) (2018). https://doi.dox.org/10.1177/155014 7718761582
13. Wang, Z., Cao, Q., Qi, H., et al.: Cost-effective barrier coverage formation in heterogeneous wireless sensor networks. Ad hoc Netw. **64**(sep.), 65–79 (2017)
14. He, S., Chen, J., Li, X., et al.: Cost-effective barrier coverage by mobile sensor networks. In: Proceedings IEEE INFOCOM 2012. IEEE (2012)
15. Saipulla, A., Westphal, C., Liu, B., et al.: Barrier coverage with line-based deployed mobile sensors. Ad Hoc Netw. **11**(4), 1381–1391 (2013)
16. Shen, C., Cheng, W., Liao, X.: Barrier coverage with mobile sensors. In: International Symposium on Parallel Architectures. IEEE (2008)
17. Chen, J., Wang, B., Liu, W., et al.: Mend barrier gaps via sensor rotation for a line-based deployed directional sensor network. In: IEEE International Conference on High Performance Computing & Communications & IEEE International Conference on Embedded & Ubiquitous Computing. IEEE (2013)
18. Mostafaei, H., Meybodi, M.R.: An energy efficient barrier coverage algorithm for wireless sensor networks (2014)
19. Chen, J., Wang, B., Liu, W., et al.: Rotating directional sensors to mend barrier gaps in a line-based deployed directional sensor network. IEEE Syst. J. **PP**(99), 1–12 (2017)
20. Wang, Z., Liao, J., Cao, Q., et al.: Barrier coverage in hybrid directional sensor networks. In: 2013 IEEE 10th International Conference on Mobile Ad-Hoc and Sensor Systems (MASS). IEEE (2013)
21. Mostafaei, H., Chowdhury, M.U., Obaidat, M.S.: Border surveillance with WSN Systems in a distributed manner. IEEE Syst. J. **12**(4), 3703–3712 (2018)
22. Tao, D., Tang, S., Zhang, H., et al.: Strong barrier coverage detection and mending algorithm for directional sensor networks. Ad Hoc Sens. Wirel. Netw. **18**(1–2), 17–33 (2013)
23. Kim, D., Kim, Y.: A new maximum fault-tolerance barrier-coverage problem in hybrid sensor network and its polynomial time exact algorithm. Ad Hoc Netw. **63**, 14–19 (2017)
24. Optimal strategies towards strong barrier coverage based on directional sensor networks. J. Chin. Comput. Syst. **035**(004), 740–745 (2014)
25. Dang, X., Li, Y., Hao, Z., Zhang, T.: A barrier coverage enhancement algorithm in 3D environment. In: Guo, S., Liu, K., Chen, C., Huang, H. (eds.) CWSN 2019. CCIS, vol. 1101, pp. 169–183. Springer, Singapore (2019). https://doi.org/10.1007/978-981-15-1785-3_13

WcAMDG: Wireless Charging and Assisted Mobile Data Gathering Algorithm in WRSNs

Zengwei Lyu[1,2], Zhenchun Wei[1,2(✉)], Xinchen Wang[1], Yang Lu[1,2(✉)], and Guowei Xu[1]

[1] School of Computer Science and Information Engineering, Hefei University of Technology, Hefei, China
`weizc@hfut.edu.cn, luyang@126.com`
[2] Engineering Research Center of Safety Critical Industrial Measurement and Control Technology, Ministry of Education, Hefei, China

Abstract. In Wireless Sensor Networks, sensor nodes near the base station need to forward data generated by the other nodes, which causes the early death of these sensor nodes. To solve the problem, some researchers used mobile sink to collect data from sensor nodes to save energy, some researchers employed mobile wireless charger to replenish energy for sensor nodes. In this paper, a Mobile Equipment (ME) with wireless charging and data collecting function is employed due to the different frequencies of data transmission and energy transfer, therefore it can save energy and replenish energy for the network simultaneously. An energy-saving coefficient is designed to balance the multi-hop transmission and the data collecting by the ME in each sensor node. Based on Lagrange Dual Decomposition and Sub-gradient Optimization methods, a distributed on-demand charging planning algorithm with assisted data collecting is proposed to optimize the charging energy in each sensor node and the routing of the WSNs. Experiments show that our proposed algorithm can effectively prolong the lifespan of network, balance the energy consumption of sensor nodes, and improve the energy utilization of the ME.

Keywords: Wireless Rechargeable Sensor Networks · Charging planning · Data gathering · Lagrange dual theory

1 Introduction

Wireless Sensor Networks (WSNs) are widely used in the field of tracking and monitoring of the environment, building facilities, animals, plants and human beings [1]. WSNs only can work for a limited time due to the limit of battery capacity. However, many applications require WSNs to be able to work continuously and efficiently without manual maintenance such as volcano monitoring, marine monitoring, and ecosystem monitoring. Although researchers have

© Springer Nature Singapore Pte Ltd. 2020
Z. Hao et al. (Eds.): CWSN 2020, CCIS 1321, pp. 57–69, 2020.
https://doi.org/10.1007/978-981-33-4214-9_5

achieved fruitful results in prolonging network lifetime, it is still the bottleneck
of network performance and the key factor in large-scale applications [2].

Some researchers are devoted to reducing energy consumption of sensor
nodes, but it will degrade the performance of network such as increasing delay
and lessening reliability. Some researches studied sensor nodes equipped with
energy harvesting modules. However, this technology strongly depends on environment that may lead to inefficiency. Other researches study Wireless Rechargeable Sensor Networks (WRSNs) [3], which employ Mobile Equipment (ME) to
replenish energy in network. In contrast to other charging techniques, wireless
charging can offer efficient and timely service without relying on unreliable environment energy [4,5].

Since the energy consumption is mainly caused by wireless data transmission
[6], in a network with static sink node, the nodes nearby sink node will quickly
consume energy when they forward mass of abundant data. And this may cause
energy hole. Even though wireless charger can supply energy for sensor nodes,
the power transmission is low-efficient owing to long distance between sink node
and sensor nodes. To improve efficiency of power transmission, we apply an ME
to gather data in the network. As a result, the load of sensors nearby sink node
will be reduced as the routing tasks are partially took by ME, and it can balance
energy consumption between the sensors.

In this paper, to provide high-performance energy replenishment, and reduce
the waste of energy due to long distance transmission and impact of energy
hole, we propose a wireless charging and assisted data gathering algorithm
(WcAMDG) to get the best charging and routing strategy which could maximize the global energy utilization. The main contributions of this paper are
summarized as follows:

1) In this paper, considering both energy replenishment and data collection, a
   path planning model is established to minimize the charging energy for sensor
   nodes to maximize the network utility.
2) Based on Lagrange Dual Decomposition and Sub-gradient Optimization
   methods, a distributed on-demand charging planning algorithm with assisted
   data collecting is proposed to optimize the charging energy in each sensor
   node and the routing of the ME.

2   Problem Formulation

2.1   Network Model

Consider a WRSN which consists of a sink node s_0, sensor nodes $S = \{s_1, s_2, ..., s_i, ..., s_N\}$, and an ME. The sink node also serves as service station
for ME to replenish energy. The sensor nodes are deployed according to the
application requirement in the target area for data sensing and submitting data
to the sink node. The battery capacity of the sensor node is E^{ini}, and if the
energy is below E^{min} the sensor node will die. The ME can charge sensor nodes
and collect data from sensor nodes at the same time. The moving energy and

charging energy carried by ME are denoted as E_v^{mo} and E_v^{ch}, respectively. The network model is shown in Fig. 1.

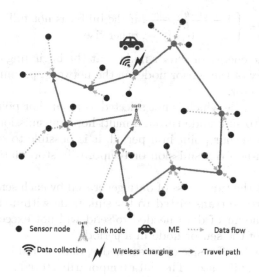

Fig. 1. The network model

Due to the limited moving energy, the maximum moving length of the ME is L_{tsp}, and the ME can only select part of the sensor nodes to replenish energy in each period. The set of the selected sensor nodes is anchor points set denoted as A. In each period, the ME starts at the service station, visits each anchor point, charges the sensor node, and collects data from the sensor node, comes back to the service station to submit the data.

2.2   Flow Routing Model and Energy-Saving Coefficient

When the energy of sensor nodes below the threshold, the sensor nodes send charging request to the ME. The ME will select some sensor nodes as the anchor points to replenish energy. Therefore, the sensor nodes in network are divided into the common sensor nodes and the anchor points. The flow rounting equation of node satisfies Eq. (1).

$$\left(g_i + \sum_{j=1}^{|N_i|} f_{ji} \right) (1 - \omega_i \varepsilon_i) = \sum_{j=1}^{|N_i|} f_{ij} \tag{1}$$

where g_i is the data generation rate of sensor node s_i in a period T, and N_i is the set of neighbor nodes that can communicate with sensor node s_i in single-hop way, and f_{ij} is data transmission rate from sensor node s_i to s_j. We use ω_i to indicate whether the sensor node is selected as an anchor point, if the sensor node s_i is anchor point $\omega_i = 1$, otherwise $\omega_i = 0$. We need to balance the multi-hop transmission and the ME collection, and an energy-saving coefficient ε_i is proposed to calculate how much data the sensor node chooses to store in buffer to be collected by ME. The energy-saving coefficient ε_i is denoted as Eq. (2)

$$\varepsilon_i = \begin{cases} 1 - \frac{(1-\theta)e_i + \theta\bar{e}}{E^{ini}} & \text{, if the buffer is not full} \\ 0 & \text{, otherwise} \end{cases} \tag{2}$$

where e_i denotes the energy of sensor node s_i at the beginning of each period, $\bar{e}$ is the average energy of the sensor nodes in the network, parameter $\theta(\theta \in [0,1])$ is the adjustment factor.

For the common node which is not selected as an anchor point in a period, it needs to send data to sink node through multi-hop transmission. For the sensor node selected as an anchor point in a period, it is possible to send data to sink node through multi-hop transmission or temporarily store data in buffer to be collected by ME.

In order to meet the timeliness of data generated by each sensor node, all the sensed data needs to be transmitted to the sink node within the period T. We assume that the amount of data needed to send will not exceed the maximum sending capability of the sensor node in a period.

Due to the limited buffer size of sensor nodes, data stored in the sensor nodes cannot exceed their buffer size. The data temporarily stored in the anchor point needs to satisfy the following constraint (3), where B_i represents the buffer size of sensor node s_i if s_i is selected as an anchor point.

$$\omega_i \varepsilon_i \left(g_i + \sum_{j=1}^{|N_i|} f_{ji} \right) \leq B_i \tag{3}$$

2.3 Energy Model

The main energy consumption of sensor nodes consists of three aspects: data perception and processing, data reception and data transmission. Denote μ_i^{gn} and μ_i^r as power dissipation of data perception and processing and data reception, respectively. Denote μ_t^{ij} and μ_t^{iv} as power dissipation of transmit data from s_i to s_j and from s_i to ME, respectively.

For each sensor node in each period, the energy consumption shall not exceed the sum of beginning energy e_i and supplement energy e_i^{ch} minus the minimum energy $E^{\min}$. Then we have

$$\left[\mu_i^r \sum_{j=1}^{|N_i|} f_{ji} + \mu_i^{gn} g_i + \mu_{iv}^t \omega_i \varepsilon_i \left(g_i + \sum_{j=1}^{|N_i|} f_{ji} \right) \right.$$
$$\left. + \mu_{ij}^t \sum_{j=1}^{|N_i|} f_{ij} \right] T \leq e_i + \omega_i e_i^{ch} - E^{\min}$$

Due to the limited energy carried by the ME, the sensor nodes charging energy and data collecting energy shall not exceed the carried energy E_v^{ch} of the ME, and it should satisfy the following constraint (5).

$$\sum_{i=1}^{N} \left[\omega_i e_i^{ch} \eta^{-1} + \mu_v^r \omega_i \varepsilon_i \left(g_i + \sum_{j=1}^{|N_i|} f_{ji} \right) T \right] \le E_v^{ch} \tag{4}$$

2.4   Optimization Problem

Since the amount of data generated during a period is a constant in the network, the less energy the ME charges sensor nodes, the higher the energy is utilized within the network. Therefore, we minimize the charging energy $U_i(\omega_i e_i^{ch})$ of each sensor node, where $U(\bullet)$ is an incremental, strictly concave and continuously differentiable function [4]. The optimization problem is formulated as OPT-1.

$$OPT - 1 : \arg\min_{f, e^{ch}} \sum_{i \in N} U_i \left(\omega_i e_i^{ch} \right)$$

$$s.t. \ (1), (3), (4), (5)$$

where the data transmission rate f_{ij} and the charging energy in each sensor node e_i^{ch} is optimization variable, and μ_i^{gn}, μ_i^r, $\mu_i^t j$, $\mu_i^t v$, g_i, T, θ are constants. The indicate variable can be obtained by the anchor point selection algorithm which will be discussed later.

3   Anchor Points Selection Algorithm

In this section, we propose a distributed algorithm to solve the problem OPT-1. We first discuss the anchor points selection algorithm. Then we propose a distributed on-demand charging planing algorithm based on Lagrange Dual Decomposition and Sub-gradient methods.

3.1   Anchor Points Selection Algorithm

In each period, ME will select a set of sensors to replenish their energy according to the on-demand request of the sensor nodes. If the energy of sensor nodes is below threshold, the sensor nodes will apply for charging. Due to the limited moving energy, the charging sequence of sensor nodes need to determine by the anchor points selection algorithm. To describe the urgency of the charging request of each sensor node. We first introduce the concept of node selection priority. Sensor nodes with higher priority will be selected as anchor points first. The priority of sensor node is denoted as

$$pr_i = \frac{|N_i|}{e_i + C_i E^{ini}} \tag{5}$$

where N_i is the number of neighbor nodes of sensor node s_i, and C_i is the number of times the sensor node s_i has been selected as an anchor point.

As shown in Fig. 2, when the energy of the sensor nodes is below threshold, the sensor nodes will send the charge request. Then the priority of these nodes is calculated by Eq. (6), and the sensor nodes are sorted according to the priority in descending order denoted as A'. The maximum m is calculated by Eq. (7), and the first m sensor nodes in A' are the set of the anchor points $A = \{\pi_1, \pi_2, ..., \pi_j, ..., \pi_m\}$.

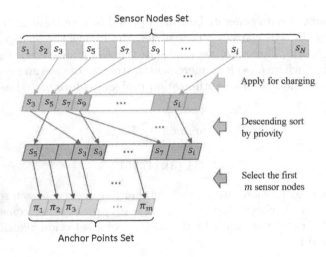

Fig. 2. Diagram of anchor points selection

$$\arg\min_m \left\{ d_{s_0,\pi_1} + \sum_{j=1}^{m-1} d_{\pi_j,\pi_{j+1}} + d_{\pi_m,s_0} \right\} \le L_{tsp} \qquad (6)$$

We use binary search method to search the maximum m in A', and the shortest travelsal path of the ME is calculated by using the TSP Nearest Neighbor algorithm [7].

3.2   Distributed On-Demand Charging Planning Algorithm

The problem OPT is a convex optimization problem, we can use Lagrange Dual Decomposition and Sub-gradient methods to solve the problem. We first introduce the Lagrange Multipliers λ_i, o_i, v_i and ξ_i for each sensor node and transmission link with respect to the constraints (1), (3), (4) and (5), respectively. The Lagrangian of the optimization problem OPT can be defined as

$$L(f_{ij}, e_i^{ch}, \lambda, o, \upsilon, \xi) = \sum_{i=1}^{N} U_i\left(\omega_i e_i^{ch}\right) + \sum_{i=1}^{N} \lambda_i \left[\left(g_i + \sum_{j=1}^{|N_i|} f_{ji}\right)(1 - \omega_i \varepsilon_i) - \sum_{j=1}^{|N_i|} f_{ji}\right]$$

$$+ \sum_{i=1}^{N} o_i \left[\omega_i \varepsilon_i \left(g_i + \sum_{j=1}^{|N_i|} f_{ji}\right) - B_i\right] + \sum_{i=1}^{N} \upsilon_i \left[\left[\mu_i^r \sum_{j=1}^{|N_i|} f_{ji}\right.\right.$$

$$+ \mu_{ij}^t \sum_{j=1}^{|N_i|} f_{ji} + \mu_i^{gn} g_i + \mu_{iv}^t \omega_i \varepsilon_i \left(g_i + \sum_{j=1}^{N_i} f_{ji}\right) - e_i - \omega_i e_i^{ch} + E^{min}\right]$$

$$+ \sum_{i=1}^{N} \xi_i \left[\omega_i e_i^{ch} \eta^{-1} + \mu_v^r \omega_i \varepsilon_i \left(g_i + \sum_{j=1}^{N} f_{ji} T\right)\right] - E_v^{ch}\right]$$

$$= \sum_{i=1}^{N} U_i\left(\omega_i e_i^{ch}\right) + \sum_{i=1}^{N} (\eta_i \xi_i - \upsilon_i)\omega_i e_i^{ch} + \sum_{i=1}^{N}\sum_{j=1}^{|N_i|} [[-\lambda_i$$

$$+ \lambda_j (1 - \omega_i \varepsilon_j) + \upsilon_j \mu_j^r] + \upsilon_i \mu_{ij}^t + \upsilon_j \mu_{jv}^t \omega_j \varepsilon_j$$

$$+ \xi_j \mu_v^r \omega_j \varepsilon_j + o_j \omega_j \varepsilon_j] f_{ij} + H$$

where

$$L_{e_i^{ch}}(e_i^{ch}, \upsilon, \xi) - \sum_{i=1}^{N} U_i\left(\omega_i e_i^{ch}\right) + \sum_{i=1}^{N} (\eta_i \eta^{-1} \quad \upsilon_i)\omega_i c_i^{vh}$$

$$L_{f_{ij}}(f_{ij}, e_i^{ch}, \lambda, o, \upsilon, \xi) = \sum_{i=1}^{N}\sum_{j=1}^{|N_i|} [-\lambda_i + \lambda_j (1 - \omega_i \varepsilon_j)$$

$$+ \upsilon_j \mu_j^r T + \upsilon_i \mu_{ij}^t T + \upsilon_j \mu_{jv}^t \omega_j \varepsilon_j T + \xi_j \mu_v^r \omega_j \varepsilon_j T + o_j \omega_j \varepsilon_j] f_{ij}$$

$$H(\lambda, o, \upsilon, \xi) = \sum_{i=1}^{N} [\lambda_i g_i(1 - \omega_i \varepsilon_j) - o_i \omega_i \varepsilon_i g_i T - o_i B_i$$

$$+ \upsilon_i g_i \mu_i^{gn} T + \upsilon_j \mu_{jv}^t \omega_j \varepsilon_j g_i T + \upsilon_i \mu_{iv}^t \omega_i g_i T$$

$$- \upsilon_i e_i + \upsilon_i E^{min} + \xi_i \mu_i^r \omega_i \varepsilon_i g_i T + \xi_i \omega_i e_i^{ch} \eta^{-1} - \xi_i E_v^{ch}]$$

$H(\lambda, o, \upsilon, \xi)$ is a constant expression. The objective function of Lagrangian dual problem of OPT is defined as $D(\lambda, o, \nu, \xi) = \min_{f_{ij}, e_i^{ch}} L(f_{ij}, e_i^{ch}, \lambda, o, \nu, \xi)$. The dual problem of the primal problem is given by Eq. (8) according to duality.

$$\max_{\lambda, \nu, \xi, o \succeq 0} D(\lambda, o, \nu, \xi) = \max_{\lambda, \nu, \xi, o \succeq 0} \min_{f_{ij}, e_i^{ch}} L(f_{ij}, e_i^{ch}, \lambda, o, \nu, \xi) \tag{7}$$

The primal problem is convex and satisfies the Slater condition, and we can use primal-dual method to obtain the optimal solution. From the dual problem, we can find that the problem can be decomposed into two independent sub-problems: the charging sub-problem and the routing sub-problem. Therefore, the problem can be solved in a distributed manner. The charging sub-problem and the routing sub-problem will be separately discussed next.

Charging Sub-problem: The charging sub-problem aims to find the amount of energy the ME charges for each anchor point in each period, which can be obtained by solving the following optimization problem OPT-C.

$$OPT - C : \min_{e^{ch} \geq 0} L_{e_i^{ch}}(e_i^{ch}, \nu, \xi)$$

$$s.t. \rho \leq e_i^{ch} \leq E^{\min} - e_i$$

From OPT-C we can see, if sensor node $\omega_i = 0$ is not selected as an anchor point, then $w_i = 0$, so we have $e_i^{ch} = 0$. If sensor node S_i is selected as an anchor point, then $\omega_i = 1$, and the charging sub-problem can be rewritten as follows.

$$\min_{e_i^{ch}=0} U_i(e_i^{ch}) + (\xi_i \eta^{-1} - \nu_i)e_i^{ch} \tag{8}$$

The charging sub-problem can be solved by introduced the Lagrange Multipliers a_i and b_i. Because the problem is concave, there is no dual gap between the solution of the dual problem and the primal problem when the KKT(Karush-Kuhn-Tucher) conditions are used.

According to the KKT conditions, the relationships of a_i and b_i and e_i^{ch} satisfy the Eq. (10), where $U_i'(e_i^{ch})$ is the first order partial derivative of $U_i(e_i^{ch})$ with variable e_i^{ch}.

$$\begin{cases} a_i \geq 0, b_i \geq 0 \\ a_i(\rho - e_i^{ch}) = 0 \\ b_i(e_i^{ch} - E^{ini} + e_i) = 0 \\ U'_i(e_i^{ch}) + (\xi_i \eta^{-1} - \nu_i) - a_i + b_i = 0 \end{cases} \tag{9}$$

According to the values of a_i and b_i, we have the following three cases. a) If $a_i > 0$ and $b_i = 0$, then we have $e_i^{ch} = \rho$, $U_i'(e_i^{ch}) + (\xi_i \eta^{-1} - \nu_i) > 0$. b) If $a_i = 0$ and $b_i > 0$, then we have $e_i^{ch} = E^{ini} - e_i$, $U_i'(e_i^{ch}) + (\xi_i \eta^{-1} - \nu_i) < 0$. c) If $a_i = 0$ and $b_i = 0$, then we have $e_i^{ch} \in [\rho, E^{ini} - e_i]$, $U_i'(e_i^{ch}) + (\xi_i \eta^{-1} - \nu_i) = 0$.

We can conclude that the value of e_i^{ch} depends on $U_i'(e_i^{ch}) + (\xi_i \eta^{-1} - \nu_i)$. As $U_i'(e_i^{ch})$ is a strict concave function, it will decrease with the increase of e_i^{ch}, then we have $U_i'(E^{ini} - e_i) \leq U_i'(e_i^{ch}) \leq U'(\rho)$. Denote $\tau = \xi_i \eta^{-1} - \nu_i$. For a given Lagrange multiplier in the current iteration, τ should be calculated first, and then the value of e_i^{ch} should be determined according to the relationship between τ, $U_i'(e_i^{ch})$ and $U'(\rho)$. So we have, if $\tau > -U_i'(E^{ini} - e_i)$, then it meets the case a), $e_i^{ch} = \rho$. If $\tau < -U_i'(\rho)$, then it meets the case b), $e_i^{ch} = E^{ini} - e_i$. Otherwise, it meets the case c), $e_i^{ch} = U_i'^{-1}(-\tau)$.

Routing Sub-problem: The purpose of solving the routing sub-problem is to get the best routing of sensor node. In practice, there will be some control information between nodes such as link status, establishment and release of connections, Lagrange multiplier exchange, etc. However, compared with the perception of data transmission, the control information are very small and the transmission frequency is very low, so the impact of this part of the control information will be ignored in routing sub-problem. The sensor node can get the route of the node by solving the following optimization problem.

$$\min_{f \succeq 0} \sum_{j=1}^{|N_i|} X_{ij} f_{ij} \tag{10}$$

where X_{ij} is the weight of the link. $X_{ij} = -\lambda_i + \lambda_j(1 - \omega_j \varepsilon_j) + v_j \mu_j^r + v_i \mu_{ij}^t + v_j \mu_{jv}^t \omega_j \varepsilon_j + \xi_j \mu_j^r \omega_j \varepsilon_j + o_j \omega_j \varepsilon_j$

It can be found that in each iteration, if the value of Lagrange multiplier has been determined, the value of X_{ij} is related to the data transmission energy consumption of the sensor node. The network can be seen as a graph $G = (S, W_{ij})$, $W_{ij} = \{X_{ij} | s_i, s_j \in S\}$, and the rounting of sensor node i the shortest path from s_i to sink node s_0 in graph G. Then the rounting of sensor nodes can be obtained by using Dijkstra algorithm.

Lagrange Multiplier Update: At each iteration, sensor node s_i updates the current Lagrange multiplier based on $\lambda_i(n)$, $v_i(n)$, $\xi_i(n)$ and $o_i(n)$ according to the following formula.

$$\lambda_i(n+1) = [\lambda_i(n) + \sigma(n)\nabla L(\lambda_i)(n)]^+ \tag{11}$$

$$v_i(n+1) = [v_i(n) + \sigma(n)\nabla L(v_i)(n)]^+ \tag{12}$$

$$\xi_i(n+1) = [\xi_i(n) + \sigma(n)\nabla L(\xi_i)(n)]^+ \tag{13}$$

$$i(n+1) = [o_i(n) + \sigma(n)\nabla L(o_i)(n)]^+ \tag{14}$$

where $\nabla L(\lambda_i)(n)$, $\nabla L(v_i)(n)$, $\nabla L(\xi_i)(n)$, $\nabla L(o_i)(n)$ is the gub-gradient of each multipliers.

$$\nabla L(\lambda_i)(n) = \left[g_i + \sum_{j=1}^{|N_i|} f_{ji}(n) \right](1 - \omega_i \varepsilon_i) - \sum_{j=1}^{|N_i|} f_{ij}(n);$$

$$\nabla L(v_i)(n) = \sum_{j=1}^{|N_i|} \mu_i^r f_{ji}(n) + \sum_{j=1}^{|N_i|} \mu_{ij}^t f_{ij}(n) + \mu_i^{gn} g_i$$

$$+ \mu_{iv}^t \omega_i \varepsilon_i \left[g_i + \sum_{j=1}^{|N_i|} f_{ji}(n) \right] - e_i - \omega_i e_i^{ch}(n) + \xi_i;$$

$$\nabla L(\xi_i)(n) = \sum_{i=1}^{N} \left[\eta^{-1} \omega_i e_i^{ch}(n) + \mu_v^r \omega_i \varepsilon_i \left(g_i + \sum_{j \in N_i} f_{ji}(n) \right) \right] - E_v^{ch}$$

$$\nabla L(o_i)(n) = \omega_i \varepsilon_i \left[g_i + \sum_{j=1}^{|N_i|} f_{ji}(n) \right] - B_i;$$

where denote $\sigma(n)$ $(0 < \sigma(n) < 1$ $)$ as gradual decline of the iterative steps, we set $\sigma(n) = 1/(10n+1)$. Regardless of the initial value of the Lagrange multiplier, the decreasing iteration step can ensure the convergence of the algorithm.

4   Simulation

4.1   Simulation Parameters Setting

100 sensor nodes are randomly deployed over a $100 \times 100\,\mathrm{m^2}$ area. The static sink node is located in the center of the area with coordinates $(50\,\mathrm{m}, 50\,\mathrm{m})$. The parameter settings are as follows. $E^{ini} = 12\,\mathrm{KJ}$, $E^{\min} = 1\,\mathrm{KJ}$, $\mu_i^r = 0.2\,\mathrm{mJ/kb}$, $\mu_i^{gn} = 0.02\,\mathrm{mJ/kb}$, $B_i = 64\,\mathrm{MB}$, $g_i = 5\text{--}10/\mathrm{s}$, $\beta = 50\,\mathrm{nJ/b}$, $\gamma = 0.0013\,\mathrm{pJ/b/m^4}$, $\alpha = 4$, $E_v^{ch} = 50\,\mathrm{kJ}$, $L_{tsp} = 400\,\mathrm{m}$, $\eta = 0.4$, $T = 3600\,\mathrm{s}$.

4.2   Performance Analysis of Anchor Point Selection Algorithm

To analyze the performance of the anchor selection algorithm, we compare the anchor selection algorithm of WcAMDG proposed in this paper with the anchor selection algorithm of WerMDG proposed in [4]. Figure 3 and Fig. 4 show the average residual energy of sensor nodes and the average residual energy standard deviation of sensor nodes of the two anchor selection algorithms, respectively. As shown in Fig. 3, compared with the anchor selection algorithm of WerMDG, the average energy reduction rate of nodes in our algorithm is slower than that of the WerMDG, and the average residual energy remains at a high level after a certain period of time.

As shown in Fig. 4, the standard deviation of the two anchor point selection algorithms are similar. The main reason is that the anchor selection algorithm

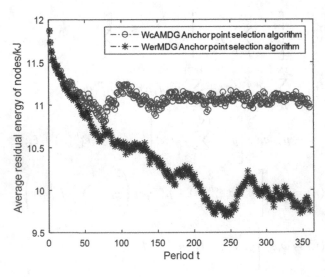

Fig. 3. Comparison of average residual energy of sensor nodes

of WerMDG only considers the residual energy of each sensor node, so that the choice of the anchor points is mostly focused on the sensor nodes with lower energy and faster energy consumption, thus the other sensor nodes cannot obtain the charging opportunity. However, our proposed algorithm not only considers the residual energy of the sensor nodes, but takes into account the fairness between sensor nodes, which avoids part of the sensor nodes being selected as anchor points frequently. Therefore, the proposed algorithm can maintain higher energy of the sensor nodes and balance the residual energy of the sensor nodes in the network.

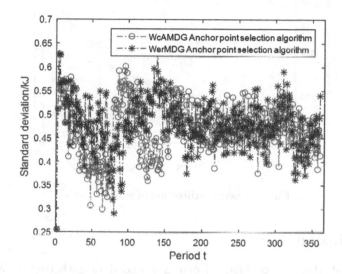

Fig. 4. Comparison of standard deviation

4.3   Performance Analysis of WcAMDG Algorithm

In order to analyze the performance of the WcAMDG algorithm, we compare it with the Mdcr algorithm proposed in [5]. Figure 5 shows the comparison between Mdcr and WcAMDG with different network scales. The number of sensor nodes in the network increases from 200 to 400, and the deployment area increases from $100 \times 100\,\mathrm{m}^2$ to $300 \times 300\,\mathrm{m}^2$.

From Fig. 5 we can see that the energy utilization of WcAMDG is much higher than that of Mdcr. This is because the energy consumption in WSNs is mainly for long-distance wireless transmission of data, and WcAMDG employs ME to replenish energy and collect data for the network which effectively reduces energy waste of long-distance wireless transmission. However, with the increase of network scale, the energy utilization of WcAMDG algorithm gradually decreases, and the energy utilization of Mdcr algorithm conversely gradually increases. The main reason is that the number of multi-hops from sensor nodes to sink node and anchor points increases when the network scale increases in WcAMDG algorithm, therefore the energy consumption for gathering the same amount of data gradually increases. While for Mdcr, as the number of sensor nodes increases, the amount of transmission data significantly increases, and the energy consumption is more evenly balanced among all the sensor nodes.

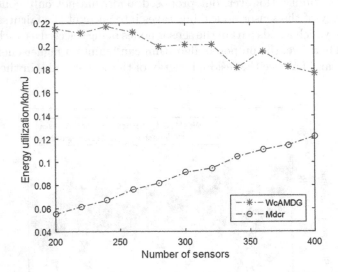

Fig. 5. Energy utilization of sensor nodes

5   Conclusion

This paper studies the problem of charging and data gathering in WRSNs in the case of ME assisted data gathering, and proposes a wireless charging and assisted mobile data gathering algorithm. The algorithm can implement ME to supplement energy for sensors and assist the sink node to gather data, so as to extend the network lifetime and reduce the occurrence of energy holes in the network. The OPT is solved by Lagrangian dual decomposition and subgradient algorithm to obtain the charge amount and routing, and compared with the previous algorithm in the simulation experiment, WcAMDG algorithm can balance energy consumption of nodes and improve energy utilization in the network. In the next work, we will further study the charging planning and routing strategies in WRSNs.

Acknowledgements. The material presented in this paper is Supported by the Fundamental Research Funds for the Central Universities with grant number [JZ2020HGQB0222, JZ2020HGQA0158].

References

1. Xu, J., Yuan, X., Wei, Z., Han, J., Shi, L., Lyu, Z.: A wireless sensor network recharging strategy by balancing lifespan of sensor nodes. In: Wireless Communications and Networking Conference, pp. 1–6 (2017)

2. Liu, F., Lu, H., Wang, T.: An energy-balanced joint routing and charging framework in wireless rechargeable sensor networks for mobile multimedia. IEEE Access **18**(6), 177637–177650 (2019)
3. Yang, Y.Y., Wang, C.: Wireless Rechargeable Sensor Networks. Springer, Berlin (2015)
4. Guo, S., Wang, C., Yang, Y.: Joint mobile data gathering and energy provisioning in wireless rechargeable sensor networks. IEEE Trans. Mob. Comput. **13**(12), 2836–2852 (2014)
5. Zhao, M., Li, J., Yang, Y.: A framework of joint mobile energy replenishment and data gathering in wireless rechargeable sensor networks. IEEE Trans. Mob. Comput. **13**(12), 2689–2705 (2014)
6. Harb, A.: Energy harvesting: State-of-the-art. Renew. Energy **36**(10), 2641–2654 (2011)
7. Lin, C., Zhou, J., Guo, C., Song, H., Wu, G., Obaidat, M.S.: TSCA: A temporal-spatial real-time charging scheduling algorithm for on-demand architecture in wireless rechargeable sensor networks. IEEE Trans. Mob. Comput. **17**(1), 211–224 (2018)
8. Shi, Y., Hou, Y.T.: Optimal base station placement in wireless sensor networks. ACM Trans. Sens. Netw. **5**(4), 1–24 (2009)

Software-Defined Multimodal Underwater Wireless Sensor Network Platform Powered by Seawater Battery

Chunjie Wang[1], Xiaochun Zhao[1], Zenghua Zhao[2]([⊠]) [iD], Wendi Xu[2], and Lin Cui[3]

[1] School of Electrical and Electronic Engineering, Tianjin University of Technology, Tianjin, China
chunjie_wang@tjut.edu.cn
[2] College of Intelligence and Computing, Tianjin University, Tianjin, China
zenghua@tju.edu.cn
[3] National Ocean Technology Centre, Ministry of Natural Resources, Tianjin, China
cuilin_oceanenergy@126.com

Abstract. Ocean exploring activities have boosted UWSN (Underwater Wireless Sensor Network) applications over the past decades. The applications have diverse requirements of network service in terms of data rates and transmission ranges. Moreover, reliable and sustainable power supply is necessary for UWSNs to fulfill a task. However, most of current UWSNs are designed for one specific application with inflexible and closed architecture, without considering power supply in the ocean. In this paper, we present a multimodal UWSN platform, Tuna, by leveraging a software-defined paradigm. Tuna supports multimodal communications covering both short-range and long-range transmission powered by seawater batteries. We design a power management module to provide Tuna with a reliable and sustainable power supply. Featuring multimodality, flexibility, reconfigurability, and energy-efficiency, Tuna is a promising one-size-fits-all solution to meet diverse requirements of ocean applications.

Keywords: Software-defined underwater wireless sensor networks · Multimodal communications · Seawater battery · Power management

1 Introduction

Underwater wireless sensor networking techniques have been applied in many ocean exploring activities over the past decades. The applications range from oil industrial to aquaculture, including instrument monitoring, pollution control, climate recording, disaster prediction, and marine life study [20]. Different applications have diverse requirements of network service in terms of data rates

This research was supported by the key project from NSFC under the grant U1701263.

© Springer Nature Singapore Pte Ltd. 2020
Z. Hao et al. (Eds.): CWSN 2020, CCIS 1321, pp. 70–83, 2020.
https://doi.org/10.1007/978-981-33-4214-9_6

and transmission ranges. For example, in marine life study, high data rates is needed to transmit real-time videos to an AUV (Autonomous Unmanned Vehicle) nearby. Whereas in pollution control scenario, for cooperative computing, one sensor node may forward a small number of scalar sensing data to another sensor kilometers away from it. In addition, whatever the application is, reliable and sustainable power supply is the unchanged requirement for UWSNs (Underwater Wireless Sensor Networks) to fulfill a task.

However, most of UWSNs are specific for one application with closed and inflexible architectural designs, which hinders the interoperability among UWSNs using different underwater communication technologies (e.g., underwater optical communications, acoustic communications, and MI (Magneto-Inductive) communications.) [5]. So far, there is not yet a one-size-fits-all UWSN solution. On the other hand, although energy-efficiency is always one of the hot topics in UWSNs, few work considers power sources available in the ocean, just assuming there is one. Hence, in this paper, we aim to address the above two challenges by designing a flexible multimodal UWSN platform, Tuna, powered by seawater battery, leveraging software-defined concept.

Software-defined UWSNs provide a promising solution to meet diverse application requirements, and are regarded as a paradigm of next generation UWSNs. The basic idea is to achieve reconfigurable (or programmable) and flexible network functionalities by software-defined architectural design [22]. SoftWater [5] is one of such network frameworks [25,28]. In SoftWater, a sensor is equipped with multiple hardware frontends, e.g., LED photodiode, acoustic transponder, and coil-antenna, to simultaneously support multiple underwater communication technologies, i.e., multimodal communications. Such feature greatly facilitates the interoperability of underwater devices and enhances the networking performance, by jointly exploiting the advantages of different underwater communication technologies.

In the light of the anticipated benefits from software-defined UWSN frameworks, there have been many research efforts toward developing software-defined UWSN platforms [9,15,22]. They are implemented based on different hardwares, e.g., USRP[1] [12,34], DSP (Digital Signal Processor) [8], FPGA (Field-Programmable Gate Arrays) [32], SBC (Single Board Computer) [13], mixture of them [11], or SoC (System on Chip, integration of a processor unit and a FPGA on one chip) [7,14]. Most of them are specified for different acoustic communications (e.g., short-rang, long-range). Ardelt et al. [7] propose a software-defined platform supporting multimodal communications. However, they target at only short-range communications. It still lacks a software-defined platform that supports underwater multimodal communications covering various transmission ranges.

Although there are many power sources available in the ocean, e.g., solar energy, wind energy, ocean wave energy, ocean thermal energy, BMFC (Benthic Microbial Fuel Cells), and seawater batteries, few of them are suitable for

---

[1] USRP is a software-defined radio device developed by Ettus, https://www.ettus.com.

UWSNs. Among them, seawater battery features high energy density, open structure, eco-friendly, and safety, which makes it suitable to support power supply for UWSNs. However, the output voltage of seawater batteries is generally around 1.6 V, which is much lower than work voltage (24 V) of most underwater sensor nodes. Furthermore, the amount of energy generated depends on the local environment. Therefore, it is challenging to provide a reliable and sustainable power for UWSNs.

In this paper, we present a software-defined UWSN platform Tuna, supporting multimodal communications (e.g., acoustic, optical and MI) with coverage of both short-range and long-range transmissions. Tuna is based on SoC as in [7,14], which makes it energy-efficiency and small-size. Unlike [7,14], Tuna adopts a motherboard-daughterboard design, where analog frontends connect to the motherboard through their daughterboards. The baseband processing (e.g., modulation, demodulation, and channel coding) shared by different communication technologies is implemented in FPGA in the motherboard, while the processing specific to them (e.g., ADC (Analog-Digital Converter), DAC (Digital-Analog Converter), PA (Power Amplifier), etc.) is put in the daughterboard. The separation of motherboard and daughterboard ensures Tuna more flexible to various communication hardware frontends, and scalable to upcoming new communications, since the difference among frontends is transparent to the motherboard thanks to the daughterboard. In this way, Tuna features multimodality, flexibility, reconfigurability, and energy-efficiency, which makes it a one-size-fits-all solution for various ocean applications, and capable of interoperating with other UWSNs.

In order to provide reliable and sustainable power supply to Tuna, we choose clean and renewable seawater battery, and design a power management module, including a boost DC (Direct Current)-DC converter, bidirectional DC-DC converter, an energy controller, and a supercapacitor. The power management module boosts the low voltage of the seawater battery to high voltages required by Tuna, and provides big current while data transmitting. Therefore, Tuna is able to fulfill long-time tasks powered by seawater batteries.

In summary, our contributions are as follows:

- We design a flexible software-defined multimodal UWSN platform Tuna. Tuna has inherent features of a software-defined platform: multimodality, flexibility, and reconfigurability. Unlike the state-of-the-art approaches, Tuna supports multimodal communications covering both short-range and long-range transmission.
- We design a power management module to provide Tuna with reliable and sustainable power based on seawater battery, a clean and renewable energy available in the ocean. To the best of our knowledge, this is the first design of UWSNs involving ocean power source and its management.

The rest of the paper is organized as follows. We survey the related work in Sect. 2. In Sect. 3, we introduce background and our motivations. In Sect. 4 we present the design of our software-defined UWSN platform Tuna. Section 5 concludes the paper.

2 Related Work

2.1 Software-Defined UWSN Platforms

There have been research efforts toward developing software-defined networking frameworks for UWSNs. From the perspective of implementation, they can be classified into two categories: a) software architecture based on commercial acoustic modems, and b) architecture involving both software and hardware.

Software Architecture Based on Commercial Acoustic Modems: SUNSET [28] and DESERT [25] are two software-defined networking frameworks that integrate simulation, emulation and experiments based on the open-source network simulators ns-2 [2] and commercial acoustic modems. Potter *et al.* propose SDOAM (Software Defined Open Architecture Modem), a high-level software architecture, based on a generalization of the classic OSI communication stack [29]. Campagnaro *et al.* design a fully reconfigurable acoustic modem based on commercial one, driven by a custom firmware version that bypasses the channel coding methods applied by the modem, and allows users to set the transmit bit rate to any desired value within a given set [10]. This type of architecture can achieve partially flexibility and reconfigurability since they are based on commercial acoustic modems.

Architecture Involving Both Software and Hardware: In recent years, researchers have proposed several studies that consider hardware development of new experimental modems with partially or fully software-defined protocol stacks. According to their hardware implementation, there are following types: USRP-based, SBC (Single Board Computer)-based, DSP (Digital Signal Processing)+FPGA-based, FPGA+DSP+SBC-based, and FPGA+ARM based architecture.

USRP-Based Architecture: Torres *et al.* propose a USRP-based architecture that exploits open-source software tools, e.g., GNU Radio [1], TinyOS [3], and TOSSIM [4], for implementing physical and data-link layer functionalities [34]. Demirors *et al.* also present a USRP-based reconfigurable acoustic modem [12]. This type of modems is easy to prototype due to open-source software and USRP device. However, they cannot be deployed in the ocean, since USRP is controlled by a computer.

FPGA+DSP-Based Architecture: FPGA is programmable, whereas DSP is good at signal processing. Therefore Sozer *et al.* implement a programmable acoustic modem in FPGA [32]. Berning *et al.* realize the software-defined radio concept in a commercial acoustic modem based on DSP [8]. Nowsheen *et al.* combine FPGA and DSP, implementing an acoustic modem [27]. However, it is hard to implement high-layer network protocols in FPGA and/or DSP.

SBC-Based Architecture: SEANet G1 is one of this type of modems. Unlike software-based framework solutions that are mainly based on interfacing and exploiting commercially available devices, SEANet G1 proposes to transform a general-purpose processor interfaced with acoustic transducers into a fully-functional acoustic network node. Since physical layer and MAC layer have time-critical tasks, it is challenging for SEATNet G1 to support high bit rate modulation schemes.

FPGA+DSP+SBC-Based Architecture: UNET-2 is such an acoustic modem [11], where FPGA is primarily responsible for packet detection, passband-baseband conversion and time-stamping. The DSP implements the physical layer signal processing and FEC coding. All higher layer functionality is implemented on the SBC running TinyCore Linux and the Java agent development framework.

FPGA+ARM-Based Architecture: This type of modem uses FPGA+ARM hardware, usually in a SoC (System on Chip) for energy efficiency and small size. SEANet G2 employes Zynq-7020 SoC, which features a dual-core ARM cortex-A9 based processor unit and a FPGA programmable logic [14]. The combination of processor and FPGA offers hardware and software reprogrammability. Ardelt *et al.* propose a modem sharing the similar architecture [7], which supports three different underwater wireless communication technologies. Unfortunately, this modem targets at short-range communications, and cannot support long-range communications.

Most of the above modems are specified for acoustic communications. Few consider multiple communication techniques [7,9,17,26]. Unlike the above solutions, our software-define UWSN platform supports multiple underwater communication technologies, covering short-range and long-range. Moreover, we consider power supply with seawater battery, which is important but ignored by most of existing work.

2.2 Power Sources for UWSNs

Power supply is a big concern for UWSN design and deployment. We focus on batteries available in the ocean. There are primarily two types of batteries suitable in the ocean: Benthic Microbial Fuel Cells (BMFCs) and seawater battery.

BMFCs are bio-electrical devices that harness the natural metabolism of microbes in marine sediments to directly produce electrical power [19]. Sediments are naturally teaming with a complex community of microbes, including the electrogenic microbes needed for MFCs, and are full of complex sugars and other nutrients that have accumulated over millions of years of microbe and animal material decay. BMFCs are viable power sources for undersea sensor and communication systems. However, it is demonstrated that the power can be generated from the microbes and the nutrients found within the sediment alone. Therefore, they supply power only for sensors deployed on the sea floor.

Seawater battery is one of the solutions for long-term sea observations. Most of seawater batteries use metal anodes and seawater as an electrolyte with cathodes. Its energy comes from electrolytic dissolution of the metal anode. Since the output voltage of seawater battery is low about 1.6 V, a power manage system is needed to convert its voltage to a higher one as application requires. Because of its open structure, seawater battery can be deployed in any depth in the sea without pressure housings. There are also emerging rechargeable seawater batteries, which make seawater battery low cost with long-cycle life [31].

Multiple power sources have been combined to provide more reliable and longer energy for UWSNs. Srujana et al. integrate energies from piezoelectric harvesting and MFCs [33], whereas Manley et al. make use of both ocean wave energy and solar energy to achieve persistent power supply for gliders [24].

In this paper, we choose seawater battery for its promising performance. We design a power control approach to manage seawater battery aiming to provide a reliable energy supply for UWSN nodes.

3   Background and Motivation

3.1   Underwater Communication Technologies: Background

The harsh underwater environment poses a great challenge for developing underwater communication systems [26]. Acoustic communication techniques have been developed for underwater communication systems and now represent a relatively mature and robust technology [17]. Acoustic systems are capable of long-range communication, but offer limited data rates and significant latency due to the speed of sound in water. Apart from acoustic communication, a couple of other technologies, like optical, magneto-inductive communications have been investigated. In the following, we illustrate some characteristics of each technology.

Underwater Acoustic Communication: Acoustic communication is a primary technique used in underwater environment. It is able to provide both short-range and long-range communications. Long-range systems that operate over several tens of kilometers have a bandwidth of only some hundreds of Hz while a short-range system operating over tens of meters or less may have up to a MHz bandwidth.

An acoustic modem consists mainly of communication system and acoustic transducers. Communication system implements primarily modulation, demodulation, and channel coding. Acoustic transducers send or receive acoustic signals transmitted in the ocean.

Underwater Optical Communication: With respect to acoustic signal transmission, optical signals have a much larger bandwidth but can propagate some tens or hundreds of meters in water, depending on the turbidity [26]. Moreover, at short ranges they offer the possibility of much higher data-rate communications, with almost zero propagation delay. The data rate can achieve 10–100 Mbps. A fading rate of about 0.15 dB/m is achievable in the blue-green band in clear water, thus the working range of underwater optical modems is on the order of 100 m in the clearest water.

An optical modem consists of an optical transmitter and a receiver. The transmitter is composed of an array of LEDs that emits 480 nm blue light or 527 nm green light. Raw data is encoded into symbols using either DPIM (Discrete Pulse Interval Modulation) or simple ON-OFF keying. The receiver consists of an avalanche photodiode with a low-noise amplifier which receives light signals and decodes them into digital data [16, 18].

Underwater Magnetic Induction: Since the radiation resistance of a coil is much smaller than that of an electric dipole, only a very small portion of energy is radiated to the far field by the coil. Due to high propagation speed of MI waves, the frequency offsets caused by Doppler effect can be greatly mitigated [9]. Compared to acoustic communication, multi-path fading is not an issue for MI-based underwater communication [6]. Moreover, without suffering from light scattering as in optical communications, the transmission range and channel quality of MI communications are independent of water quality factors such as water turbidity.

An MI modem usually consists of an RF front-end, analog-to-digital/digital-to-analog converter (ADC/DAC), modulator, and equalizer [6]. In addition, since MI channel is insensitive to multipath fading, Doppler effect, and underwater acoustic noise, an extremely high-order modulation scheme and corresponding channel equalization scheme can be jointly designed based on the underwater MI channel models, which can provide high data rate MI communication links under water.

Motivation: We summarize the characteristics of acoustic, optical, and MI underwater communications in Table 1. We can see that the three communication techniques are different in terms of transmission range, data rate, and latency. They are complementary in underwater sensor networking applications. From the respective of implementation, although their modems have different senders and receivers for different analog signals (e.g., acoustic, optical, and MI), they share modulation and demodulation schemes in common. This motivates us to design a flexible UWSN platform supporting multiple communication techniques to meet diversity application requirements.

Table 1. Characteristics of underwater communication technologies.

Tech.	Comm. ranges	Data rates	Latency	Energy consumption
Acoustic	~Km	~Kbps	667 ms/Km	100 bits/J
Optical	10–100 m	~Mbps	0.03 ms/Km	30,000 bits/J
MI	10–100 m	~Mbps	0.03 ms/Km	-

3.2   Seawater Battery

Seawater batteries have advantages of high energy density, open structure, eco-friendly and safety, which make it suitable to support power supply for UWSN nodes. However, the overall cell voltage of seawater batteries depends on the salinity and oxygen concentration in the water and is generally around 1.6 V. The power generation of seawater batteries ranges from a few milliwatts to several watts [21]. They cannot directly support a network node in UWSNs to work. This motivates us to design a power control system to manage the seawater battery so as to supply reliable power for UWSNs.

4   Software-Defined UWSN Platform Design

We first explain our fundamental design principles, and then detail the platform architecture.

4.1   Design Principles

The design of UWSN platform should adhere to the following principles.

- **Meeting diverse requirements of various applications.** Different ocean applications have different requirements in terms of data rates and transmission ranges. A UWSN should be designed to meet all of these requirements, rather than being application oriented.
- **Multimodality.** There are multiple underwater wireless communication technologies (e.g., underwater acoustic, optical, and MI communication) at present, and new communication technologies will be developed in the future. Each communication technique has its unique characteristics and thus suitable for different applications. For example, underwater acoustic communication features low dat rate yet long transmission range. Whereas underwater optical and MI communications can achieve high data rate in short range. These communication technologies cannot replace each other, and thus will co-exist in a long run. Therefore, A UWSN should support multiple underwater communication technologies simultaneously, i.e., working in a multimodal communication mode. Moreover, UWSNs should interoperate with each other.
- **Flexibility.** A UWSN should be flexible to allow different communication hardware connection, and can adopt new communication hardwares. It should be easy to exchange different communication hardwares without redesign of UWSN node hardware.
- **Reconfigurability.** A UWSN should be reconfigurable at run time, in order to adapt to underwater channel environments and interoperate with other UWSNs.
- **Energy efficiency.** Power supply is very costly since it is difficult to deploy and maintain a power source in the ocean. Therefore, a UWSN should be energy-efficiency from its hardware to software, especially network protocols.
- **Using clean and renewable energy, easy to obtain from the ocean.** Power sources used by a UWSN should be clean and renewable, i.e., eco-friendly, and are easy to obtain from the ocean.

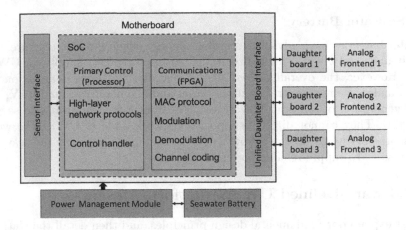

Fig. 1. Platform functional architecture.

4.2 Software-Defined Multimodal UWSN Platform Architecture

Based on the design principles, we present a software-defined multimodal UWSN platform, Tuna. The functional architecture is illustrated in Fig. 1.

From hardware to software, platform Tuna is designed by leveraging software-defined concept and modularization as well. From the perspective of hardware, Tuna consists of a motherboard and several daughterboards. The motherboard adopts a SoC, which combines a general-purpose processor and a FPGA on a single chip, making it energy-efficiency and small-size. The motherboard is responsible for general-purpose processing and common communication functionalities by means of software-defined approaches. Furthermore, the motherboard provides interfaces to sensors and daughterboards. Through daughterboards, the motherboard can be equipped with multiple frontends. The frontends include LED photodiode, acoustic transducer, coil-antenna, *etc.*, to simultaneously support different underwater communication technologies, e.g., underwater optical communications, acoustic communications, MI communications, and other upcoming new ones. Frontends input analog signals to daughterboards and vice versa. Since analog signals may be acoustic, light, or electro-magnetic, the daughterboard has to be designed specifically according to the signal characteristics. The separative design of motherboard and daughterboard enables Tuna to support multiple communication techniques easily, just by connecting different daughterboards to the motherboard.

From the perspective of software, platform Tuna is mainly comprised of three modules: primary control module, communication module, and power management module. The primary control module handles general-purpose commands, and high-layer network protocols (e.g., application layer, transport layer, network layer, and non-time-sensitive part of MAC protocols). The primary control module is implemented in the general-purpose processing unit by leveraging software-defined methodologies. The communication module is implemented in

FPGA and exploits SDR (Software-Defined Radio) technologies to implement time-sensitive part of MAC protocols, and physical layer protocols (e.g., modulation, demodulation, and channel coding). By means of SDR, the communication module can respond frontends quickly and support reconfiguration at run-time. The power management module manages seawater battery and supplies reliable power to motherboard and daughterboards.

In this way, our software-defined UWSN platform Tuna benefits multimodality, flexibility, reconfigurability, and energy-efficiency. Such features greatly facilitate the interoperability of underwater devices and enhance the networking performance by jointly exploiting the advantages of different underwater communication technologies [5].

Primary Control Module: The primary control module runs Linux operating system and is in charge of data processing and of executing software-defined functionalities. The high-layer network protocols are implemented in this module, including part of MAC functions, network, transport and application layer functions.

In software-defined paradigm, network functions are separated into two planes: data plane and control plane [23]. The data plane comprehends the data transmission and forwarding functions. In general, the data plane is instantiated as flow tables in routers, switches and firewalls, as well as circuits that encode and decode signals for transmission. The control plane consists of functions controlling the network behavior (e.g., network paths, forwarding, signaling and others). Examples of control planes are routing protocols, network middle box configuration such as firewall configuration.

Among SoC chips, Xilinx Zynq 7020 SoC is a promising candidate with a dual-core ARM cortex-A9 based processor unit and a FPGA, which has been adopted in SEANet G2 [14] and in [7]. The Xilinx Evaluation board offers a 1 GB of DDR3 SDRAM and 128 MB of Flash memory. Moreover, it supports a rich set of I/O peripherals, including two I^2C blocks that can operate both as master and slaves, and 118 GPIO pins to enable connectivity with virtually any sensors, data converters, and memories. Therefore, we are implementing a prototype in Xilinx Evaluation board to verify our design.

Software-Defined Multimodal Communication Module: The communication module offers time-sensitive MAC functionalities and baseband processing (e.g., modulation, demodulation, and channel coding). It is implemented in a FPGA, which makes it programmable and enables SDR. In this way, the baseband processing for a variety of different underwater wireless communication techniques is programmed in software in advance, and is capable of switching among them at run-time. Therefore, our software-defined UWSN platform Tuna supports multimodal communication mode covering short-range and long-range transmissions.

In addition, we put the communication module in the motherboard. The motherboard offers interfaces to daughterboards. The daughterboards are

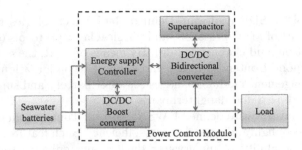

Fig. 2. Power management module.

designed specifically for different frontends (e.g., acoustic transducers, photo-diode, coil antenna). The frontends are analog. The daughterboards primarily consist of ADC, DAC, low-noise amplifier, and (or) power amplifier. They take in charge of converting digital signals to analog signals during sending phase, and converting analog signals to digital signals during receiving phase.

Seawater Battery Power Management Module: Seawater battery generates electric with output voltage less than 1.6 V, whereas our motherboard and frontends require higher voltage of 5 V and 24 V. In addition, seawater battery is unreliable because of its dependence on environmental conditions. To address this issue, a power management module is needed between the seawater battery and the UWSN node. Thus the harvested energy from the seawater battery is transferred to the node with the boosted voltage to meet node requirements. As shown in Fig. 2, the power management module consists of DC-DC boost converter, DC-DC bidirectional converter, supercapacitor, and energy supply controller. The power management module is designed to accommodate the unique features of seawater battery and achieves better energy conversion efficiency as well.

For designing high-efficiency seawater battery power system, a suitable DC-DC converter is required. A normal boost converter converts a DC voltage to a higher DC voltage. Among DC-DC converter topologies, interleaved boost converter is considered as a promising solution for seawater battery power systems due to its excellent electrical performance [30]. Interleaved boost converter offers good performance in terms of reducing ripple contents with high efficiency, fast transient response, and reliability. Interleaved boost converter consists of several boost converters connected in parallel and controlled by an interleaved method which has the same switching frequency and phase.

We design a DC-DC boost converter as shown in Fig. 3a. The design of interleaved boost converter involves selection of inductors, capacitor, and power switches. Four phases are utilized since ripple contents reduce with increase in the number of phases. Further increasing the number of phases leads to higher complexity of the circuit. Therefore four phases are selected to trade off between ripple content reduction and circuit complexity.

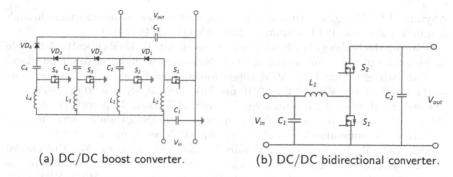

(a) DC/DC boost converter.   (b) DC/DC bidirectional converter.

Fig. 3. DC/DC converters.

A supercapacitor has very high capacitance. The capacitance density or energy density is an important property of a supercapacitor, which refers to the amount of charges that can be stored per unit. We adopt a bidirectional DC-DC converter to connect a supercapacitor and a node. The topology of the bidirectional DC-DC converter is illustrated in Fig. 3b. The bidirectional DC-DC is responsible for recharging and discharging the supercapacitor. When the node needs high power during transmissions, the bidirectional DC-DC converter discharges the supercapacitor to provide power for the node. When the supercapacitor has insufficient voltage, the bidirectional DC-DC converter recharges it from the seawater battery.

5   Conclusions

We design a software-defined UWSN platform, Tuna, which supports multimodal communications including acoustic, optical and MI, covering both short-range and long-range transmissions. Tuna is powered by clean and renewable seawater battery. Through power management, the seawater battery can provide reliable and sustainable power for Tuna. Tuna features multimodality, flexibility, reconfigurability, and energy-efficiency, which makes it a promising one-size-fits-all solution for various ocean applications. Our work is still at an early stage, and we are working to implement Tuna and will verify its performance by field experiments in the near future.

References

1. Gnuradio. https://www.gnuradio.org/
2. Ns2. http://nsnam.sourceforge.net/wiki/index.php/Main_Page
3. Tinyos. http://www.tinyos.net/
4. Tossim. http://networksimulationtools.com/tossim/
5. Akyildiz, I.F., Wang, P., Lin, S.: Softwater: Software-defined networking for next-generation underwater communication systems. Ad Hoc Netw. **46**(4), 1–11 (2016)

6. Akyildiz, I.F., Wang, P., Sun, Z.: Realizing underwater communication through magnetic induction. IEEE Commun. Mag. **53**(11), 42–48 (2015)
7. Ardelt, G., Mackenberg, M., Markmann, J., Esemann, T., Hellbrück, H.: A flexible and modular platform for development of short-range underwater communication. In: Proceedings of the 11th ACM International Conference on Underwater Networks and Systems, WUWNET 2016, pp. 35:1–35:8. ACM, New York (2016)
8. Berning, F., Radtke, T., Rautenberg, S., Motz, M., Nissen, I.: A realization of the software defined radio concept in an underwater communication modem. In: 2014 Underwater Communications and Networking (UComms), pp. 1–5 (2014)
9. Campagnaro, F., Francescon, R., Casari, P., Diamant, R., Zorzi, M.: Multimodal underwater networks: Recent advances and a look ahead. In: Proceedings of the International Conference on Underwater Networks and Systems, WUWNET 2017, pp. 4:1–4:8. ACM, New York (2017)
10. Campagnaro, F., Francescon, R., Kebkal, O., Casari, P., Kebkal, K., Zorzi, M.: Full reconfiguration of underwater acoustic networks through low-level physical layer access. In: Proceedings of the International Conference on Underwater Networks and Systems, WUWNET 2017. ACM, New York (2017)
11. Chitre, M., Topor, I., Koay, T.: The UNET-2 modem – an extensible tool for underwater networking research. In: OCEANS 2012, pp. 1–7 (2012)
12. Demirors, E., Sklivanitis, G., Santagati, G.E., Melodia, T., Batalama, S.N.: A high-rate software-defined underwater acoustic modem with real-time adaptation capabilities. IEEE Access **6**, 18602–18615 (2018)
13. Demirors, E., Shankar, B.G., Santagati, G.E., Melodia, T.: Seanet: A software-defined acoustic networking framework for reconfigurable underwater networking. In: Proceedings of the 10th International Conference on Underwater Networks and Systems, WUWNET 2015, pp. 11:1–11:8. ACM, New York (2015)
14. Demirors, E., Shi, J., Guida, R., Melodia, T.: Seanet g2: Toward a high-data-rate software-defined underwater acoustic networking platform. In: Proceedings of the 11th ACM International Conference on Underwater Networks and Systems, WUWNET 2016, pp. 12:1–12:8. ACM, New York (2016)
15. Dol, H.S., Casari, P., van der Zwan, T., Otnes, R.: Software-defined underwater acoustic modems: Historical review and the NILUS approach. IEEE J. Oceanic Eng. **42**(3), 722–737 (2017)
16. Doniec, M., Vasilescu, I., Chitre, M., Detweiler, C., Hoffmann-Kuhnt, M., Rus, D.: Aquaoptical: A lightweight device for high-rate long-range underwater point-to-point communication. In: OCEANS 2009, pp. 1–6 (2009)
17. Farr, N., Bowen, A., Ware, J., Pontbriand, C., Tivey, M.: An integrated, underwater optical/acoustic communications system. In: OCEANS 2010, pp. 1–6 (2010)
18. Gois, P., Sreekantaswamy, N., Basavaraju, N., Rufino, M., Sebastião, L., Botelho, J., Gomes, J., Pascoal, A.: Development and validation of blue ray, an optical modem for the MEDUSA class AUVs. In: 2016 IEEE Third Underwater Communications and Networking Conference (UComms), pp. 1–5 (2016)
19. Guzman, J.J., Cooke, K.G., Gay, M.O., Radachowsky, S.E., Girguis, P.R., Chiu, M.A.: Benthic microbial fuel cells: long-term power sources for wireless marine sensor networks. In: Carapezza, E.M. (ed.) Sensors, and Command, Control, Communications, and Intelligence (C3I) Technologies for Homeland Security and Homeland Defense IX, vol. 7666, pp. 586–596. International Society for Optics and Photonics, SPIE, Florida (2010)
20. John Heidemann, M.S., Zorzi, M.: Underwater sensor networks: Applications, advances and challenges. Philos. Trans. R. Soc. **370**(1958), 158–175 (2012)

21. Liu, Q., Yan, Z., Wang, E., Wang, S., Sun, G.: A high-specific-energy magnesium/water battery for full-depth ocean application. Int. J. Hydrogen Energy **42**(36), 23045–23053 (2017)
22. Luo, H., Wu, K., Ruby, R., Liang, Y., Guo, Z., Ni, L.M.: Software-defined architectures and technologies for underwater wireless sensor networks: A survey. IEEE Commun. Surv. Tutorials **20**(4), 2855–2888 (2018)
23. Macedo, D.F., Guedes, D., Vieira, L.F.M., Vieira, M.A.M., Nogueira, M.: Programmable networks–from software-defined radio to software-defined networking. IEEE Commun. Surv. Tutorials **17**(2), 1102–1125 (2015)
24. Manley, J., Willcox, S.: The wave glider: A persistent platform for ocean science. In: OCEANS 2010 IEEE SYDNEY, pp. 1–5 (2010)
25. Masiero, R., Azad, S., Favaro, F., Petrani, M., Toso, G., Guerra, F., Casari, P., Zorzi, M.: Desert underwater: An ns-miracle-based framework to design, simulate, emulate and realize test-beds for underwater network protocols. In: OCEANS 2012, pp. 1–10 (2012)
26. Moriconi, C., Cupertino, G., Betti, S., Tabacchiera, M.: Hybrid acoustic/optic communications in underwater swarms. In: OCEANS 2015 - Genova, pp. 1–9 (2015)
27. Nowsheen, N., Benson, C., Frater, M.: A high data-rate, software-defined underwater acoustic modem. In: OCEANS 2010, pp. 1–5 (2010)
28. Petrioli, C., Petroccia, R., Spaccini, D.: Sunset version 2.0: Enhanced framework for simulation, emulation and real-life testing of underwater wireless sensor networks. In: Proceedings of the Eighth ACM International Conference on Underwater Networks and Systems, WUWNET 2013, pp. 43:1–43:8. ACM, New York (2013)
29. Potter, J., Alves, J., Furfaro, T., Vermeij, A., Jourden, N., Merani, D., Zappa, G., Berni, A.: Software defined open architecture modem development at CMRE. In: 2014 Underwater Communications and Networking (UComms), pp. 1–4 (2014)
30. Rahavi, J.S.A., Kanagapriya, T., Seyezhai, R.: Design and analysis of interleaved boost converter for renewable energy source. In: 2012 International Conference on Computing, Electronics and Electrical Technologies (ICCEET), pp. 447–451 (2012)
31. Senthilkumar, S., Go, W., Han, J., Thuy, L., Kishor, K., Kim, Y., Kim, Y.: Emergence of rechargeable seawater batteries. J. Mater. Chem. A **7**(44), 25305–25313 (2019)
32. Sozer, E., Stojanovic, M.: Reconfigurable acoustic modem for underwater sensor networks. In: WUWNET 2006, pp. 101–104 (2006)
33. Srujana, B.S., Neha, Mathews, P., Harigovindan, V.: Multi-source energy harvesting system for underwater wireless sensor networks. Procedia Comput. Sci. **46**, 1041–1048 (2015)
34. Torres, D., Friedman, J., Schmid, T., Srivastava, M.B., Noh, Y., Gerla, M.: Software-defined underwater acoustic networking platform and its applications. Ad Hoc Netw. **34**, 252–264 (2015)

Non-ideal Characteristics of Low-Cost Radio Transceivers in Wireless Sensor Networks

Wei Liu[1] (ID), Jian Xie[1] (ID), Daqing Zheng[1]([✉]) (ID), Jinwei Xu[1] (ID), Rong Luo[2] (ID), and Shunren Hu[1] (ID)

[1] School of Electrical and Electronic Engineering, Chongqing University of Technology, Chongqing 400054, China
zdq2016@cqut.edu.cn
[2] Department of Electronic Engineering, Tsinghua University, Beijing 100084, China

Abstract. Some important supporting techniques for wireless sensor networks including link quality estimation, channel modeling and node localization depend on the accuracy of transceiver parameters such as transmit power and receive power. Unfortunately, the low-cost transceivers used by sensor nodes are non-ideal and usually cannot provide accurate and consistent parameter values. As far as we know, there is still no systematical study on the non-ideal characteristics of such transceivers in the literature. In this paper, accuracy and consistency of transmit power, receive power and channel frequency are evaluated through measurements. The results show that channel frequency has good accuracy and consistency. The measured receive power has little difference from the actual input power. Its calibration curve is approximately linear, although there are relatively obvious nonlinear regions. For a single node, there is nearly no difference between the calibration curves of different channels. However, there are obvious offsets between different nodes. Actual transmit power is much lower than the nominal one. There are not only significant differences between the calibration curves of different nodes, but also certain differences between different channels of a single node. It means that calibration of the transmit power is more difficult than the receive power. Fortunately, these calibration curves are overall offset and can be calibrated by only measuring the offset of a single power point. The results also show that if these parameters are not calibrated carefully, performance of link quality estimation, channel modeling and node localization would be affected inevitably.

Keywords: Wireless sensor networks · Low-cost transceiver · Non-ideal characteristics · Calibration model · Transmit power · Receive power · Channel frequency

1 Introduction

As a new data acquisition method, wireless sensor networks (WSNs) can be used to collect a variety of information from the deployed area. These networks have been successfully used in many fields, such as military surveillance, environmental monitoring,

© Springer Nature Singapore Pte Ltd. 2020
Z. Hao et al. (Eds.): CWSN 2020, CCIS 1321, pp. 84–97, 2020.
https://doi.org/10.1007/978-981-33-4214-9_7

industrial control, home automation, and so on [1]. For WSNs, link quality estimation [2, 3], channel modeling [4–6] and node localization [7–9] are important supporting techniques, which depend on the accuracy of transceiver parameters such as transmit power and receive power.

Sensor nodes typically employ low-cost radio transceivers, such as CC2420 [10] and CC1101 [11] provided by TI, and AT86RF230 [12] and ATmega256RFR2 [13] provided by Microchip. These transceivers are usually non-ideal: on one hand, there are manufacturing tolerances for these transceivers. On the other hand, the matching circuits also affect the actual parameter values. As a result, the actual transmit power is often inconsistent with the nominal value, and the measured receive power is often inconsistent with the input value. And what is worse, the transmit power of sensor nodes is very low, only several milliwatts. Consequently, this inconsistency will lead to greater impact. Therefore, it is necessary to study the non-ideal characteristics of such low-cost transceivers.

At present, a few works have studied the non-ideal characteristics of such transceivers. However, these works mainly focused on analyzing the relationship between the measured receive power and the actual one. They paid less attention to the relationship between the actual transmit power and the nominal one. Based on this, this paper systematically studied the non-ideal characteristics of such transceivers through actual measurements, including consistency of the actual transmit power, measured receive power and actual channel frequency, as well as the differences of different channels and nodes. The contributions of this paper are as follows: 1) Consistency of transmit power, receive power and channel frequency is analyzed; 2) Impacts of the channel on the non-ideal characteristics of transmit power and receive power are studied; 3) Impacts of the node on the non-ideal characteristics of transmit power and receive power are studied.

The results in this paper show that: 1) Channel frequency has good accuracy and consistency. 2) The measured receive power has little difference from the actual input power. Its calibration curve is approximately linear, although there are relatively obvious nonlinear regions. 3) Chen et al. pointed out that there are non-injective regions in the calibration curve of receive power [14]. However, no similar result appears in this paper. Therefore, their conclusions are only valid for specific transceivers. 4) For a single node, there is nearly no difference between the calibration curves of different channels. However, there are obvious offsets between different nodes. 5) Actual transmit power is much lower than the nominal one. 6) There are not only significant differences between the calibration curves of different nodes, but also certain differences between different channels of a single node. It means that calibration of the transmit power is more difficult than the receive power. Fortunately, these calibration curves are overall offset and can be calibrated by only measuring the offset of a single power point.

The rest of this paper is organized as follows. In Sect. 2, related works are given. This is followed by experimental setup in Sect. 3. Experimental results are given in Sect. 4 and non-ideal characteristics of the transmit power and receive power are analyzed comprehensively. Finally, conclusions are presented and suggestions are made for future works.

2 Related Works

Transmit and receive power of wireless sensor nodes are two important physical layer parameters, which are widely used in link quality estimation, channel modeling, node localization and so on. For example, channel modeling requires measurement of path loss at different distances, which can be obtained by subtracting the receive power from transmit power. Actual nodes are typically used in WSNs for path loss measurements, rather than instruments such as signal generators and spectrum analyzers. The reasons are twofold. On one hand, actual nodes can better reflect true channel propagation characteristics [5]. On the other hand, measuring instruments are difficult to be moved and powered in outdoor environments [15]. For example, Cheffena et al. established an empirical path loss model in the outdoor snowy environment by using the nominal transmit power and measured receive power of CC2500 [4]. Similarly, by using the nominal transmit power and measured receive power of XBee Pro, Olasupo et al. established empirical path loss models in the outdoor grass and parking environment respectively [5, 6]. Chong et al. established an empirical path loss model in the flat and irregular terrain by using the nominal transmit power and measured receive power of CC1101 [15].

Transmit and receive power are also used for sensor node localization. For example, Passafiume et al. proposed a calibration-free real-time indoor localization method, which used the measured receive power of CC2430 to estimate the node location [7]. Zheng et al. constructed a fingerprint based localization and tracking method by using the measured receive power of CC2530 [8]. Tomic et al. used the transmit power and receive power to calculate the path loss between nodes, and performed 3D node localization by combining the angle-of-arrival measurements. They assumed that all nodes have identical transmit power [9].

In brief, nominal values were typically used as the transmit power, while measured values provided by transceiver were typically used as the receive power. However, the low-cost transceivers used by sensor nodes are non-ideal and usually cannot provide accurate and consistent parameter values. Unfortunately, existing works completely ignore the impacts of non-ideal characteristics of transmit and receive power. Although Chong et al. had used spectrum analyzer to calibrate the measured receive power of CC1101 and pointed out that its accuracy is ±2.03 dB, they did not deeply study the non-ideal characteristics of transmit and receive power [15].

At present, a few works have studied the non-ideal characteristics of low-cost transceivers. However, these works mainly focused on analyzing the relationship between the measured receive power and the actual one. They paid less attention to the relationship between the actual transmit power and the nominal one. For example, Chen et al. first pointed out that the measured receive power is non-ideal. They pointed out that there are nonlinear and non-injective regions between the measured receive power and the actual input one for CC2420 and AT86RF230. At the same time, they also claimed that the calibration curve is consistent for the same type of transceiver, that is to say, the measured receive power could be calibrated by using a uniform calibration model [14]. Zheng et al. measured the receive power of CC2420 under different environmental noise levels, and found that there are two nonlinear regions in the receive power calibration curve of CC2420 [2]. Jayasri et al. pointed out that the measured receive power of CC2550 are nonlinear, but they did not give a calibration curve between the measured receive power and actual input one [3].

In addition, some transceiver datasheets also mention the non-ideal characteristics of receive power. For example, the CC2420 datasheet gives a calibration curve for the measured receive power, and it is clear that there are multiple nonlinear regions [10]. The CC1101 datasheet gives calibration curves for the measured receive power at different data rates. It can be seen that linearity is good when the input power is in the range of [−100 dBm, −25 dBm], but there are still multiple nonlinear regions [11]. The ATmega256RFR2 datasheet also gives a calibration curve, and it is clear that there are multiple nonlinear regions [13]. However, the AT86RF230 datasheet does not give calibration curves for the measured receive power [12]. At the same time, these datasheets completely ignore the non-ideal characteristics of transmit power.

Based on CC2430, Zhang et al. studied the influence of operating voltage variation on the receive power, and found that the higher the voltage, the greater the receive power. However, they did not consider the non-ideal characteristics of transmit and receive power [18]. Fang et al. studied the hardware consistency of CC2420 using 20 nodes, and pointed out that the actual transmit power of different nodes with 0 dBm nominal value has a maximum difference of 0.93 dBm, while the maximum difference of receive power is 2 dBm under the same conditions [16]. He et al. studied the accuracy of the measured receive power and the transmit power control for CC1100 and ADF7020, and pointed out that the measurement accuracy of ADF7020 decreases with the receive power, while that of CC1100 has no obvious relationship with the receive power. At the same time, the linearity of CC1100's transmit power curve is much better than ADF7020 [17]. Although these works considered the non-ideal characteristics of transmit and receive power, they did not consider the impacts of channel and node variation on these non-ideal characteristics.

In summary, existing works mainly focus on analyzing the non-ideal characteristics of the receive power, and does not systematically study the non-ideal characteristics of such transceivers, including the non-ideal characteristics of transmit power, the impacts of channel and node variation on these characteristics and so on.

3   Experimental Setup

This paper analyzes the non-ideal characteristics through actual measurements using the ATmega256RFR2 transceiver [13]. ATmega256RFR2 is compatible with IEEE 802.15.4 standard and operates in the 2.4 GHz band. Transmit power can be adjusted through the Transceiver Transmit Power Control Register [13]. 16 nominal transmit powers from −16.5 dBm to 3.5 dBm are provided.

ATmega256RFR2 provides the measured receive power by accessing the PHY_ED_LEVEL register [13]. The valid values of this register are 0–83. A value of 0 means that the input power is less than −90 dBm. Resolution of the receive power measurement is 1 dB. For a valid register value, the receive power can be calculated as follows, where ED is the value of the PHY_ED_LEVEL register:

$$P_{RF} = -90 + ED\,[dBm] \tag{1}$$

ATmega256RFR2 also provides channel settings in accordance with IEEE 802.15.4 standard. Channels 11–26 of the 2.4 GHz band can be selected, and the frequency of channel k can be calculated as follows:

$$F_C = 2405 + 5(k - 11)MHz \tag{2}$$

where $k = 11, 12, ..., 26$.

Seven ATmega256RFR2 Xplained Pro nodes are chosen, which are official prototype platforms provided by Microchip [19]. In order to study the non-ideal characteristics of receive power, a Rigol DSG3030 high frequency signal generator is used to generate input signals with known power. In order to study the non-ideal characteristics of transmit power and channel frequency, a Rohde & Schwarz FSVR7 spectrum analyzer is used to measure the output signals. Experimental environment is shown in Fig. 1. An N-type interface to SMA interface adapter cable is used to connect the instrument and the node. Attenuation of the cable is approximately constant in the 2.4 GHz band, which is 0.47 dB measured by the Agilent N9915A network analyzer. All the measurements compensate for this attenuation.

4   Experimental Results Analysis

This section gives the experimental results. For the sake of space consideration, only the results of typical channels and nodes are given. Other channels and nodes have the same characteristics or trends. Therefore, it does not affect the acquisition of relevant conclusions.

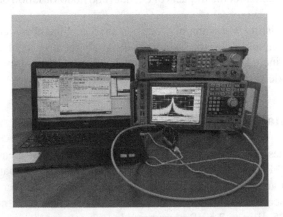

Fig. 1. The experimental environment.

4.1   Accuracy and Consistency of the Channel Frequency

There are good consistencies for the channel frequencies of different nodes. Meanwhile, the measured frequencies are very close to the nominal ones, as shown in Fig. 2. The differences between the actual channel frequencies and the nominal ones are in the range of −0.08 MHz to 0.06 MHz, as shown in Fig. 3. The absolute mean error is only 0.02 MHz and its variance is only 0.0005. These differences are almost negligible considering the 2.4 GHz frequency band and 2 MHz channel bandwidth.

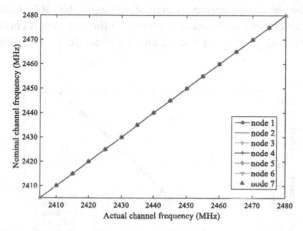

Fig. 2. Relationship between the actual channel frequencies and the nominal ones.

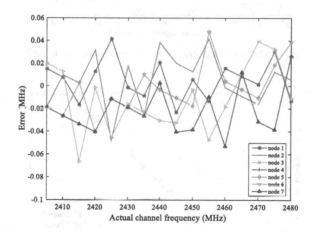

Fig. 3. Differences between the actual channel frequencies and the nominal ones.

4.2 Accuracy and Consistency of the Receive Power

Receive Power Characteristics of Single Node Under Typical Channels
Calibration curves of the receive power for node 2 and node 7 under typical channels are shown in Figs. 4 and 5, respectively. Among them, horizontal axis is the actual input power generated by signal generator, and vertical axis is the measured value provided by transceiver. It can be seen that the measured receive power has little difference from

the actual one. For node 2, when the actual input power is greater than −5 dBm, the measured value is constant at −7 dBm. When the actual input power is less than −89 dBm, the measured value is constant at −90 dBm. For node 7, the corresponding points are (−7 dBm, −7 dBm) and (−91 dBm, −90 dBm), respectively. This is almost consistent with the valid measurement range of ATmega256RFR2. It can also be seen that there are relatively obvious nonlinear regions in the calibration curves, such as the [−45 dBm, −30 dBm] interval for node 2 and the [−60 dBm, −45 dBm] interval for node 7.

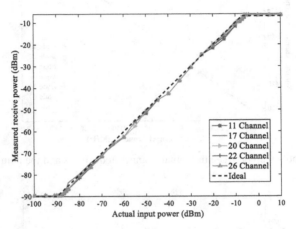

Fig. 4. Calibration curves of the receive power for node 2.

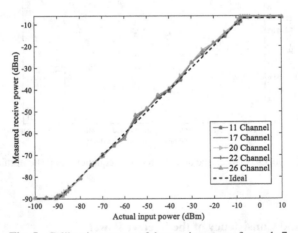

Fig. 5. Calibration curves of the receive power for node 7.

In terms of the differences between different channels, although the measured values of some power points under different channels have 0–3 dB differences, there are no obvious overall offsets between these curves. Considering the measurement accuracy of transceiver itself, it is reasonable to consider that the calibration curves under different channels are consistent and a uniform calibration model can be used.

Receive Power Characteristics of Different Nodes Under Typical Channels
Calibration curves of the receive power under channel 11 and 26 for different nodes are shown in Figs. 6 and 7, respectively. It can be seen that the measured values on some power points differ by a maximum of 6 dB for different nodes. Meanwhile, there are relatively obvious overall offsets between these curves. These offsets are consistent for different channels. For example, node 4 has the lowest measured power under channel 11 and 26, which also appears under other channels. At the same time, the nonlinear regions of different nodes are also different.

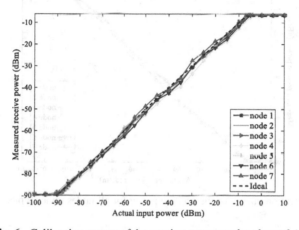

Fig. 6. Calibration curves of the receive power under channel 11.

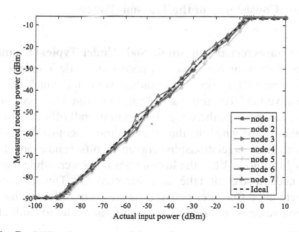

Fig. 7. Calibration curves of the receive power under channel 26.

Overall Characteristics of the Receive Power

For the sake of clarity, Fig. 8 shows the calibration curves for all nodes under typical channels. Channels of the same node are represented with the same color and line type. It can be seen that there are relatively obvious offsets for different nodes. This again shows that a calibration curve obtained for a specific node cannot be used to calibrate other nodes, even if they have the same type of transceiver. This is in complete contrast to the conclusion in [14], which claims that the receive power can be calibrated using a uniform calibration model. This indicates that whether a uniform calibration model can be used depends on the type of the transceiver employed.

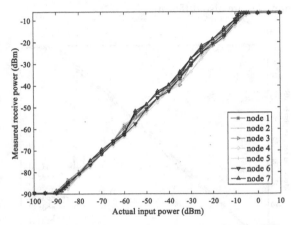

Fig. 8. Calibration curves of the receive power for all nodes under typical channels.

4.3   Accuracy and Consistency of the Transmit Power

Transmit Power Characteristics of Single Node Under Typical Channels

Calibration curves of the transmit power for node 1 and node 3 under typical channels are shown in Figs. 9 and 10, respectively. Among them, horizontal axis is the nominal transmit power, and vertical axis is the actual value measured by spectrum analyzer. As can be seen from these figures, there are significant overall offsets between the curves under different channels. Meanwhile, the offset is almost identical for each power point. However, there is no obvious relationship between the offset and channel frequency. For example, channel 11 of node 1 has the lowest transmit power, while that of node 3 has the largest. Other nodes also exhibit the same characteristics. This shows that for a single node, although there are differences between the curves of different channels, only one constant calibration value is required to use a uniform model to calibrate the transmit power.

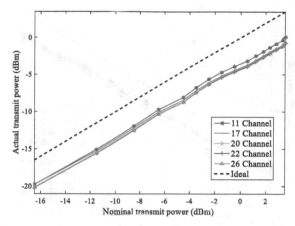

Fig. 9. Calibration curves of the transmit power for node 1.

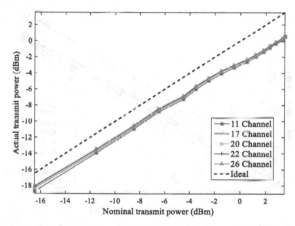

Fig. 10. Calibration curves of the transmit power for node 3.

Transmit Power Characteristics of Different Nodes Under Typical Channels

Calibration curves of the transmit power under channel 11 and 26 for different nodes are shown in Figs. 11 and 12, respectively. As can be seen from these figures, there are huge differences for the actual transmit power of different nodes. For example, for channel 11 and 3.5 dBm nominal value, the actual transmit power of node 4 is 2.06 dBm, while that of node 1 is only 0.09 dBm.

At the same time, there are obvious overall offsets between the calibration curves under the same channel. However, the differences between nodes under different channels are not the same. For example, the actual transmit power of node 4 at each nominal power point is about 1.97 dB higher than that of node 1 under channel 11, but the offset under channel 26 is about 2.2 dB.

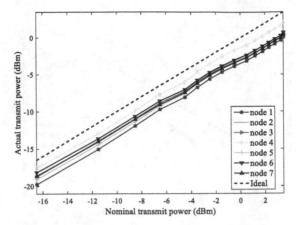

Fig. 11. Calibration curves of the transmit power under channel 11.

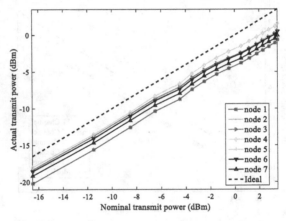

Fig. 12. Calibration curves of the transmit power under channel 26.

Overall Characteristics of the Transmit Power

For the sake of clarity, Fig. 13 shows the calibration curves for all nodes under typical channels. Channels of the same node are represented with the same color and line type. It can be seen that for the same nominal transmit power, the actual transmit power of different nodes is different, and is much lower than the nominal one. There are not only significant differences between the calibration curves of different nodes, but also certain differences between different channels of a single node. It means that in practical applications, using nominal transmit powers will introduce large errors. Meanwhile, calibration of the transmit power is more difficult than the receive power. A calibration curve obtained for a specific node under a specific channel cannot be used to calibrate other nodes, even other channels of the same node. Fortunately, these transmit power calibration curves are overall offset and can be corrected by only measuring the offset of a single power point.

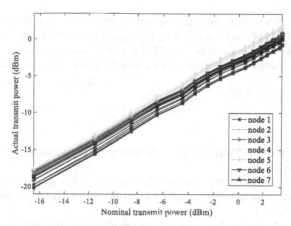

Fig. 13. Calibration curves of the transmit power for all nodes under typical channels.

5 Conclusions and Future Works

Accuracy and consistency of the transceiver parameters such as transmit power and receive power are critical for link quality estimation, channel modeling and node localization in WSNs. However, the non-ideal characteristics of commonly used low-cost transceivers always make the actual transmit power inconsistent with the nominal value, and the measured receive power inconsistent with the input value. This paper systematically studied the non-ideal characteristics of such transceivers through actual measurements. The results show that for the selected transceiver, channel frequency has good accuracy and consistency, but there is certain degree of inconsistency for the receive power and transmit power.

For the receive power, there are relatively obvious nonlinear regions in the calibration curves. For a single node, there is nearly no difference between the calibration curves under different channels. However, there are obvious offsets between different nodes. Therefore, a calibration curve obtained for a specific node cannot be used to calibrate other nodes, even if they have the same type of transceiver. For the transmit power, its calibration is more difficult than the receive power. There are not only significant differences between the calibration curves of different nodes, but also certain differences between different channels of a single node. This means that each channel of each node requires a special calibration model. Fortunately, these calibration curves are overall offset and can be calibrated by only measuring the offset of a single power point.

Future works can be divided into three aspects: First, more in-depth study on the non-ideal characteristics of such transceivers will be done, such as the impacts of operating voltage on the transmit power and receive power. Second, actual impacts of such non-ideal characteristics on the performance of link quality estimation, channel modeling and node localization will be explored. Third, calibration models for typical transceivers would be constructed, and performance improvements after the introduction of calibration will be analyzed.

Acknowledgment. This work is supported in part by National Natural Science Foundation of China under Grant No. 61601069 and in part by Chongqing Research Program of Basic Research and Frontier Technology under Grant No. cstc2017jcyjAX0254 and No. cstc2016jcyjA0515. The authors would like to thank the anonymous reviewers for their valuable comments and suggestions.

References

1. Prasad, P.: Recent trend in wireless sensor network and its applications: a survey. Sens. Rev. **35**(2), 229–236 (2015)
2. Zheng, G., Han, D., Zheng, R., Schmitz, C., Yuan, X.: A link quality inference model for IEEE 802.15.4 low-rate WPANS. In: IEEE Global Telecommunications Conference, pp. 1–6. IEEE, Houston (2011)
3. Jayasri, T., Hemalatha, M.: Link quality estimation for adaptive data streaming in WSN. Wirel. Pers. Commun. **94**, 1543–1562 (2016)
4. Cheffena, M., Mohamed, M.: Empirical path loss models for wireless sensor network deployment in snowy environments. IEEE Antennas Wirel. Propag. Lett. **16**, 2877–2880 (2017)
5. Olasupo, T.O., Otero, C.E., Olasupo, K.O., Kostanic, I.: Empirical path loss models for wireless sensor network deployments in short and tall natural grass environments. IEEE Trans. Antennas Propag. **64**(9), 4012–4021 (2016)
6. Olasupo, T.O., Otero, C.E., Otero, L.D., Olasupo, K.O., Kostanic, I.: Path loss models for low-power, low-data rate sensor nodes for smart car parking systems. IEEE Trans. Intell. Transp. Syst. **19**(6), 1774–1783 (2017)
7. Passafiume, M., Maddio, S., Cidronali, A.: An improved approach for RSSI-based only calibration-free real-time indoor localization on IEEE 802.11 and 802.15.4 wireless networks. Sensors **17**(4), 717–755 (2017)
8. Zheng, K., et al.: Energy-efficient localization and tracking of mobile devices in wireless sensor networks. IEEE Trans. Veh. Technol. **66**(3), 2714–2726 (2017)
9. Tomic, S., Beko, M., Dinis, R.: 3-D target localization in wireless sensor network using RSS and AoA measurements. IEEE Trans. Veh. Technol. **66**(4), 3197–3210 (2017)
10. Texas Instruments Inc.: CC2420 Datasheet. https://www.ti.com/lit/ds/symlink/cc2420.pdf. Accessed 13 May 2020
11. Texas Instruments Inc.: CC1101 Datasheet. http://www.ti.com/lit/ds/symlink/cc1101.pdf. Accessed 16 May 2020
12. Microchip Technology Inc.: AT86RF230 Datasheet. http://ww1.microchip.com/downloads/en/DeviceDoc/doc5131.pdf. Accessed 13 May 2020
13. Microchip Technology Inc.: ATmega256RFR2 Datasheet. http://ww1.microchip.com/downloads/en/DeviceDoc/Atmel-8393-MCU_Wireless-ATmega256RFR2-ATmega128RFR2-ATmega64RFR2_Datasheet.pdf. Accessed 18 May 2020
14. Chen, Y., Terzis, A.: On the mechanisms and effects of calibrating RSSI measurements for 802.15.4 radios. In: Silva, J.S., Krishnamachari, B., Boavida, F. (eds.) EWSN 2010. LNCS, vol. 5970, pp. 256–271. Springer, Heidelberg (2010). https://doi.org/10.1007/978-3-642-11917-0_17
15. Chong, P.K., Kim, D.: Surface-level path loss modeling for sensor networks in flat and irregular terrain. ACM Trans. Sens. Netw. **9**(2), 1–32 (2013)
16. Fang, Z., Zhao, Z., Geng, D., Xuan, Y., Du, L.: RSSI variability characterization and calibration method in wireless sensor network. In: IEEE International Conference on Information and Automation, pp. 1532–1537. IEEE, Harbin (2010)

17. He, Y., Flikkema, P.G.: System-level characterization of single-chip radios for wireless sensor network applications. In: IEEE 10th Annual Wireless and Microwave Technology Conference, pp. 1–5. IEEE, Clearwater (2009)
18. Zhang, R., Guo, J., Chu, F., Song, Y.: Influence of supply voltage of node on RSSI-based localization performance and calibration technique. In: Jiang, L. (ed.) ICCE2011. AISC, vol. 110, pp. 409–416. Springer, Heidelberg (2011). https://doi.org/10.1007/978-3-642-25185-6_53
19. Microchip Technology Inc.: ATmega256RFR2 Xplained Pro User Guide. http://ww1.microc hip.com/downloads/en/DeviceDoc/Atmel-42079-ATMEGA256RFR2-Xplained-Pro_User-Guide.pdf. Accessed 13 May 2020

Basic Theory and Application of Internet of Things

An Automatic Extraction Method of Traffic Network Boundary Based on Neighbor Node Information of IoV

Mingcai Zheng[1]($^{\boxtimes}$), Xiaochao Zhao[1], Han Gu[1], Jinbing Zheng[2], and Kefeng Li[1]

[1] Hunan First Normal University, Changsha 410205, Hunan, China
dysfzmc@163.com
[2] Forty-Eighth Institute of China Electronics Technology Group Corporation,
Changsha 410111, Hunan, China

Abstract. In order to extract boundary information of traffic network quickly, an automatic extraction method of traffic network boundary based on the neighbor information of transportation vehicles in traffic network, namely TNBAE-NI, is proposed. Firstly, the real-time distributed scene of traffic vehicles is extracted from the traffic trajectory data of traffic vehicles. Secondly, the enhanced distributed scene of traffic vehicles is formed by superposition of multiple real-time distributed scenes at different times. Thirdly, the uniform distributed scene of traffic vehicles is constructed by removing and interpolating nodes in the enhanced distributed scene. Lastly, the boundary nodes of traffic network are identified based on the statistical characteristics of neighbor Vehicle nodes in the uniform distributed scene, and the traffic network boundaries are produced by exploiting the interconnection of adjacent boundary nodes in the traffic network. The theoretical analysis and simulation results show that the TNBAE-NI method can obtain enough accurate traffic network boundaries with relatively lightweight computation.

Keywords: Traffic trajectory data · Neighbor information · Traffic network boundary · Automatic extraction · Distributed scene

1 Introduction

With the development of transportation system, the coverage density and coverage breadth of traffic network are increasing, and the dynamic changes often occur due to traffic network planning, construction and other reasons. So, it becomes more difficult to grasp the real-time distribution information of traffic network. At the same time, with the popularization of navigation services and the rise of new technologies such as unmanned driving, the demand for real-time distribution information of traffic network is increasing. The real-time automatic acquisition method of accurate distribution information of traffic network has gradually attracted people's attention and become one of the focuses in the field of information technology. Quick and accurate acquisition of real-time distribution information of traffic network will play an important role in many aspects such as Transportation Information Service, traffic network planning, unmanned

© Springer Nature Singapore Pte Ltd. 2020
Z. Hao et al. (Eds.): CWSN 2020, CCIS 1321, pp. 101–114, 2020.
https://doi.org/10.1007/978-981-33-4214-9_8

driving, etc. It is of practical significance to study the automatic extraction method of traffic network boundary.

2 Related Works

Distribution information of traffic network plays an important role in the application of Transportation Information Service [1–3], navigation [4–6], unmanned driving [7–9], traffic network planning [10–12] and so on [13, 14]. With the continuous expansion of the scale of traffic network, the extraction method of traffic network distribution information has gradually changed from manual acquisition to automatic acquisition by machine, which benefits from the rapid development of information technology. Traffic network distribution information is closely related to the location information of traffic vehicles in the course of driving. Traffic network distribution information can be extracted from the location information of traffic vehicles in the traffic network. Therefore, location technology, information transmission technology and intelligent data analysis technology of trajectory location data have become the key technologies for automatic extraction of traffic network distribution information [15–17]. With the development of positioning technologies such as GPS, BDS and cooperative self-localization [18, 19], as well as the increasing in coverage breadth and coverage density of traffic vehicles and transportation infrastructure, the ubiquitous intelligent sensing method of location information of traffic vehicles has been basically available. At the same time, with the continuous extension of the coverage area of Internet, mobile communication network, satellite communication network, ad hoc network and other communication networks [20], especially the emergence of ubiquitous interconnected Internet of Vehicles (IoV) technology [21], the ubiquitous transmission routes of real-time location information of traffic vehicles have also been available. The real-time location information of traffic vehicles can be continuously aggregated into the transportation information storage server to form the big traffic data of transportation trajectory [22], which provides sufficient basic data source for automatic extraction of distribution information of traffic network. Benefit from the development of big data analysis technology [23] and image processing technology [24], it is not difficult to automatically extract traffic network distribution information [25] from the traffic trajectory data. As for the automatic extraction of traffic network boundary, it can be realized by using edge detection technology [26] in image processing technology. However, the huge scale of traffic network and the huge amount of traffic trajectory data [27] bring about extremely high computational burden during automatic extraction of traffic network. It is necessary to find other lightweight automatic extraction method of traffic network. According to the neighbor node information of traffic vehicles contained in the traffic trajectory data, this paper proposes an lightweight automatic extraction method of traffic network based on the neighbor node information, namely TNBAE-NI, which completes the ubiquitous perception and ubiquitous transmission of traffic vehicles' trajectory location information in the ubiquitous interconnected Internet of Vehicles, and the boundary information of traffic network is extracted by simple calculation in the automatic extraction server. The automatic extraction of traffic network boundary information is realized with lower computational complexity and higher real-time performance.

3   Description of TNBAE-NI

3.1   Overall Scheme of TNBAE-NI

The purpose of this paper is to automatically extract the boundary of traffic network based on the statistical information of traffic vehicle's neighbor nodes contained in the traffic trajectory data. In order to obtain useful and efficient statistical information of the neighbor nodes, such treatments as Real-time distributed scene generation of traffic vehicles, enhanced distributed scene generation of traffic vehicles and uniform distributed scene generation of traffic vehicles should be completed before the neighbor node information statistics of traffic vehicle and the boundary extraction of traffic network. In uniform distributed scene, the boundary node and non-boundary node of traffic network have distinct statistical characteristics. For example, the number of neighbor nodes in the same radius circular neighborhood is quite different between boundary node and non-boundary node, and the average location of the neighbor nodes of boundary node in the some radius circular neighborhood is different from the geometric center of the neighborhood, but the average location of the neighbor nodes of non-boundary node in the same radius circular neighborhood is near to the geometric center of the neighborhood, and so on. Each of these can be used as the basis for boundary extraction of traffic network. However, considering that the uniform distributed scene can't be absolutely uniform, both the number of neighbor nodes and the average location of neighbor nodes are taken into adoption in TNBAE-NI. The algorithm flow of TNBAE-NI is shown in Fig. 1.

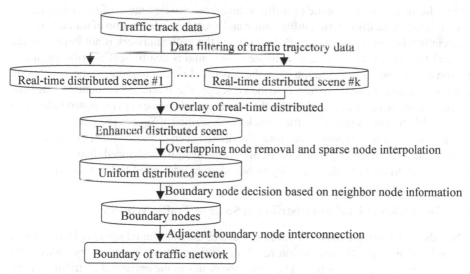

Fig. 1. The algorithm flow of TNBAE-NI

3.2   Generation of Real-Time Distributed Scene of Traffic Vehicles

Traffic trajectory data contains information as described in {vehicle ID, time, location}, which records the location of a certain traffic vehicle at a certain time, and can be used for automatic extraction of traffic network distribution information. In the traffic trajectory data, the location information of a traffic vehicle at different times reflects the trajectory information of the vehicle. This can be represented by a data combination as described in $S_{ID} = \{$Vehicle ID, Time 1, Location 1, Time 2, Location 2,...$\}$. The trajectory data of a single vehicle reflects the distribution of part of the traffic network to a certain extent, but it can't accurately reflect the entire boundary of the traffic network, nor can it reflect the complete distribution of the traffic network. The location information of different vehicles at a certain time constitutes the real-time distributed scene of traffic vehicles in the traffic network. When the density of traffic vehicles in the traffic network at a certain time is large enough, it can be used to automatically extract the distribution information and the boundary of the traffic network. The real-time distributed scene of traffic vehicles in the traffic network can be obtained from the traffic trajectory data, and only the ID and location information of traffic vehicles need to be searched by time from the traffic trajectory data. Data combination as described in $S_K = \{$time k, vehicle ID1, location 1, vehicle ID2, location 2,...$\}$ can be used to represent the real-time distributed scene of traffic vehicles at "k" time. Node "n" in the "k" time real-time distributed scene can be marked as node (k, n).

3.3   Generation of Enhanced Distributed Scene of Traffic Vehicles

The real-time distributed scene of traffic vehicles at a single time is often insufficient to reflect the accurate distribution information and boundary information of traffic network. Especially when the density of traffic vehicles in the traffic network is not large enough, the real-time distributed scene at a single time contains insufficient distribution information and boundary information of traffic network. In order to increase the distribution density of traffic vehicles in the distributed scene, the moderate amount of real-time distributed scenes at different times in the recent period can be superimposed to form an enhanced distributed scene of traffic vehicles as described in $S_{KM} = \{S_{K1}, S_{K2}, ..., S_{Km}\}$. The number of superimposed real-time distributed scenes should make the density of traffic vehicles in the neighborhood of any location in the enhanced distributed scene large enough to improve the accuracy of boundary extraction of traffic network.

3.4   Generation of Uniform Distributed Scene of Traffic Vehicles

When the distribution density of vehicle nodes in the distributed scene is large enough and uniform enough, the extraction result of traffic network boundary by lightweight method can be accurate enough. Therefore, the nodes in the enhanced distributed scene should be processed as follows to form a uniform distributed scene of traffic vehicles.

1) Removal of Overlapping Nodes
The enhanced distributed scene is formed by overlapping multiple real-time distributed scenes at different times. There may be overlapping or near overlapping vehicle nodes

in a very small neighborhood of some a certain location, which is not conducive to the lightweight automatic extraction of traffic network boundary and needs to be removed. Whether the node (k, n) in the enhanced distributed scene is removed or not is marked with $F_V (k, n)$, and the default value of "1" is taken before removal. When the value of "0" is taken, it means that the node (k, n) does not participate in the automatic extraction of traffic network boundary, namely, it is removed. For a valid node (i, j) marked with "1", if there is a neighbor node (k, n) in the sufficiently small neighborhood, then the node (k, n) is marked as an invalid node and takes "0" value according to formula (1), namely, the node (k, n) is removed.

$$F_V(k, n) = \begin{cases} 0, \text{ if } d_{(k,n)-(i,j)} \le \varepsilon_d \\ 1, \text{ if } d_{(k,n)-(i,j)} > \varepsilon_d \end{cases} \tag{1}$$

Where, $d_{(k, n)-(i, j)}$ is the geometric distance between the node (k, n) and the node (i, j), ε_d is the adopted threshold of neighborhood radius when overlapping or near overlapping node is removed, and its value takes into account the accuracy requirements of traffic network boundary extraction and the distribution density of vehicle nodes.

2) Statistics of Minimum Spacing between Node and Neighbor Node
In order to determine the uniformity of node distribution in the enhanced distributed scene after removing the overlapping or near overlapping nodes, the distance $d(k, n)$ between the valid node (k, n) and the nearest neighbor node (i, j) in its neighborhood is calculated according to formula (2).

$$d(k, n) = \begin{cases} min\{d_{(k,n)-(i,j)}\}, \text{ if } \begin{cases} F_V(k, n) = 1 \\ F_V(i, j) = 1 \end{cases} \\ \infty, \text{ others} \end{cases} \tag{2}$$

Where, the function min{ } means to take the minimum value from the set.

Then, the minimum D_{min} and the maximum D_{max} of the minimum spacing $d(k, n)$ of all valid nodes in the enhanced distributed scene are searched according to formula (3) and formula (4) separately. The difference between the minimum spacing D_{min} and the maximum spacing D_{max} can reflect the uniformity of the enhanced distributed scene after removing the overlapping or near overlapping nodes.

$$D_{min} = min\{d(k, n)\} \tag{3}$$

$$D_{max} = max\{d(k, n)\} \tag{4}$$

Where, the function max{ } means to take the maximum value from the set.

3) Node Interpolation in Sparse Region
In order to make the distribution of the valid nodes as uniform as possible in the enhanced distributed scene after removing overlapping or near overlapping nodes, and considering the principle of equal division, when $D_{max} > 1.5D_{min}$, the node interpolation operation is implemented in the enhanced distributed scene. One or more nodes are interpolated on

the connection line between the node and its nearest neighbor node when the geometric distance between them is greater than 1.5Dmin, and the principle of equal interval interpolation is adopted. If the distance $d(k, n)$ between the valid node (k, n) and its nearest valid neighbor node (i, j) is greater than 1.5Dmin, one or more new nodes need to be interpolated at equal intervals between them. The number of interpolated nodes is estimated according to formula (5).

$$N(k, n) = \frac{d(k, n)}{D_{min}} + 0.5 - 1, \ \ if \ d(k, n) > 1.5D_{min} \tag{5}$$

Where, the comparison threshold takes 1.5D_{min} according to the principle of equal division.

The insertion position of the interpolated node is calculated according to formula (6).

$$\begin{cases} x(k_{max} + 1, L + l) = x(k, n) + l\frac{x(i,j) - x(k,n)}{N(k,n) + 1} \\ y(k_{max} + 1, L + l) = y(k, n) + l\frac{y(i,j) - y(k,n)}{N(k,n) + 1} \end{cases} \tag{6}$$

Where, k_{max} denotes the maximum number of real-time distributed scenes used to superposition in the process of the enhanced distributed scene generation, $k_{max} + 1$ denotes the serial number of the special scene formed by the interpolated nodes, L denotes the number of previously interpolated nodes, l denotes the increment of the number of new interpolated nodes, and takes value in the interval $1 - N(k, n)$.

3.5 Statistics of Neighbor Node Information

Neighbor node information mainly includes the number of neighbor nodes and the average location of neighbor nodes in a circular neighborhood with a certain radius. These can be used as the statistical value of neighbor node information when extracting the boundary of traffic network.

1) Radius Determination of Circular Neighborhood
The circular neighborhood used to calculate the information of neighbor nodes should make the statistical value of neighbor nodes of boundary node significantly different from the statistical value of non-boundary node, which is closely related to the distribution density and uniformity of vehicle nodes. The distribution density of vehicle nodes can be reflected by the minimum distance between directly adjacent nodes, and the distribution uniformity of vehicle nodes can be reflected by the difference between the minimum distance D_{min} and the maximum distance D_{max}. When determining the radius of the circular neighborhood, the nearest neighbor spacing of valid nodes in the uniform distributed scene is recalculated according to formula (2), and then the minimum neighbor spacing D_{minN} and the maximum neighbor spacing D_{maxN} in the uniform distributed scene are re-searched according to formula (3) and formula (4) separately. Then, the radius of the circular neighborhood is taken according to formula (7).

$$R = D_{maxN} + (D_{maxN} - D_{minN}) \tag{7}$$

2) Statistics of the Number of Neighbor Nodes

In the uniform distributed scene of vehicle nodes, the number of neighbor nodes in the same area of circular neighborhood can be used as the basis to distinguish the boundary nodes from the non-boundary nodes. In a circular neighborhood with radius R, the number of neighbor nodes of node (k, n) is counted according to formula (8).

$$N_N(k, n) = \begin{cases} N_N(k, n) + 1, & \text{if } \begin{cases} d_{(k,n)-(i,j)} \leq R \\ k \neq i \text{ or } n \neq j \end{cases} \\ N_N(k, n), & \text{others} \end{cases} \tag{8}$$

After counting the number of neighbor nodes for each valid node in the uniform distributed scene, then, in order to identify the degree of uniformity of node distribution, the number of minimum neighbor nodes N_{min} and the number of maximum neighbor nodes N_{max} in the uniform distributed scene are searched by formula (9) and formula (10), respectively.

$$N_{min} = \min\{N_N(k, n)\} \tag{9}$$

$$N_{max} = \max\{N_N(k, n)\} \tag{10}$$

3) Statistics of the Average Location of Neighbor Nodes

In the uniform distributed scene of vehicle nodes, the average location of neighbor nodes in the circular neighborhood of each valid node can be used as the basis to distinguish the boundary nodes from the non-boundary nodes. In a circular neighborhood with radius R, the average location of neighbor nodes of the node (k, n) is calculated according to formula (11), and the average location of neighbor nodes for one valid node (k, n) is recorded as a virtual node $(\bar{k}, \bar{n})$.

$$\begin{cases} \bar{x}(k, n) = \begin{cases} \frac{\sum_R x(i,j)}{N_N(k,n)}, & \text{if } \begin{cases} d_{(k,n)-(i,j)} \leq R \\ k \neq i \text{ or } n \neq j \end{cases} \\ x(k, n), & \text{others} \end{cases} \\ \bar{y}(k, n) = \begin{cases} \frac{\sum_R y(i,j)}{N_N(k,n)}, & \text{if } \begin{cases} d_{(k,n)-(i,j)} \leq R \\ k \neq i \text{ or } n \neq j \end{cases} \\ y(k, n), & \text{others} \end{cases} \end{cases} \tag{11}$$

3.6 Marking of Boundary Node Based on Number of Neighbor Nodes

In the uniform distributed scene of vehicle nodes, the number of neighbor nodes of boundary node is less than that of non-boundary node. Considering that the actual uniform distributed scene may not be absolutely uniform, the identification flag $B_N(k,n)$ of boundary node based on the number of neighbor nodes is marked as "1" according to formula (12).Otherwise, marked as "0".

$$B_N(k, n) = \begin{cases} 1, & \text{if } N_N(k, n) < N_{min} + \varepsilon_n(N_{max} - N_{min}) \\ 0, & \text{others} \end{cases} \tag{12}$$

Among them, the value of ε_n is assigned between 0–1 according to the distribution density and the distribution uniformity of vehicle nodes in the uniform distributed scene, which is generally 0.5.

3.7 Marking of Boundary Node Based on Average Location of Neighbor Nodes

In the uniform distributed scene of vehicle nodes, the location of each node is the geometric center of its neighborhood. The boundary node is usually far away from the average location of its neighbor nodes in the neighborhood, but the non-boundary node is usually nearer to the average location of its neighbor nodes in the neighborhood. Therefore, boundary nodes and non-boundary nodes can be distinguished according to the distance between the node (k, n) and its virtual node $(\bar{k}, \bar{n})$. Considering that the actual uniform distributed scene may not be absolutely uniform, the identification flag $B_p(k, n)$ of boundary node based on the average location of its neighbor nodes is marked as "1" or "0" according to formula (13).

$$B_P(k, n) = \begin{cases} 1, & if\ d_{(k,n)-(\bar{k},\bar{n})} < D_{minN} \\ 0, & others \end{cases} \tag{13}$$

3.8 Comprehensive Marking of Boundary Node and Boundary Extraction

Because the distribution of vehicle nodes in the uniform distributed scene is not necessarily absolutely uniform, there may be a certain misjudgment rate when identifying boundary nodes according to the number of neighbor nodes or the average location of neighbor nodes. In order to make the identification of boundary nodes as accurate as possible, both the number of neighbor nodes and the average location of neighbor nodes are all used as the basis for identifying boundary nodes of traffic network. Only those nodes meeting the two criteria are eventually marked as boundary nodes, namely, the comprehensive identification flag $B(k, n)$ is marked as "1" or "0" according to formula (14).

$$B(k, n) = \begin{cases} 1, & if\ \begin{cases} B_N(k, n) = 1 \\ B_P(k, n) = 1 \end{cases} \\ 0, & others \end{cases} \tag{14}$$

After identifying out the boundary nodes of traffic network, the boundary of traffic network can be obtained by connecting the adjacent boundary nodes of the traffic network.

4 Simulation Analyses

The simulation scenario adopts two types of traffic network, one is the "⊕" type traffic network, the other is the "#" type traffic network. A certain number of nodes are randomly distributed in the traffic network. In the simulation scenario, the "⊕" type traffic network can represent the trajectory of various directions of traffic network, and the "#" type traffic network can represent the most common traffic network. Through the formation of real-time distributed scene of traffic vehicles, enhancement of real-time distributed scene and homogenization of enhanced distributed scene, the uniform distributed scene for traffic network boundary extraction is obtained. Then, the information of neighbor nodes in the uniform distributed scene is counted, and the traffic network boundary nodes are judged out and the boundary line of traffic network is extracted. Finally, the boundary extraction error of traffic network is analyzed. The simulation results of each stage and the extracted boundary of traffic network are shown in Figs. 2, 3, 4, 5 and 6, and the boundary extraction errors of traffic network are shown in Table 1 and Figs. 7 and 8.

Figure 2 shows the real-time distributed Scene of vehicle nodes at a given time in the traffic network. As can be seen from the graph, the distribution density of vehicle nodes at each location may not be high enough and uneven, which can't guarantee that the distribution of traffic network boundary can be accurately reflected by the real-time distributed scene.

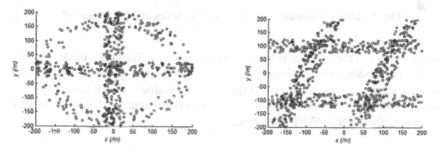

Fig. 2. Real-time distributed scene of vehicle nodes

Figure 3 shows the enhanced distributed scene of vehicle nodes for the traffic network. After overlapping the real-time distributed scenes of vehicle nodes at multiple times, the distribution density of vehicle nodes at each location in the traffic network can be large enough to accurately reflect the distribution of traffic network boundary.

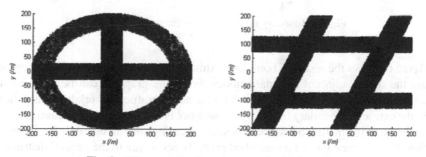

Fig. 3. Enhanced distributed scene of vehicle nodes

Figure 4 shows the uniform distributed scene of vehicle nodes. By deleting the overlapping or near overlapping nodes and interpolating nodes in node sparse regions in the enhanced distributed scene, the uniform distributed scene of vehicle nodes is obtained. In the figure, the nodes marked as "1" form the uniform distributed scene of vehicle nodes, and the nodes marked as "0" are the deleted overlapping or near overlapping nodes.

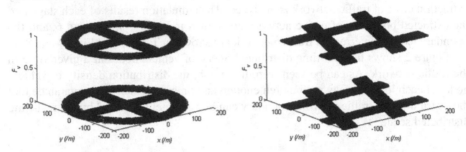

Fig. 4. Uniform distributed scene of vehicle nodes after homogenization

Figure 5 shows the result of boundary node extraction. The nodes marked as "0" are non-boundary nodes, and the nodes marked as "1" are boundary nodes. From the graph, it can be seen that the automatic extraction result of traffic network boundary nodes is consistent with the actual distribution of road network boundary, which shows that the extraction method TNBAE-NI is feasible.

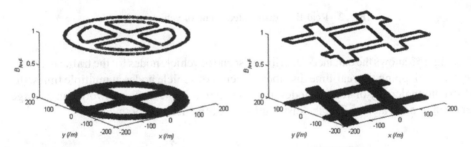

Fig. 5. Boundary node extraction from vehicle nodes

Figure 6 shows the result of boundary extraction of traffic network formed by connecting the direct adjacent boundary nodes. From the graph, it can be seen that the extraction result is basically consistent with the actual traffic network boundary. In the graph, the extracted boundary line of traffic network is not very smooth because the node density in the uniform distributed scene is not high enough for the sake of lightweight calculation. If necessary, it can be smoothed properly according to the general distribution characteristics of traffic network.

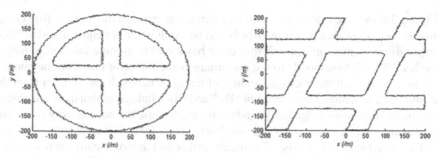

Fig. 6. Boundary extraction result of traffic network

Table 1 lists the boundary extraction errors of traffic network based on different extraction rules. It can be seen that the extraction error under the comprehensive extraction rules is small, and monotonically decreases with the increase of node density. The results of extraction error will be illustrated in conjunction with Fig. 7 and Fig. 8.

Table 1. Boundary extraction error with different node density

Node density	On neighbor-number		On average location		On comprehensive	
	$d_{\text{N-B-MAX}}$	$d_{\text{N-B-MS}}$	$d_{\text{N-B-MAX}}$	$d_{\text{N-B-MS}}$	$d_{\text{N-B-MAX}}$	$d_{\text{N-B-MS}}$
0.025	15.4884	7.2059	23.5749	10.4001	13.4884	5.6525
0.0500	13.7250	6.0814	24.3375	9.7081	11.5797	4.8150
0.1000	14.0452	5.1560	24.7595	8.0674	9.9963	3.9633
0.1500	24.9607	8.9073	23.3488	6.3411	7.2299	3.0454
0.2000	24.9951	12.3546	24.9228	6.5922	6.5842	2.4796
0.2500	24.9665	13.5526	24.9665	7.1266	5.7593	2.1872
0.3000	24.9613	13.3312	24.9933	6.7764	4.9159	2.1010
0.3500	24.9897	13.4789	24.9454	6.4667	4.5303	1.8486
0.4000	24.9614	13.6911	24.9258	6.7690	4.4863	1.7844
0.4500	24.9978	13.8225	24.2290	4.6782	4.1899	1.8628
0.5000	24.9960	13.7793	24.8792	6.4972	4.3655	1.8041
0.5500	24.9442	14.0869	24.7621	5.2356	4.2283	1.6322
0.6000	24.9685	13.9829	24.7027	6.6115	4.0871	1.5717
0.6500	24.9969	14.1406	24.9425	8.4398	4.5161	1.4565
0.7000	24.9933	14.3687	24.8349	4.4288	4.0162	1.4446
0.7500	24.9876	14.0561	24.9614	6.6295	3.7762	1.4041
0.8000	24.9881	14.3345	24.7781	6.1793	3.0196	1.2951
0.8500	24.9948	14.4972	24.9323	8.0337	3.0058	1.2412
0.9000	24.9967	14.2051	24.8505	6.3056	3.1212	1.2055
0.9500	24.9755	14.3258	24.9439	5.6462	3.0729	1.0548
1.0000	24.9969	14.2480	24.9731	5.5140	2.7790	0.9048

Figure 7 shows the maximum boundary extraction error. In the figure, "B_N" corresponds to the maximum extraction error based on the number of neighbor nodes, "B_P" corresponds to the maximum extraction error based on the average location of neighbor nodes, "B_{N+P}" corresponds to the maximum extraction error based on the number of neighbor nodes and the average location of neighbor nodes. It can be seen from the figure that there is always a large error in "B_N" and "B_P", indicating that there are always non-boundary nodes misjudged as boundary nodes, because the node density in the distributed scene after homogenization is not absolutely uniform. Different from "B_N" and "B_P", the extraction error of "B_{N+P}" is much smaller and monotonically decreases with the increase of node density. This shows that the nodes judged as boundary nodes in "B_{N+P}" are all located near the traffic network boundary, and with the increase of node density, the judgment of boundary nodes is more accurate.

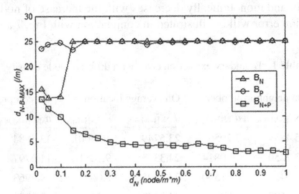

Fig. 7. Maximum boundary extraction error

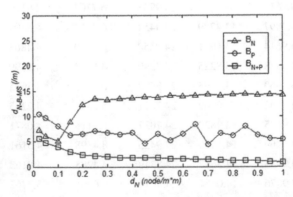

Fig. 8. Mean square value of boundary extraction error

Figure 8 shows the mean square value of boundary extraction error. In the figure, "B_N" corresponds to the mean square value of extraction error based on the number of neighbor nodes, "B_P" corresponds to the mean square value of extraction error based on the average location of neighbor nodes, "B_{N+P}" corresponds to the mean square value of extraction error based on the number of neighbor nodes and the average location of neighbor nodes. It can be seen from the figure that the mean error of "B_{N+P}" is much smaller than that of "B_N" and "B_P", and decreases with the increase of node density. However, the mean error of "BN" and "BP" is not only relatively large, but also does not decrease with the increase of node density.

5 Conclusions

With the continuous expansion of the scale of traffic network, the computational cost of automatic boundary extraction of the traffic network increases sharply. In this paper, a lightweight automatic boundary extraction method based on neighbor node information from the traffic trajectory data is proposed. One of the purposes of this method is to reduce the computational complexity. If want to further improve the extraction accuracy, we can consider increasing node density and using more complex neighbor node interpolation method, so that the uniform distributed scene after interpolating nodes can fill the traffic network more evenly and more densely. For super-large scale traffic network, if want to improve the real-time performance of boundary extraction, we can consider regional statistics and distributed processing.

Acknowledgements. This work is supported by the Natural Science Foundation of Hunan Province under Grant No. 2017JJ2056.

References

1. Zhao, J., Zhou, X.: Improving the operational efficiency of buses with dynamic use of exclusive bus lane at isolated intersections. IEEE Trans. Intell. Transp. Syst. **20**(2), 642–653 (2018)
2. Xu, B., Ban, X.J., Bian, Y., et al.: Cooperative method of traffic signal optimization and speed control of connected vehicles at isolated intersections. IEEE Trans. Intell. Transp. Syst. **20**(4), 1390–1403 (2019)
3. Guo, Y., Ma, J., Xiong, C., et al.: Joint optimization of vehicle trajectories and intersection controllers with connected automated vehicles: Combined dynamic programming and shooting heuristic approach. Transp. Res. Part C: Emerg. Technol. **98**, 54–72 (2019)
4. Chen, W., Liu, Y.: Gap-based automated vehicular speed guidance towards eco-driving at an un-signalized intersection [J]. Transp. Metrica B: Transp. Dyn. **7**(1), 147–168 (2019)
5. Luo, W., Lin, L., Wang, K.C.P.: Automated pavement horizontal curve measurement methods based on inertial measurement unit and 3D profiling data. J. Traffic Transp. Eng. **3**(2), 137–145 (2016)
6. Bichiou, Y., Rakha, H.A.: Developing an optimal intersection control system for automated connected vehicles. IEEE Trans. Intell. Transp. Syst. **20**(5), 1908–1916 (2018)
7. Guo, H., Shen, C., Zhang, H., et al.: Simultaneous trajectory planning and tracking using an MPC method for cyber-physical systems: a case study of obstacle avoidance for an intelligent vehicle. IEEE Trans. Industr. Inf. **14**(9), 4273–4283 (2018)
8. Hu, L., Zhong, Y., Hao, W., et al.: Optimal route algorithm considering traffic light and energy consumption. IEEE Access **6**, 59695–59704 (2018)

9. Hu, X., Chen, L., Tang, B., et al.: Dynamic path planning for autonomous driving on various roads with avoidance of static and moving obstacles. Mech. Syst. Sig. Process. **100**, 482–500 (2018)
10. He, F.F., Yan, X.D., Liu, Y., et al.: A traffic congestion assessment method for urban road networks based on speed performance index. Procedia Eng. **137**, 425–433 (2016)
11. Chen, T.B., Zhang, P., Gao, S.: Research on the dynamic target distribution path planning in logistics system based on improved artificial potential field method-fish swarm algorithm. In: The 30th Chinese Control and Decision Conference, Liaoning: Control and Decision, pp. 4388–4392 (2018)
12. Ugnenko, E., Uzhvieva, E., Voronova, Y.: Simulation of traffic flows on the road network of urban area. Procedia Eng. **134**, 153–156 (2016)
13. Stipancic, J., Miranda-Moreno, L., Saunier, N., Labbe, A.: Network screening for large urban road networks: using GPS data and surrogate measures to model crash frequency and severity. Accid. Anal. Prev. **12**(5), 290–301 (2019)
14. Hu, W., Nie, C., Qiu, Z., et al.: A route guidance method based on quantum searching for real-time dynamic multi-intersections in urban traffic networks. Acta Electronica Sinica **46**(1), 104–109 (2018). (in Chinese)
15. Zhao, X., Zheng, J., Li, K., et al.: Automatic extraction of traffic network based on ubiquitous interconnected vehicular sensor networks. Commun. Technol. **51**(9), 2176–2181 (2018). (in Chinese)
16. Wang, S., Zhang, H.: A method of urban built-up area boundary recognition based on vehicle track data. Bull. Surv. Map. (1), 56–59, 64 (2019)
17. Lu, H.: Research on road network construction and augmentation based on GNSS vehicle trajectories. Acta Geodaetica Cartogr. Sin. **48**(2), 268–270 (2019)
18. Sui, X., Li, Y., Shen, J., et al.: High-accurate positioning method of BDS/GPS tight combination under complicated environment. J. Navigat. Positioning **7**(1), 83–87 (2019)
19. Güler, S., Fidan, B.: Target capture and station keeping of fixed speed vehicles without self-location information. Eur. J. Control **43**(9), 1–11 (2018)
20. Ahuja, K., Khosla, A.: Network selection criterion for ubiquitous communication provisioning in smart cities for smart energy system. J. Netw. Comput. Appl. **127**(1), 82–91 (2018)
21. Huang, Z., Li, M., Tian, R., et al.: Dynamic data compression strategy based on internet of vehicle. Comput. Sci. **45**(11), 304–311 (2018)
22. Zhang, X., Yuan, Z., Zhang, H., et al.: Research on preprocessing method for traffic trajectory big data. Comput. Eng. **45**(6), 26–31 (2019)
23. Ji, L., Chen, K., Yu, Y., et al.: Vehicle type mining and application analysis based on urban traffic big data. J. Comput. Appl. **39**(5), 1343–1350 (2019)
24. Liu, Y., Yan, Z.: Review of Lattice Boltzmann method for image processing. J. Image Graph. **22**(12), 1623–1639 (2017)
25. Lv, Y., Li, Y., Fan, H., et al.: Research on road boundary extraction based on conjunction feature of vehicle-borne LiDAR point cloud. Geogr. Geo-Inf. Sci. **35**(1), 30–37 (2019)
26. Wu, H., Lin, X., Li, X., et al.: Land parcel boundary extraction of UAV remote sensing image in agricultural application. J. Comput. Appl. **39**(1), 298–304 (2019). (in Chinese)
27. Li, X., Luo, Q., Meng, D.: Traffic flow-big data forecasting method based on spatial-temporal weight correlation. Acta Scientiarum Naturalium Universitatis Pekinensis **53**(4), 775–782 (2017)

Mission-Oriented Joint Multi-channel and Timeslot Allocation in Data Center Network

Yanhong Yang[✉], Xuanxuan Xu, and Shaozhong Cao

School of Information Engineering, Beijing Institute of Graphic Communication, Beijing 102600, China
yangyanhong@bigc.edu.cn

Abstract. Joint multi-channel and slots allocation is widely adopted to improve the efficiency of wireless sensor networks. For the data center (DC) network, data transmissions are not only delivered to the sink but also the DC in the network. The traditional methods are sink first collects data, then forward to DC nodes, which inevitably brings data delay. Suppose it can meet the data acquisition requirements of the DCs without affecting the normal aggregation process, which will have practical significance in factory monitoring. In this paper, we propose a Joint Channel and Slot Allocation scheme (JCSDC) for mission-oriented Data Center in WSN. Compared to the existing works, 1) we introduce a novel joint allocation scheme which maximizes the parallelism transmission in each timeslot; 2) we modify transmission directions to build up shortcuts for datacenters. Finally, we conduct simulation experiments. The results show that JCSDC can significantly improve the packet delay without incurring data clustering process compared to the current works.

Keywords: WSN · Industrial monitoring · Joint channel slot allocation

1 Introduction

In recent years, wireless sensor networks have been widely used in many application fields, such as building monitoring, industrial equipment monitoring, and agricultural monitoring [1]. Although network transmission is easily affected by the environment, such as noise interference caused by metal equipment in factories, its wireless superiority, and low cost have driven the deployment of more factories. Most WSN are mission-oriented, where the sink node plays a vital role in collecting data with a tolerant real-time requirement. In these networks, most of them are task-driven, so it is necessary to ensure the timeliness of transmission, and the transmission mode is direct to the sink.

Multi-channel communication is an effective approach to improve transmission reliability and efficiency for WSN [2]. With the application of wireless in factories, the types of network nodes have become more abundant, and data center (DC) nodes have emerged to monitor the operational status of surrounding nodes in real-time in the network. In our cooperation with Beiren, we hope to provide direct access to tablet computers in the data center. Gao et al. [3] proposed a novel prioritized channel allocation scheme for different paths and channels, which jointly considers the deadline

© Springer Nature Singapore Pte Ltd. 2020
Z. Hao et al. (Eds.): CWSN 2020, CCIS 1321, pp. 115–125, 2020.
https://doi.org/10.1007/978-981-33-4214-9_9

requirement. Soua et al. [4] proposed a simple and efficient distributed joint channel and timeslot assignment for raw convergecast in multi-channel wireless sensor networks. In mission-oriented networks, Zhang et al. [5] analyze queuing modeling for delay packets in multi-hop communications where the packet arrival rate and service rate are both generally distributed.

It is not very efficient to directly use the existing methods on the data center network. Data send to the sink node according to the current techniques, and the DC node needs to wait until the sink node forwards the data to itself, or by accessing the cloud server. In this way, it is difficult to ensure the timeliness of data in the DC node (explained with an illustrative example in Sect. 2.) It is better to build the path directly to DC, but it cannot affect the state of the original sink to collect data.

JCSDC was implemented in simulation experiments. The evaluation results show that compared to the existing works, JCSDC significantly reduces data latency to the DC and does not incur additional impact on sink nodes. The main contributions of this paper are summarized as follows.

1) Use the dynamic programming method to assign sink collection links maximum the transmissions of nodes by assigning them with different channels and timeslots.
2) Propose a distributed method to build shortcuts for DC that can quickly expand other latest allocation algorithms.
3) We implement in simulation. Although it has not been tested in real testbed, it can still demonstrate the efficiency of the work. In the future, we will implement it in the factory in Bei Ren.

The rest of this paper is organized as follows. Section 2 presents the motivation of our work with illustrative examples. Section 3 offers the design details of JCSDC. Section 4 evaluates JCSDC with simulation experiments. Section 5 presents related works, and Sect. 6 concludes this work.

2   Motivation

In this section, we use an example to illustrate our work on the impact of joint assignment in the DC network. In our cooperation project with a printing machine manufacturer in Beijing, the DC node is a tablet attached to the machine. They raised a problem that DCs need to get data sensing part of the equipment around, and if acquired from a sink node or access cloud server will bring more considerable delay.

Joint Multi-channel and Timeslot Allocation. In Fig. 1, the topology is a 3-hop network. Every node needs to transmit and forward periodically generated data to sink. The sink node acts as a gateway to upload data to a local server or cloud server. DC node 6 requires data of node 4 and node 5 in real-time. Figure 2 demonstrates the assignment result of data collection. It cost at least six timeslots to collect all the data. Node 6 has to wait until the next chance when the sink forwards the data by downlink in the next superframe period. Otherwise, in Fig. 3, we use idle timeslots to complete the data transmission from nodes 4 and 5 to node 6, but it does not affect the initial data collection process. Node 6 received all the data at the fourth timeslot without waiting for the forwarding of the sink. (We did not show the link from the sink to other nodes, it will wait for the next superframe cycle.)

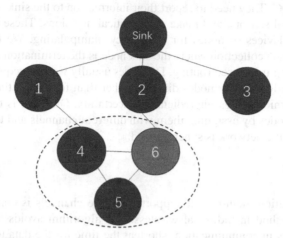

Fig. 1. An example of the topology of a sensor network.

Channel 0	5->4	2->sink	2->sink	1->sink	1->sink	1->sink
Channel 1	6->2	4->1	4->1			
Channel 2	3->sink					
	Timeslot 1	Timeslot 2	Timeslot 3	Timeslot 4	Timeslot 5	Timeslot 6

Fig. 2. Traditional assignment.

Channel 0	5->4	2->sink	2->sink	1->sink	1->sink	1->sink
Channel 1	6->2	4->1	4->1	4->6		
Channel 2	3->sink	5->6				
	Timeslot 1	Timeslot 2	Timeslot 3	Timeslot 4	Timeslot 5	Timeslot 6

Fig. 3. Build shortcuts for DC.

Increase Transmit Slots. Based on the above analysis of existing works, we identify an optimization opportunity as follows. With the present works, on the one hand, potential shortcuts to DC can be scheduled in advance as they are predictable. At the same time, there are some slots left unused after the link scheduling. Our main idea is to use those remaining spare slots for paths to DC in a probable manner. The detailed design will be discussed in Sect. 3.

3   Design of JCSDC

With the improvement of node performance, some nodes in the network act as the responsibility of DC. They need to report their information to the sink node, collect the information of local sensors, and make some critical decisions. These devices include typical handheld devices or nodes for emergency manipulating. We focus on event-driven multi-hop data collection where the sink node is the termination of all the sensor nodes by a spanning tree-based routing. DC nodes usually want to acquire the information of the surrounding sensor nodes directly, rather than forward it through downlink communication, which brings unpredictable uncertainty. Our goal is to multiplex the transmissions of nodes by assigning them with different channels and timeslots to sink and DC assuming the network is synchronized.

3.1   Overview

The TDMA allocation method that supports multiple channels is considered to be a highly reliable method in industrial wireless. Our algorithm avoids the primary and secondary conflicts in communication, shortens the time for the data to reach the sink node and DC as much as possible. JCSDC consists of two assignment rounds. The first round (Sect. 3.3) aims to assign links with different timeslots and channels in order to maximize the parallelized packet delivery. After the first round, the links from all nodes to sink nodes are established. The second round (Sect. 3.4) is to develop shortcuts to DC, and based on the original allocation corresponding timeslot and channel are allocated simultaneously.

3.2   Assumptions and Symbols Notations

Similar to the definitions in Incel et al. [12], the following constraints should be satisfied to complete the data transmission from all the sensor nodes to the sink [11].

Constraint 1: All the data packets must be collected by the sink node at the end of the last timeslot.

Constraint 2: Any node, including the sink, can only transmit or receive data, but not simultaneously, at any timeslot.

Constraint 3: When interfered by some other node over channel $c1$, a sensor node cannot communicate with any node unless a different channel $c2$ ($c1 \neq c2$) is used.

Each node is configured with a transmitter-receiver, which occupies a channel and a timeslot during transmission. We focus on event-driven multi-hop data collection where the data are. The notations used throughout this paper are summarized in Table 1.

Table 1. Notations.

Symbols	Notations
v_i	The node in the network with ID i
$M(v_i)$	Maximum number parallelized of links
max	The calculation to choose the maximum item
$H(v_i)$	Children nodes for v_i
h_1	The first child node
h_f	The last child node
DC	Datacenter
N	Total number of nodes in Network
Nei(DC)	Set of DC's neighbor node
w	Index of the possibility of data transmission
P_{t_begin}	The time packet p produced
P_{t_end}	The time packet p received by the destination

3.3   Joint Channel Slot Assignment for Sink

After the network node completes the joined process, the sensor node sends the location information and neighbor information to the sink node. According to the network topology information, it constructs the routing tree for data transmission. It then allocates the timeslots according to the maximum and parallel chain way of each timeslot according to the dynamic allocation algorithm. The idea is similar to my previous work [11]. The recursive equation of dynamic programming is (1). In the process of code implementation, we adopt a bottom-up strategy. When the value of w in the formula is 1, it indicates that there is data to be transmitted; otherwise, it is 0. Then, the channel allocation adopts the minimum available channel.

$$M(v_i) = \max \begin{cases} w + \sum_{x \in H(v_i) \cap x \neq h_1} M(x) + \sum_{y \in H(h_1)} M(y) \\ \vdots \\ w + \sum_{x \in H(v_i) \cap x \neq h_i} M(x) + \sum_{y \in H(h_i)} M(y) \\ \vdots \\ w + \sum_{x \in H(v_i) \cap x \neq h_f} M(x) + \sum_{y \in H(h_f)} M(y) \\ \sum_{x \in H(v_i)} M(x) \end{cases} \tag{1}$$

v_i is a node in the network. $M(v_i)$ represents the maximum number of links that can communicate in parallel in the topology of the root node v_i. $H(v_i)$ represents a collection of children nodes for v_i. $h_1 \in H(v_i)$ represents the first child node, $h_i \in H(v_i)$ represents the i-th child node, $h_f \in H(v_i)$ represents the last child node. The routing graph determines the number of child nodes, and the number of child nodes of each node is inconsistent.

3.4 Joint Channel Slot Assignment for DC

The data center node broadcasts the presence message of the data center node. The message contains the network address of the data center node and sends in contention timeslots in the form of broadcast. The response from the neighboring node includes approval or rejection. The default value of the response from the adjacent node is consent. In exceptional cases, it sends a rejection response. If a rejection response is received, the DC will resend the data center message after waiting for a specified period.

Based on the scheduling result by Sect. 3.3, it finds idle timeslots and channel to DC shortcut. First, a set *Nei (DC)* of nodes is obtained and sorted by the response time. Each node belonging to the set negotiates with the DC from the smallest unused timeslot and gradually increases the timeslot until it finds an available timeslot without collision. Then check whether the assignment meets the conditions of the channel and if there is no available channel, continue to increase the timeslot.

Until all the nodes that need to allocate the link have obtained the link, peripheral nodes form two data packets of sensor data generated in each cycle, one to the sink node and the other to the data center node.

4 Performance Evaluation and Analysis

In this paper, the performance of JCSDC has evaluated simulations in terms of cycle average data transmission delay (CAD). The smaller the value of CAD, the lower the delay, and the higher the efficiency of the algorithm. The data transmission delay calculates the difference between the generation time and the time it is received. For the sink node, it will collect the data from the node in the network. When the sink gets data from one of the nodes, it can calculate the data transmission delay. Then data from multiple nodes can calculate an average value of data delay, which is the sum of all the delay divided by the number of nodes to determine the performance of the algorithm. However, it should be noted that sometimes the data will not be received within a cycle [6]. If only the first cycle is counted, it will cause the node should receive ten packets, but only received nine packages, the average delay is not an accurate value and is underestimated. In this case, we used the following calculation method:

$$CAD = \frac{\sum_{n=1}^{N} P_{t\_end} - P_{t\_begin}}{N * \text{cycles}} \tag{2}$$

We compare the performance of JCSDC with Wave [3] and ReDCA [4] in simulation. Wave is the latest work on channel allocation for low power wireless networks. It adopts a simple and efficient joint channel and a timeslot assignment algorithm. ReDCA is another state-of-art work using the assignment order is determined by calculating the path assignment order, and the influence of link quality on the path is also considered. Compared with those, JCSDC further considers the whole network performance optimization.

We first evaluate the performance of JCSDC in C++ with a small-scale network contains 20 nodes, which are randomly deployed in an area. One node is the sink node, and the other nodes are source nodes. Data from source nodes traverse to the sink node through a specific path based on the least hop count.

Then we evaluate the performance of the medium-scale network of 100 nodes. The other nodes generate 100 packets and transmit them to the sink through a spinning tree, and sixteen channels are all used.

4.1 Small-Scale Network

We simulated a 20-point network where the node numbered 0 is a sink node. The network adopts random distribution, evenly distributed in the area of 50×50. The maximum communication distance of the node is 20. The length of the superframe is 64.

Figure 4 shows a comparison of the five algorithms. Algorithms wave and ReDCA complete the transfer to the sink node, then forward down to DC, whose average CAD is 48 timeslot delay. The wave shortcut and ReDCA shortcut algorithms are extended by us to add shortcuts to DC using the method mentioned in Sect. 3.4. It is evident that after the shortcut is constructed, the CAD that reaches the data center node is reduced by 91%. Each node act as a DC, the X-axis indicates the DC node number.

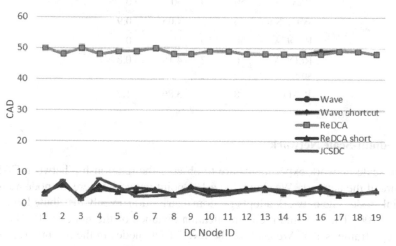

Fig. 4. Comparison of CAD.

Figure 5 shows the results of the comparison as a bar graph. Table 2 shows the analysis of test statistics, which lists the maximum, minimum, average, and standard deviation of CAD. When the DC node ID is 1, 6, 9, 10, 11, 12, 15, 18, JCSDC is better than the other two algorithms, and when the ID is 2, 4, 5, the performance is worse. The reason is that the algorithm allocation strategies are different, and JCSDC may not be able to achieve the best allocation for each DC node. But overall, the average CAD value of JSDCS is 3.85, the CAD value of Wave shortcut is 4.05, and the CAD value of ReDCA is 4.18. JSDCS reduces the CAD by 4.9% and 7.9%, respectively, compared to the other two algorithms.

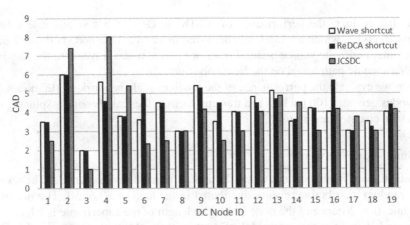

Fig. 5. Comparison of CAD with three algorithms with shortcuts.

Table 2. Statistical data comparison of algorithm CAD.

Algorithms	Max	Min	Average	STDEV
Wave	50	50	50	0
Wave Short	6	2	4.05	0.9
ReDCA	50	50	50	0
ReDCA short	6	2	4.18	0.8
JCSDC	8	1	3.86	1.7

4.2 Medium-Scale Network

Medium-scale network experiments are to observe the relationship between CAD and the nature of the network. We simulated a 100-point network where the node numbered 0 is a sink node. The network adopts random distribution, evenly distributed in the area of 100 × 100. The maximum communication distance of the node is 20. The length of the superframe is 128. We analyze the level of DC nodes in the routing tree and the number of neighbors.

DC Level Impact on CAD. To establish the communication link from all nodes to sink nodes, the routing tree created by the breadth-first strategy is adopted. Among them, level refers to the minimum hops to the sink node. Figure 6 shows that the algorithm of JCSDC is better than other algorithms. By the time it reaches level 4, the advantage is reduced. Because the node at level 4 is far from the sink node, there is less interference and less amount of communication data, which is easier to find the first shortcuts to DC.

The Number of DC's Neighbor Impact on CAD. Figure 7 shows a comparison of CAD between different algorithms. The X-axis is the number of neighbors. It can be seen

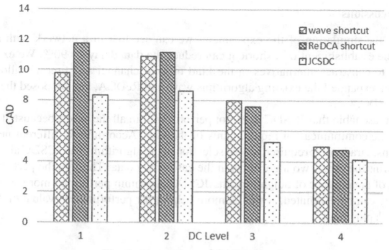

Fig. 6. Comparison of CAD by level.

that as the number of neighbors increases, the CAD value of JCSDC increases accordingly. The reason is that due to a large number of neighbors, there is a high probability of communication competition. When constructing a shortcut, the original link needs to be preferentially maintained, so the required delay is increased. It can be seen from the figure that the JCSDC algorithm is superior to other algorithms when the number of neighbors is less than 14. The other two algorithms also showed an upward trend as the number of neighbors increased, but it was not smooth.

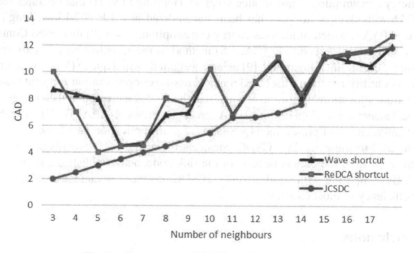

Fig. 7. Comparison of CAD by neighbor numbers.

4.3 Discussions

Through the simulation of the experiment, we can see that in a network with a data center, the establishment of a shortcut can reduce the data delay by 90%. We explored the way to construct alternatives in the kind of joint channel and timeslot allocation algorithm, expanded the existing algorithms wave and ReDCA, and proposed the state-of-art JCSDC.

It is reasonable that JCSDC does not perform well in all the cases, because it needs to meet the communication requirements of the sink. According to different network conditions, a tradeoff is required for the selection of the algorithm. The JCSDC algorithm outperforms the other two algorithms in the case of big data. Through the performance analysis of the number of neighbors, the JCSDC algorithm performed more smoothly. The delay can be estimated, which is more helpful for performance evaluation before network deployment.

5 Related Works

In reality, packet loss will lead to that the transmissions are deferred to the next duty cycle [6] when the length is not long enough for lots of retransmissions, which will incur a full-cycled delay. Otherwise, there will be considerable delay incurred for the links without packet losses as the slot lengths are the same for all links.

Joint Channel and timeslot allocation in multi-channel wireless sensor networks have been extensively studied in many years. This work was not accessible due to the assignment was NP-hard [13]. Collotta [7] proposed flexible IEEE 802.15.4 Deadline-Aware Scheduling for DPCSs Using Priority-Based CSMA-CA aim at minimizing the total energy consumption. Time slotted Channel Hopping (TSCH) that operates based on TDMA with channel hopping has been standardized in IEEE 802.15.4e, Jung [14] introduced PAAS, which minimizes energy consumption. Eisen [8] discussed Control-Aware Low Latency Scheduling (CALLS) method to meet control based goals under tight latency constraints. Jagannath [9] using a weighted virtual queue (VQ) to construct the network utility function, discussed a new cross-layer optimization for joint routing and spectrum allocation algorithm. Some research adopted aggregation technology. For example, Latency-controlled End-to-End Aggregation Protocol (LEAP) [10] that enables explicit enforcement of pre-defined QoS targets for an application data flow.

Compared to these works, JCSDC considers the actual requirements deployed in the factory, ensured the data collection of the sink node, and established a shortcut for the DC. By comparing with similar works, JCSDC has more advantages, stability, and higher efficiency in most cases.

6 Conclusions

In this paper, we propose a novel joint channel and timeslot assignment scheme for a mission-oriented data center network, which maximizes the parallel packet delivery and builds shortcuts to the data center. A dynamic programming scheme is proposed to find the maximum number of nodes that can transmit in parallel. Then, without changing the link allocation, a method to add a shortcut to the data center is proposed. Simulation experiments are conducted, implying that JCSDC outperforms the state-of-art works.

Acknowledgment. This work is supported by the Scientific research project of the Beijing Municipal Education Committee (KM 201810015010, KZ 202010015021) and Daxing Technology Development Project (KT 201901162).

References

1. Coates, A., Hammoudeh, M., Holmes, K.G.: Internet of things for buildings monitoring: experiences and challenges. In: the International Conference on Future Networks and Distributed Systems. ACM (2017)
2. Yafeng, W., et al.: Realistic and efficient multi-channel communications in wireless sensor networks. In: 27th Conference on Computer Communications, pp. 1193–1201. IEEE INFOCOM (2008)
3. Weifeng, G., et al.: Reliable channel allocation for mission oriented low-power wireless networks. In: IEEE Conference on Computer Communications Workshops (INFOCOM WKSHPS), pp. 70–75. IEEE INFOCOM (2018)
4. Soua, R., Minet, P., Livolant, E.: A distributed joint channel and slot assignment for convergecast in wireless sensor networks. In: the International Conference on New Technologies, Mobility and Security (2014)
5. Bowu, Z., et al.: Queuing modeling for delay analysis in mission oriented sensor networks under the protocol interference model. In: 2nd ACM Annual International Workshop on Mission-Oriented Wireless Sensor Networking, pp. 11–20. ACM (2013)
6. De Guglielmo, D., Anastasi, G., Seghetti, A.: From IEEE 802.15.4 to IEEE 802.15.4e: a step towards the internet of things. In: Gaglio, S., Re, G.L. (eds.) Advances onto the Internet of Things. Advances in Intelligent Systems and Computing, vol. 260. Springer, Cham (2014). https://doi.org/10.1007/978-3-319-03992-3_10
7. Collotta, M., et al.: Deadline-aware scheduling for DPCSs using priority-based CSMA-CA. In: Computers in Industry, vol. 65, no. 8, pp. 1181–1192. Flexible IEEE 802.15.4 (2014)
8. Eisen, M., et al.: Control aware radio resource allocation in low latency wireless control systems. Internet Things J. 6(5), 7878–7890 (2019). IEEE
9. Jagannath, J., et al.: Design and experimental evaluation of a cross-layer deadline-based joint routing and spectrum allocation algorithm. IEEE Trans. Mob. Comput. 18(8), 1774–1788 (2019)
10. Chiariotti, Federico, et al.: LEAP: A Latency Control Protocol for Multi-Path Data Delivery with Pre-Defined QoS Guarantees. IEEE INFOCOM 2018 - IEEE Conference on Computer Communications Workshops (INFOCOM WKSHPS), pp. 166–171(2018)
11. Yanhong, Y., et al.: Optimal time and channel assignment for data collection in wireless sensor networks. Int. J. Sens. Netw. 28(3), 165–178 (2018)
12. Incel, O.D., et al.: Fast data collection in tree-based wireless sensor networks. IEEE Trans. Mob. Comput. 11(1), 86–99 (2012)
13. Srinivasan, K., Dutta, P., Tavakoli, A., Levis, P.: An empirical study of low-power wireless. ACM Trans. Sens. Netw. 6(2), 16:1–16:49 (2010)
14. Jung, J., et al.: Parameterized slot scheduling for adaptive and autonomous TSCH networks. In: Conference on Computer Communications Workshops, pp. 76–81 (2018)

Power Minimization in Wireless Powered Fog Computing Networks with Binary Offloading

Han Li[1,2], Yang Lu[1,2]($\boxtimes$), Ke Xiong[1,2]($\boxtimes$), Xi Yang[3], Yu Zhang[4],
Duohua Wang[5], and Ning Wei[5]

[1] School of Computer and Information Technology,
Beijing Jiaotong University, Beijing 100044, China
kxiong@bjtu.edu.cn
[2] Beijing Key Laboratory of Traffic Data Analysis and Mining, Beijing Jiaotong
University, Beijing 100044, China
[3] School of Information, Beijing Wuzi University, Beijing 101149, China
[4] State Grid Energy Research Institute Co., Ltd., Beijing 102209, China
[5] ZTE Corporation, Xi'an 710065, China

Abstract. This paper investigates the power minimization design for a
multi-user wireless powered fog computing (FC) network, where a hybrid
access point (HAP) (integrated with a fog server) charges the multiple
energy-limited wireless sensor devices (WSDs) via wireless power transfer
(WPT). With the harvested energy, each WSD accomplishes its computation task by itself or by the fog server with a binary offloading mode.
A power minimization problem is formulated by jointly optimizing the
time assignment (for WPT and tasks offloading) and the WSDs' computation mode selection (local computing or FC) under constraints of
energy causality and computation rate requirement. Due to the integer and coupling variables, the considered problem is non-convex and
difficult to solve. With successive convex approximate (SCA) method,
a threshold-based algorithm is designed in terms of the WSDs' channel gains. Simulation results show that the proposed algorithm is able
to achieve the same performance of the enumeration-based algorithm
with very low computational complexity. Moreover, it is observed that
the channel gains have a great impact on computation mode selection.
Specifically, the WSDs with good channel gains prefer local computing
while the WSDs with poor channel gains prefer FC, which is much different from the existing sum computation rate maximization designs.

Keywords: Binary offloading · Fog computing · Power minimization ·
Successive convex approximate · Wireless power transfer

This work was supported in part by ZTE Corporation, in part by the Self-developed
project of State Grid Energy Research Institute Co., Ltd. (Ubiquitous Power Internet
of Things Edge Computing Performance Analysis and Simulation Based on Typical
Scenarios, No. SGNY202009014) and also in part by the Beijing Intelligent Logistics
System Collaborative Innovation Center (No. BILSCIC-2019KF-07).

© Springer Nature Singapore Pte Ltd. 2020
Z. Hao et al. (Eds.): CWSN 2020, CCIS 1321, pp. 126–139, 2020.
https://doi.org/10.1007/978-981-33-4214-9_10

1   Introduction

With the development of Internet of Things (IoTs), more and more latency-intensive and computation-intensive applications are appearing, which bring huge computing burden to the wireless sensor devices (WSDs) [1,2]. To improve the computation capabilities of WSDs in IoTs, fog computing (FC) (or mobile edge computing (MEC)) has been regarded as one of the most promising technologies [3,4]. With FC, WSDs are allowed to offload part or all of the computation tasks to their surrounding fog servers acted by access points (APs), base stations (BSs) and personal computers (PCs) via either partial offloading or binary offloading modes.

On the other hand, to provide controllable and stable energy supply for battery-limited WSDs in IoTs, wireless power transfer (WPT) has been attracting increasing interests [5–7]. To inherit the benefits of both FC and WPT, some works began to investigate WPT-enabled FC systems, see e.g., [8–13]. In [8], computation rate of system was maximized and partial offloading was employed, where however, only single user was considered. In [9–11], the multi-user systems were investigated, but their goals were to maximize the computation rate. As green communication has become a basic requirement in 5G networks [14], some works began to investigate power-minimization design for WPT-enabled FC systems [12,13]. In [12], the total energy consumption of AP was minimized under constraints of users' individual computation latency. In [13], the required energy was minimized under constraints of computation, communication and energy harvesting requirements. In [12] and [13], only the partial offloading mode was considered.

It is noticed that in practical systems, some computation tasks are not arbitrarily divisible. Therefore, in this paper, we investigate the power minimization design for multi-user WPT-enabled FC systems where the binary offloading mode is employed at each WSD rather than the partial offloading one.

The **contributions** of our work are summarized as follows. *First*, a power minimization problem is formulated by jointly optimizing the time assignment and the individual computation mode selection under constraints of energy causality and computation rate requirement. *Second*, due to the integer variables introduced by computation mode selection and coupling variables in constraints, the considered problem is non-convex and without known solution approach. With successive convex approximate (SCA) method, a threshold-based algorithm in terms of the WSDs' channel gains is designed. *Third*, simulation results show the validity and efficiency of the proposed algorithm. It is shown that the proposed algorithm is able to achieve the same performance of the enumeration-based algorithm with very low computational complexity. It is also shown that, in order to reduce the transmit power of the HAP, the WSDs with good channel gains prefer local computing while the WSDs with poor channel gains prefer FC, which is much different from the existing sum computation rate maximization designs. Meanwhile, WSDs with better channel gains require shorter offloading time.

The rest of the paper is organized as follows. Section 2 describes the system model and formulates the optimization problem. Section 3 presents the proposed algorithm. Simulation results are provided in Sect. 4 and Sect. 5 concludes this paper.

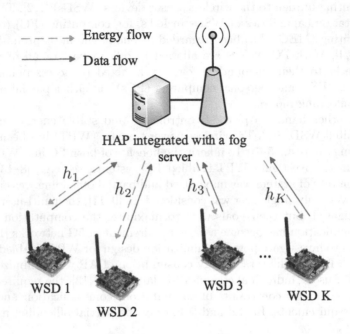

Fig. 1. System model.

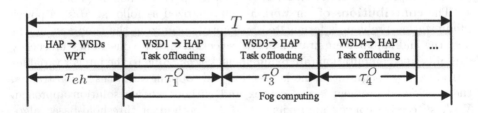

Fig. 2. Time assignment frameworks.

2   System Model

2.1   Network Model

Consider a multi-user wireless powered FC network as shown in Fig. 1, which consists a single-antenna HAP and a set $\mathcal{K} \triangleq \{1, ..., K\}$ of single-antenna WSDs.

The HAP first charges the multiple energy-limited WSDs via WPT, and then, with the harvested energy, each WSD accomplishes its computation task by local computing or offloading the task to the HAP with a binary offloading mode.

Block fading channel model is assumed so that the channel coefficient is assumed to remain unchanged within each time block T but may independently changes from one block to the next. In order to explore the achievable performance limits of this system, perfect channel state information (CSI) and the WSDs' computation rate requirements are assumed to known by the HAP.

2.2   EH Model

For clarity, the time assignment framework is shown in Fig. 2, where τ_{eh} is the time used for WPT, and τ_i^U is that used for offloading of the i-th WSD. In the first phase with time interval of τ_{eh} ($\tau_{eh} \leq T$), the harvested energy at the i-th WSD can be given by [11]

$$E_i^{eh} = \eta P_{\text{HAP}} h_i \tau_{eh}, \ i \in \mathcal{K}, \tag{1}$$

where $\eta \in (0,1)$ represents the constant EH efficiency factor, P_{HAP} denotes the transmit power at the HAP, and h_i denotes the channel gain between the HAP and the i-th WSD.

2.3   Computing Model

Let $s_i = \{0,1\}$, $\forall i \in \mathcal{K}$ denote the index of computation mode at the i-th WSD, where $s_i = 0$ and $s_i = 1$ represent the local computing mode and FC mode, respectively.

1) Local computing mode: If the local computing mode is selected, since the EH and computing circuits of each WSD are independent and communication is not involved in local computing, WSDs with local computing mode can harvest energy and compute simultaneously [11]. Thus, whole T can be used for local computing. Let τ_i^L denote the computation time of the i-th WSD with $0 \leq \tau_i^L \leq T$. As a result, the achievable computation rate of the i-th WSD with local computing mode (bit/s) is given by

$$R_i^L = \frac{f_i \tau_i^L}{\varepsilon T}, \tag{2}$$

where constant ε denotes the number of CPU cycles needed to process one bit of raw data, and f_i denotes computing speed (cycle/s) of the i-th WSD's processor. Then, the required energy can be modeled by $k_i f_i^3 \tau_i^L$ [15], where k_i represents the micro-processor's computation energy efficiency coefficient. To ensure a sustainable operation of the WSD, the energy consumption of the i-th WSD with local computing should satisfy

$$k_i f_i^3 \tau_i^L \leq E_i^{eh}. \tag{3}$$

2) FC mode: If the FC mode is selected, each WSD can offload its task to the HAP in its assigned time slot. Let δb_i be the number of bits offloaded to the HAP, where b_i represents the amount of raw data and $\delta > 1$ represents the communication overhead in data offloading. Thus, b_i can be given by

$$b_i = \frac{B\tau_i^O}{\delta} \log_2 \left(1 + \frac{P_i^O h_i}{\sigma^2} \right),$$ (4)

where B denotes the communication bandwidth, P_i^O denotes the transmit power at the i-th WSD, τ_i^O denotes the offloading time allocated to the i-th WSD, and σ^2 denotes the noise power. Correspondingly, the achievable computation rate of the i-th WSD with FC mode can be given by

$$R_i^O = \frac{B\tau_i^O}{\delta T} \log_2 \left(1 + \frac{P_i^O h_i}{\sigma^2} \right).$$ (5)

After offloading, the computing tasks are computed at the HAP, and HAP sends back the results to the corresponding WSDs. Here, the time spent on computing tasks and sending results by the HAP are neglected like [11]. That is, the WSDs with FC mode satisfies that

$$\sum_{i=1}^{K} \tau_i^O + \tau_{eh} \leq T.$$ (6)

Meanwhile, the energy consumption of the i-th WSD with FC mode is constrained by

$$P_i^O \tau_i^O \leq E_i^{eh}.$$ (7)

2.4 Problem Formulation and Analysis

Our goal is to minimize the transmit power at the HAP under constraints of energy causality and computation rate requirement, which is mathematically formulated as

$$\mathbf{P}_1: \min_{P_{\mathrm{HAP}}, s, \tau_{eh}, \tau^L, \tau^O, f, P^O} P_{\mathrm{HAP}}$$ (8)

$$\text{s.t. } \sum_{i=1}^{K} \tau_i^O + \tau_{eh} \leq T,$$ (8a)

$$\tau_{eh} \geq 0, \tau_i^O \geq 0,$$ (8b)

$$P_i^O \geq 0,$$ (8c)

$$0 \leq \tau_i^L \leq T, 0 \leq f_i \leq f_i^{\max},$$ (8d)

$$(1 - s_i)k_i f_i^3 \tau_i^L + s_i P_i^O \tau_i^O \leq \eta P_{\mathrm{HAP}} h_i \tau_{eh},$$ (8e)

$$(1 - s_i)\frac{f_i \tau_i^L}{\varepsilon T} + s_i \frac{B\tau_i^O}{\delta T} \log_2 \left(1 + \frac{P_i^O h_i}{\sigma^2} \right) \geq R^{req},$$ (8f)

$$s_i = \{0, 1\}, \forall i \in \mathcal{K},$$ (8g)

where $f_i^{\max}$ denotes the maximum CPU frequency of the i-th WSD, $\boldsymbol{s} = [s_1, s_2, ..., s_K]$, $\boldsymbol{f} = [f_1, f_2, ..., f_K]$, $\boldsymbol{\tau}^L = [\tau_1^L, \tau_2^L, ..., \tau_K^L]$, $\boldsymbol{\tau}^O = [\tau_1^O, \tau_2^O, ..., \tau_K^O]$ and $\boldsymbol{P}^O = [P_1^O, P_2^O, ..., P_K^O]$. Constraint (8e) means that the energy consumption of each WSD cannot exceed its harvested energy. Constraint (8f) means that each WSD needs to process R^{req}-bit raw data at least over T.

3   Solution Approach

Due to the binary variables $\boldsymbol{s}$ and the coupling variables in constraints (8e) and (8f), problem $\mathbf{P}_1$ is non-convex and cannot be directly solved with known methods. It is observed that the optimization of computing frequency $\boldsymbol{f}$ and time $\boldsymbol{\tau}^L$ for WSDs with local computing mode can be independent of the optimization of the transmit power $\boldsymbol{P}^O$ for WSDs with FC mode due to the binary offloading mode. Specifically, we have the following lemmas.

Lemma 1. *The minimum transmit power P_{HAP}^* is achieved when $\tau_i^{L^*} = T$ and $f_i^* = (\frac{E_i^{eh}}{k_i T})^{\frac{1}{3}}$ for WSDs with local computing mode.*

Proof. The minimum P_{HAP}^* should satisfy energy requirements of all WSDs, i.e., $P_{HAP}^* \geq \frac{k_i f_i^3 \tau_i^L}{\eta h_i \tau_{eh}}$, $\forall i \in \{i | s_i = 0\}$ and $P_{HAP}^* \geq \frac{P_j^O \tau_j^O}{\eta h_j \tau_{eh}}$, $\forall j \in \{j | s_j = 1\}$. Notice that the minimum P_{HAP}^* depends mainly on the high-consumption WSD who requires HAP to set the highest P_{HAP}. Without loss of generality, we assume the l-th WSD with local computing is the high-consumption one. Its rate requirement is $\frac{f_l \tau_l^L}{eT} \geq R^{req}$, and the energy requirement is $k_l f_l^3 \tau_l^L$. Then, $f_l \geq \frac{R^{req} eT}{\tau_l^L}$. Note that f_l monotonically increases when τ_l^L decreases, and the energy requirement $k_l f_l^3 \tau_l^L$ increases as f_l^3 plays a major role. Thus, by setting $\tau_l^L = T$, one can obtain a smaller energy requirement, and further requiring a smaller $\bar{P}_{HAP}$. For $\forall i \neq l$, setting $\tau_i^L = T$ only decreases its energy requirement. When a FC mode WSD is the high-consumption one. Setting $\tau_i^L = T$ for all local computing mode WSDs, only decreases their energy requirements without increasing the minimum P_{HAP}^*. Thus, $\tau_i^{L^*} = T$.

Then, we prove $f_i^* = (\frac{E_i^{eh}}{k_i T})^{\frac{1}{3}}$ via contradiction. Suppose that a WSD who selects local computing mode can always exhaust the harvested energy with T if operating at the maximum CPU frequency, i.e.,

$$E_i^{eh} = \eta P_{HAP} h_i \tau_{eh} < k_i f_i^{\max^3} T. \tag{9}$$

Without loss of generality, we assume the l-th WSD with local computing mode is the high-consumption one. Suppose $\{P_{HAP}^*, \boldsymbol{s}^*, \tau_{eh}^*, \boldsymbol{\tau}^{L^*}, \boldsymbol{\tau}^{O^*}, \boldsymbol{f}^*, \boldsymbol{P}^{O^*}\}$ is the optimal solution to problem $\mathbf{P}_1$, where $\tau_l^{L^*} = T$ and $f_l^* < (\frac{E_l^{eh}}{k_l T})^{\frac{1}{3}} = (\frac{\eta P_{HAP}^* h_l \tau_{eh}^*}{k_l T})^{\frac{1}{3}}$. Then, one can obtain a smaller $\bar{P}_{HAP}$ by making the equation $f_l^* = (\frac{\eta \bar{P}_{HAP} h_l \tau_{eh}^*}{k_l T})^{\frac{1}{3}}$ holding true, and energy constraints and rate constraints of all WSDs are still satisfied. This contradicts with the assumption that $\{P_{HAP}^*, \boldsymbol{s}^*, \tau_{eh}^*, \boldsymbol{\tau}^{L^*}, \boldsymbol{\tau}^{O^*}, \boldsymbol{f}^*, \boldsymbol{P}^{O^*}\}$ is the optimal solution to problem $\mathbf{P}_1$.

For $\forall i \neq l$, setting $f_i^* = (\frac{E_i^{eh}}{k_i T})^{\frac{1}{3}}$ only increases its computing rate with same harvested energy. When a FC mode WSD is the high-consumption one, setting $f_i^* = (\frac{E_i^{eh}}{k_i T})^{\frac{1}{3}}$ for all WSDs with local computing mode, only increases their computing rate without increasing the minimum P_{HAP}^*. Thus, Lemma 1 is proved.

Lemma 2. *The minimum transmit power P_{HAP}^* is achieved when $P_i^{O^*} = \frac{E_i^{eh}}{\tau_i^O}$ for WSDs with FC mode.*

Proof. This lemma is proved via contradiction. Suppose $\{P_{HAP}^*, s^*, \tau_{eh}^*, \tau^{L^*}, \tau^{O^*}, f^*, P^{O^*}\}$ is the optimal solution to problem P_1, where $P_i^{O^*} < \frac{E_i^{eh}}{\tau_i^{O^*}} = \frac{\eta P_{HAP}^* \tau_{eh}^* h_i}{\tau_i^{O^*}}$, $\forall i = \{i | s_i = 1\}$. Then, one can obtain a bigger $\bar{P}_i^O$ by making the equation $\bar{P}_i^O \tau_i^{O^*} = \eta P_{HAP}^* \tau_{eh}^* h_i$ holding true, where the rate constraint is over satisfied. In this case, the i-th WSD can offload with a shorter time $\bar{\tau}_i^O$ and all WSDs have longer $\bar{\tau}_{eh}$ to EH. As a result, one can obtain a smaller $\bar{P}_{HAP}$ to satisfy all energy and rate constraints. This contradicts with the assumption that $\{P_{HAP}^*, s^*, \tau_{eh}^*, \tau^{L^*}, \tau^{O^*}, f^*, P^{O^*}\}$ is the optimal solution to problem P_1. Therefore, Lemma 2 is proved.

By substituting $\tau_i^{L^*} = T$, $f_i^* = (\frac{E_i^{eh}}{k_i T})^{\frac{1}{3}}$ and $P_i^{O^*} = \frac{E_i^{eh}}{\tau_i^O}$ into problem P_1, it could be simplified to the following problem P_2, i.e.,

$$P_2: \min_{P_{HAP}, s, \tau_{eh}, \tau^O} P_{HAP} \tag{10}$$

$$\text{s.t. } (1 - s_i)\mu_1 \left(\frac{h_i}{k_i T}\right)^{\frac{1}{3}} (\tau_{eh} P_{HAP})^{\frac{1}{3}}$$

$$+ s_i \mu_2 \tau_i^O \ln\left(1 + \frac{\mu_3 h_i^2 \tau_{eh} P_{HAP}}{\tau_i^O}\right) \geq R^{req}, \tag{10a}$$

$$+ (8a), (8b), (8g),$$

where $\mu_1 \triangleq \frac{\eta^{\frac{1}{3}}}{\varepsilon}$, $\mu_2 \triangleq \frac{B}{\delta \ln(2) T}$ and $\mu_3 \triangleq \frac{\eta}{\sigma^2}$. However, problem P_2 is still non-convex. By introducing two new variables, i.e., $e^x = P_{HAP}$ and $e^y = \tau_{eh}$, and substituting them into problem P_2, one has that

$$P_3: \min_{x, s, y, \tau^O} e^x \tag{11}$$

$$\text{s.t. } \sum_{i=1}^K \tau_i^O + e^y \leq T, \tag{11a}$$

$$\tau_i^O \geq 0, \tag{11b}$$

$$(1 - s_i)\mu_1 \left(\frac{h_i}{k_i T}\right)^{\frac{1}{3}} (e^{x+y})^{\frac{1}{3}}$$

$$+ s_i \mu_2 \tau_i^O \ln\left(1 + \frac{\mu_3 h_i^2 e^{x+y}}{\tau_i^O}\right) \geq R^{req}, \tag{11c}$$

$$s_i = \{0, 1\}, \forall i \in \mathcal{K}. \tag{11d}$$

The constraint (11c) is still non-convex, via defining $\alpha \triangleq e^{x+y}$, problem $\mathbf{P}_3$ is further equivalently expressed to be

$$\mathbf{P}_4 : \min_{x,s,y,\tau^O,\alpha} \quad e^x \tag{12}$$

$$\text{s.t. } (1 - s_i)\mu_1 \left(\frac{h_i}{k_iT}\right)^{\frac{1}{3}} \alpha^{\frac{1}{3}}$$

$$+ s_i\mu_2\tau_i^O \ln\left(1 + \frac{\mu_3 h_i^2 \alpha}{\tau_i^O}\right) \geq R^{req}, \tag{12a}$$

$$e^{x+y} \geq \alpha, \tag{12b}$$

$$\alpha \geq 0. \tag{12c}$$

$$(11a), (11b), (11d).$$

Now, the constraint (12a) is convex, but the introduced constraint (12b) is non convex. So, we transform it into the following inequality, i.e.,

$$\frac{1}{\alpha} \geq e^{-x-y}. \tag{13}$$

Assuming that $\bar{\alpha}$ is the feasible points of problem $\mathbf{P}_4$, the lower bound of $1/\alpha$ is be given by

$$\frac{1}{\alpha} \geq \frac{1}{\bar{\alpha}} - \frac{1}{\bar{\alpha}^2}(\alpha - \bar{\alpha}). \tag{14}$$

Then, the restrictive constraint of (12b) is given by

$$\frac{1}{\bar{\alpha}} - \frac{1}{\bar{\alpha}^2}(\alpha - \bar{\alpha}) \geq e^{-x-y}. \tag{15}$$

By replacing constraint (12b) with (15), problem $\mathbf{P}_4$ can be approximately transformed to be

$$\mathbf{P}_5 : \min_{x,s,y,\tau^O,\alpha} \quad e^x \tag{16}$$

$$\text{s.t. } \frac{1}{\bar{\alpha}} - \frac{1}{\bar{\alpha}^2}(\alpha - \bar{\alpha}) \geq e^{-x-y} \tag{17}$$

$$(11a), (11b), (11d), (12a), (12c).$$

The problem $\mathbf{P}_5$ is still non-convex due to discrete constraint (11d). However, when the s is fixed, problem $\mathbf{P}_5$ reduces to a convex problem, which can be solved by using standard convex optimization solvers. In order to find the optimal solution $\{P_{\text{HAP}}^*, s^*, \tau_{eh}^*, \tau^{O^*}\}$, one can enumerate all the 2^K possible values of s and find the one who yield the smallest P_{HAP}.

Previous works have pointed out, in the WPT assisted networks with TDMA adopted in the uplink, there exists a doubly near-far phenomenon [16,17]. That is, the farther the WSD is from the HAP, the less energy it receives. So, it has to transmit with higher power to achieve the same rate as the nearby WSDs. Therefore, the WSD with worst channel gain has the greatest impact on the system performance. Based on such an observation, we have the following Lemma 3.

Lemma 3. *The optimal s^* has a threshold structure, if there exists the i-th WSD who selects the local computing mode, i.e., $s_i^* = 0$, all WSDs whose channel gains are better than him select the local computing mode.*

Proof. Without loss of generality, suppose $h_1 \geq h_2 \geq \dots \geq h_N$. Let $\{P_{HAP}^*, s^*, \tau_{eh}^*, \tau^{O^*}\}$ be the optimal solution to problem $\mathbf{P_2}$. Now prove this lemma via contradiction. If the j-th WSD, $j < i$, selects local computing mode, due to the broadcast nature of wireless communications, the harvested energy exceeds its required energy, because it has same rate requirement with the i-th WSD. If the j-th WSD, $j < i$, selects FC mode, then $\tau_j^{O^*} > 0$. Then, by setting $\bar{\tau}_i^O = 0$, all WSDs can have a longer $\bar{\tau}_{eh}$ to EH. As a result, one can obtain a smaller $\bar{P}_{HAP}$ and all energy and rate constraints are still satisfied. This contradicts with the assumption that $\{P_{HAP}^*, s^*, \tau_{eh}^*, \tau^{O^*}\}$ is the optimal solution to problem $\mathbf{P_2}$. Thus, Lemma 3 is proved.

Following Lemma 3, one can sort the WSDs in a descending order with their channel gains at first. Then, only $(K+1)$ possible values of s, i.e., $[1, 1, 1, ..., 1]'$, ... , $[0, ..., 0, 1, ..., 1]'$, ... , $[0, 0, 0, ..., 0]'$ need to be considered. By solving problem $\mathbf{P_5}$ $(K+1)$ times under $(K+1)$ fixed s, the smallest P_{HAP}^* can be obtained. For clarity, this algorithm is summarized in Algorithm 1.

Algorithm 1: Threshold-based algorithm for solving Problem $\mathbf{P_2}$

Initialize the number of WSDs K and other initialization parameters,
e.g. h_i's and R^{req};
Sort WSDs in descending channel order from 1 to K;
for $n = 0 : K$ **do**

   if $n = 0$ **then**
      | $s = [1, 1, 1, ..., 1]'$;
   else
      | $s(n) = 0$;
   end
   Set $q = 1$ and given $\bar{\alpha}$;
   repeat;
   Obtain $\{x^*(q), y^*(q), \tau^{O^*}(q), \alpha^*(q)\}$ via solving Problem $\mathbf{P_5}$ under s ;
   Update $\bar{\alpha}(q) = e^{x+y}$, $q = q + 1$;
   Until the pre-defined stopping criterion is met;
   Obtain $P_{HAP}^*(n) = e^{x^*}(q)$, $\tau_{eh}^*(n) = e^{y^*}(q)$ and $\tau^{O^*}(n) = \tau^{O^*}(q)$;

end
Return the minimal $P_{HAP}^*(n)$

---

4   Numerical Results

This section provides some simulation results to validate our analysis and evaluate the system performance. The simulation scenario is shown in Fig. 3. In the simulations, the EH efficiency factor η is set as 0.5. The path loss is modelled by the free-space path loss model [10]

$$h_i = A_d \left(\frac{3 * 10^8}{4\pi f_c d_i} \right)^{\psi}, \ \forall i \in \mathcal{K}, \tag{18}$$

where $A_d = 4.11$ represents the antenna gain, $f_c = 915\,\text{MHz}$ represents the transmission frequency, d_i represents the distance between the HAP and the i-th WSD, and $\psi \geq 2$ represents the path loss exponent. Without loss of generality, the time block length T is set as $1\,\text{s}$, the number of WSDs K is set as 8, and the rate requirements of all the WSDs R^{req} is set as $30000\,\text{bit/s}$. For WSDs with local computing mode, the computation energy efficiency coefficient k_i is set as 10^{-29}, and the number of CPU cycles needed to process one bit of raw data ε is set as 1000. For WSDs with FC mode, the bandwidth B is set as $2\,\text{MHz}$, the communication overhead δ is set as 1.2, and the noise power σ^2 is set as $10^{-10}\,\text{W}$. For clarity, the specific simulation parameters are shown in Table 1, which remain unchanged unless otherwise specified.

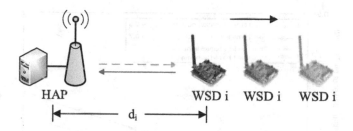

Fig. 3. Illustration of the simulation scenarios.

Table 1. Simulation parameters.

Parameters	Notation	Values
The EH efficiency factor	η	0.5
The transmission frequency	f_c	915 MHz
The time block length	T	1s
The number of WSDs	K	8
The rate requirements	R^{req}	30000 bit/s
The computation energy efficiency coefficient	k_i	10^{-29}
The number of CPU cycles needed to process one bit of raw data	ε	1000
The bandwidth	B	2 MHz
The communication overhead	δ	1.2
The noise power	σ^2	10^{-10} W

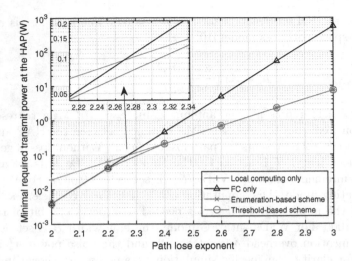

Fig. 4. The minimal required power at the HAP compared with different schemes versus the path loss exponent.

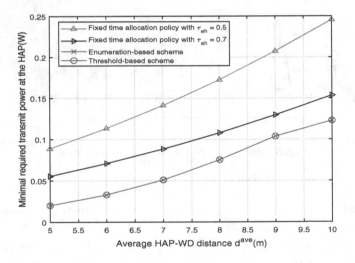

Fig. 5. The minimal required power at the HAP compared with different schemes versus the average distance from the HAP to WSDs.

Figure 4 compares the proposed scheme and two benchmark schemes, i.e., local computing only scheme and FC only scheme, in terms of the path lose exponent ψ, where $d_i = 3 + 1(i-1)$m, $i = 1, ..., 8$. For comparison, the result of enumeration-based algorithm is also plotted. It is observed that as ψ increases, the required transmit power of the four schemes increases significantly. It is also observed that the FC only scheme is better than the local computing only scheme with a relatively small ψ, and the local computing only scheme is better than the FC only scheme with a relatively large ψ. The reason is, as ψ increases, the capacities are greatly degraded by the poor wireless channel gains. For all values of ψ, the proposed algorithm shows the best performance, which is able to achieve the same performance of the enumeration-based algorithm. Thus, optimizing mode selections can obtain significant performance gains.

Figure 5 compares the proposed scheme and the fixed time allocation schemes in terms of the average distance from the HAP to WSDs. For the fixed time allocation schemes, τ_{eh} is set as 0.5 and 0.8, respectively, and the rest time is equally allocated to each WSDs. The WSDs are deployed along a straight line equidistantly within a range $[d^{ave} - 3.5, d^{ave} + 3.5]$, where d^{ave} is the average distance from all WSDs to the HAP, and the distance between each two neighboring WSDs is 1 m. It is observed that as d^{ave} increases, the required transmit power of the two schemes increases significantly, and for all d^{ave}, the proposed scheme is superior to the fixed time allocation schemes. Thus, optimizing time assignment can obtain significant performance gains.

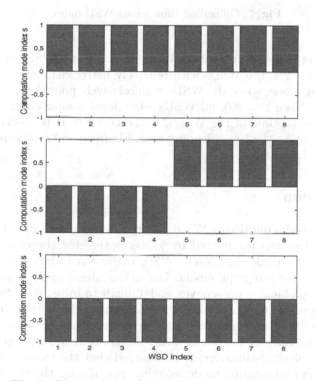

Fig. 6. Computing mode selection versus WSD index.

Figure 6 shows the optimal computing mode selections in terms of path loss exponent ψ, i.e., $\psi = 2.0$ (the top figure), $\psi = 2.4$ (the middle figure) and $\psi = 3.0$ (the bottom figure), where $d_i = 1 + 0.5(i-1)m$, $i = 1, ..., 8$. For clarity, we use $s_i = 1$ and $s_i = -1$ to denote that the i-th WSD selects FC mode and

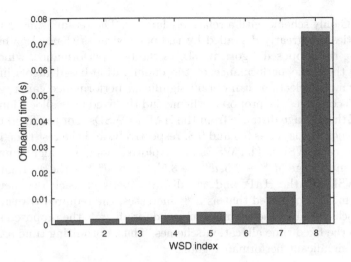

Fig. 7. Offloading time versus WSD index.

local computing mode, respectively. When $\psi = 2.0$, all WSDs select the FC mode. When $\psi = 2.4$, the WSDs with relatively better channel gains select the local computing mode, while the WSDs with relatively poor channel gains select the FC mode. When $\psi = 3.0$, all WSDs select local computing mode. Figure 7 plots the offloading time of the WSDs, where $\psi = 2.0$. It is observed that the better channel gains, the less offloading time. Figures 6 and 7 are consistent with the analysis in Lemma 3.

5   Conclusion

This paper studied a multi-user WPT powered network with FC. A power minimization problem was formulated by jointly optimizing the time assignment, and the computing mode selection of WSDs under constraints of energy causality and computation rate requirement. Due to the integer and coupling variables, the considered problem is non-convex and difficult to solve. With SCA method, a threshold-based algorithm was designed in terms of the WSDs' channel gains. Simulation results demonstrated that the proposed algorithm is able to achieve the same performance of the enumeration-based algorithm with very low computational complexity. Moreover, it is observed that the channel gains have a great impact on computation mode selection. Specifically, the WSDs with good channel gains prefer local computing while the WSDs with poor channel gains prefer FC, which is much different from the existing sum computation rate maximization designs. Besides, the better channel gains, the less offloading time.

References

1. Wu, W., Zhou, F., Hu, R.Q., Wang, B.: Energy-efficient resource allocation for secure NOMA-enabled mobile edge computing networks. IEEE Trans. Commun. **68**(1), 493–505 (2020)
2. Zheng, H., Xiong, K., Fan, P., Zhong, Z., Letaief, K.B.: Fog-assisted multiuser SWIPT networks: local computing or offloading. IEEE Internet Things J. **6**(3), 5246–5264 (2019)
3. Barbarossa, S., Sardellitti, S., Lorenzo, P.D.: Communicating while computing: distributed mobile cloud computing over 5G heterogeneous networks. IEEE Sig. Process. Mag. **31**(6), 45–55 (2014)
4. Li, B., Zhang, Y., Xu, L.: An MEC and NFV integrated network architecture. ZTE Commun. **15**(2), 19–25 (2017)
5. Xu, J., Zeng, Y., Zhang, Y.: UAV-enabled wireless power transfer: trajectory design and energy optimization. IEEE Trans. Wireless Commun. **17**(8), 5092–5106 (2018)
6. Zheng, H., Xiong, K., Fan, P., Zhou, L., Zhou, Z.: SWIPT-aware fog information processing: local computing vs. fog offloading. Sensors **18**(10), 3291–3307 (2018)
7. Huang, Y., Clerckx, B., Bayguzina, E.: Waveform design for wireless power transfer with limited feedback. IEEE Trans. Wireless Commun. **17**(1), 415–429 (2018)
8. Zheng, H., Xiong, K., Fan, P., Zhong, Z.: Wireless powered communication networks assisted by multiple fog servers. In Proceeding IEEE ICC Workshops, Shanghai, China, pp. 1–6 (2019)
9. Wang, F.: Computation rate maximization for wireless powered mobile edge computing. In: Proceeding APCC, Perth, Australia, pp. 1–6 (2017)
10. Zeng, M., Du, R., Fodor, V., Fischione, C.: Computation rate maximization for wireless powered mobile edge computing with NOMA. In: Proceeding of IEEE WoWMoM, Washington DC, USA, pp. 1–9 (2019)
11. Bi, S., Zhang, Y.J.: Computation rate maximization for wireless powered mobile-edge computing with binary computation offloading. IEEE Trans. Wircl. Commun. **17**(6), 4177–4190 (2018)
12. Wang, F., Xu, J., Wang, X., Cui, S.: Joint offloading and computing optimization in wireless powered mobile-edge computing systems. IEEE Trans. Wirel. Commun. **17**(3), 1784–1797 (2018)
13. Liu, J., Xiong, K., Fan, P., Zhong, Z., Letaief, K.B.: Optimal design of SWIPT-aware fog computing networks. In: Proceedings IEEE INFOCOM Workshops, Paris, France, pp. 13–19 (2019)
14. Lu, Y., Xiong, K., Fan, P., Ding, Z., Zhong, Z., Letaief, K.B.: Global energy efficiency in secure MISO SWIPT systems with non-linear power-splitting EH model. IEEE J. Sel. Areas Commun. **37**(1), 216–232 (2019)
15. Wang, Y., Sheng, M., Wang, X., Wang, L., Li, J.: Mobile-edge computing: partial computation offloading using dynamic voltage scaling. IEEE Trans. Commun. **64**(10), 4268–4282 (2016)
16. Ju, H., Zhang, R.: Throughput maximization in wireless powered communication networks. IEEE Trans. Wirel. Commun. **13**(1), 418–428 (2014)
17. Liu, L., Zhang, R., Chua, K.C.: Multi-antenna wireless powered communication with energy beamforming. IEEE Trans. Commun. **62**(12), 4349–4361 (2014)

Efficient Transmission of Multi Satellites-Multi Terrestrial Nodes Under Large-Scale Deployment of LEO

Wei Sun and Bin Cao(✉)

Harbin Institute of Technology (Shenzhen), Shenzhen 518055, China
sunwei.hc@qq.com, caobin@hit.edu.cn

Abstract. In this paper, a novel uplink satellite-terrestrial network (STN) under the large-scale deployment of satellites is proposed to achieve efficient transmission of satellite-terrestrial data. In this network framework, spectrum utilization is improved by appropriate spectrum reuse and optimization to achieve matching transmission of multi terrestrial nodes (TNs) -multi satellite nodes (SNs). We formulate the optimization problem with maximizing system sum rate as optimization objective while considering TNs' power and rate constraints. The original optimization problem is a highly non-convex optimization problem. We divide the optimization problem into node association subproblem and resource allocation subproblem, where resource allocation problem mainly includes channel allocation and power allocation. We propose a Matching and Lagrangian dual combination algorithm (MLCA) to solve the 0–1 combinatorial programming, wherein we use a matching algorithm and transform the original problem into convex subproblems via the Lagrangian dual method. Finally, simulation results are performed to verify the advantages of the proposed algorithm.

Keywords: STN · Matching algorithm · Non-convex optimization

1 Introduction

With the rapid deployment of terrestrial information networks, on one hand, the user experience of wireless services have annually improved. On the other hand, the large-scale development of terrestrial networks is gradually reaching its bottleneck, wherein a global seamless coverage is notable. Recently, the Space-Air-Terrestrial Integrated Information Network (SATIIN) attracts tremendous attention from both academia and industry [1]. Generally, SATIIN consists of satellites in different orbits and integrates with air and terrestrial information infrastructures. In such a way, SATIIN can exceedingly extend the coverage area

Supported by the General Project of Guangdong Natural Science Foundation nos. 2020A1515010851, and the General Project of Shenzhen Natural Science Foundation nos. JCYJ20190806142414811.

Z. Hao et al. (Eds.): CWSN 2020, CCIS 1321, pp. 140–154, 2020.
https://doi.org/10.1007/978-981-33-4214-9_11

and provide flexible transmission. For achieving global networking and real-time access via low earth orbit (LEO) satellites, SpaceX [2] and OneWeb [3] are on the way to launch thousands of LEO satellites to facilitate seamless and high-speed communication services. Thus, the efficient satellite-terrestrial transmission paradigms and key-enabling technologies have become hot research topics in this very area.

Some related works have investigated the satellite-terrestrial transmission resource allocation, e.g., [4] performed the joint allocation of transmission and computing resources, and proposed a joint computation and transmission resource allocation scheme. [5] and [6] studied the collaborative data download problem by using Inter-Satellite Link (ISL). Huang et al. analyzed how to collect data from IoT gateways via LEO satellites on a time-varying uplink in an energy-efficient manner, and proposed an online algorithm based on Lyapunov optimization theory [7]. [8] and [9] proposed a terrestrial-satellite network architecture to achieve efficient data offloading in ultra-dense LEO deployment. In [10] and [11], the optimization problem of joint sub-channel and power allocation in a heterogeneous uplink orthogonal frequency division multiple access (OFDMA) based network is studied. In [12], Zhang et al. proposed a resource allocation scheme for co-channel femtocells, aiming to maximize the capacity. In [13] and [14], application of matching algorithm in resource allocation is introduced.

In general, the current work rarely considers the resource allocation problem under the dense deployment of LEO satellites. In this paper, we mainly focus on the satellite-terrestrial nodes matching and transmission resource allocation under the dense deployment of LEO satellite and propose an simple and efficient algorithm conbining matching algorithm and duality theory.

The rest of the paper is organized as follow. In Sect. 2, we describe the system model of satellite-terrestrial networks under the deployment of large scale LEO and formulation the optimization problem with the objective of maximizing the total system rate under the consideration of multiple constraints. In Sect. 3, we propose the method of satellite-terrestrial nodes association and resource allocation, we solve the problem of user and channel association by using matching algorithm, and solve the power allocation problem by Lagrangian dual iteration. Simulation results are presented in Sect. 4, and at last, we conclude the whole paper in Sect. 5.

2 System Model and Problem Formulation

In this section, we mainly present the system model and problem formulation. With the large-scale deployment of LEO satellites, in order to further improve its spectrum utilization, it is necessary to perform spectrum multiplexing. Referring to spectrum multiplexing in terrestrial cellular systems, we consider that the whole satellite frequency band can be divided into N segments, which are multiplexed by N groups of satellites. Because the main focus of this paper is the problem of resource allocation, this paper doesn't study the detailed spectrum multiplexing scheme. It mainly studies the problem of resource allocation between satellites that reuse the same frequency segment after the spectrum multiplexing scheme is determined.

2.1   System Model

As shown in Fig. 1, we consider an OFDMA based STN wherein LEO satellites provide transmission services to TNs. Since the frequency spectrum is divided into orthogonal sub-bands, the satellites can be divided into $\mathcal{N} = \{1, 2, ...N\}$ groups and satellites in different groups use different frequency segments, but satellites in the same group reuse the same frequency segment. So in this paper, we think that the shared frequency group of satellites has been divided, and we only discuss satellites in one frequency group, all of which share the same frequency.

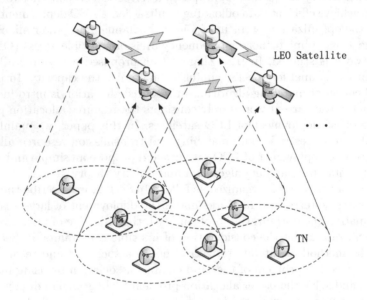

Fig. 1. Multi-satellite multi-TN uplink transmission network.

We focus on LEO satellite accessing control and resource allocation in the uplink of terrestrial nodes. Due to the pre-planned orbit of each satellite, its altitude, speed, and position information are known to all terrestrial nodes in each time slot. For convenience, we adopt a quasi-static method to split a time period into multiple time slots, during each of which the position of a satellite and the channel between satellite and terrestrial nodes is unchanged, and we assume that LEO satellites have knowledge about channel state information of terrestrial nodes.

In group n, we consider the frequency segment n with bandwidth B divided into a set $\mathcal{K} = \{1, 2, ..., K\}$ of orthogonal subchannels, which are reused by LEO satellites. It should be noted that due to the mobility of LEO satellites, there is a certain Doppler shift in the frequency. We think that the frequency bands mentioned in this paper have been compensated. To better depict the satellite-terrestrial nodes association and subchannel allocation, we introduce a binary matrix $\mathbf{Y}$ where the element $y_{i,j,k} = 1$ indicates that TN i is associated with LEO satellite j over subchannel k and $y_{i,j,k} = 0$ otherwise, so $y_{i,j,k}$ includes two physical meanings of satellite-terrestrial node association and channel assignment. Additionally, let $\mathcal{I}_j$ be the set of TNs associated with the satellite j, $\mathcal{I}_j \subset \mathcal{I}$. Although the spectrum allocation scheme between satellites and TN is optimized to a certain degree when deploying LEO satellites, co-frequency interference is unavoidable due to the inherent characteristics of satellite transmission. Denote $h_{i,j,k}$ as the channel gain of the TN i-satellite j link over subchannel k with both the large-scale fading and the shadowed-Rician fading taken into consideration. Assuming that the subchannel k of the satellite j is allocated to the TN i, then the received signal-to-interference-noise-radio(SINR) on this subchannel can be expressed by

$$R_{i,j,k} = \log_2 \left(1 + \frac{p_{i,j,k}|H_{i,j,k}|^2}{\sum\limits_{i' \neq i} \sum\limits_{j' \neq j} y_{i',j',k} p_{i',j',k} |H_{i',j,k}|^2 + N_0} \right) \tag{1}$$

where $p_{i,j,k}$ is the transmit power of TN i to satellite j over subchannel k, the total gain of the TN i to satellite j over subchannel k is $H_{i,j,k} = h_{i,j,k}\sqrt{G_{i(j),j}L_{i,j}}$, with both the large-scale fading $L_{i,j,k}$, the shadowed-Rician fading $h_{i,j,k}$ and the antenna gain of TN i - $G_{i(j),j}$ taken into consideration. As shown in [15], $G_{i(j),j}$ is the antenna gain of TN i towards satellite j and the $G_{i'(j'),j}$ is the off-axis antenna gain of TN i' to satellite j when the transmission target direction of TN i' is towards satellite j'. N_0 is the power spectrum density of the Additive White Gaussian Noise (AWGN).

2.2   Problem Formulation

Through the above analysis, we know that there are many issues to be considered for the uplink transmission of multi satellite-multi terrestrial nodes under the large-scale deployment of LEO. So, in this paper, satellite-terrestrial node association, channel assignment and power allocation problem are formulated as an optimization problem that aims to maximize the overall STN throughput as follows:

$$OPT1 : \max_{\mathbf{y},\mathbf{p}} \left\{ \sum_{j \in \mathcal{J}} \sum_{i \in \mathcal{I}} \sum_{k \in \mathcal{K}} y_{i,j,k} R_{i,j,k} \right\} \tag{2}$$

$$s.t. \sum_{i \in \mathcal{I}_j} y_{i,j,k} \leq 1, \quad \forall j \in \mathcal{J}, k \in \mathcal{K} \tag{3}$$

$$\sum_{k \in \mathcal{K}} y_{i,j,k} p_{i,j,k} \leq P_{\max}, \quad \forall i \in \mathcal{I} \tag{4}$$

$$\sum_{k \in \mathcal{K}} y_{i,j,k} R_{i,j,k} \geq R_{\min}, \quad \forall i \in \mathcal{I}, j \tag{5}$$

$$y_{i,j,k} = \{0,1\}, \quad \forall i \in I_j, j, k \tag{6}$$

where constraint (3) guarantees that each subchannel can be allocated to at most one TN in a satellite; constraint (4) imply that the transmit power of each TN is less than the limit of maximum transmit power; constraint (5) sets the QoS requirement $R_{\min}$ to ensure the QoS of TN; constraint (6) represents the value of the channel and user association.

3   Satellite-Terrestrial Nodes Association and Resource Allocation

It is observed that the OPT is a mixed integer and non-linear optimization problem because it contains both binary variable $\mathbf{Y}$ and continuous variables $\mathbf{P}$. Thus, first, it is hard to find the global centralized optimal solution for this problem. Hence to proceed with solving the optimization problem, we adopt a suboptimal approach and split the optimization problem into two sub-problems. Firstly, each TN needs to find an appropriate satellite to establish a connection. Then we consider the resource allocation for the satellite-terrestrial transmission.

3.1   Satellite-Terrestrial Nodes Association

As mentioned, $\mathbf{Y}$ includes two physical features of satellite-terrestrial node association and channel assignment. In this section, we first study the association of the satellite-terrestrial node, i.e., we determine TN i associates with which satellite in which group. For simplicity, we express $y_{i,j,k}$ as $y_{i(j),j,k}$. Note that nodes association not only determines whether TN i connects to satellite j or satellite j' in group n, but also determines whether TN i associates with group n or n'. Since the association of satellite-terrestrial nodes is a binary variable, and we convert it to a many-to-one matching problem. The utility function of TNs is expressed as:

$$TSLIST_i^j = \log(1 + \sum_k \frac{p_{i,j,k} |H_{i,j,k}|^2}{\sum_{j' \neq j} y_{i,j',k} p_{i,j',k} |H_{i,j',k}|^2 + N_0}) \tag{7}$$

Since the objective is to maximize the overall system rate, when a TN needs to select a satellite, it should consider the average received SINR over all subchannels. After each TN makes a request to the satellite based on its own utility function, satellite will also make a judgment based on its own utility function. The utility function of satellites is defined as follows

$$STLIST_j^i = \log(\sum_k p_{i,j,k} |H_{i,j,k}|^2) \tag{8}$$

where it only relates to the channel gain. Our proposed TN-Satellite Matching algorithm is listed in Algorithm 1.

Algorithm 1. Satellite-Terrestrial Nodes Matching Algorithm

Input: TNs set TN, G, SNs set SAT, Maximum number of SAT_j matching-$N_j^{\max}$
Output: Matching relationship X
  Initialization:
  Building TNs' and satellites' preference lists $TSLIST$ and $STLIST$, $t = 0$
  initialization Unmatched TN set $UNmatch$ and Matching relationship X
  TNs request process:
  for all TN_i **do**
    TN_i finds those SAT_j that does not meet the number of matching and have not rejected TN_i, update $TSLIST_i$
    TN_i sends an access request to the most preferred SAT based on its preference list $TSLIST_i$
  end for
  Satellite decision process:
  for all SAT_j **do**
    if Matched number of SAT_j-$N_j^{t-1} \leq N_j^{\max}$ **then**
      SAT_j counts the number of requested TN_i-P_j^t in this iteration t.
      According to the $SATLIST_j$, accept maximum number of $N_j^{\max} - N_j^{t-1}$ requests from TN in descending order
      Remove accepted TN_i from the unmatched list $UNmatch$ to establish a match $X_{i,j} = 1$. Any TN_i more than $P_j^t + N_j^{t-1} - N_j^{\max}$ will be rejected
    else
      Reject all
    end if
  end for
  if $UNmatch$ is not empty **then**
    Switch to step 4 and $t = t + 1$
  end if

3.2 Satellite-Terrestrial Resource Allocation

After the satellite-terrestrial nodes association is determined, the original optimization problem $OPT1$ becomes a channel and power resource allocation problem. The optimization can be formulated as:

$$OPT2: \max_{\mathbf{y},\mathbf{P}} \left\{ \sum_{j \in \mathcal{J}} \sum_{i \in \mathcal{I}_j} \sum_{k \in \mathcal{K}} y_{i(j),j,k} R_{i(j),j,k} \right\} \tag{9}$$

$$s.t. \sum_{i \in \mathcal{I}_j} y_{i(j),j,k} \leq 1, \quad \forall j \in \mathcal{J}, k \in \mathcal{K} \tag{10}$$

$$\sum_{k \in \mathcal{K}} y_{i(j),j,k} P_{i(j),j,k} \leq P_{\max}, \quad \forall i \in \mathcal{I}_j, j \tag{11}$$

$$\sum_{k \in \mathcal{K}} y_{i(j),j,k} R_{i(j),j,k} \geq R_{\min}, \quad \forall i \in \mathcal{I}_j, j \tag{12}$$

$$y_{i(j),j,k} = \{0,1\}, \quad \forall i \in I_j, j, k \tag{13}$$

Considering that excessive interference will seriously affect the transmission quality, making the whole network meaningless. At the same time, in order to facilitate the solution design and also derive an efficient resource allocation algorithm, we consider an upper bound for the interference term and impose the following constraint to the $OPT2$ which is given by:

$$\sum_{j' \neq j} \sum_{i' \in I_{j'}} y_{i'(j'),j,k} p_{i'(j'),j,k} h_{i'(j'),j,k} \leq I_{th}, \quad \forall j, k \tag{14}$$

Then $R_{i(j),j,k}$ becomes

$$R_{i(j),j,k} = \log_2 \left(1 + \frac{p_{i,j,k} |H_{i,j,k}|^2}{I_{th} + N_0} \right) \tag{15}$$

where I_{th} is the maximum tolerable inter-satellite interference temperature parameter. Note that by varying the value of I_{th}, the amount of interference can be controlled in each subcarrier by resource allocator to improve the system performance.

Considering the computational complexity, we adopt a suboptimal approach and decouple these two subproblems. Firstly, channel allocation is performed, followed by power allocation based on channel allocation.

Channel Allocation. The optimization problem is an NP-hard problem; however, since the problem contains only one binary variable. Thus, we propose the Indefinite number of many-to-one matching algorithm. Note that the co-channel interference at satellites from satellite-terrestrial uplinks in other satellites is fixed, so we can decompose the subchannel allocation problem of the whole network into J independent sub-problem and solve in order. The following we assume that subchannel allocation is performed for satellite j.

Each TN that associated with LEO satellite j obtains the utility of subchannel as:

$$GCLIST_{i(j)}^k = R_{i(j),j,k} \tag{16}$$

where TN i propose its utility of subchannel k based on the equivalent data rate, it is reasonable because each TN would like to obtain then higher data rate.

Similarly, each subchannel that belong to LEO satellite j has its utility of TN that associated with LEO satellite j, the utility function is expressed as:

$$CLIST_{i(j)}^k = \frac{R_{i(j),j,k} - R_{\min}}{\varphi R_{i(j),j,k} \sum_{j' \neq j} p_{i(j),j',k} |H_{i(j),j',k}|^2} \tag{17}$$

Since each TN has its QoS requirement $R_{\min}$ to ensure the QoS of TN, we must ensure if channel k is assigned to TN i, the minimum rate limit $R_{\min}$ of TN

i can be met, so we quantify the difference between achieved rate and minimum rate limit and expressed as $\frac{R_{i(j),j,k}-R_{\min}}{R_{i(j),j,k}}$. At the same time, for subchannel k of satellite j, it must reduce the co-channel interference caused to other satellites during allocation, and it is expressed as $\sum_{j'\neq j} p_{i(j),j',k}\left|H_{i(j),j',k}\right|^2$, where φ is a weighted parameter that ensure the co-channel interference to other satellites can play a role in the utility function $CLIST$.

The specific Subchannel-TN matching algorithm is shown in the Algorithm 2.

Algorithm 2. Indefinite Number Of Channel Matching Algorithm

Input: TNs set $TN \in SAT_j$, G, Channel set of SAT_j-CH
Output: Matching relationship C
  Initialization:
  Building TNs' and Channels' preference lists $GCLIST$ and $CLIST$, $t = 0$,
  $N_j^{\min} = \lfloor |Ch|/|GS| \rfloor$
  Initialization Unmatched Channel set $UNmatch$ and Matching relationship C
  TNs request process:
  for all TN_i do
    if Matched number of $N_j^{t-1} \leq N_j^{\min}$ **then**
      TN_i finds those CH_k that haven't met the number of matching and haven't
      rejected TN_i, update $GCLIST_i$
      TN_i sends an access request to the most preferred CH based on its preference
      list $GCLIST_i$
    else
      TN perform step.7 and step.8 sequentially
    end if
  end for
  Channel decision process:
  for all CH_k do
    if Matched number of CH_k-$N_j^{t-1} \leq 1$ **then**
      CH_k counts the number of requested TN_i-P_j^t in this iteration t.
      According to the $CLIST_k$, accept requests from the most preferred TN
      Remove accepted CH_k from the unmatched list $UNmatch$ and establish a
      match $C_{i,j} = 1$. Then all remaining requests from TN_i will be rejected
    else
      Reject all
    end if
  end for
  if $UNmatch$ is not empty **then**
    Switch to step 4 and $t = t + 1$
  end if

Power Allocation. After allocates the subchannel, the power allocation scheme needs to be optimized to coordinate interference and improve the overall performance of the satellite-terrestrial uplink network.

We can solve the optimization by using the Lagrangian dual decomposition method. The Lagrangian function is given by

$$
\begin{aligned}
L(\mathbf{P}, \boldsymbol{\lambda}, \boldsymbol{\mu}, \boldsymbol{\omega}) \\
= \sum_j \sum_{i \in I_j} \sum_k R_{i(j),j,k} + \sum_j \sum_{i \in I_j} \lambda_{i,j} \left(p_{\max} - \sum_k y_{i(j),j,k} p_{i(j),j,k} \right) \\
+ \sum_j \sum_{i \in I_j} \mu_{i,j} \left(\sum_k y_{i(j),j,k} R_{i(j),j,k} - R_{min} \right) \\
+ \sum_j \sum_k \omega_{j,k} \left(I_{th} - \sum_{j' \neq j} \sum_{i' \in I_{j'}} y_{i'(j'),j,k} p_{i'(j'),j,k} h_{i'(j'),j,k} \right)
\end{aligned}
\tag{18}
$$

where $\boldsymbol{\lambda}, \boldsymbol{\mu}, \boldsymbol{\omega}$ are the Lagrange multiplies vectors for constraints (11), (12) and (14) in $OPT2$ respectively. The boundary constraints (13) in $OPT2$ will be absorbed in the Karush-Kuhn-Tucker (KKT) conditions to be shown later. Thus, the Largrangian dual function is defined as:

$$
g(\boldsymbol{\lambda}, \boldsymbol{\mu}, \boldsymbol{\omega}) = \max_{\mathbf{P}} L(\mathbf{P}, \boldsymbol{\lambda}, \boldsymbol{\mu}, \boldsymbol{\omega})
\tag{19}
$$

And the dual problem can be expressed as:

$$
\min_{\boldsymbol{\lambda}, \boldsymbol{\mu}, \boldsymbol{\omega}} g(\boldsymbol{\lambda}, \boldsymbol{\mu}, \boldsymbol{\omega})
\tag{20}
$$

$$
s.t. \boldsymbol{\lambda}, \boldsymbol{\mu}, \boldsymbol{\omega} > 0
\tag{21}
$$

Considering irrelevance between different channels, we decompose the optimization problem into $K \times J$ independent subproblems based on the number of channels K and the number of satellites J, and the dual problem can be solved iteratively with solving the subproblem in order. Accordingly, the Lagrangian function is rewritten as:

$$
\begin{aligned}
L(\mathbf{P}, \boldsymbol{\lambda}, \boldsymbol{\mu}, \boldsymbol{\omega}) = \sum_k \sum_j L_{k,j}(\mathbf{P}, \boldsymbol{\lambda}, \boldsymbol{\mu}, \boldsymbol{\omega}) \\
+ \sum_j \sum_{i \in I_j} \lambda_{i,j} p_{\max} - \sum_j \sum_{i \in I_j} \mu_{i,j} R_{min} + \sum_j \sum_k \omega_{j,k} I_{th}
\end{aligned}
\tag{22}
$$

where

$$
\begin{aligned}
L_{k,j}(\mathbf{P}, \boldsymbol{\lambda}, \boldsymbol{\mu}, \boldsymbol{\omega}) \\
= \sum_{i \in I_j} (1 + \mu_{i,j} y_{i(j),j,k}) R_{i(j),j,k} - \sum_{i \in I_j} \lambda_{i,j} y_{i(j),j,k} p_{i(j),j,k} \\
- \omega_{j,k} \sum_{j' \neq j} \sum_{i' \in I_{j'}} y_{i'(j'),j,k} p_{i'(j'),j,k} h_{i'(j'),j,k}
\end{aligned}
\tag{23}
$$

According to the KKT conditions, we can get the optimal power allocated to TN_i that served by satellite j at subchannel k as follows:

$$
p_{i(j),k}^* = \left[\frac{(1 + \mu_{i,j})}{\ln 2 (\lambda_{i,j} + \sum_{j' \neq j} \sum_{i' \in I_{j'}} \omega_{j',k} h_{i(j),j',k})} - \frac{I_{th} + \sigma^2}{h_{i(j),j,k}} \right]^+
\tag{24}
$$

where $[x]^+ = \max(0, x)$.

To find the Lagrangian multiplies, we use the sub-gradient method:

$$\lambda(t+1) = [\lambda(t) - \tau_{\lambda(t)}(P_{\max} - \sum_k y_{i(j),j,k}P_{i(j),j,k})]^+ \tag{25}$$

$$\mu(t+1) = [\mu(t) - \tau_{\mu(t)}(R_{\min} - \sum_{k \in \mathcal{K}} y_{i(j),j,k}R_{i(j),j,k})]^+ \tag{26}$$

$$\begin{aligned}\omega(t+1) \\ = [\omega(t) - \tau_{\omega(t)}(I_{th} - \sum_{j' \neq j} \sum_{i' \in I_{j'}} y_{i'(j'),j,k}P_{i'(j'),j,k}h_{i'(j'),j,k})]^+ \end{aligned} \tag{27}$$

4   Simulation Results

In this section, the performance of our proposed algorithm is investigated through simulation. We consider a spectrum sharing satellite-terrestrial uplink transmission system which consists of $J = 4$ LEO satellites and $I = 200$ TNs. All satellites in the system share the same frequency band on Ka-band and the total bandwidth is 400MHz. We set the numbers of subchannels as 80 in the sense. The small-scale fading over Ka-band is modeled as Shadowed-Rician fading reference as [14]. Meanwhile, we also consider the free-space path loss and set the off-axis antenna gain of the TN's directional antenna as [15]. Unless otherwise mentioned in the following, the simulation parameters are shown in Table 1.

Table 1. Simulation parameter table

Height of Orbit	1000 km
Service radius	30 km
Maximum transmit power of each TN	3 W
Minimum rate requirement	10 Mbps
Antenna gain	43.3 dbi
Ka-band carrier frequency	30 GHz
Bandwidth	400 MHz

In the real communication scenario, in order to make full use of the scarce satellite communication window, sometimes only the TNs with better channel conditions will be adopted for satellite-terrestrial transmission, so more than the MLCA algorithm mentioned above, we also proposed the algorithm that without the minimum rate constraint (WJPCA), and the power and channel are allocated jointly. Figure 2 presents the convergence of the proposed MLCA algorithm, we select the WJPCA algorithm and the CRPA (Channel Random And Power Average Algorithm) algorithm as the comparative simulation algorithm. And from the figure, we can see that MLCA and WJPCA algorithm all can achieve good convergence. Since the MLCA algorithm needs to maximize the total system rate on the basis of guaranteeing the minimum rate constraint of each TN, therefore, the total rate is lower than the WJPCA algorithm, because the WJPCA will allocate as many resources as possible to TNs with good channel conditions, which will inevitably lead to an increase in the overall system rate.

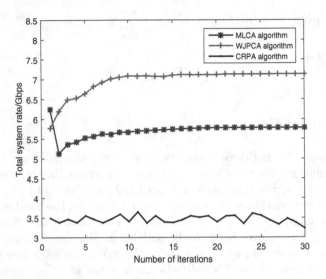

Fig. 2. Total system rate v.s. Number of iterations.

However, although MLCA algorithm has a lower overall system rate, it guarantees access by more TNs and achieves the performance improvement on the number of access. In the same process as Fig. 2, the relationship diagram of the number of TNs access to satellites is shown in Fig. 3 below,

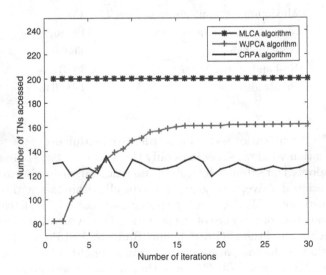

Fig. 3. Number of TNs accessed v.s. Number of iterations.

From the Fig. 3, we can see our proposed MLCA algorithm has a great performance improvement of the number of access TNs, this is due to the MLCA algorithm guarantees that each user can obtain a certain number of subchannels when allocating subchannels to meet the minimum rate constraint.

Changes in the range of TN's location will also affect the overall system throughput, In Fig. 4, we simulated the total throughput of the satellite-terrestrial transmission system at different service radius R, we set a combination of 4 satellites and 200 ground nodes, and there are 50 subchannels. We simulated the system when the radius R of the local nodes ranged from 30 km to 100 km. The overall rate is shown in Fig. 4 below:

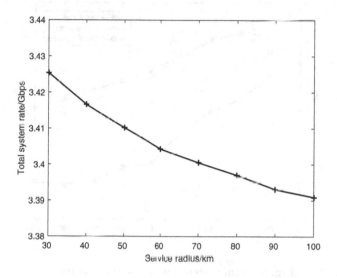

Fig. 4. Total system rate v.s. Service radius.

Obviously, changes in the ground service radius will affect the overall rate, it can be seen from Fig. 4 that when the radius R of the service area changes from 30 km to 100 km, the total data rate gradually decreases. As the distance increases, the overall channel conditions become worse and worse. The off-axis angle will become larger and larger, and the off-axis gain will gradually decrease, causing the co-channel interference to be reduced to a certain extent, but the overall trend is still downward. This is mainly due to the height of satellite flight is 1000 km, according to the calculation of the Pythagorean theorem, the distance between the LEO satellites and the TNs has not changed much when the change of radius R is not too large. In the calculation of the off-axis angle that causes the off-axis gain, the off-axis angle is related to the distance, but if the off-axis angle itself is not too large, the change of the off-axis angle will not cause a large reduction in the off-axis gain, and the change of the interference will not be very large. As the distance increases, the overall channel fading variation will be larger than the off-axis gain variation, resulting in a decrease in the overall system rate. When R is large enough, the reduction of the total system rate will be more obvious, but when R is large enough, the scenario mentioned in this paper will not exist, so the upper limit of the simulation considered is set to 100 km.

At last, we analysis system performance with different numbers of ground nodes, considering the system with 4 satellites and 80 sub-channels, the total system rate under different numbers of TNs is simulated. As follow in Fig. 5, we choose Particle swarm optimization (PSO) algorithm and CRPA algorithm as the comparative simulation algorithm.

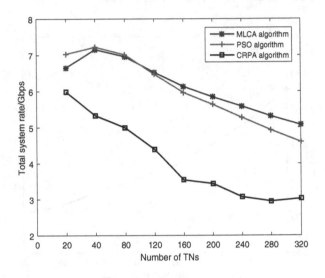

Fig. 5. Total system rate v.s. service radius.

From the Fig. 5 we can find that the total system rate in the three different algorithms all decrease with the increase of the number of TNs, This is because the model considers four independent satellite systems, each satellite sharing the same frequency band, and when each TNs transmit to one satellite, it also causes co-channel interference to other satellites. Because an uplink system is considered in this paper, each TN has its own maximum transmit power, and the maximum transmit power is also equal in an order of magnitude. When the number of TNs in the system is not large, the total rate will increase with the increase of the number of TNs. But when the number of TNs in the system rises to a certain degree, the effect of the power variance of equal magnitude will be reduced, and the change of the channel will affect the rate more significantly. The more TNs there are, the more TNs need to be guaranteed to meet the minimum rate constraint, and more and more resources will be allocated from TNs with better channel conditions to TNs with poor channel conditions. Compare to the variance of power at this time, the difference between good and bad channel conditions has a greater impact on the overall system rate, and the rate of TNs with good channel condition will decrease, and the rate of TNs with bad channel condition will increase, thereby meeting their minimum rate requirements. This guarantees that all TNs can access to satellites and meet the minimum rate constraint, but the final total rate will decrease. We can also clearly see from the Fig. 5 that compared with PSO algorithm and CRPA algorithm, our proposed MLCA algorithm achieves a great improvement on the performance of the overall system rate.

5   Conclusion

We studied the uplink transmission of multi TNs -multi SNs to achieve efficient transmission of STN under large scale development of LEO satellites. After the optimization problem of maximizing the total system rate is established, we proposed a Matching and Lagrangian dual combination algorithm to solve the satellite-terrestrial nodes association and resource allocation. We showed that the proposed algorithm can achieve efficient matching and resource allocation though matching algorithm, non-convex conversion and Lagrangian dual iteration. The proposed algorithm has many desirable properties. First, it improves total system rate to a certain extent while ensuring that the number of TNs that can be accessed to the satellite. Second, we analyze the relationship between the total system rate and the number of ground nodes, the service radius. Third, our algorithm will reach a stable matching and converge after a small number of iterations, which is relatively simple to use.

References

1. Yu, Q., Wang, J., Bai, L.: Architecture and critical technologies of space information networks. J. Commun. Inf. Networks **1**(3), 1–9 (2016)
2. SpaceX Non-Geostationary Satellite System, Federal Commun. Commissions, Washington, DC, USA (2016)
3. OneWeb Non-Geostationary Satellite System, Federal Commun. Commissions, Washington, DC, USA (2016)
4. He, L., Li, J., Sheng, M., et al.: Joint allocation of transmission and computation resources for space networks. In: 2018 IEEE Wireless Communications and Networking Conference (WCNC), pp. 1–6. IEEE (2018)
5. Jia, X., Lv, T., He, F., et al.: Collaborative data downloading by using intersatellite links in LEO satellite networks. IEEE Trans. Wireless Commun. **16**(3), 1523–1532 (2017)
6. Lv, T., Liu, W., Huang, H., et al.: Optimal data downloading by using inter-satellite offloading in LEO satellite networks. In: 2016 IEEE Global Communications Conference (GLOBECOM), pp. 1–6. IEEE (2016)
7. Huang, H., Guo, S., Liang, W., et al.: Online green data gathering from Geo-distributed IoT networks via LEO satellites. In: 2018 IEEE International Conference on Communications (ICC), pp. 1–6. IEEE (2018)
8. Di, B., Zhang, H., Song, L., et al.: Ultra-dense LEO: integrating terrestrial-satellite networks into 5G and beyond for data offloading. IEEE Trans. Wirel. Commun. **18**(1), 47–62 (2018)

9. Di, B., Zhang, H., Song, L., et al.: Data offloading in ultra-dense LEO-based integrated terrestrial-satellite networks. In: 2018 IEEE Global Communications Conference (GLOBECOM), pp. 1–6. IEEE (2018)

10. Soleimani, B., Sabbaghian, M.: Cluster-based resource allocation and user association in mmWave femtocell networks. IEEE Trans. Commun. **PP**(99), 1–1 (2018)

11. Khamidehi, B., Rahmati, A., Sabbaghian, M.: Joint sub-channel assignment and power allocation in heterogeneous networks: an efficient optimization method. IEEE Commun. Lett. 1–1 (2016)

12. Zhang, H., Jiang, C., Beaulieu, N.C., et al.: Resource allocation in spectrum-sharing OFDMA femtocells with heterogeneous services. IEEE Trans. Commun. **62**(7), 2366–2377 (2014)

13. Bayat, S., Li, Y., Song, L., et al.: Matching theory: applications in wireless communications. IEEE Signal Process. Mag. **33**(6), 103–122 (2016)

14. Abdi, A., Lau, W.C., Alouini, M.S., et al.: A new simple model for land mobile satellite channels: first-and second-order statistics[J]. IEEE Trans. Wireless Commun. **2**(3), 519–528 (2003)

15. ITU-R S.1428, Reference FSS earth station radiation patterns for use in interference assessment involving non-GSO satellite in frequency bands between 10.7 GHz and 30 GHz (2000)

Internet of Things Security and Privacy Protection

Sensor Fusion Based Implicit Authentication for Smartphones

Dai Shi and Dan Tao[✉]

School of Electronic and Information Engineering, Beijing Jiaotong University,
Beijing 100044, China
dtao@bjtu.edu.cn

Abstract. Implicit authentication, as a novel identity authentication mechanism, has received widespread attention. However, the performance of implicit authentication still needs to be improved. In this paper, we propose a sensor fusion based implicit authentication system to enhance the protection level of the identity authentication mechanism for smartphone. First, the sensor used to characterize user behavior is determined by analyzing the authentication performance of each sensor. Then, considering the practicability of the system, one-class classification algorithm One-Class Support Vector Machine (OC-SVM) is used to train the authentication model. Finally, the decision function of each sensor is weighted and fused to deliver a result. Based on the actual data set of 7,500 samples collected from 75 participants, the effectiveness of the system is verified in different operating environments and varied passwords. The results show that the proposed system can improve the accuracy of identity authentication effectively.

Keywords: Implicit authentication · Pattern lock · Sensor fusion · OC-SVM

1 Introduction

With the widespread usage of smartphones, a large amount of private information is stored on the phone, so a convenient and reliable identity authentication system for smartphones is necessary. Pattern lock is widely used because of its memorability [1]. However, it is vulnerable to acoustic attack [2] and video-based attack [3], etc., which will weaken the security of pattern lock. With the enrichment of smartphone sensors, researchers have attempted to use multiple sensors to record user interaction data during pattern input. The user's behavior data is formed in daily life, which is unique and difficult to be imitated. Through the authentication analysis of the user's unlocking behavior characteristics, the method of transparently implementing user identity authentication is called implicit authentication [4].

At present, some scholars have carried out research on implicit authentication [5–10]. Implicit authentication records the user's behavior information

© Springer Nature Singapore Pte Ltd. 2020
Z. Hao et al. (Eds.): CWSN 2020, CCIS 1321, pp. 157–168, 2020.
https://doi.org/10.1007/978-981-33-4214-9_12

through sensors built into the phone. The collected behavior information is automatically authenticated in the background of the mobile phone. In the existing implicit authentication system, to improve the authentication performance, feature extraction and feature selection are carried out on the original data collected by the sensors, but the performance of implicit identity authentication still needs to be improved. A feature vector is usually thus initiated based on the features extracted from each sensor data and input into the authentication model for identity authentication. However, the features extracted by the sensors often contain some confusing information, which leads to classification errors and weakens the authentication performance. Based on the above background, we propose a novel sensor fusion based implicit authentication system, SFIA, for smartphone. When the user draws the pattern, the smartphone utilizes sensors to automatically collect information about the user's behavior. If the pattern matches correctly, the mobile phone background will authenticate the collected behavior data. Only when the pattern matches correctly and the behavior data is legal, the access request can be passed.

The contributions of this paper are summarized as follows:

1) We propose a pattern lock security enhancement method, SFIA. This method uses the user's behavior information as an identification mark to assist in identity authentication. Even if the impostor steals the user's pattern, the mobile phone would not be unlocked due to different behavior characteristics.

2) To further improve the authentication performance, we propose an implicit authentication method based on sensor fusion on the basis of in-depth analysis of commonly used sensors on smartphones. The decision level fusion of the behavioral data collected by multiple sensors is carried out to reduce the classification errors caused by single decision.

3) Based on the actual data set, we evaluated the performance of SFIA system from two perspectives: different operating environments and varied passwords. The results show that the implicit authentication method based on sensor fusion can achieve higher authentication performance.

The remainder of this paper is organized as follows. Section 2 overviews the related work. In Sect. 3, we design an SFIA framework, and propose an authentication algorithm based on sensor fusion. Then, the simulation experiments are performed and experimental results are given in Sect. 4. Finally, we conclude this paper in Sect. 5.

2   Related Work

As a privacy security protection mechanism, implicit authentication is often used to assist traditional authentication methods in forming a two-factor authentication mechanism to improve the security of authentication mechanism. With the widespread usage of pattern lock, the implicit authentication mechanism based on pattern lock has attracted more and more attention.

Angulo et al. [5] extracted time features as authentication markers, and realized about 10.39% average Equal Error Rate (EER) by adopting the Random Forest classifier algorithm. Similarly, Alpar et al. [6] also use only time features for authentication. Based on the previous studies, Liu et al. [7] introduced more behavioral characteristics, including time, pressure, size and angle keystroke feature, and determined the optimal combination of these features through a series of experiments to achieve an EER of 3.03%. Similar to Liu et al., literatures [8,9] used touch screen and accelerometer to extract users' behavioral characteristics, so as to realize pattern Lock's security enhancement scheme. Ku et al. [10] introduced more comprehensive sensors, used touch screen, accelerometer, gyroscope and magnetometer for feature extraction, and utilized recursive feature elimination for feature selection to remove features with poor authentication performance. They achieved the EER of 2.66% (sitting), 3.53% (walking), and 5.83% (combined).

The above research put all the features into a feature vector, which is the input of the authentication model for identity authentication. However, the features extracted by sensors often contain some confusing information. These confusing information, which is mainly derived from the low sensitivity of the extracted sensor features to some users, leads to classification errors and weakens the authentication performance. To effectively avoid the classification errors caused by the single authentication of the decision algorithm for user legality judgments, we propose an implicit authentication system based on sensor fusion. This is a decision-level fusion algorithm that makes final decisions by fusing the verification results of various sensors to improve identity authentication performance.

3 System Design

3.1 System Design Overview

The framework of SFIA is illustrated in Fig. 1. It mainly consists of two phases: the training phase and the authentication phase. In the training phase, the system collects the behavior data to extract features when the owner inputs the correct password serially. The extracted features are sent to the authentication model construction module for model training. The trained model is stored on the phone for authentication during the authentication phase.

In the authentication phase, when the unlocking behavior is executed, the system will automatically collect the user's behavior information and determine whether the user's unlock password is correct. If the password is wrong, the request is rejected. When the unlock password is correct, the system analyzes the collected behavior information to determine the user's identity. In more detail, the system extracts features from the collected behavior data and inputs the extracted features into the authentication model for user authentication. Only when the user's decision making is legal, the user's unlock request will be allowed.

3.2 Data Acquisition

The built-in sensors of smartphones are often used to characterize user behavior information. To obtain the user's behavior data, we developed an Android application to collect the sensor information when the user is unlocking. Accelerometer measures the acceleration applied to the phone, including gravity. Gravity sensor measures the force of gravity applied to the phone. Gyroscope measures phone's rate of rotation. Linear accelerometer measures the acceleration applied to the phone, excluding the impact of gravity. Magnetometer measures the ambient geomagnetic field. Orientation sensor measures degrees of rotation of the phone. Rotation vector sensor measures the orientation of a device. The touch screen is used to record the duration, pressure and position information of the touch operation.

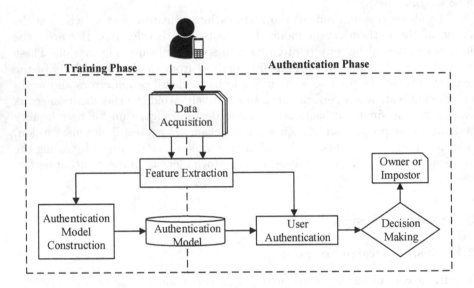

Fig. 1. The framework of SFIA.

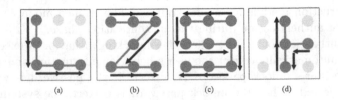

Fig. 2. The four preset passwords of our system.

To verify the authentication performance of SFIA comprehensively, we collected behavior data under different operating environments and varied passwords. Related research shows that most users prefer to set graphics related to letters or numbers as passwords [9]. Considering the password complexity and user preferences, we preset four passwords to evaluate the effectiveness of SFIA, as illustrated in Fig. 2, namely password L, password Z, password S and password T. We collected the behavior data of 75 participants using the given device (Huawei Nova2S, MI5). The specific statistical information is described in Table 1.

Table 1. The statistical information of participants

Environment	Properties		Population
Sitting	Age	18–23	36
		24–30	10
		31–55	4
	Gender	Male	23
		Female	27
Walking	Age	18–23	10
		24–30	12
		31–55	3
	Gender	Male	14
		Female	11

3.3 Feature Extraction

The dimension of behavioral data collected directly from each sensor is huge, which is not conducive to the later identification, so feature extraction is necessary. We extract more meaningful features from the raw behavioral data to help the classifier gain a deeper understanding of the data. The rhythm and pressure of the user when drawing the pattern are unique. We extracted 10 features from the touch screen, which are listed in Table 2. Furthermore, the smartphone might shake, tilt, and rotate due to the user's unlocking operation. This information can be detected using sensors built into the phone. We utilize 7 related sensors to record the behavior information when unlocking, and the features extracted by each sensor are listed in Table 3.

3.4 Sensor Selection

With the development of mobile communication and sensor technology, more sensors are built into smartphones. These sensors can provide raw data with high frequency and high precision for device shake detection. Different sensors are used for various purposes. They can be used to detect the tilt of the device or the rotation of the device. Moreover, the authentication accuracy of the behavior

Table 2. Features from the touch screen

Feature	Description
Duration	Time duration of each point
Moving time	Duration of moving from the previous point to the next point
Pressure_mean	Mean value of touch pressure
Pressure_std	Standard deviation of touch pressure
Pressure_sk	Skewness of touch Pressure
Pressure_ku	Kurtosis of touch Pressure
Position_mean	Mean value of each axis of touch position
Position_std	Standard deviation of each axis of touch position
Position_sk	Skewness of each axis of touch position
Position_ku	Kurtosis of each axis of touch position

Table 3. Features from each sensor

Feature	Description
Mean	Mean value of each axis
Standard deviation	Standard deviation of each axis
Skewness	Skewness of each axis
Kurtosis	Kurtosis of each axis
Range	Difference between the maximum and minimum value of each axis
Interquartile range	Difference between the 75% and 25% quartiles of each axis
Energy	Intensity of each axis
Entropy	Sample entropy of each axis

data collected by different sensors is also disparate. Hence, the sensor selection is one of the keys to achieve sensor-based user identity authentication.

We adopt EER to evaluate the authentication performance of each sensor to help us select the optimal sensor for implicit authentication. EER is one of the widely used performance metrics in the implicit authentication system. The value of EER is determined by finding the point where False Acceptance Rate (FAR) and False Rejection Rate (FRR) are equal. In our research, we collected the behavior data of 8 sensors including touch screen. Figure 3 illustrates the authentication performance of different sensors in both sitting and walking operating environments. Among them, TS for touch screen, Acc for accelerometer, Gra for gravity sensor, Gyr for Gyroscope, Lacc for Linear accelerometer, Mag for magnetometer, Ori for orientation sensor and RV for rotation vector sensor. We found that the magnetometer, orientation sensor and rotation vector sensor have excellent authentication performance while sitting, but these three sensors

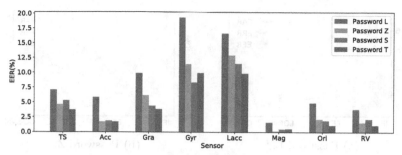

(a) Authentication performance of different sensors during sitting.

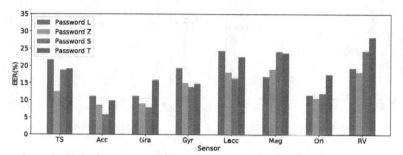

(b) Authentication performance of different sensors during walking.

Fig. 3. Authentication performance of different sensors.

are used for the rotation detection of the phone. Considering the information redundancy caused by multiple selections of the same type sensor, we finally select magnetometer, accelerometer, and touch screen for behavioral data collection while sitting. Similarly while walking, accelerometer, gravity sensor and orientation sensor are used for behavioral data collection because of their better performance. Accelerometer and gravity sensor are utilized to record the movement such as shaking and tilting. The orientation sensor is adopted to record the rotation direction of the mobile phone. Note that data collection of 8 sensors is only needed in the process of sensor selection, while only behavioral data collection of 3 sensors in the corresponding environment is needed in the actual scene. That is, sensor selection is only an experimental analysis before system development. When the system is developed, the optimal selection of sensors would be employed for data collection.

3.5 Authentication Model Construction

Authentication model construction is the key module of implicit authentication. Due to the uniqueness of behavior habits, the feature vectors of different users are dissimilar. The authentication model distinguishes the owner from the impostor by analyzing the feature vectors. The identity authentication model based

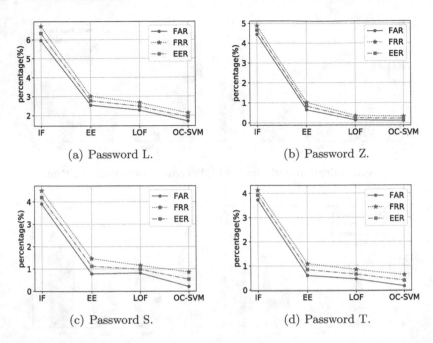

(a) Password L.   (b) Password Z.

(c) Password S.   (d) Password T.

Fig. 4. Authentication performance with different classification algorithms.

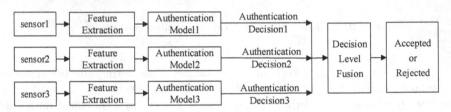

Fig. 5. The authentication framework of the sensor fusion algorithm.

on binary classification algorithms needs to provide both the feature vectors of owner and impostor for model training. Nevertheless, in practice, the owner's feature vector is easy to obtain, but it is difficult to obtain the feature vectors of all impostors in advance [11]. Based on this background, we use one-class classification algorithm to build the authentication model, which only ask the owner's feature vectors for model training to distinguish the owner from impostors. Here we have tried different one-class classification algorithm: Isolated Forest (IF), Elliptic Envelope (EE), Local Outlier Factor (LOF) and OC-SVM. The user authentication results are shown in Fig. 4. We used OC-SVM with better authentication performance to build the authentication model.

To further improve authentication performance, we propose an identity authentication framework based on sensor fusion, as illustrated in Fig. 5. The feature vector extracted by each sensor is input as a single individual to the

OC-SVM classifier for authentication, and the corresponding decision function $f_i(y)$ is obtained. Finally, $f_i(y)$ is fused according to the corresponding weight to determine the user's identity.

In our system, we determine the weight of each sensor based on its authentication contribution. Then, according to formula (1), we can get the fused decision function $g(y)$:

$$g(y) = \sum_{i=1}^{n} f_i(y) \times \frac{\frac{1}{EER_i}}{\sum_{i=1}^{n} \frac{1}{EER_i}} \tag{1}$$

where, EER_i is the equal error rate obtained by authenticating of the ith sensor. n is the number of sensors used in data collection.

Finally, the user's identity is determined according to the decision rules of formula (2):

$$y \in \begin{cases} \text{owner,} & g(y) \geq 0 \\ \text{impostor,} & g(y) < 0 \end{cases} \tag{2}$$

When the $g(y)$ is less than 0, the unknown user is considered to be an impostor and its access is denied; otherwise, the unknown user is considered to be the owner and the phone is unlocked.

4 Performance Evaluation

4.1 Experiment Settings

To verify the effectiveness of SFIA, we collect data on the unlocking behavior of 75 participants. 50 participants are required to collect data during sitting, and the other 25 participants are required to collect data during walking. Participants are asked to draw each preset password 25 times. In the end, we collect 7,500 samples for the experiment. In the experiment, we set each participant as the owner for model training, and other participants in the same operating environment as impostors for attack experiment. The experimental results of all participants are averaged as the authentication performance of SFIA to better summarize the universality of the system. Moreover, 5-fold cross-validation is used to train the OC-SVM authentication model to effectively avoid overfitting problems Here we choose Radial Basis Function (RBF) kernel for model training.

4.2 Effectiveness of Sensor Fusion

The decision-making method of the existing research is to combine the features extracted by multiple sensors into a feature vector and input it into the identity authentication model for identity verification. However, the features extracted by sensors often contain some confusable information, which leads to the fact that such a single verification to determine the user's legitimacy weakens the authentication performance. To effectively avoid the classification errors caused by single verification of the decision algorithm, sensor fusion is introduced to improve the fault tolerance of the authentication decision algorithm.

Table 4. Authentication performance with (without) sensor fusion

(a) Sitting.

	FAR(%)	FRR(%)	EER(%)
Password L	1.4328 (1.701)	1.909 (2.1267)	1.6709 (1.9138)
Password Z	0.038 (0.112)	0.2008 (0.3231)	0.1194 (0.2176)
Password S	0.1951 (0.2033)	0.5443 (0.858)	0.3697 (0.5307)
Password T	0.1669 (0.1706)	0.4957 (0.629)	0.3313 (0.3998)
Average	0.4582 (0.5460)	0.7875 (0.8725)	0.6228 (0.7093)

(b) Walking.

	FAR(%)	FRR(%)	EER(%)
Password L	8.27 (8.4767)	9.4 (9.5)	8.835 (8.9883)
Password Z	6.4367 (6.49)	7.5667 (7.85)	7.0017 (7.17)
Password S	4.69 (5.1433)	6.45 (7.0167)	5.57 (6.08)
Password T	9.8267 (10.31)	11.05 (11.4833)	10.4383 (10.8967)
Average	7.3059 (7.4842)	8.6167 (8.9625)	7.9613 (8.2234)

Based on the actual data set, we conduct comparative experiments on the identity authentication system with or without sensor fusion to illustrate the effectiveness of SFIA. The experimental results are summarized in Table 4. We can find that no matter in different operating environments or varied passwords, the performance of the identity authentication system with sensor fusion is more outstanding. More specifically, the introduction of sensor fusion resulted in the average EER of the four passwords decreased by 12.2% during sitting, while the average EER decreased by 3.2% during walking. Furthermore, we find that in the same system, the authentication performance in the sitting environment is better than that in the walking environment. In the sitting environment, the user's torso remains relatively static, which interferes less with the collection of behavioral data. On the contrary, in the walking environment, the user's body shaking interferes with the distinction of subtle behavior differences, resulting in the degradation of the authentication performance.

Table 5. Comparison with existing authentication approaches

Scheme	Training data	Sensor Fusion	EER[a]
Angulo et al. [5]	Owner & Impostors	-	S:5.5790%, D:9.4395%
Ku et al. [10]	Owner & Impostors	-	S:2.6030%, D:10.8865%
SFIA	Owner	✓	S:0.6228%, D:7.9613%

[a] S for sitting and W for walking.

4.3   Comparison with Existing Methods

We compare the SFIA system with the existing implicit authentication methods based on pattern lock, which are reproduced in our data set. The comparison results are depicted in Table 5. Angulo et al. [5] extracted two types of time features to characterize the unlocking behavior data of users, and used the Random Forest for identity authentication. Ku et al. [10] used more sensors to characterize the unlocking behavior data of users and used Naive Bayes for identity authentication. In these research methods, all the features are combined into a feature vector for authentication decision. There are more misjudgments in a single decision, which leads to a decline in authentication performance. By analyzing the authentication performance of various sensors, we propose a sensor fusion based authentication method SFIA to improve the authentication performance. The experimental results show that the SFIA system shows more excellent authentication performance.

5   Conclusion

To improve the security of password protection mechanism, implicit authentication has been widely studied, but the authentication accuracy still needs to be improved. We propose the SFIA, an implicit authentication mechanism based on sensor fusion. The experimental results show that it is helpful to improve the authentication performance by fusing the decision function of each sensor. Among them, the performance improvement is higher in sitting environment, with an average reduction of 12.2% for the four passwords. More generally, regardless of different operating environments or varied passwords, SFIA can achieve better authentication results. This sufficiently indicates the effectiveness of the SFIA mechanism.

Acknowledgement. This work was supported by the National Natural Science Foundation of China under Grant No.61872027 and the Open Research Fund for the State Key Laboratory of Integrated Services Networks in China (No. ISN21 16).

References

1. Andriotis, P., Oikonomou, G., Mylonas, A., Tryfonas, T.: A study on usability and security features of the Android pattern lock screen. Inf. Comput. Secur. **24**(1), 53–72 (2016)
2. Zhou, M., Wang, Q., Yang, J., et al.: PatternListener: Cracking Android Pattern Lock Using Acoustic Signals. In Proceedings of the 2018 ACM SIGSAC Conference on Computer and Communications Security, pp. 1775–1787 (2018)
3. Guixin, Y., Zhanyong, T., Dingyi, F., et al.: A video-based attack for android pattern lock. ACM Trans. Priv. Secur. **21**(4), 1–31 (2018)
4. Mahfouz, A., Mahmoud, T.M., Eldin, A.S.: A survey on behavioral biometric authentication on smartphones. Inf. Secur. Tech. Rep. **37**, 28–37 (2017)

5. Angulo, J., Wästlund, E.: Exploring touch-screen biometrics for user identification on smart phones. In: Proceedings of Privacy and Identity Management for Life, pp. 130–143 (2012)
6. Alpar, O.: Intelligent biometric pattern password authentication systems for touch-screens. Expert Syst. Appl. **42**(17–18), 6286–6294 (2015)
7. Liu, C.L., Tsai, C.J., Chang, T.Y., et al.: Implementing multiple biometric features for a recall-based graphical keystroke dynamics authentication system on a smart phone. J. Netw. Comput. Appl. **53**, 128–139 (2015)
8. Meng, W., Li, W., Wong, D.S., et al.: TMGuard: a touch movement-based security mechanism for screen unlock patterns on smartphones. In: Proceedings of Applied Cryptography and Network Security, pp. 629–647 (2016)
9. Ganesh, S.M., Vijayakumar, P., Deborah, L.J.: A secure gesture based authentication scheme to unlock the smartphones. In Proceedings of 2017 Second International Conference on Recent Trends and Challenges in Computational Models (ICRTCCM), pp. 153–158 (2017)
10. Ku, Y., Park, L.H., Shin, S., et al.: Draw It as shown: behavioral pattern lock for mobile user authentication. IEEE Access **7**, 69363–69378 (2019)
11. Wang, R., Tao, D.: Context-aware implicit authentication of smartphone users based on multi-sensor behavior. IEEE Access **7**, 119654–119667 (2019)

Local Centroid Distance Constrained Representation-Based K-Nearest Neighbor Classifier

Yingying Zhao[1], Yitong Liu[2], Xingcheng Liu[1,3]([✉]), and En Zou[3]

[1] School of Electronics and Information Technology, Sun Yat-sen University,
Guangzhou 510006, China
`isslxc@mail.sysu.edu.cn`
[2] School of Data and Computer Science, Sun Yat-sen University,
Guangzhou 510006, China
[3] School of Information Science, Xinhua College of Sun Yat-sen University,
Guangzhou 510520, China

Abstract. The K-Nearest Neighbor (KNN) algorithm is widely studied for its simplicity and ease of understanding. However, classical KNN follows the principle of simple majority voting and treats each neighbor equally. In fact, the degree of importance for each neighbor is different, so the principle of simple majority voting would reduce the accuracy of classification without being improved of it. To overcome this problem, we propose a local centroid distance constrained representation-based KNN classifier (LCDR-KNN). K nearest training samples are selected from each class to form a sample subset, the distance from the centroid of the k nearest neighbors of each class to the unknown sample is served as the constraint. The representation coefficient of each neighbor in this subset is obtained with the method of Collaborative representation(CR), and it is used as the weight of neighbor voting. Compared with the conventional or state-of-the-art algorithms, the proposed algorithm have great advantages on condition of the different k values and the optimal k value.

Keywords: K-nearest neighbor(KNN) · Collaborative representation(CR) · Representation coefficient · Weight

1 Introduction

Classification is an important research direction in the field of Artificial Intelligence. There are many classic classification models, such as Support Vector Machine [1], Decision Tree [2], Bayesian classifier [3], etc. The KNN [4] is also a

Supported by the National Natural Science Foundation of China (Grant Nos. 61873290 and 61572534), the Special Project for Promoting Economic Development in Guangdong Province (Grant No. GDME-2018D004), and the Science and Technology Program of Guangzhou, China (Grant No. 202002030470).

Z. Hao et al. (Eds.): CWSN 2020, CCIS 1321, pp. 169–180, 2020.
https://doi.org/10.1007/978-981-33-4214-9_13

very important classification model. It has received a lot of attention since it was proposed in 1967, and it has become one of the top ten algorithms for machine learning. The classic KNN makes a simple statistic on the number of different classes in k neighbors to obtain the class of unknown samples. This approach is easy to understand, but it will cause many problems.

For example, different k values have a great influence on the performance of the algorithm, so many researchers are committed to finding an optimal k value for different unknown samples. Among them, some researchers obtain the optimal k value of each training sample by sparse reconstruction of the training samples or classifying the ones, then the optimal k values of training samples are used as labels, the feature is invariant, to train a classification model to get the optimal k of unknown samples [5–7]. However, these methods need to learn the k value of the unknown sample, which will greatly increase the running time. In addition, the location distribution of neighbors is different, and the importance of classification for unknown samples is also different. Therefore, a local mean-based k-nearest neighbor method (LMKNN) was proposed by using the local mean vector to classify unknown samples [8]. Further, the methods of weighting multiple local mean vectors were proposed to determine the classes of unknown samples [9,10]. How to assign weights to neighbor samples has always been a concern. The simplest method is to assign weights to neighbors samples according to their distance to the unknown sample, but this method is not completely correct. The reason is that sometimes the relatively distant neighbors may be more important for classification. Therefore, the method of CR is used in our proposed algorithm to obtain the weight of each neighbor. The unknown sample is re-represented by its neighbor samples, and the representation coefficient of each neighbor can be considered as its contribution to the reconstruction of the unknown sample. A large representation coefficient means that there is a high similarity between the neighbor sample and the unknown sample, so this neighbor will get a relatively large weight in the classification.

Collaborative representation based classification (CRC) is a method for image recognition. In CRC, the unknown sample is represented by all the training samples, the regularized residual in different classes are used for classification. It is proposed on the basis of sparse representation classification (SRC) [11]. In the objective function of SRC, the L_1 norm is used to control the sparsity of representation coefficients, so that the weights are concentrated on a small number of samples. L_1-minimization cannot be solved directly, although there are many fast L_1-minimization iterative solutions, compared to L_2-minimization, the solution of L_1-minimization is time-consuming [12].

Many researchers have done a lot of work on the basis of CR [13,14]. However, most CR-based methods are proposed for image recognition, and some problems will be encountered when directly used in data classification. A large number of samples that are irrelevant to classification will also have representation coefficients, which makes data classification difficult, especially for class imbalanced data sets. Due to a large number of samples in the majority class, it is easier to represent unknown samples, which is unfair to the minority class, and it is easy to make the classification result more biased to the majority class.

Therefore, we choose k neighbor samples nearest to the unknown sample from each class. This method can eliminate the interference of distant samples in advance, so that representation coefficients are concentrated on a small number of samples. What's more, the number of training samples used for each class to represent the unknown sample is the same, which is fair for classification. The main contributions of this paper are outlined as follows:

(1) Assigning weights to neighbors of unknown samples by using the method of CR. Moreover, the uneven distribution of data samples is considered. The same number of neighbors are taken from each class to represent the unknown sample, and representation coefficients are concentrated on a small number of samples.
(2) The distance between the local mean vector (ie, the centroid) and the unknown sample is used as the constraint for CR, so that different classes compete with each other. The class with short centroid distance has a great advantage in competition.

The rest of the paper is organized as follows. The related works are summarized and demonstrated in Sect. 2. In Sect. 3, we propose a local centroid distance constrained representation-based KNN classifier. In Sect. 4, we analyze the proposed algorithm. The conducted simulations and the corresponding results are presented in Sect. 5. Finally, we draw a conclusion in Sect. 6.

2 Related Works

In this section, we briefly review CRC and a local mean representation-based K-nearest neighbor classifier (LMRKNN) [16]. The LMRKNN is a method that combines KNN with CRC.

We assume that the set of n training samples within c classes is denoted as $X = [x_1, x_2, ..., x_n] = [X_1, X_2, ..., X_c]$, where $X_i = [x_{i1}, x_{i2}, ..., x_{in_i}]$ represents the set of n_i training samples in i-th class, c_i. x_{ih} denotes the nearest h-th training sample to unknown sample in i-th class. The unknown sample is represented as y.

2.1   CRC

Suppose the unknown sample can be represented linearly by all the training samples:

$$\hat{S} = \arg\min_{S}\{\|y - XS\|_2^2 + \gamma\|S\|_2^2\}, \tag{1}$$

where γ is a regularized parameter. The solution of Eq. (1) can be easily and analytically derived as

$$\hat{S} = (X^T X + \gamma I)^{-1} X^T y, \tag{2}$$

where I is an identity matrix. The class-specific representation residual and coefficient vector are used in classification, the regularized residual is computed:

$$r_i = \frac{\|y - X_i \hat{S}_i\|_2}{\|\hat{S}_i\|_2}, i = 1, 2, ...c. \tag{3}$$

where $\hat{S}_i$ represents the representation coefficient vector of the i-th class neighbor samples. The unknown sample is classified as the class with the smallest regularized residual r_i.

$$c_y = \arg\min_{c_i} r_i, i = 1, 2, ...c. \tag{4}$$

2.2 LMRKNN

K nearest neighbors are selected from each class, the set of k-nearest neighbors from class c_i is denoted as $X_{ik} = [x_{i1}, x_{i2}, ..., x_{ik}]$. The categorical k-local mean vectors are computed by using k-nearest neighbors from each class:

$$m_{ih} = \frac{1}{h} \sum_{j=1}^{h} x_{ij}, h = 1, ...k. \tag{5}$$

Let $M_i = [m_{i1}, m_{i2}, ..., m_{ik}]$ denotes the set of k-local mean vector in class c_i. The k local mean vector in class c_i is used to represent the unknown sample y linearly, the representation coefficient vector S_i is solved by constraining the l_2-norm regularization item of S_i as follows:

$$\hat{S}_i = \arg\min_{S_i} \{\|y - M_i S_i\|^2 + \gamma \|S_i\|^2\}. \tag{6}$$

The set of representation coefficients $\hat{S}_i$ for class c_i can be easily derived as:

$$\hat{S}_i = (M_i^{\mathrm{T}} M_i + \gamma I)^{-1} M_i^{\mathrm{T}} y, i = 1, 2, ...c. \tag{7}$$

The class specific representation residual is computed:

$$r_i = \|y - M_i \hat{S}_i\|^2, i = 1, 2, ...c. \tag{8}$$

According to the above idea, the representation residuals of each class are calculated, the unknown sample y is classified into the class that has the minimum representation residual in Eq. (8) among all classes.

$$c_y = \arg\min_{c_i} r_i, i = 1, 2, ...c. \tag{9}$$

3   The Proposed Method

In this section, we give a detailed introduction to our proposed method. First, k training samples nearest to unknown sample are selected from each class using Euclidean distance.

$$d(y, x_{it}) = \sqrt{(y - x_{it})^{\mathrm{T}}(y - x_{it})}, i = 1, 2, ..., c,$$
$$t = 1, 2, ..., n_i. \tag{10}$$

These $N = c*k$ training samples are used to form a neighbor sample subset, $\tilde{X} = [x_{11}, ..., x_{1k}, ..., x_{i1}, ..., x_{ik}, ..., x_{c1}, ..., x_{ck}]$. The unknown sample is represented by its neighbor sample subsets:

$$\hat{S} = \arg\min_{S}\{\|y - \tilde{X}S\|_2^2 + \gamma\|S\|_2^2\}. \tag{11}$$

The distribution of neighbor samples relative to unknown samples in each class is important for judging the class of unknown sample, so we add the constraint of the local mean vector (i.e. centroid) to the objective function, so that different classes compete with each other when representing the unknown sample:

$$\hat{S} = \arg\min_{S}\{\|y - \tilde{X}S\|_2^2 + \gamma_1\|S\|_2^2 + \gamma_2\sum_{j=1}^{N} s_j^2\|y - u_j\|_2\}, \tag{12}$$

where s_j represents the representation coefficient of the j-th neighbor sample in $\tilde{X}$, u_j represents the local mean vector composed of k neighbors of the class to which the j-th neighbor sample belongs, $u_j(j = 1, 2, ..., N)$ is the same within a class, and for each class, $u_i(i = 1, 2, ..., c)$ is represented as:

$$u_i = \frac{1}{k}\sum_{h=1}^{k} x_{ih}, i = 1, 2, ...c, \tag{13}$$

where, the class of neighbor sample x_{ih} is i.

Next, the representation coefficient S is derived. It is easy to conclude that the derivation of the first two terms is $-2\tilde{X}^{\mathrm{T}}(y - \tilde{X}S)$ and $2\gamma_1 S$. Let $f(S) = \gamma_2\sum_{i=1}^{N} s_j^2\|y - u_j\|_2$, Since $f(S)$ does not directly contain S, the derivative of each term s_j in the S is obtained, that is, obtain $\frac{\partial f(S)}{\partial S}$ by solving $\frac{\partial f(S)}{\partial s_k}$:

$$\frac{\partial f(S)}{\partial s_k} = \frac{\partial}{\partial s_k}(\gamma_2 s_k^2\|y - u_k\|_2) = 2\gamma_2 s_k\|y - u_k\|_2. \tag{14}$$

Thus,

$$\frac{\partial f(S)}{\partial S} = \begin{bmatrix} \frac{\partial}{\partial s_1} \\ \vdots \\ \frac{\partial}{\partial s_N} \end{bmatrix} = \begin{bmatrix} 2\gamma_2 s_1 \|y - u_1\|_2 \\ \vdots \\ 2\gamma_2 s_N \|y - u_N\|_2 \end{bmatrix}$$

$$= 2\gamma_2 \begin{bmatrix} \|y - u_1\|_2 & \cdots & 0 \\ \vdots & \ddots & \vdots \\ 0 & \cdots & \|y - u_N\|_2 \end{bmatrix} \begin{bmatrix} s_1 \\ \vdots \\ s_N \end{bmatrix} \tag{15}$$

$$= 2\gamma_2 M S.$$

Overall, the derivative of Eq. (12) is:

$$-2\tilde{X}^T(y - \tilde{X}S) + 2\gamma_1 S + 2\gamma_2 M S = 0. \tag{16}$$

The representation coefficient can be easily obtained:

$$\hat{S} = (\tilde{X}^T\tilde{X} + \gamma_1 I + \gamma_2 M)^{-1} X^T y, \tag{17}$$

where, $M = \begin{bmatrix} \|y - u_1\|_2 & \cdots & 0 \\ \vdots & \ddots & \vdots \\ 0 & \cdots & \|y - u_N\|_2 \end{bmatrix}$, $u_j = \frac{1}{k}\sum_{h=1}^{k} x_{ih}, i = 1, 2, ..., c.$ u_j is

the same within a class i. The representation coefficients of k nearest samples are obtained for each class, the representation coefficient of each neighbor sample is equivalent to its weight in the classification. And the k representation coefficients for each class are added separately:

$$W_i = \sum_{h=1}^{k} \hat{s}_{ih}, i = 1, 2, ...c, \tag{18}$$

where $\hat{s}_{ih}$ denotes the representation coefficient of h-th neighbor from i-th class. The unknown sample is classified to the class with the largest sum of coefficients:

$$c_y = \arg\max_{c_i} W_i, i = 1, 2, ...c. \tag{19}$$

The pseudo-code of LCDR-KNN is shown in Algorithm 1.

Algorithm 1. LCDR-KNN

Input: A training set: X, unknown sample: y, the size of neighbor: k.
Output: The class of unknown sample c_y.
1: The number of class, c and number of samples in each class, $[n_1, n_2, ..., n_c]$ is obtained using the training set, X.
2: **for** i=1 to c **do**
3:      **for** t=1 to n_i **do**
4:          $d(y, x_{ih}) = \sqrt{(y - x_{it})^{\mathrm{T}}(y - x_{it})}, t = 1, 2, ..., n_i.$
5:      **end for**
6: **end for**
7: K nearest training samples of each class, $[x_{i1}, x_{i2}, ..., x_{ik}]$, and the subset of training sample, $\tilde{X}$ are obtained.
8: **for** j=1 to N **do**
9:      $u_j = \frac{1}{k}\sum_{h-1}^{k} x_{ih}, i = 1, 2, ...c.$
10: **end for**
11: $M = \begin{bmatrix} \|y - u_1\|_2 & \cdots & 0 \\ \vdots & \ddots & \vdots \\ 0 & \cdots & \|y - u_N\|_2 \end{bmatrix}$
12: $\hat{S} = (\tilde{X}^{\mathrm{T}}\tilde{X} + \gamma_1 I + \gamma_2 M)^{-1} X^{\mathrm{T}} y$
13: **for** i=1 to c **do**
14:      $W_i = \sum_{h=1}^{k} \hat{s}_{ih}.$
15: **end for**
16: $c_y = \arg\max_{c_i} W_i, i = 1, 2, ...c$
17: Return c_y.

---

4   Algorithm Analysis

In this section, the proposed algorithm is analyzed from two aspects: KNN and CRC, respectively.

Firstly, from the KNN point of view, it is equivalent to selecting k nearest training samples from each class. These k nearest training samples have different positions and distances relative to the unknown sample, so their importance to classification is different. The calculated representation coefficients S equal to the weights of neighbor samples. So the sum of weights of k neighbor samples in each class is calculated, and the unknown sample is classified into the class with the largest sum of weights.

To obtain the weights (i.e. represent coefficients, S), $N = c * k$ training samples are used to re-represent the unknown sample. If a training sample can better represent the unknown sample, then the weight of this training sample is larger. What's more, centroid distances are added to the objective function, so that different classes compete with each other, the sample with short centroid distance is dominant in competition.

Secondly, from the CRC perspective: we can see that the first two terms of the objective function Eq. (12) are in the same form as the ones of CRC. The CRC represents the unknown sample with all the training samples, but our method is to select k nearest neighbors from each class to form a sample subset to represent the unknown sample. The proposed method, relative to the CRC, calculates the Euclidean distance to find k samples nearest to the unknown sample, which can better find the class of the unknown sample. Because some training samples are far away from unknown samples, their similarity with unknown samples is very low. In this way, the interference of these samples can be eliminated first before calculating the representation coefficients. Thus, without using the L_1 norm to control its sparsity, the representation coefficients can be concentrated on a few samples. We can see the third term of the objective function Eq. (12), which is to add a centroid constraint to the CRC objective function. From the objective function, we can see that if the distance between the unknown sample and the local centroid of the class is short, the representation coefficient s_j will be larger, whereas, the representation coefficient s_j will be smaller. In other words, if the unknown sample is close to the local centroid of k training sample of a certain class, it is more competitive and the assigned representation coefficient is larger.

5   Numerical Experiments

To demonstrate the effectiveness of the proposed algorithm, we compared our proposed algorithm with previous algorithms: CRC[12], MLP-SCG[17], KNN[4], LMPNN[15], MLMKHNN[9] and LMRKNN[16]. Among these comparison algorithms, MLP-SCG is a feedforward multi-layer perception (MLP) using the Scaled Conjugate Gradient (SCG) learning algorithm, which is the most popular classification algorithm in recent years. LMPNN, MLMKHNN and LMRKNN are the state-of-the-art KNN improved algorithms. Experiments were performed on the UCI data sets and the KEEL data sets. The characteristics of data sets used in the experiments are shown in Table 1, where, WDBC is short for Wisconsin diagnostic breast cancer data set.

Table 1. The data sets in the experiments.

Data set	Sample number	Feature number	Class number	Ratio
Vehicle	846	18	4	199:212:217:218
Seeds	210	7	3	70:70:70
Diabetes	768	8	2	268:500
DNAtest	1186	180	3	290:303:603
Ecoli	307	7	4	35:52:77:143
Vote	435	16	2	168:267
Bupa	345	6	2	145:200
Wine	178	13	3	48:59:71
Wdbc	569	30	2	212:357

All data sets were standardized prior to experiments: each feature was standardized so that its mean is equal to 0 and variance is equal to 1 to increase data comparability. In addition, each data set was split into 10 copies, 1 for the test set, and the remaining 9 for the training set. The average of ten cross-validation tests as the final result. The method of data sets processing and the division of data sets for different algorithms were consistent. We chose the optimal value of parameter γ_1 and γ_2 for each data set from seven candidate values: 0.0001, 0.001, 0.01, 0.1, 1, 10, and 100.

First, the accuracy of the algorithms with different k values was compared. The accuracy was calculated by classifying the correct number of samples in the test set divided by the total number of test samples. Figure 1 shows the accuracy of different algorithms under different data sets when the k values are taken from 1 to 20.

From Fig. 1, we can see that for data sets: vehicle, seeds and wine, our proposed algorithm can guarantee the optimal classification performance regardless

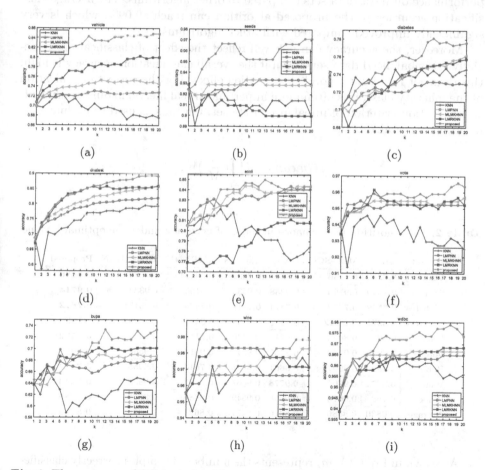

Fig. 1. The accuracy of different algorithms under different data sets when the k values are taken from 1 to 20: (a) Vehicle. (b) Seeds. (c) Diabetes.(d) DNAtest. (e) Ecoli. (f) Vote. (g)Bupa. (h)Wine. (i)Wdbc.

of the k value. And the performance improvement is obvious compared with other algorithms. While the performance improvement of other data sets is not as obvious as the advantages of these three data sets, our proposed algorithm always guarantees the optimal classification effect on the whole, and it is very competitive.

Then, the performance of algorithm under the optimal k value was compared. Combined with the results shown in Fig. 1, k values range from 1 to 20, the highest accuracy for each algorithm was compared. The results of the comparison are shown in Table 2. As we can find in Table 2, compared to Fig. 1, there are two additional comparison algorithms: CRC and MLP-SCG, this is because CRC and MLP-SCG use all training samples for prediction, so there is no parameter k, no need for comparison under different k values. From Table 2, we can see that in the case of optimal performance, our proposed algorithm has the best performance on most data sets compared to other algorithms. The average classification accuracy of the proposed algorithm can reach 89.09%, which is very significantly improved compared with other algorithms.

Moreover, the accuracy can not well reflect the effect of classification. Especially for imbalanced data sets, even if the overall classification accuracy is high, this does not represent a good classification effect. For the correct classification of the minority class, it is often more important in real life. So in our experiment, the evaluation criterion of imbalanced data set, Gmeans, is used to evaluate the performance of algorithms.

$$Gmeans = (\prod_{i=1}^{c}(\frac{m_i}{M_i}))^{\frac{1}{c}}. \tag{20}$$

Table 2. The algorithm performance in terms of accuracy under the optimal k value.

Data set	CRC	MLP-SCG	KNN	LMPNN	LMRKNN	MLMKHNN	Proposed
Vehicle	0.7232	0.7886	0.7246	0.7305	0.7968	0.7529	**0.8486**
Seeds	0.7619	0.9195	0.9238	0.9333	0.9190	0.9333	**0.9714**
Diabetes	0.6549	0.7652	0.7474	0.7317	0.7578	0.7617	**0.7812**
DNAtest	0.5371	**0.9042**	0.7959	0.8195	0.8591	0.8600	0.8945
Ecoli	0.5082	0.8065	0.8212	0.8440	0.8114	0.8441	**0.8502**
Vote	0.7045	0.9448	0.9455	0.9545	0.9614	0.9568	**0.9659**
Bupa	0.5825	0.6607	0.6661	0.6811	0.7013	0.6955	**0.7334**
Wine	0.8771	0.9705	0.9778	0.9667	0.9833	0.9833	**0.9944**
Wdbc	0.798	0.9670	0.9666	0.9649	0.9684	0.9666	**0.9789**
Average	0.6830	0.8586	0.8410	0.8474	0.8621	0.8616	**0.8909**

As shown in Eq. (20), m_i represents the number of samples correctly classified in i-th class test samples, M_i represents the number of i-th class test samples. The solution of Gmeans can be understood as the arithmetic square root of the product of the accuracy of different classes.

Table 3. The algorithm performance in terms of Gmeans under the optimal k value.

Data set	CRC	MLP-SCG	KNN	LMPNN	LMRKNN	MLMKHNN	Proposed
Vehicle	0.7045	0.7715	0.6746	0.6903	0.7871	0.7221	**0.8386**
Seeds	0.7733	0.9241	0.929	0.9351	0.9358	0.9351	**0.9743**
Diabetes	0.2529	0.7070	0.6786	0.6807	0.7239	0.7267	**0.7452**
DNAtest	0.1452	**0.8974**	0.8288	0.8096	0.8263	0.8282	0.8763
Ecoli	0	0.6981	0.7394	0.7751	0.7617	0.7786	**0.7882**
Vote	0.4982	0.9415	0.948	0.9526	0.9591	0.9538	**0.9623**
Bupa	0.2427	0.5865	0.6491	0.6535	0.6682	0.6744	**0.7034**
Wine	0.8771	0.9703	0.979	0.9649	0.9833	0.9852	**0.9961**
Wdbc	0.8106	0.9617	0.9567	0.9581	0.9623	0.9609	**0.9753**
Average	0.4783	0.8286	0.8204	0.8244	0.8453	0.8406	**0.8733**

The comparison results of Gmeans for different algorithms are shown in Table 3. Like the previous comparison of accuracy, which is also compared with the Gmeans corresponding to the optimal k value of each algorithm. We can see from Table 3 that the performance of the proposed algorithm has been significantly improved. Furthermore, we can see that the classification effect of CRC is relatively poor, it is because the CRC uses all samples to represent unknown samples. It seeks to improve the overall classification performance by sacrificing the accuracy of the minority class, which is unfair to the samples of the minority class. It may even cause all the samples of the minority class to be misclassified, so for the data set, ecoli, the Gmeans is 0.

6   Conclusion

In this paper, a KNN algorithm based on centroid distance constraint representation is proposed. To get the contribution of different neighbor samples to the classification, the method of CR is used to obtain the weight of each neighbor sample. To make each class compete with each other, the distance from the centroid of neighbor samples in each class to unknown sample is used as the constraint. In the proposed algorithm, different neighbor samples have different weights, and the position relation of unknown sample relative to each class is taken into account in the calculation of weights. Extensive experiments have been performed on the UCI and the KEEL data sets, the results of which show that compared to the previous four related KNN-based algorithms, the proposed algorithm is more competitive in the case of different k values. With the optimal k value emloyed, the proposed algorithm outperforms those algorithms based on the CR, the neural network and the KNN in terms of accuracy and Gmeans.

References

1. Wu, X., Zuo, W., Lin, L., Jia, W., Zhang, D.: F-SVM: combination of feature transformation and SVM learning via convex relaxation. IEEE Trans. Neural Networks Learn. Syst. **29**(11), 5185–5199 (2018)

2. Safavian, S.R., Landgrebe, D.: A survey of decision tree classifier methodology. IEEE Trans. Syst. Man, Cybern. **21**(3), 660–674 (1991)
3. Jiang, L., Zhang, L., Li, C., Wu, J.: A correlation-based feature weighting filter for Naive Bayes. IEEE Trans. Knowl. Data Eng. **31**(2), 201–213 (2019)
4. Cover, T.M., Hart, P.E.: Nearest neighbor pattern classification. IEEE Trans. Inf. Theor. **13**(10), 21–27 (1967)
5. Mullick, S.S., Datta, S., Das, S.: Adaptive learning-based K-Nearest Neighbor classifiers with resilience to class imbalance. IEEE Trans. Neural Networks Learn. Syst. **29**(11), 5713–5725 (2018)
6. Garciapedrajas, N., Castillo, J.A., Cerruelagarcia, G.: A proposal for local k values for k-nearest neighbor rule. IEEE Trans. Neural Networks Learn. Syst. **28**(2), 470–475 (2017)
7. Zhang, S., Li, X., Zong, M., Zhu, X., Wang, R.: Efficient KNN classification with different numbers of nearest neighbors. IEEE Trans. Neural Networks Learn. Syst. **29**(5), 1774–1785 (2018)
8. Mitani, Y., Hamamoto, Y.: A local mean-based nonparametric classifier. Pattern Recogn. Lett. **27**(10), 1151–1159 (2006)
9. Pan, Z., Wang, Y., Ku, W.: A new k-harmonic nearest neighbor classifier based on the multi-local means. Expert Syst. Appl. **67**, 115–125 (2017)
10. Gou, J., Ma, H., Ou, W., Zeng, S., Rao, Y., Yang, H.: A generalized mean distance-based K-nearest neighbor classifier. Expert Syst. Appl. **115**, 356–372 (2019)
11. Wright, J., Yang, A.Y., Ganesh, A., Sastry, S., Ma, Y.: Robust face recognition via sparse representation. IEEE Trans. Pattern Anal. Mach. Intell. **31**(2), 210–227 (2009)
12. Zhang, L., Yang, M., Feng, X.: Sparse representation or collaborative representation: which helps face recognition?. In: Proceedings of the 2011 International Conference on Computer Vision, pp. 471–478. IEEE, Barcelona (2011)
13. Waqas, J., Yi, Z., Zhang, L.: Collaborative neighbor representation based classification using l2-minimization approach. Pattern Recogn. Lett. **34**(2), 201–208 (2013)
14. Li, W., Tramel, E.W., Prasad, S., Fowler, J.E.: Nearest regularized subspace for hyperspectral classification. IEEE Trans. Geosci. Remote Sens. **52**(1), 477–489 (2014)
15. Gou, J., Zhan, Y., Rao, Y., Shen, X., Wang, X., He, W.: Improved pseudo nearest neighbor classification. Knowl. Based Syst. **70**, 361–375 (2014)
16. Gou, J., Qiu, W., Yi, Z., Xu, Y., Mao, Q., Zhan, Y.: A local mean representation-based K-nearest neighbor classifier. ACM Trans. Intell. Syst. **10**(3), 29.1–29.25 (2019)
17. Moller, M.F.: Original contribution: a scaled conjugate gradient algorithm for fast supervised learning. Neural Netw. **6**(4), 525–533 (1993)

A Novel Mixed Sampling Algorithm for Imbalanced Data Based on XGBoost

Shu-Xu Zhao[1(✉)], Xiao-long Wang[1], and Qing-sheng Yue[2]

[1] College of Electronic and Information Engineering, Lanzhou Jiaotong University, Lanzhou 730070, China
zhaoshuxu@163.com
[2] Lanzhou University of Arts and Science, Lanzhou 730000, China

Abstract. In the classification processing of imbalanced datasets, the current method causes the classification surface to shift as the imbalance of sample categories, which results in the classifier's performance degradation. To this end, we propose a novel hybrid sampling ensemble algorithm (EEBS-XGBoost) based on XGBoost. The algorithm can make full use of the easily overlooked potential information in the undersampling of majority class samples; and promote the density of minority class samples in the boundary area. Finally, we get a robust classifier with better performance by building multiple balanced sample sets with which to train multiple differentiated subclassifiers. The experimental results show that this algorithm can effectively improve the classification of minority class than other methods in processing imbalanced datasets.

Keywords: Imbalanced datasets · XGBoost · Ensemble learning · Classification

1 Introduction

The design principles maximize the overall classification accuracy of traditional classification algorithms, but which makes the classification surface bias in dealing with imbalanced data classification [1, 2]. Usually, the misclassification cost of a few samples is relatively high, which leads to the classification effect not being as expected.

Sample sampling technology is a processing method of the data layer, in which the process of sampling and classifier training are independent of each other and have universality. This method obtains a relatively balanced dataset by undersampling and oversampling. Random undersampling will cause the classification information lost, resulting in a reduction in classification accuracy. Han et al. [3] proposed BorderlineSMOTE (BSO1), which generates new minority samples in the boundary area instead of using SMOTE on all minority samples. Nevertheless, it does not consider the differences between the boundary samples. Yang Yi et al. [4] proposed an improved BSO1 method, which sets different upsampling rates by the specific distribution of boundary samples; and increases the number of minority samples by nearestneighbor interpolation. He et al. [5] proposed the ADA-SYN method, which uses a minority sample's distribution density to decide automatically the number of new samples generated. Yu et al. [6] proposed

Z. Hao et al. (Eds.): CWSN 2020, CCIS 1321, pp. 181–196, 2020.
https://doi.org/10.1007/978-981-33-4214-9_14

ACOSampling, which uses the optimized ant colony search algorithm to evaluate the importance of the majority samples, which retains the majority of samples with high stress in undersampling.

The small number of minority samples is the main reason for the low classification accuracy of unbalanced data. The overlapping of minority and majority classes on the boundary increases the difficulty of classification. Ensemble learning [7, 8] has the advantages of strong generalization and high parallelism, which can make full use of a small number of samples and overcome the performance limitations of a single learning algorithm, thereby improving the classification ability of the model. Yu [9] et al. cited a DBN-based resampling SVM integration strategy, which was applied to credit classification of imbalanced data, and changed the weights of different categories by introducing a revenue-sensitive revenue matrix to make the results more reasonable. Castellanos [10] proposed to use the Smooth algorithm for data generation, thereby balancing the data set of samples encoded as strings. Liu [11] combined the semi-supervised sampling method with the triangular center of gravity theory, and oversampling the positive samples can solve the problem of data imbalance. Tao et al. [12] proposed the asBagging algorithm that combines random undersampling with the Bagging ensemble learning model. In literature [13], Chawla et al. combined SMOTE with the Boosting model proposed the SMOTE Boost method. Liu et al. [14] proposed the EasyEnsemble (EE) ensemble learning algorithm, using Bagging to fuse random downsampling with the AdaBoost algorithm to compensate for the loss of sample information caused by random downsampling. At the same time, the AdaBoost base classifier improves the generalization ability of the classification results. For the problem of category imbalance, EasyEnsemble has the advantage of low-time complexity and high utilization rate of minority data, which provides useful ideas for this article.

Aiming at the shortcomings of the majority sampling method of unbalanced data, by reasonably increasing the number of minority samples to make their samples are balanced. We proposed a hybrid sampling ensemble learning algorithm, EEBS-XGBoost, combined with EasyEnsemble and Borderline-SMOTE2, to solve the performance degradation of imbalanced data classification.

2   Extreme Gradient Boosting and Borderline-SMOTE2

2.1   Extreme Gradient Boosting

Extreme Gradient Boosting (XGBoost) is an improved and efficient machine learning ensemble algorithm based on the gradient boosting tree (GBDT) [16] proposed by Chen Tianqi [15]. Its high accuracy and high performance are superior to other similar algorithms. XGBoost uses CPU multi-threading for parallel computing, which improves the efficiency of the algorithm. Using Taylor's second-order expansion of the loss function makes the efficiency and accuracy of finding the optimal solution higher. Regular terms are added to the objective function to weigh the model's complexity to avoid overfitting. Suppose that the model has K decision trees,

$$\hat{y}_i = \sum_{k=1}^{K} f_k(X_i), \ f_k \in F \tag{1}$$

where F is the set corresponding to all regression trees. Therefore the objective function is:

$$L(\phi) = \sum_i l(\hat{y}_i, y_i) + \sum_k \Omega(f_k) \tag{2}$$

where l enotes the loss function to describe the difference between the predicted value $\hat{y}_i$ and the true value y_i, Ω is the complexity of the tree, that is the regular term.

$$\Omega(f) = \gamma T + \frac{1}{2}\lambda\|w\|^2 \tag{3}$$

where T represents the number of leaf nodes in the current regression tree, w denotes the weight of the leaf nodes. Using the boosting method, keep the previous model unchanged and add a new function to the model to make the objective function as small as possible.

$$\hat{y}_i^{(0)} = 0$$
$$\hat{y}_i^{(1)} = f_1(x_i) = \hat{y}_i^{(0)} + f_1(x_i)$$
$$\hat{y}_i^{(2)} = f_1(x_i) + f_2(x_i) = \hat{y}_i^{(1)} + f_2(x_i)$$
$$\ldots\ldots$$
$$\hat{y}_i^{(t)} = \sum_{k=1}^t f_k(x_i) = \hat{y}_i^{(t-1)} + f_t(x_i) \tag{4}$$

where $\hat{y}_i^{(t)}$ is the predicted value of the ith sample in the tth round, the newly added function is $f_t(x_i)$. The objective function is

$$L^{(t)} = \sum_{i=1}^n l(y_i, \hat{y}_i^{(t-1)} + f_t(X_i)) + \Omega(f_t) + \text{constant} \tag{5}$$

Using Taylor's second-order expansion of the loss function to approximate the objective function, then

$$L^{(t)} \approx \sum_{i=1}^n [l(y_i, \hat{y}^{(t-1)}) + g_i f_t(X_i) + \frac{1}{2}h_i f_t^2(X_i)] + \Omega(f_t) + \text{constant} \tag{6}$$

where

$$g_i = \partial_{\hat{y}^{(t-1)}} l(y_i, \hat{y}^{(t-1)}) \tag{7}$$

$$h_i = \partial_{\hat{y}^{(t-1)}}^2 l(y_i, \hat{y}^{(t-1)}) \tag{8}$$

Removing the constant, we have

$$\tilde{L}^{(t)} = \sum_{i=1}^n [g_i f_t(X_i) + \frac{1}{2}h_i f_t^2(X_i)] + \Omega(f_t) \tag{9}$$

Define that $I_j = \{i|q(x_i) = j\}$ as the sample set of leaf node j

$$\tilde{L}^{(t)} = \sum_{i=1}^{n} [g_i f_t(X_i) + \frac{1}{2}h_i f_t^2(X_i)] + \gamma T + \frac{1}{2}\lambda \sum_{j=1}^{T} \omega_j^2$$

$$= \sum_{j=1}^{T} [(\sum_{i \in I_j} g_i)\omega_j + \frac{1}{2}(\sum_{i \in I_j} h_i + \lambda)\omega_j^2] + \gamma T \qquad (10)$$

where γ is the penalty value.

Partial derivation of the objective function yield

$$\omega_j^* = -\frac{\sum_{i \in I_j} g_i}{\sum_{i \in I_j} h_i + \lambda} \qquad (11)$$

Substituting formula (11) in objective function, then

$$\tilde{L}^{(t)}(q) = -\frac{1}{2}\sum_{j=1}^{T} \frac{(\sum_{i \in I_j} g_i)^2}{\sum_{i \in I_j} h_i + \lambda} + \gamma T \qquad (12)$$

Computing the gain

$$L_{split} = \frac{1}{2}[\frac{(\sum_{i \in I_L} g_i)^2}{\sum_{i \in I_L} h_i + \lambda} + \frac{(\sum_{i \in I_R} g_i)^2}{\sum_{i \in I_R} h_i + \lambda} - \frac{(\sum_{i \in I} g_i)^2}{\sum_{i \in I} h_i + \lambda}] - \gamma \qquad (13)$$

which is the score of subtrees in the left and right minus the score obtained without splitting. Adding a threshold γ to restrict the growth of the tree. And the tree node would not be split while the gain is less than γ. In formula (3), γ is the coefficient of the leaf node, representing pre-pruning while optimizing the objective function.

2.2 Borderline-SMOTE2

Borderline-SMOTE2 (BSO2) inherits the SMOTE algorithm's idea, using the neighbor information of the entire training set to find neighbors in the majority and minority samples. Choosing a random number between 0 and 0.5 prevents the newly generated samples from being too close to the majority decision area, ensuring that the newly created samples are closer to the minority sample than the minority neighbor sample. BSO2 effectively avoids the propagation of original noise information on the new sample set and improves the classification performance. However, the time complexity increasing with adding most class sample information in calculating K nearest neighbors.

Algorithm1 BSO2

Input : the minority sample P, the majority sample N, imbalanced ratio IR, sampling rate SR, training set S, Nearest neighbor parameter K.

1 . Take the samples of N and P from S to form the majority class training sample S^- and the minority class training sample S^+.

2 . Let T be an empty set.

3 . Let S^{new} empty.

4 . For $i = 1 : P$

5 .   Find the corresponding sample x_i in S^+.

6 .   Find the K nearest neighbors of x_i in S, recoding the number of majority
        neighbors as N^{maj}.

7 .   If $K / 2 \le N^{maj} < K$, then $T = T \cup x_i$.

8 . End

9 . For $i = 1 : P \times SR$

10 .   Randomly select a main sample x in T set.

11 .   Find the K nearest neighbor of the main sample x in S and place it in the
         neighbor sample set S^{Ner}.

12 .   Randomly choose a number from 1 to K, finding the corresponding main
         neighbor sample x' in S^{Ner}.

13 .   Let the new minority sample x^{new} : $x^{new} = x + rand \times (x' - x), rand \in [0, 0.5]$

14 . $S^{new} = S^{new} \cup x^{new}$

15 .   Let S^{Ner} empty.

16 . End

Output : $S = S \cup S^{new}$

2.3 EasyEnsemble

EasyEnsemble(EE) algorithm combines random downsampling and the AdaBoost algorithm using the Bagging strategy in which the base classifier selects the AdaBoost algorithm to improve classification accuracy and generalization ability. It compensates for the loss of information of majority class samples caused by random downsampling, and with the advantages of low time complexity and high utilization of minority class data.

Algorithm2 EasyEnsemble(EE)

Input : Training set $D = \{(x_1, y_1), (x_2, y_2), \cdots, (x_m, y_m)\}$, the number of base classifier N in the Bagging, the number of base classifier M and learning algorithm L in the AdaBoost and testing smaple x'.

1 . Divide the original training set D to obtain the minority class sample set S^+ and the majority class sample set S^- .

2 . For i=1:N

3 .   Randomly select a subset S_i^- , let $\left|S_i^-\right| = \left|S_i^+\right|$

4 . $S_i = S_i^- \cup S_i^+$

5 .   Train an AdaBoost ensemble classifier H_i composed of M base classifiers on S_i, and record the weight ω_{ij} of each base classifier L_{ij} and the integrated decision threshold θ_i .

6 . End

Output : Prediction class label of testing sample:

$$y' = \text{sgn}(\sum_{i=1}^{N} \sum_{j=1}^{M} \omega_{ij} L_{ij}(x) - \sum_{i=1}^{N} \theta_i)$$

3   EEBS-XGBoost Algorithm

3.1   Proposal of Algorithm Strategy

The ensemble learning technique has higher classification accuracy and generalization ability than a single classifier, which widely used in the classification problem of imbalanced data. To make full use of the original information of the majority and minority samples, proposing a novel hybrid sampling ensemble algorithm based on EEBS-XGBoost, in which the EE algorithm to downsample the majority samples, BSO2 algorithm to upsample the minority samples and XGBoost as the new base classifier. Describing the algorithm as follows.

- First, through the EE downsampling algorithm, multiple subsets of majority samples are randomly drawn from multiple category samples independently. Add a new sampling rate threshold, making the number of samples in the subclass of the majority sample is proportional to the number of samples in the first minority class.
- Combine the extracted subsets of the majority samples with the minority sample sets, respectively. Upsampling minority samples with imbalance rate, sampling rate threshold, and BSO2 algorithm to generate new minority samples with reasonably controlled, and increase the number of minority samples.
- Form a balanced training subset of multiple categories at last. To improve the classification performance of a single base classifier, using the XGBoost with better classification performance to replace the AdaBoost base classifier in the original EE algorithm.

- Using a grid search to find the optimal parameter combination of each base classifier in training the base classifier, and feedback in real-time, timely adjust each XGBoost base classifier to achieve a single better classification performance. The trained multiple XGBoost base classifiers are integrated into the final robust classifier using the weighted voting method.

Figure 1 is the framework of the EEBS-XGBoost algorithm. For the majority class sample N and the minority class sample P in the training subset, m different sample subsets N_m and P_m are newly generated by the EE and BSO2 algorithms and combined to form a balanced data set. Adding different feature combinations to each XGBoost base classifier for training makes each base classifier have diversity. To make the classification performance of each XGBoost base classifier better, adjusting the model parameters in time through the Grid Search algorithm in training classifiers. Use the weight ω_{ij} of the base classifier h_{ij} and the integration decision threshold θ_i (the segmentation value of the sample category label) to perform weighted voting integration. Adjusting the integration strategy through the validation set to generate a robust classifier, and finally, make predictions on the test data.

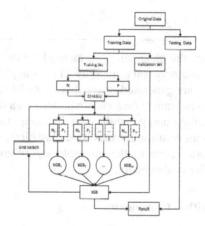

Fig. 1. EEBS-XGBoost famework

Algorithm 3 : EEBS-XGBoost

Input : the minority sample P, the majority sample N, imbalanced ratio IR, number of randomly sampled subsets n , the number of iterations per training XGBoost classifier t_i , sampling rate threshold r

1 . For $i = 1:n$

2 . Randomly sample from N to get a subset N_i, let $r|N_i| = |P|$.

3 . $P_s = BSO2(P, IR, r)$

4 . $P' = P + P_s$

5 . Train the ensemble classifier H_i consisting of t_i base classifiers with N_i and P',
ω_{ij} is weight of each XGBoost base classifier h_{ij} , θ_i is ensemble decision
threshold. $H_i(x) = \text{sgn}(\sum_{j=1}^{t_i} \omega_{ij} h_{ij}(x) - \theta_i)$

6 . End

Output : Final ensemble model H

$$H(x) = \text{sgn}(\sum_{i=1}^{n}\sum_{j=1}^{t_i} \omega_{ij} h_{ij}(x) - \sum_{i=1}^{n} \theta_i)$$

Each base classifier uses the undersampling method for the majority class samples without information lost; the necessary minority class samples are all retained, and new minority class samples are generated reasonably in the EEBS-XGBoost algorithm. Therefore the classifier can be trained on a class-balanced data set. XGBoost is a lifting tree model with robust learning and generalization. Training multiple newly generated category balance subsets can result in various base classifiers, which can improve the prediction result and generalization of the ensemble algorithm, and the classification performance of the classifier is also better.

3.2 Evaluation of Algorithm Complexity

The time cost of the EEBS-XGBoost algorithm mainly consists of sample sampling cost and base classifier training cost. Suppose n is the number of subsets obtained by the majority class downsampling through the EE algorithm, p is the number of samples of the minority class, and t is the number of iterations of the classifier. When upsampling minority samples, the BSO2 algorithm synthesizes a new minority sample based on the k nearest neighbor algorithm, the time complexity is approximately equal to $O(p^2)$. The time complexity of the n subsets obtained by downsampling the majority of classes through the EE algorithm is $O(n)$. XGBoost as the base classifier in model training, using the sparse greedy algorithm to find the optimal split point with the training data stored in a block structure, and the data has been pre-sorted in each column at the beginning. Therefore, the optimal split point of each layer can be obtained only by scanning the blocks to replace rearrange on each node. So the time complexity is $O(Kd\|X\|_0 + \|X\|_0 \log R)$, where K is the total number of trees, d is the maximum depth of the tree, $\|X\|_0$ is the number of non-missing entries in the training data, and R is the maximum number of rows in each storage block. As the original sparse greedy algorithm doesn't use block storage. It is needed to resort the data on each column to find the optimal split at each node. This ends up incurring a time complexity at each layer that is approximated by $O(\|X\|_0 \log n)$, where n is the maximum length of sorting lists at each layer. Multiplying by K trees and d layers per tree, the original time complexity is $O(Kd\|X\|_0 \log n)$. With the block structure, since the data is already pre-sorted by every column at the start, it does not need to resort at each node. Then the time complexity down to $O(Kd\|X\|_0)$. $O(\|X\|_0 \log R)$ is the one time preprocessing cost that can be amortized.

The EE algorithm has a lower time cost than the BSO2 algorithm and the XGBoost-based classifier with mixed sampling. The time complexity of the EEBS-XGBoost algorithm can be approximated as:

$$t \times O(p^2 + Kd\|X\|_0 + \|X\|_0 \log R) \tag{14}$$

4 Experimental Analysis

4.1 Data Set

Use two different data sets to verify the performance of the proposed model in classifying minority classes in an imbalanced data set. The credit card data set (Credit Card) uses the UCI public data set [17], with an imbalance rate of 4.52, which contains information on arrears payment, demographic factors, credit data, payment history, billing statements and other information of credit card customers in Taiwan. The credit fraud data set (Credit Card) is provided by ULB Machine Learning Laboratories [18]. The data set contains the transactions of a European bank credit card within two days. The data category is hugely unbalanced, with an imbalance rate of 577.88, which is highly uneven data and fraud. The volume accounts for 0.172% of all transactions. Divide the original data; the ratio of the training set to the test set is 7:3 (Table 1).

Table 1. ULB credit card fraud dataset

	Data set	Total number	Positive class	Negative class	Imbalanced rate
Credit Card	Raw data	30000	6636	23364	4.52
	Training set	21000	4636	16364	
	Test set	9000	2000	7000	
Credit Card	Raw data	284807	492	284315	577.88
	Trainset	199364	345	199019	
	Test set	85443	147	85296	

4.2 Evaluation Index

In imbalanced data sets, the minority class is called the positive type (P), and the majority class is called the negative type (N). The traditional classification algorithm aims to maximize the correct rate, and it is easy to ignore the classification accuracy of positive samples. Because positive samples are more important than negative, selecting several measurement methods based on the confusion matrix as performance evaluation indicators for unbalanced data sets (Table 2).

Table 2. ULB credit fraud data confusion matrix

Actual type	Prediction	
	Negative type	Positive type
Negative type	TN	FP
Positive type	FN	TP

The global classification accuracy is of little significance to the positive class, which can examine and weigh the classification accuracy of the negative type. The accuracy rate and the recall rate are opposed to each other. One value is higher, with the other is lower. $F - value$ is the balanced relationship between precision rate and recall rate, and β is the importance of recall rate relative to precision rate. $G - mean$ represents the geometric mean of the true rate (TPR) and true negative rate (TNR). When the two are close, the G-mean value is the largest. The Receiver Operating Characteristic Curve (ROC) curve formed by "sorting" the decision output value of each sample, used to describe the model's resolving power. The vertical axis is the true positive rate (TPR), and the horizontal axis is the false positive rate (FPR), the points on the curve are arranged from the origin to the decision value from small to large. The larger the AUC value, the better the classification performance of the model. The evaluation defines as follows.

$$Accuracy = \frac{TP + TN}{TP + TN + FP + FN} \tag{15}$$

$$Precision = \frac{TP}{TP + FP} \tag{16}$$

$$Recall = \frac{TP}{TP + FN} = Sensitivity = TPR \tag{17}$$

$$FPR = \frac{FP}{TN + FP} \tag{18}$$

$$Specificity = \frac{TN}{TN + FP} = TNR \tag{19}$$

$$F-value = \frac{(1 + \beta^2) \times Precision \times Recall}{\beta^2 \times Precision + Recall} \tag{20}$$

$$G-mean = \sqrt{Sensitivity \times Specificity} \tag{21}$$

4.3   Experiment Setting

Split the original data to generate training data and test data with a ratio of 7:3, and then split the training data with a rate of 8:2 to create a training set and a verification set. Each model uses a grid search and 10-fold cross-validation on the training set to obtain the best parameters. At the same time, it performs verification on the verification set. The final model gains Recall, Gmean, AUC, and other values on the test data to repeat this process. We choose the maximum G-mean as the model parameter optimization goal, considering the IR rate is not high in using the Credit Card data set, and the classification threshold is 0.5. Using Credit Fraud data, a highly unbalanced set, in conducting credit card fraud detection, considering that the number of positive samples is relatively small, only 0.172% of the total number of samples, the model training should pay more attention to the classification of positive samples. Using the maximum Recall value as the model parameter optimization goal and set the classification threshold to 0.6.

Experiment 1: Under-five sampling strategies, selecting six algorithms: Logistic Regression (LR), Decision Tree (DT), AdaBoost (Ada), Gradient Lifting Decision Tree (GBDT), Random Forest (RF), XGBoost (XGB), respectively, conduct experiment. The sampling strategy is as follows.

- Origin: P and N do not carry out any operation, which directly used for training.
- Oversampling(OS): P performs random upsampling to $P : N = 1 : 1$.
- SMOTE:Upsampling with SMOTE algorithm and $P : N = 1 : 1$.
- Undersampling(US): N performs random upsampling, $P : N = 1 : 1$.
- EasyEnsemble(EE):Random downsampling i times with replacement from N to get the subset N_i, $|N_i| = |P|$, the classifier uses $N_i + P$ for training.

Experiment 2: XGBoost as a classifier is combined with five sampling strategies to evaluate the classification performance of the data set; the experimental setup is as follows.

- Undersampling+Oversampling+XGBoost(UO-XGB): N randomly downsamples to get subset N', and P randomly upsamples to get P', $P' : N' = 1 : 1.5$. XGBoost uses P' and N' for training.
- Undersampling+SMOTE+XGBoost (US-XGB):N randomly downsamples to get subset N', making $|N'| = 2|P|$ P gets P' through the SMOTE algorithm, then $|P'| = 1.5|P|$, XGBoost uses $P + P'$ and N' for training.
- EasyEnsemble+SMOTE+XGBoost (ES-XGB): N samples i times through the EE algorithm to obtain the subset N_i, and $|N_i| = 2|P|$. P gets P' through the SMOTE algorithm, making $|P'| = 1.5|P|$. XGBoost uses $P + P'$ and N' for training.
- EasyEnsemble+Borderline-SMOTE1+XGBoost(EB-XGB):N samples i times through the EE algorithm to obtain the subset N_i,$|N_i| = 2|P|$.P gets P' through the BSO1 algorithm, and $|P'| = 1.5|P|$. XGBoost uses $P + P'$ and N' for training.
- EasyEnsemble+Borderline-SMOTE2+XGBoost(EEBS-XGB):N samples i times through the EE algorithm to get subset N_i so that $|N_i| = 2|P|$.P gets P' through the BSO1 algorithm, making $|P'| = 1.5|P|$. XGBoost uses $P + P'$ and N' for training.

4.4   The Experimental Result and Performance Evaluation

In Fig. 2, from the perspective of the classifier's classification effect, after performing random upsampling, SMOTE, random downsampling, and EE sampling strategies, Random Forest and XGBoost perform equally well, both of which have achieved excellent results in the model. The data sampling strategy, SMOTE, random downsampling,and EE have greatly improved the Recall value compared with other sampling methods; notably, the EE algorithm performs best.

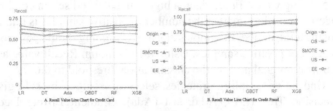

Fig. 2. Recall value line chart for credit data

Table 3 and Table 4 compared XGB with LR, DT, Ada, GBDT, RF, and other algorithms, respectively, and obtained Recall and G-mean values on the experimental data set. Compared with different sampling methods on SMOTE, random downsampling, and EE, the Recall value and G-mean value are improved, in which EE performs best, proving that the ensemble learning algorithm EE has high classification performance for minority class in imbalanced data set. Among all the classifiers, XGBoost performs best under the same sampling strategy, with higher Recall and G-mean values.

Table 3. Recall value for all models

		Origin	OS	SMOTE	US	EE
Credit Card	LR	0.4120	0.5678	0.6138	0.5761	0.6478
	DT	0.4248	0.5446	0.5968	0.5461	0.6132
	Ada	0.4502	0.5355	0.5821	0.5798	0.6103
	GBDT	0.4223	0.5461	0.6014	0.5652	0.6296
	RF	0.4771	0.5676	0.6297	0.6048	0.6503
	XGB	0.4539	0.5614	0.6348	0.5997	0.6562
Credit Fraud	LR	0.5983	0.5983	0.5983	0.5983	0.8519
	DT	0.5954	0.6815	0.7961	0.8518	0.9037
	Ada	0.6781	0.7185	0.8440	0.8668	0.8741
	GBDT	0.6011	0.7333	0.8369	0.8467	0.8963
	RF	0.6809	0.7481	0.8741	0.8794	0.9037
	XGB	0.6353	0.7778	0.8816	0.8618	0.9185

Table 4. G-Mean values for all models

		Origin	OS	SMOTE	US	EE
Credit Card	LR	0.5170	0.6089	0.6367	0.6705	0.6837
	DT	0.5322	0.5722	0.6072	0.6589	0.6564
	Ada	0.5239	0.5770	0.6130	0.6635	0.6600
	GBDT	0.5057	0.5871	0.6224	0.6413	0.6759
	RF	0.5832	0.6139	0.6564	0.6725	0.6935
	XGB	0.5609	0.6160	0.6751	0.6694	0.6880
Credit Fraud	LR	0.7734	0.8775	0.9248	0.9246	0.9207
	DT	0.7714	0.8253	0.8921	0.9149	0.9376
	Ada	0.8234	0.8475	0.9141	0.9151	0.9151
	GBDT	0.7750	0.8563	0.9128	0.8894	0.9235
	RF	0.8251	0.8649	0.9307	0.9112	0.9122
	XGB	0.7970	0.8818	0.9367	0.9147	0.9399

Table 5. All Xgboost ensemble model results

		UO-XGB	US XGB	US-XGB	EB-XGB	EEBS-XGB
Credit Card	Acc	0.7624	0.7387	0.7046	0.7021	0.6921
	Recall	0.5976	0.6547	0.6715	0.6679	0.6805
	Prec	0.4727	0.4290	0.4023	0.3956	0.4018
	F1	0.5165	0.5278	0.5049	0.4904	0.5098
	AUC	0.7624	0.7491	0.7652	0.7505	0.7683
	Gmean	0.6807	0.6949	0.6987	0.6955	0.7003
	Runtime(s)	0.6369	0.8910	4.1776	4.2196	4.2366
Credit Fraud	Acc	0.9995	0.9537	0.9644	0.9440	0.9208
	Recall	0.8027	0.9184	0.9129	0.9320	0.9483·
	Prec	0.9008	0.0331	0.0434	0.0281	0.0205
	F1	0.8489	0.0639	0.0828	0.0546	0.0402
	AUC	0.9784	0.9770	0.9794	0.9799	0.9821
	Gmean	0.8959	0.9359	0.9383	0.9380	0.9344
	Runtime(s)	26.1576	0.6175	3.7418	3.8858	5.9228

As shown in Table 5, using XGBoost as the base classifier and the same US strategy for most type samples, SMOTE has a higher score than the model OS, because SMOTE is different from OS, in which filled new samples in the neighborhood interval of the minority samples instead of copying a few samples. The majority of samples using EE has a higher Recall value than the US model when using the same SMOTE algorithm in upsampling for minority samples. However, due to the generation of multiple subsets, the time complexity becomes more substantial and takes the longest time. Using BSO1 and BSO2 models can obtain relatively high Recall values because the two have improved the SMOTE algorithm. BSO2 uses the neighborhood information of the entire training set instead of BSO1 only uses the similar neighbor information of a small number of samples to generate new samples. Therefore, the EEBS-XGBoost integrated the BSO2 algorithm, whose classification performance is relatively good.

In Fig. 3 A, the UO-XGB model uses the highly unbalanced data set Credit Fraud for experiments. The strategy adopted by which causes the newly generated minority classes to have disadvantages with large numbers, prolonged time consumption, and low classification performance. Therefore, this figure does not show its performance. As shown in Fig. 2, the higher the Recall value, the lower the Precision value, using the Credit Fraud dataset for experiments. This phenomenon occurs because TP increases a little with FP an exponential growth, resulting in a decrease of the Precision value, which caused by the small number of minority samples, the high imbalance rate, and the hugely imbalanced data.

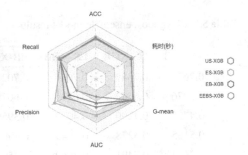

Fig. 3. Radar chart of XGBoost ensemble models

From Fig. 4, we can see that in the highly unbalanced data, using the maximum Recall value as the model's optimization goal for model training, XGBoost significantly improves the classification performance through grid search to optimize parameters. Compared with other models, the EEBS-XGBoost model proposed in this paper can obtain a more considerable AUC value and the largest ROC curve area.

In short, XGBoost performs better than other classifiers. The EEBS-XGBoost model proposed in this paper can achieve better classification results for minority classes on imbalanced data sets than other methods.

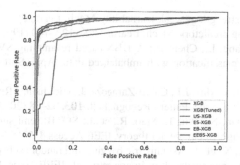

Fig. 4. ROC curve of ensemble models

5 Conclusions

The hybrid sampling integrated learning algorithm based on XGBoost makes the new samples synthesized by the minority class more reasonably close to the minority sample area. The algorithm makes full use of the easily ignored useful information in undersampling the majority samples, training multiple balanced subsets of data samples through multiple XGBoost classifiers to improve the classification performance. Experimental results show that the classification accuracy of the algorithm for imbalanced data is better than other methods. The experiment obtained a higher Recall value, but lower Precision. The next step is to consider how to achieve a better balance between the two in the imbalanced data. Besides, in highly imbalanced data, there is a considerable gap between the number of minority samples and the majority of samples. The obtained FN value is small, and the FPR cannot be changed quickly. As a result, the TPR initially gets a more considerable value, making the ROC curve to reflect the real situation objectively. For highly imbalanced data, we should consider designing more effective evaluation indicators.

References

1. Sun, Y., Wong, A.K.C., Kamel, M.S.: Classification of imbalanced data: a review. Int. J. Pattern Recogn. Artif. Intell. **23**(04), 687–719 (2009)
2. Drummond, C., Robert, C.H.: C4. 5, class imbalance, and cost sensitivity: why under-sampling beats over-sampling. In: Workshop on learning from imbalanced datasets II, August 2003, pp. 1–8 (2003)
3. Han, H., Wang, W.Y., Mao, B.H.: Borderline-SMOTE: a new over-sampling method in imbalanced data sets learning. In: International Conference on Intelligent Computing. Springer, August 2005, pp. 878–887
4. 杨毅, 卢诚波, 徐根海. 面向不平衡数据集的一种精化 Borderline-SMOTE 方法. 复旦学报: 自然科学版, **5**, 537–544 (2017)
5. He, H., Bai, Y., Garcia, E.A., et al.: ADASYN: adaptive synthetic sampling approach for imbalanced learning. In: IEEE International Joint Conference on Neural Networks, pp. 1322–1328, June 2008
6. Yu, H., Ni, J., Zhao, J.: ACOSampling: an ant colony optimization-based undersampling method for classifying imbalanced DNA microarray data. Neurocomputing **101**(2), 309–318 (2013)

7. Schapire, R.E.: The strength of weak learnability. Mach. Learn. **5**(2), 197–227 (1990)
8. Breiman, L.: Bagging predictors. Mach. Learn. **24**(2), 123–140 (1996)
9. Yu, L., Zhou, R., Tang, L., Chen, R.: A DBN-based resampling SVM ensemble learning paradigm for credit classification with imbalanced data. Appl. Soft Comput. **69**, 192–202 (2018)
10. Castellanos, F.J., Valero-Mas, J.J., Calvo-Zaragoza, J., RicoJuan, J.R.: Oversampling imbalanced data in the string space. Pattern Recogn. Lett. **103**, 32–38 (2018)
11. Liu, D., Qiao, S., Han, N., Wu, T., Mao, R., et al.: SOTB: semi-supervised oversampling approach based on trigonal barycenter theory. IEEE Access **8**, 50180–50189 (2020)
12. Tao, D., Tang, X., Li, X., et al.: Asymmetric bagging and random subspace for support vector machines-based relevance feedback in image retrieval. IEEE Trans. Pattern Anal. Machine Intell. **28**(7), 1088–1099 (2006)
13. Chawla, N.V., Lazarevic, A., Hall, L.O., et al.: SMOTEBoost: improving prediction of the minority class in boosting. In: European Conference on Principles of Data Mining and Knowledge Discovery, pp. 107–119, September 2003
14. Liu, X.Y., Wu, J., Zhou, Z.H.: Exploratory undersampling for class-imbalance learning. IEEE Trans. Syst. Man, Cybern. Part B (Cybernetics), **39**(2), 539–550 (2009)
15. Chen, T., Carlos, G.: Xgboost: a scalable tree boosting system. In: Proceedings of the 22nd ACM SIGKDD International Conference on Knowledge Discovery and Data Mining, pp. 785–794, August 2016
16. Friedman, J.H.: Greedy function approximation: a gradient boosting machine. Ann. Stat. **29**(5), 1189–1232 (2001)
17. Lichman, M.. UCI machine learning repository .[http://archive.ics.uci.edu/ml]. Irvine, CA: University of California, School of Information and Computer Science (2007)
18. Dal Pozzolo, A., Caelen, O., Johnson, R.A., et al.: Calibrating probability with undersampling for unbalanced classification. In: IEEE Symposium Series on Computational Intelligence, pp. 159–166, December 2015

Privacy-Preserving and Secure Average Consensus

Yalian Wu[✉], Jiaqi Zhao, Jinbiao Luo, and Qingyu Yang

School of Automation and Electronic Information Xiangtan University,
Xiangtan 411105, Hunan, China
201921001958@smail.xtu.edu.cn

Abstract. Average consensus is the key to distributed networks, widely used in distributed sensor networks, smart grid energy management and automatic control. In the traditional average consensus algorithm, the explicit exchange of status values with its neighbors through real identity will lead to the leakage of node status information and privacy issues. This paper proposes a novel confidential interaction scheme. In this method, the group signature scheme is applied to the consensus interaction process to provide anonymity for the nodes, and at the same time to encrypt the exchanged information, so as to ensure the privacy of the nodes, and also ensure that the consensus state reaches an accurate value. Besides, our scheme can also trace the dishonest nodes in the interaction process. Finally, the effectiveness of the proposed scheme is illustrated by numerical simulation.

Keywords: Average consensus · Privacy · Security · Group signature

1 Introduction

In the past few decades, consensus has been extensively developed. It instructs individual nodes to reach an agreement about an interest through interaction without a computing center [1]. The consensus algorithm has attracted many researchers due to its wide application in the multi-node system [1,2], data fusion [3] and other fields. In recent years, embedded systems and wireless communication technologies have developed rapidly, especially the emergence of large-scale sensor networks and the Internet of Things. The average consensus is on automatic control, signal processing, smart grid distributed energy management and scheduling [4], distribution sensor network [5] and other fields find more and more applications.

The most commonly used consensus protocol is the average consensus algorithm, which guarantees that the state of all nodes converges to the average of their initial values [6]. In the traditional average consensus algorithm relies on the exchange of explicit state values between adjacent nodes, and follows the time-invariant update algorithm to achieve the required consistency [7,8]. There are two problems with this method. First, the explicit exchange of state values

© Springer Nature Singapore Pte Ltd. 2020
Z. Hao et al. (Eds.): CWSN 2020, CCIS 1321, pp. 197–208, 2020.
https://doi.org/10.1007/978-981-33-4214-9_15

will lead to the leakage of state values containing sensitive information. Secondly, if a node understands the update rules of consensus, it means that it will be able to infer the state values of all nodes. For privacy reasons, nodes participating in the consensus prefer to protect their initial state from being disclosed.

In the database literature, the security and privacy issues of consensus have received considerable attention. Most of the schemes are to blur the state by adding noise to the state to mask the true state value of the node. The idea of differential privacy is proposed in [9]. The author first proposed a differential private consensus algorithm in [10]. Their consensus algorithm converges to random values, not the average of the initial state. The author in [11] uses differential privacy to inject irrelevant noise into the average consensus. In [12], the injection of correlated (relative to uncorrelated) noise is proposed, in which nodes are added to the network asymptotically minus their initial offset values. Another common method is to use cryptographic techniques to solve, for example, homomorphic encryption [13,14]. In [14], the author proposed a new method of applying homomorphic cryptography to the interactive protocol, which can ensure true average convergence.

However, the vast majority of methods use the real identity of the nodes to interact to achieve an average consensus. In this way, the initial state can correspond to the true identity of the node, which leads to privacy leakage. In order to solve privacy and security issues, a novel privacy protection scheme based on group signature security and privacy protection consensus is proposed. Note that the group signature scheme has been applied to various applications, such as the in-vehicle self-organizing network [15] to solve privacy issues under the strong assumption.

The contributions of this paper are as follows: 1) This paper provides anonymity for the nodes participating in the interaction to ensure the privacy of the node, and uses signatures to ensure the integrity of the interactive information; 2) The dishonest node can be traced by confirming the signature information of the node; 3) Encrypt and decrypt the message by using two algorithms ENCRYPT and DECRYPT.

The remainder of this paper will be organized as described below. Reviews the average consensus problem and bilinear groups in Sect. 2. In Sect. 3, adds the privacy protection scheme of this paper to the consensus interaction process. Section 4 discusses privacy guarantees and security mechanisms. Section 5 introduces the simulation. Gives the conclusion of this paper in Sect. 6.

2   Background

2.1   Average Consensus

Consider a network of N nodes composed of an undirected and connected graph $G = (V, E, A)$, which $V = \{1, 2, \cdots, N\}$ is expressed as a set of nodes; $E \subset V \times V$ is expressed as a set of edges, representing the connection between nodes; $A = [a_{i_j}]$ is a weighted adjacency matrix of the network.

We assume that each node has an initial state $x_i[0]$, and the node v_i interacts with all its neighbors through the network. Its neighbor set is expressed as

$$N_i = \{j \in |(i, j) \in E\} \tag{1}$$

Then, in order to reach an average consensus, that is, the state of all nodes $x_i[k](i = 1, 2, \cdots, N)$ converges to the average value of the initial state of the nodes, namely $\frac{\sum_{j=1}^{N} x_j[0]}{N}$. Nodes use a common average consensus update rule to update the status

$$x_i[k + 1] = x_i[k] + \varepsilon \sum_{v_i \in N_i} a_{ij}(x_j[k] - x_i[k]) \tag{2}$$

2.2 Bilinear Pairing

We follow the concepts related to bilinear mapping mentioned by Boneh, Lynn and Shacham [16]:

1) G_1 and G_2 are additive cyclic group of order;
2) g_1 and g_2 are the generators of G_1 and G_2 respectively;
3) $e : G_1 \times G_2 \to G_T$ is a bilinear pair, it is a mapping, and meets the following conditions:
   - Bilinearity: There are two elements $n, m \in \mathbb{Z}$ in $\mathbb{Z}$, when $p_1 \in G_1, p_2 \in G_2$ has $e(p_1^m, p_2^n) = e(p_1, p_2)^{mn}$.
   - Non-degeneracy: $e(g_1, g_2) \neq 1$.
   - Computability: The function e is computable.

3 Security Interaction Protocol

In this section, in order to protect the privacy and security of nodes, we propose a secure interaction scheme. Our scheme uses group signature [17] to sign messages transmitted by nodes, and uses two algorithms to encrypt and decrypt the original message in the interaction process. Our solution provides the anonymity of the node, the essence of which is to hide the one-to-one mapping relationship between the real identity of the node and the identity used in the communication, so as to achieve node anonymity and thus protect the node privacy. In addition, our solution also meets other security requirements, such as message integrity and resistance to collusion attacks.

In 1991, Chaum and Heyst proposed the concept of group signatures [17]. With the deepening of research, group signature scheme is continuously improved. Camenisch introduced a group signature algorithm suitable for large-scale groups in [18], but this scheme ignores the revocation mechanism. Cpopescu [19] proposed a new ID-based group signature, which is based on the binaural pairing of algebraic curves. Unfortunately, this scheme is linkable; that is, it can distinguish whether the same signer generates two different group signatures. Therefore, we chose a short group signature scheme [16] suitable for the consensus process, which has the characteristics of short signatures and saving communication bandwidth.

The secret interaction scheme will be described in detail below. Specifically, the secret interaction scheme consists of six stages, which are described in the following paragraphs.

3.1 System Setup

Consider the bilinear groups G_1 and G_2, their corresponding generators g_1 and g_2, as shown in Sect. 2. Then make the SDH hypothesis applies to (G_1, G_2) and the Linear hypothesis applies to G_1. This scheme uses two hash functions $H : \{0,1\}^* \to \mathbb{Z}_p^*$ and $H_1 : \{0,1\}^k \to \{0,1\}^k$.

Randomly select two numbers $h \xleftarrow{R} G_1 \{1_{G_1}\}$ and $h_0 \xleftarrow{R} G_2 \{1_{G_2}\}$, and random numbers $\xi_1, \xi_2 \xleftarrow{R} \mathbb{Z}_p^*$. Then set $u, v \in G_1$ make $u^{\xi_2} = v^{\xi_2} = h$, and set $h_1, h_2 \in G_2$ make $h_1 = h_0^{\xi_1}, h_2 = h_0^{\xi_2}$. Select $\gamma \xleftarrow{R} \mathbb{Z}_p^*$ and set $w = g_2^\gamma$. The group public key is $gpk = (g_1, g_2, h, u, v, w)$. The group private key of the group administrator (the party who can track the signature) is $gmsk = (\xi_1, \xi_2)$. Where γ is only owned by the private key issuer. This way the system is initialized.

3.2 Confidential Interaction Protocol

Considering the general situation, we use the interactive process of nodes to specify this solution, as shown in Fig. 1.

1) Node registration: First add the node to the group, and the MM (member manager) generates a tuple (A_i, x_i) based on the node's identity ID_i, which is used as the node's private key $gsk[i]$. Then use γ, MM calculates $x_i \leftarrow H(\gamma, ID_i) \in \mathbb{Z}_p^*$ and then sets $A_i \leftarrow g_1^{1/(\gamma + x_i)}$. Finally, MM will store a pair (A_i, ID_i), and sends back the message password pwd, complete the node registration.

   Note that, MM does not require storage x_i and x_i can be calculated by γ and ID_i, which saves storage space.

   When nodes in the network transmit messages, they use the same pwd to improve communication efficiency.

2) Encrypt message: due to the symmetry, only the transmission process of the node v_1 is shown. In the network, the message encrypted mes' by the node v_1 and transmitted to v_2.

   Make $f \in \mathbb{Z}_p^*$ and calculate

$$F = fg_1 \tag{3}$$

$$F' = e(F, pwd) = e(fg_1, pwd) \tag{4}$$

$$t = H(F') = H(e(fg_1, pwd)) \tag{5}$$

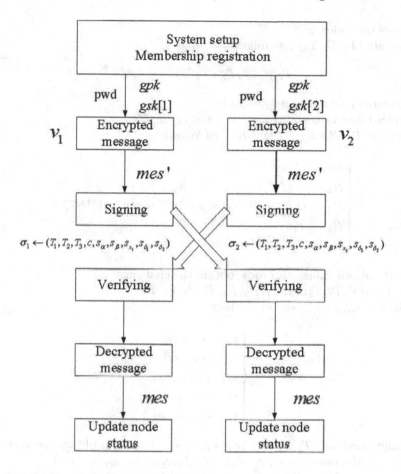

Fig. 1. Description of the distribution of security interaction schemes.

Let $message \in M$ (where M is the set of messages that can be signed) be and assume

$$m_1 = message \oplus t \tag{6}$$

$$m_2 = mes \oplus H_1(message) \tag{7}$$

The encrypted information of the original information mes' is

$$mes' = (m_1, m_2) \tag{8}$$

3) Signing: given encrypted message mes' , using the group public key $gpk = (g_1, g_2, h, u, v, w)$ and private key pair $gsk[i] = (A_i, x_i)$, the node v_1 sign on mes', the signing process consists of the following calculation.

a) Choose the index $\alpha, \beta \xleftarrow{R} \mathbb{Z}_p^*$.
b) Calculate (T_1, T_2, T_3) , as follows

$$T_1 \leftarrow u^\alpha, T_2 \leftarrow v^\beta, T_3 \leftarrow A_i h^{\alpha+\beta} \tag{9}$$

c) Calculate $\delta_1 \leftarrow x_i \alpha$ and $\delta_2 \leftarrow x_i \beta$.
d) Extract blind values $r_\alpha, r_\beta, r_{x_i}, r_{\delta_1}$ and r_{δ_2} in $\mathbb{Z}_p^*$.
e) Calculate R_1, R_2, R_3, R_4 and R_5 , as follows:

$$\begin{cases} R_1 \leftarrow u^{r_\alpha} \\ R_2 \leftarrow v^{r_\beta} \\ R_3 \leftarrow e(T_3, g_2)^{r_{x_i}} \cdot e(h, w)^{-r_\alpha - r_\beta} \cdot e(h, g_2)^{-r_{\delta_1} - r_{\delta_2}} \\ R_4 \leftarrow T_1^{r_{x_i}} \cdot u^{-r_{\delta_1}} \\ R_5 \leftarrow T_2^{r_{x_i}} \cdot v^{-r_{\delta_2}} \end{cases} \tag{10}$$

f) Use the above values and mes' obtain the challenger c,
$c \leftarrow H(mes', T_1, T_2, T_3, R_1, R_2, R_3, R_4, R_5) \in \mathbb{Z}_p^*$
g) Calculate $s_\alpha, s_\beta, s_{x_i}, s_{\delta_1}, s_{\delta_2}$, where

$$\begin{cases} s_\alpha = r_\alpha + c\alpha \\ s_\beta = r_\beta + c\beta \\ s_{x_i} = r_{x_i} + cx_i \\ s_{\delta_1} = r_{\delta_1} + c\delta_1 \\ s_{\delta_2} = r_{\delta_2} + c\delta_2 \end{cases} \tag{11}$$

h) Finally, combine (T_1, T_2, T_3) and $s_\alpha, s_\beta, s_{x_i}, s_{\delta_1}, s_{\delta_2}$ to obtain the group signature of the message σ , $\sigma \leftarrow (T_1, T_2, T_3, c, s_\alpha, s_\beta, s_{x_i}, s_{\delta_1}, s_{\delta_2})$
4) Verification: After the node v_2 receives the group signature, the node first verifies the security and integrity of the message. The node first reconstructs the signature $(\widehat{R}_1, \widehat{R}_2, \widehat{R}_3, \widehat{R}_4, \widehat{R}_5)$ according to the following steps to perform signature verification. To determine whether a member of the trusted group signs the message:

$$\begin{cases} \widehat{R}_1 \leftarrow u^{s_\alpha}/T_1^c \\ \widehat{R}_2 \leftarrow v^{s_\beta}/T_2^c \\ \widehat{R}_3 \leftarrow e(T_3, g_2)^{s_{x_i}} \cdot e(h, w)^{-s_\alpha - s_\beta} \cdot e(h, g_2)^{-s_{\delta_1} - s_{\delta_2}} \cdot \\ \qquad\qquad (e(T_3, w)/e(g_1, g_2))^c \\ \widehat{R}_4 \leftarrow T_1^{s_{x_i}} \cdot u^{-s_{\delta_1}} \\ \widehat{R}_5 \leftarrow T_2^{s_{x_i}} \cdot v^{-s_{\delta_2}} \end{cases} \tag{12}$$

Then, recalculate from $\widehat{c}$. $\widehat{c} \leftarrow H(mes', T_1, T_2, T_3, \widehat{R_1}, \widehat{R_2}, \widehat{R_3}, \widehat{R_4}, \widehat{R_5})$
The node v_2 gets $\widehat{c}$ and verifies that it is the same as c in the signature σ. If so, the node believes that the information comes from a trusted group member and the information has not been changed. If not, the node v_2 ignores the message.

5) Decrypt message: After verifying the group signature, the encrypted message mes' is received, and the node v_2 uses pwd decryption mes' to obtain the original message

$$t' = H(e(fg_1, pwd)) \tag{13}$$

The original message can be obtained by the following formula

$$message = m_1 \oplus t' \tag{14}$$

$$mes = m_2 \oplus H_1(message) \tag{15}$$

6) Consensus process: After the node v_2 (corresponding v_1) obtains the original message, it will use (2) to update its status accordingly.
7) Node traceability: In many applications, nodes rely on accurate consensus values to achieve data fusion or energy management. Many nodes do not conduct honest data exchange in order to protect their privacy, which will lead to the destruction of consensus results. In this case, the true identity generated by the signature needs to be traced back. MM first verifies the validity of the signature and then calculates A_i by using the following equation $A_i \leftarrow T_3/(T_1^{\xi_1} \cdot T_2^{\xi_2})$ It can search records (A_i, ID_i) to find node identity ID_i.

4   Analysis of Privacy and Security

The two concepts of privacy and security are often used interchangeably in the literature. Among them, Privacy is considered unobservable, and security involves a wider range of issues, including understanding the node state and using the system to cause damage. Both concepts are essentially related to an honest but curious opponent. And our solution can face the dishonest nodes in the network and trace them back.

Privacy protection and communication security are important requirements in the consensus network. In this section, we evaluate from the aspects of privacy and security.

In terms of privacy protection, require opponents to find no the scope of private value, and defines privacy protection as an attacker cannot uniquely determine the value to be protected. Our solution provides anonymity for the node, hides the identity of the node, does not use the real identity for communication within the network, and also provides encryption and decryption algorithms to protect the message. Even if the attacker intercepts the message, he cannot uniquely determine the identity of the node, thereby achieving privacy protection.

As far as security is concerned, our solution achieves the following four aspects:

1) Unforgeability: Only valid nodes within the group can sign on behalf of the group. It is impossible to forge a valid group signature; otherwise, the assumption of SDH will be contradictory. Thereby preventing information tampering and protecting the integrity of the information.

2) Anonymity: In our algorithm, the group signature is $\sigma \leftarrow (T_1, T_2, T_3, c, s_\alpha, s_\beta, s_{x_i}, s_{\delta_1}, s_{\delta_2})$, where $s_\alpha, s_\beta, s_{x_i}, s_{\delta_1}, s_{\delta_2}$ is a random number and T_1, T_2, T_3, c also is a random number, these randomness causes our signature messages to be random. Therefore, the attacker cannot obtain any information of the sending node, so the privacy of the sending node can be prevented from being leaked.

3) Unlinkability: compare two different group signatures $\sigma \leftarrow (T_1, T_2, T_3, c, s_\alpha, s_\beta, s_{x_i}, s_{\delta_1}, s_{\delta_2})$, the random number selected by the interactive node is different, so the T_1, T_2, T_3 of messages sent before and after the same node are different. At the same time, the T_1, T_2, T_3 of messages sent by different nodes are completely independent, so they are not linkable.

4) Traceability: The member administrator can verify the validity of the signature and find the actual information sender through the node identity recovery process. The group signature $\sigma \leftarrow (T_1, T_2, T_3, c, s_\alpha, s_\beta, s_{x_i}, s_{\delta_1}, s_{\delta_2})$ is valid, so the member administrator can first export $A_i \leftarrow T_3/(T_1^{\xi_1} \cdot T_2^{\xi_2})$ to trace the identity of the node.

The safety comparison between this scheme and the schemes [12,13] and [14] is shown in Table 1. The three schemes can meet the privacy requirements of nodes in the average consensus. However, [12,13] and [14] cannot provide unforgeability, and thus cannot guarantee the integrity of the interactive information. Since this scheme introduces a group signature scheme, it provides the ability to trace dishonest nodes. Therefore, this scheme is superior to existing schemes in terms of unforgeability and traceability.

Table 1. Security Comparison.

Schemes	Privacy	Unforgeability	Traceability
[12]	√	×	×
[13]	√	×	×
[14]	√	√	×
this scheme	√	√	√

5 Numerical Simulation

In this section, the simulation shows the consensus results under the confidential interaction scheme. Simulate a network composed of four nodes connected in an undirected graph. Two different node topologies are set as shown in Fig. 2 and Fig. 3 respectively. We set the step size and the initial states of the four nodes are set to 1, 4, 2, and 6, respectively. The four nodes interact under the privacy protection algorithm we proposed, and each node updates the state of the node according to formula (3). The simulation results show that the nodes in the network can reach average consensus under different topologies, corresponding to Fig. 4 and Fig. 5.

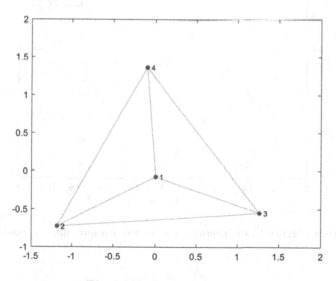

Fig. 2. Network topology a.

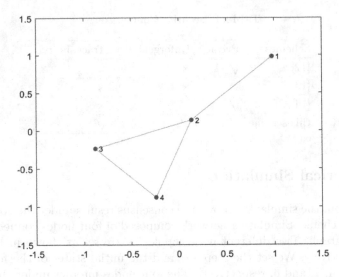

Fig. 3. Network topology b.

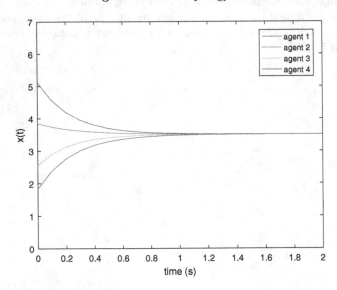

Fig. 4. Convergence to the average consensus(corresponding to topology a).

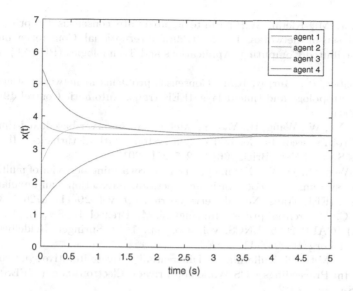

Fig. 5. Convergence to the average consensus(corresponding to topology b).

6   Conclusion

Aiming at the network average consensus problem, this paper proposes a security and privacy protection protocol to protect the security and privacy of nodes. Compared with the existing data confusion-based average consensus scheme, most of the above average consensus methods use real identities for consensus interaction, and we use an improved group signature scheme to apply to the consensus interaction process, which provides anonymity for nodes and thus achieves protection Their initial state guarantees the integrity of the interactive information. This solution can also trace the dishonest nodes that provide false information. Finally, the privacy and security of the algorithm are analyzed and the performance of the algorithm is verified by simulation.

References

1. Olfati-Saber, R., Fax, J.A., Murray, R.M.: Consensus and cooperation in networked multi-agent systems. Proc. IEEE **95**(1), 215–233 (2007)
2. Cao, Y.C., Yu, W.W., Ren, W., Chen, G.R.: An overview of recent progress in the study of distributed multi-agent coordination. IEEE Trans. Ind. Inform. **9**(1), 427–438 (2013)
3. Olfati-Saber, R., Shamma, J.S.: Consensus filters for sensor networks and distributed sensor fusion. In: Proceedings of the 44th IEEE Conference on Decision and Control/European Control Conference (CCDECC), pp. 6698–6703 (2005)
4. Zhao, C., Chen, J., He, J., Cheng, P.: Privacy-preserving consensus-based energy management in smart grids. In: IEEE Transactions on Signal Processing, vol. 66, no. 23, pp. 6162–6176 (2018)

5. O'Connor, M., Kleijn, W.B.: Finite approximate consensus for privacy in distributed sensor networks. In: 2019 20th International Conference on Parallel and Distributed Computing, Applications and Technologies (PDCAT), pp. 75–77 (2019)

6. Olfati-Saber, R., Murray, R.M.: Consensus problems in networks of agents with switching topology and time-delays. IEEE Trans. Automatic Control **49**(9), 1520–1533 (2004)

7. Wei, X., Yu, W., Wang, H., Yao, Y., Mei, F.: An observer-basedfixed-time consensus control for second-order multi-agent systems with disturbances. IEEE Trans. Circuits Syst. II Exp. Briefs, **66**(2), 247–251 (2019)

8. Hu, H., Wen, G., Yu, W., Xuan, Q., Chen, G.: Swarming behavior of multiple euler-lagrange systems with cooperation-competition interactions: an auxiliary system approach. IEEE Trans. Neural Netw. Learn. Syst, vol. **29**(11), 5726–5737 (2018)

9. Dwork, C.: Differential privacy. In: Bugliesi, M., Preneel, B., Sassone, V., Wegener, I. (eds.) ICALP 2006. LNCS, vol. 4052, pp. 1–12. Springer, Heidelberg (2006). https://doi.org/10.1007/11787006_1

10. Huang, Z., Mitra, S, Dullerud, G.: Differentially private iterative synchronous consensus. In: Proceedings CCS Workshop Privacy Electron. Soc. (WPES), Raleigh, NC, USA, July 2012

11. Nozari, E., Tallapragada, P., Cortes, J.: Differentially private average consensus: obstructions, trade-offs, and optimal algorithm design. Automatica **81**(7), 221–231 (2017)

12. Mo, Y., Murray, R.M.: Privacy preserving average consensus. IEEE Trans. Autom. Control **62**(2), 753–765 (2017)

13. Yin, T., Lv, Y., Yu, W.: Accurate privacy preserving average consensus. IEEE Trans. Circ. Syst. II Express Briefs, **67**(4) 690–694 (2020)

14. Ruan, M., Gao, H., Wang, Y.: Secure and privacy-preserving consensus. IEEE Trans. Automatic Control **64**(10), 4035–4049 (2019)

15. Lin, X., Sun, X., Ho, P., Shen, X.: GSIS: a secure and privacy-preserving protocol for vehicular communications. IEEE Trans. Vehicular Technol. **56**(6), 3442–3456 (2007)

16. Boneh, D., Boyen, X., Shacham, H.: Short group signatures. In: Franklin, M. (ed.) CRYPTO 2004. LNCS, vol. 3152, pp. 41–55. Springer, Heidelberg (2004). https://doi.org/10.1007/978-3-540-28628-8_3

17. Chaum, D., van Heyst, E.: Group signatures. In: Davies, D.W. (ed.) EUROCRYPT 1991. LNCS, vol. 547, pp. 257–265. Springer, Heidelberg (1991). https://doi.org/10.1007/3-540-46416-6_22

18. Camenisch, J., Stadler, M.: Efficient group signature schemes for large groups. In: Kaliski, B.S. (ed.) CRYPTO 1997. LNCS, vol. 1294, pp. 410–424. Springer, Heidelberg (1997). https://doi.org/10.1007/BFb0052252

19. Popescu, C.: An efficient ID-based group signature scheme. Studia Univ. Babes-Bolyai, Informatica, vol. XLVII, no. 2, pp. 29–38 (2002)

Privacy-Preserving Scheme Based on Group Signature in Smart Grid

Yalian Wu[✉], Jinbiao Luo, Jiaqi Zhao, and Qingyu Yang

School of Automation and Electronic Information, Xiangtan University,
Xiangtan 411105, Hunan, China
201921002064@smail.xtu.edu.cn

Abstract. Smart grid is a typical cyber-physical fusion system, which combines power system engineering technology and communication information technology. Compared with traditional power grids, smart grids involve more complex interaction processes. The interaction of information poses a certain threat to the privacy of users. However, most of the existing privacy-preserving schemes are not secure and cannot resist internal or external attacks well. In order to solve the existing challenges, this article proposes a privacy-preserving scheme based on group signatures, applying elliptic curve cryptography to ensure user privacy and data integrity and authenticity. We use the ProVerif verification tool to formally analyze and verify the scheme, and compare it with other schemes to prove the safety and correctness of the proposed scheme. At the same time, our solution has good scalability and low computing and storage costs.

Keywords: Smart grid · Privacy-preserving · Safety

1 Introduction

The concept of the smart grid was born in 2006. It uses modern digital technologies such as modern communication technology, smart sensor technology, information technology, and intelligent control technology to achieve energy optimization. Compared with the traditional power grid, the smart grid has the characteristics of bidirectional flow of power and information, and in the case of improving energy utilization and efficiency, the grid not only has stronger security and stability, but also has a high degree of automation and self-repair ability [1].

In order to maintain the instantaneous supply and demand the balance of electric energy, the smart grid needs to regularly collect user's electricity consumption data, and analyze and process it. Therefore, each user will be equipped with a smart meter with real-time measurement and two-way communication functions to collect the user's electricity consumption data, and upload the collected data within a specified time. All electricity consumption data is transmitted to the control center through a secure channel, and the power grid makes decisions after analyzing and processing the data, thereby realizing energy scheduling. Obviously, the user's electricity consumption data contains a lot of sensitive

© Springer Nature Singapore Pte Ltd. 2020
Z. Hao et al. (Eds.): CWSN 2020, CCIS 1321, pp. 209–220, 2020.
https://doi.org/10.1007/978-981-33-4214-9_16

information. If these data are obtained by a malicious attacker, the user's personal information will be disclosed, and the attacker can even infer the user's electricity consumption habits and lifestyle habits based on the electricity consumption data [2]. Therefore, how to protect the user's electricity data while ensuring the efficient operation of the smart grid has always been a research hotspot.

In view of the above problems, this paper proposes a data aggregation scheme combining group signature technology and ECC encryption algorithm to protect the privacy of users. The main contributions of this article are as follows:

(1) Apply group signature technology [14,15] to make the scheme anonymous, unforgeable and traceable. The difficulty of solving discrete logarithms makes it impossible for attackers to obtain the user's identity information, and it is difficult to tamper with and forge the data, ensuring the authenticity and integrity of the data.
(2) The proposed scheme can effectively resist internal and external attacks such as replay attacks, collusion attacks, man-in-the-middle attacks, data forgery, and false data injection attacks, and achieve the purpose of protecting user privacy.
(3) In terms of security, in addition to the theoretical analysis of the proposed scheme, the ProVerif tool is also used for formal verification.

1.1 Related Work

In recent years, many studies on the privacy and security of smart grids have been published to resist various attacks in the process of information interaction, such as replay attacks, false data injection (FDI) attacks, man-in-the-middle attacks, and data forgery. However, most of these schemes often only target one of these attacks, and cannot effectively protect the authenticity and integrity of electricity consumption data and ensure the privacy of users.

In [3], Gong et al. designed a scheme to ensure the privacy, integrity and availability of data based on incentive demand response combined identity recognizable signature and partially blind signature to achieve efficient anonymity. That is to verify the authenticity of the data without revealing the signer's true identity, thereby protecting the user's private information. However, it cannot well resist internal and external attacks such as replay attacks and fake data injection attacks. In [4], Tan et al. proposed a smart grid privacy protection scheme based on pseudonyms, which can resist false data injection attacks. This solution uses the DH key exchange method to authenticate the smart meter, and uses a function constructed by the group key, time, and number of smart meters to generate a virtual ID. Each smart meter uses a virtual ID to send data, so that the energy provider cannot easily associate consumption information with the identified user without exposing the original ID. But it only considers FDI attacks and is vulnerable to other types of attacks. In [5], He et al. proposed a smart grid anonymous key distribution (AKD) scheme using elliptic curve cryptography based on identity cryptography. The proposed solution does not need to go through a trusted third party, provides mutual authentication between participants and ensures the anonymity of smart meters. However, this solution is mainly aimed at external attacks such as replay attacks and intermediate attacks, and cannot resist internal attacks. In [6], Garcia et al. combined Paillier homomorphic encryption and additive secret sharing to construct a protocol for fraud detection with privacy protection, which preserves the privacy of personal energy measurement. The author in [7] proposed an encryption of a single measurement value based on additive homomorphic encryption while allowing the power supplier to access the corresponding set of decrypted values, enabling direct connection and data exchange between the e-commerce and the user, while retaining the latter's Privacy. In [8], Li et al. proposed a distributed incremental data aggregation scheme by constructing an aggregation tree, combined with encryption technology to protect data transmission, so that all meters participate in aggregation without seeing any intermediate results or final results. However, none of the solutions proposed in [6–8] can well resist man-in-the-middle attacks and false data injection attacks, and cannot ensure the authenticity and integrity of the data.

Reference [9] adopts homomorphic encryption technology, bilinear pairing and identity-based signature to protect users' privacy. Although the use of identity-based signatures guarantees the integrity and authenticity of the data, compared with existing solutions, its computation and communication overhead will be relatively large. Reference [10] uses identity-based sequential aggregation signature (IBSAS) to protect users' privacy and ensure the authenticity and integrity of data, but the author of reference [19] proves that using IBSAS does not prevent attackers from forging signatures.

2   Scheme Design

2.1   System Architecture

The scheme proposed in this paper mainly includes four entities, namely SM, Gateway (GW), Control Center (CC), and Trusted Third Party (TTP). As shown in Fig. 1, each user installs a smart meter, and each residential area contains a GW to aggregate the user's electricity consumption data and send it to the CC.

1. SM: Each user in the residential area will install a smart meter, which can detect and collect the power consumption data of the device and send it to the gateway, and at the same time exchange keys with the control center.
2. GW: Validate the data sent by SM, and aggregate the data after verification and transmit it to the control center. With the help of gateways, the control center can reduce the communication overhead and computing costs with users.
3. CC: With powerful computing capabilities, you can verify and decrypt the data in the GW and analyze it. Based on the analysis results, CC makes decisions on the processes of power generation, transmission and distribution, and responds to the dynamic requirements on the demand side.

4. TTP: Generate public and private keys, distribute the public key to SM, and send the private key to CC. In addition, TTP is credible and does not participate in the aggregation process.

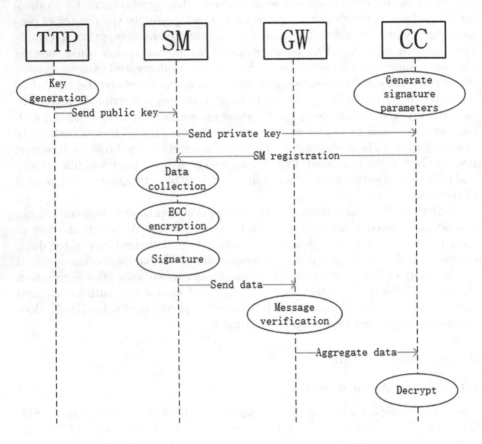

Fig. 1. System architecture of the proposed scheme.

2.2 Proposed Solution

Our proposed scheme introduces the group signature technology on the basis of the ECC encryption algorithm, and at the same time improves the data transmission process, adding a hash operation message verification code (HMAC) and time stamp T to ensure the security of the transmission process. The whole scheme is mainly composed of four phases: initialization, data encryption and signature, signature verification and aggregation, and data decryption.

Initialization Phase. At this stage, smart meters, gateways, control centers, and Trusted third party complete initialization.

1) Key generation

Step 1. TTP selects a large prime number p, and the elliptic curve E on the finite field F_p is $E(a,b) : y^2 = x^3 + ax + b$, A base point $P \in E(F_p)$, where $a, b \in F_p$, $4a^3 + 27b^2 (\mathrm{mod} p) \neq 0$, $E(F_p)$ is the set of all points on curve E, n is the order of P.

Step 2. TTP selects a random number $s_{pri}(s_{pri} < n)$ as the private key, generates a public key $s_{pub} = s_{pri} \cdot P$, and sends the public key to the smart meter in the residential area, and the private key is sent to the control center.

2) Create a group and add members

The group public key and group private key of the group signature are generated by the group center (GC). In the scheme, the control center is the group center.

Step 1. Establishment of the system

(1) The GC randomly selects lp bit prime numbers p' and q' secretly so that $p = 2p' + 1, q = 2q' + 1$ is a prime number and let $n = pq$.
(2) The GC randomly selects $a, a_0, g, h \in QR(n)$.
(3) The GC randomly chooses $x \in Z_{p'q'}$ secretly, let $y = g^x \bmod n$. The group public key is $Y = (n, a, a_0, y, g, h)$, and the private key is $S = \left(p'q', x\right)$.

Step 2. Joining members

(1) User U_i generates a private value $\tilde{x}_i \subset [0, 2^{\lambda_1}]$, a random integer $\tilde{r} \in [0, n^2]$, calculates $C_1 = g^{\tilde{x}_i} h^{\tilde{r}}$, sends C_1 to GC, and proves the correctness of C_1.
(2) GC check $C_1 \in QR(n)$. If yes, the GC randomly selects α_i and $\beta_i \in [0, 2^{\lambda_1}]$ and sends (α_i, β_i) to U_i.
(3) U_i calculates $x_i = 2^{\lambda_1} + (\alpha_i \tilde{x}_i + \beta_i \bmod 2^{2^{\lambda_1}})$, sends $C_2 = a^{x_i} \bmod n$ to GC, and U_i proves to GC:
i. The discrete logarithm of C_2 to a is within Δ, where $\Delta = [2^{\lambda_1} - 2^{\lambda_2}, 2^{\lambda_1} + 2^{\lambda_2}]$.
ii. Knowing that u, v, w makes u within $[-2^{\lambda_1}, 2^{\lambda_1}]$, satisfying:

$$\begin{cases} a^u = C_2/a^{2^{\lambda_1}} \\ C_1^{\alpha_i} g^{\beta_i} = g^u (g^{2^{\lambda_2}}) h^w \end{cases} \tag{1}$$

(4) GC check $C_2 \in QR(n)$. If yes and the above proof is correct, the GC selects a prime number $e_i \in \Gamma$, calculates $A_i = (C_2 a_0)^{1/e_2}$, and sends it to the U_i member certificate (A_i, e_i).
(5) U_i verify as follow:

$$a^{x_i} a_0 = A_i^{e_i} \bmod n \tag{2}$$

Data Encryption and Signing Phase. At this stage, the smart meter uses a public key to encrypt the collected data, and then uses a group certificate to produce a group signature.

1) Data encryption
   The smart meter generates a random integer $r(r < n)$ and encrypts the data m to be transmitted with the public key to obtain the ciphertext $C_s = \{rP, m + rs_{pub}\}$.

2) Signature
(1) Generate a random number $w \in {}_R\{0,1\}^{2lp}$ and calculate $T_1 = A_i y^w$ mod n, $T_2 = g^w$ mod n, $T_3 = g^{e_i} h^w$ mod n.
(2) Randomly select r_1, r_2, r_3, r_4, where,

$$\begin{cases} r_1 \in \pm\{0,1\}^{\varepsilon(\gamma_2+k)} \\ r_2 \in \pm\{0,1\}^{\varepsilon(\lambda_2+k)} \\ r_3 \in \pm\{0,1\}^{\varepsilon(\gamma_1+2lp+k+1)} \\ r_4 \in \pm\{0,1\}^{\varepsilon(2lp+k)} \end{cases} \tag{3}$$

calculate $d_1, d_2, d_3, d_4, c, s_1, s_2, s_3, s_4$ as follow:

$$\begin{cases} d_1 = T_1^{r_1}/(a^{r_2}y^{r_3}) \\ d_2 = T_2^{r_1}/g^{r_3} \\ d_3 = g^{r_4} \\ d_4 = g^{r_1}h^{r_4} \\ c = H(g \parallel h \parallel a_0 \parallel a \parallel T_1 \parallel T_2 \parallel T_3 \parallel d_1 \parallel d_2 \parallel d_3 \parallel d_4 \parallel m) \\ s_1 = r_1 - c(e_i - 2^{\gamma_1}) \\ s_2 = r_2 - c(x_i - 2^{\lambda_1}) \\ s_3 = r_3 - ce_i w \\ s_4 = r_4 - cw \end{cases} \tag{4}$$

(3) Output signature $\sigma_i = (c, s_1, s_2, s_3, s_4, T_1, T_2, T_3)$, sign data $M_i \leftarrow (C_s \parallel T)$ with timestamp T, and send $M_i \parallel \sigma_i (i = 1, 2, ..., n)$ to GW.

Signature Verification and Aggregation Phase. At this stage, the GW performs signature verification on the data sent from the SM. If the message verification is successful, the data is aggregated and sent to the CC.

1) Verify signature
   Calculate

$$c' = H(g \parallel y \parallel a_0 \parallel a \parallel T_1 \parallel T_2 \parallel T_3 \parallel a_0^c T_1^{s_1 - c2^{\gamma_1}}/(a^{s_2 - c2^{\lambda_1}} y^{s_3})) \text{ mod } n \parallel$$
$$(T_2^{s_1 - c2^{\gamma_1}}/g^{s_3}) \text{ mod } n \parallel T_2^c g^{s_4} \text{ mod } n \parallel (T_3^c g^{s_1 - c2^{\gamma_1}} h^{s_4} \text{ mod } n) \parallel m)$$

The condition for successful signature verification is, if and only if $c' = c$, and s_1, s_2, s_3, s_4 satisfying:

$$\begin{cases} s_1 \in \pm\{0,1\}^{\varepsilon(\gamma_2+k)+1} \\ s_2 \in \pm\{0,1\}^{\varepsilon(\lambda_2+k)+1} \\ s_3 \in \pm\{0,1\}^{\varepsilon(\gamma_1+2lp+k+1)+1} \\ s_4 \in \pm\{0,1\}^{\varepsilon(2lp+k)+1} \end{cases} \tag{5}$$

2) Data aggregation

Step 1. After successfully verifying the signature of the smart meter, the gateway will perform the following operations to aggregate the received data:

$$M = \prod_{i=1}^{n} M_i \qquad (6)$$

Step 2. Generate a hash-based message verification code (HMAC) to report the aggregated data to the control center:

$$HMAC = (M, T) \qquad (7)$$

Data Decryption Phase. The control center verifies the integrity of the message through calculation, and after decryption, decrypts the following operations to obtain user data:

$$m + rs_{pub} - s_{pri} rP = m + rs_{pri}P - s_{pri} rP = m \qquad (8)$$

3   Security Analysis

3.1   Anonymity

There is a probabilistic polynomial time algorithm K that produces a safety parameter l_G. For any polynomial time algorithm P, it is computationally infeasible to solve the strong RSA problem. That is, under the strong RSA assumption, the GC sends a certificate (A_i, e_i) to the member U_i, and the signature $(c, s_1, s_2, s_3, s_4, T_1, T_2, T_3)$ output at the signing stage. In solving the problem of discrete logarithms on the elliptic curve, it is impossible for any attacker to calculate T_1, T_2, T_3 from (A_i, e_i), thus ensuring user's anonymity.

3.2   Unforgeability

In the scheme, C_1 is based on the knowledge signature of the representatives of g and h, to ensure that the signer knows his certificate, but does not disclose a little related content. In other words, to calculate a valid authorized signature, the signer needs to have the certificate (A_i, e_i), otherwise it is necessary to solve the discrete logarithm to obtain the certificate, which is computationally infeasible, so the signature is unforgeable to prevent information from being tampered with, The purpose of protecting its integrity and authenticity, thereby resisting false data injection attacks.

3.3   Traceability and Resistance to Joint Attacks

The GC can use the private key to open the group signature to determine the identity of the signer. Group members cannot prevent the opening of a legal group signature. Even if the group members colluded together, a legal group signature that cannot be tracked cannot be generated.

3.4 Resilient to Replay Attack and Man-in-the-middle Attack

If an external attacker uses a replay attack, the original timestamp T will be changed to T'. During the message verification, the original T and are compared, and the message is tampered with, resulting T' in the verification failure, thereby resisting the replay attack. At the same time, if there is a third party C acting as both communication parties for messaging, the two communication parties do not know that they are sharing communication with C, but our solution has the possibility of mutual authentication and message modification, so it can resist man-in-the-middle attacks.

3.5 Formal Verification of Security Using ProVerif

ProVerif is a widely used automated cryptographic protocol simulation tool that supports multiple cryptographic primitives, such as encryption and signature in public key cryptography, hash function and DH key agreement, defined by rewriting rules or equations. It can prove a variety of security attributes, including: confidentiality, authentication, process equivalence, etc. The verification process is as follows: query the security attributes that need to be proven in the protocol, and when the protocol has the security attributes inquired, the query result outputs true, otherwise, it outputs false. The protocol proposed in this article has been implemented in the ProVerif simulation tool, and the query results are shown in Fig. 2. In the figure, the first three respectively show that the group public key Y and private keys sk1 and sk2 cannot be obtained by the attacker, which proves the correctness and confidentiality of the proposed scheme and ensures that the user's electricity data is difficult to obtain by others. The last two output results show that our scheme can resist replay attacks and simulated attacks.

4 Comparative Analysis

4.1 Performance Analysis

In the size of the key, the 160-bit ECC algorithm has the same security strength as the 1024-bit DH, RSA, DSA and other algorithms. Therefore, a smaller key size requires less storage space, lower power consumption, and more bandwidth and computational cost savings.

On the Windows 10 Professional operating system with 4.0 GB RAM and Intel Core i5 3.30 GHz processor, as described in [20], the execution time of different calculation methods is shown in Table 1. Among them, t_{sed}, t_{aed}, t_m, t_{mul}, t_{add}, t_h, t_H respectively represent symmetric encryption or decryption, asymmetric encryption or decryption, modular power, point multiplication, point addition, hash operation, HMAC operation.

According to the execution time given in Table 1, our scheme is compared with the scheme proposed in [12,13,16–18] in terms of computational cost. As shown in Table 2, in terms of calculation cost, our scheme is second only to literature [18] and [13]. In addition, Fig. 3 describes the computational cost of different numbers of key agreements.

```
Verification summary:

Query not attacker(Y[]) is true.

Query not attacker(sk1[]) is true.

Query not attacker(sk2[]) is true.

Query inj-event(endU1) ==> inj-event(startU1) is true.

Query inj-event(endU2) ==> inj-event(startU2) is true.
```

Fig. 2. The verification result from the ProVerif tool.

Table 1. Execution time of different calculation methods

t_{sed}	t_{aed}	t_m	t_{mul}	t_{add}	t_h	t_H
0.0046 ms	3.85 ms	3.85 ms	2.226 ms	0.0288 ms	0.0023 ms	0.0046 ms

Table 2. Comparison of calculation costs

Scheme	Operations	Computational cost (ms)
[16]	$4t_{sed} + 6t_m + 2t_h + 2t_H$	23.1322
[17]	$4t_m + 4t_{aed} + 2t_H$	30.8092
[18]	$2t_{aed} + 4t_{sed} + 2t_H + 2t_{mul}$	12.175
[12]	$8t_{mul} + 4t_{add} + 8t_h$	17.9416
[13]	$5t_{mul} + 5t_H + t_{add}$	11.1818
Ours	$2t_{aed} + 2t_m + 2t_H$	15.4092

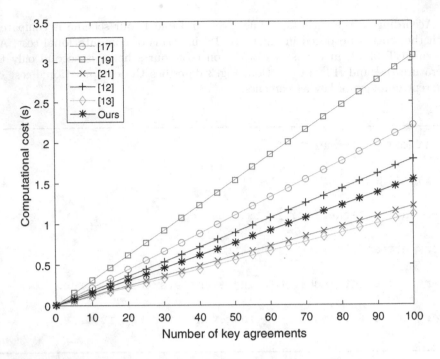

Fig. 3. The computational costs for different number of key agreements.

4.2   Security Analysis

Our scheme is compared with the scheme proposed in [3,9,11–13] in terms of security. It can be seen from Table 3, the scheme proposed in this paper has better performance in security.

Table 3. Security comparison

	[3]	[9]	[11]	[12]	[13]	Ours
Anonymity	√	×	×	×	×	√
Resilient to replay attacks	×	√	√	√	√	√
Resilient to man-in-the-middle	×	√	√	√	√	√
Resilient to FDI attacks	×	√	√	×	×	√
Resilient to data forgery	×	√	√	√	√	√
Traceability	×	×	×	×	×	√
Authentication	√	√	√	√	√	√

5   Conclusion

Privacy security is an important point that cannot be ignored in the smart grid. In this paper, we propose a data aggregation scheme for smart grid. The scheme uses group signature technology and ECC encryption algorithm to protect the integrity and authenticity of data, and can resist various types of internal and external attacks, providing a strong guarantee for the privacy of users and the security of data. In addition, under the condition of not changing the group's public key, the signature length, signature algorithm, verification algorithm and opening algorithm will not increase with the increase of the number of group members, which makes our scheme have good scalability.

References

1. Morello, R., Mukhopadhyay, S., Liu, Z., et al.: Advances on sensing technologies for smart cities and power grids: a review. IEEE Sens. J. **17**, 7596–7610 (2017). https://doi.org/10.1109/JSEN.2017.2735539
2. Mohamed Amine, F., Leandros, M., Helge, J., et al.: A systematic review of data protection and privacy preservation schemes for smart grid communications. Sustain. Cities Soc. **38**, 806–835 (2017)
3. Gong, Y.M., Cai, Y., Guo, Y.X., et al.: A privacy-preserving scheme for incentive-based demand response in the smart grid. IEEE Trans. Smart Grid **7**, 1304–1313 (2016)
4. Tan, X.B., Zheng, J.Y., Zou, C., et al.: Pseudonym-based privacy-preserving scheme for data collection in smart grid. Int. J. Ad Hoc Ubiquit. Comput. **22**, 48–56 (2016)
5. Wang, L.N., Wang, H.Q., Khan, M., He, D.B.: Lightweight anonymous key distribution scheme for smart grid using elliptic curve cryptography. IET Commun. **10**, 1795–1802 (2016)
6. Garcia, F.D., Jacobs, B.: Privacy-friendly energy-metering via homomorphic encryption. In: Cuellar, J., Lopez, J., Barthe, G., Pretschner, A. (eds.) STM 2010. LNCS, vol. 6710, pp. 226–238. Springer, Heidelberg (2011). https://doi.org/10.1007/978-3-642-22444-7_15
7. Felix, G.M., Christoph, S., Osman, U., et al.: Do not snoop my habits: preserving privacy in the smart grid. IEEE Commun. Mag. **50**, 166–172 (2012)
8. Li, F.J., Luo, B., Liu, P.: Secure and privacy-preserving information aggregation for smart grids. IJSN **6**, 28–39 (2011)
9. Li, H., Lin, X., Yang, H., Liang, X., et al.: EPPDR: an efficient privacy-preserving demand response scheme with adaptive key evolution in smart grid. IEEE Trans. Parallel Distrib. Syst. **25**, 2053–2064 (2014). https://doi.org/10.1109/TPDS.2013.124
10. Hur, J.B., Koo, D., Shin, Y.: Privacy-preserving smart metering with authentication in a smart grid. Appl. Sci. **5**, 1503–1527 (2015)
11. Badra, M., Zeadally, S.: Lightweight and efficient privacy-preserving data aggregation approach for the smart grid. Ad Hoc Netw. **64**, 32–40 (2017)
12. Abbasinezhad-Mood, D., Nikooghadam, N.M.: Design and hardware implementation of a security-enhanced elliptic curve cryptography based lightweight authentication scheme for smart grid communications. Future Gener. Comput. Syst. **84**, 47–57 (2018). https://doi.org/10.1016/j.future.2018.02.034

13. Mahmood, K., Chaudhry, S., Naqvi, H., et al.: An elliptic curve cryptography based lightweight authentication scheme for smart grid communication. Future Gener. Comput. Syst. **81**, 557–565 (2017). https://doi.org/10.1016/j.future.2017.05.002
14. Ateniese, G., Camenisch, J., Joye, M., Tsudik, G.: A practical and provably secure coalition-resistant group signature scheme. In: Bellare, M. (ed.) CRYPTO 2000. LNCS, vol. 1880, pp. 255–270. Springer, Heidelberg (2000). https://doi.org/10.1007/3-540-44598-6_16
15. Kong, W., Shen, J., Vijayakumar, P., et al.: A practical group blind signature scheme for privacy protection in smart grid. J. Parallel Distrib. Comput. **136**, 29–39 (2019)
16. Mahmood, K., Chaudhry, S., Naqvi, H., Shon, T., et al.: A lightweight message authentication scheme for smart grid communications in power sector. Comput. Electr. Eng. **52**, 114–124 (2016)
17. Sule, R., Katti, R.S., Kavasseri, R.G.: A variable length fast message authentication code for secure communication in smart grids. In: 2012 IEEE Power and Energy Society General Meeting, pp. 1–6 (2012)
18. Zhang, L.P., Tang, S.Y., Luo, H.: Elliptic curve cryptography-based authentication with identity protection for smart grids. PloS One **11**, 1334–1345 (2016)
19. Hwang, J.Y., Yung, M., Lee, D.H.: Universal forgery of the identity-based sequential aggregate signature scheme. In: Proceedings of the 4th International Symposium on Information, Computer, and Communications Security, January 2009, pp. 157–160 (2019). https://doi.org/10.1145/1533057.1533080
20. Yanik, T., Kilinc, H.: A survey of SIP authentication and key agreement schemes. IEEE Commun. Surv. Tutor. **16**, 1005–1023 (2014)

Perception and Positioning

Device-Free Activity Recognition: A Survey

Mingzhi Pang[1], Xu Yang[1], Jing Liu[1], Peihao Li[1], Faren Yan[1],
and Pengpeng Chen[1,2(✉)]

[1] School of Computer Science and Technology, China University of Mining
and Technology, Xuzhou 221116, China
{MingzPang,yang_xu,jingl,lph,08183005,chenp}@cumt.edu.cn
[2] China Mine Digitization Engineering Research Center,
Ministry of Education, Xuzhou 221116, China

Abstract. With the increasing number of WIFI hotspots and video surveillance equipment deployed, device-free activity recognition based on video and WIFI signals has attracted widespread attention. In order to better understand the current device-free human motion recognition work and the future development trend of device-free perception, this paper provides a detailed review of existing video-based and WIFI-based related work. Meanwhile, the principle of device-free activity recognition is deeply analyzed. We have compared the existing work in different aspects. Finally, by analyzing the shortcomings of the existing methods, the future research direction of device-free motion recognition is proposed.

Keywords: Device-free human activity recognition · Video · WIFI

1 Introduction

With the rapid development of computer science, computing technology is changing from machine centered mode to human centered mode. Its core idea is to realize the perception and reasoning of human body behavior by machine and make humans become a part of the computing link, so human behavior perception and analysis technology are of vital importance.

In fact, since the past few decades, people have been constantly creating new technologies to achieve more effective perception and analysis of human behavior. Gesture recognition gait recognition action emotion recognition, and behavior analysis technology has been gradually applied to daily life. Recently, human activity recognition has attracted widespread attention, and many researchers are doing in-depth research for the reason that it can be applied to various applications such as human-computer interaction [1], elderly monitoring [2], gesture control [3], and security surveillance [4].

This work was supported by the National Natural Science Foundation of China under Grant 51774282 and Grant 51874302.

For human activity recognition, many solutions have been proposed previously, and they can be categorized into two classes: device-based activity recognition and device-free activity recognition. For device-based activity recognition methods, users are required to carry devices such as mobile phones or special sensors. The disadvantages of this approach include that it is not convenient for the user to carry the device, and it is expensive. Therefore, many researchers shift their attention to device-free activity recognition in recent years. This kind of method can complete action recognition without any device carried by users.

Device-free human activity recognition methods can be boiled down into two categories: video-based and WIFI-based methods. Video-based methods have been studied for long because of its intuitiveness [5]. Deep convolutional neural network is used to extract temporal-spatial information [6–8]. This method achieves good recognition accuracy. However, not every place and scene is suitable for the camera. For example, cameras are hardly used or forbidden in places where privacy has the highest priority. Cameras are also nearly useless in places with dim light. As a result, key information could not be detected by means of common cameras in these places, and corresponding solutions are needed. That is one reason for WIFI-based activity recognition attracting attention.

As early as 2000, Bahl et al. [9] proposed Radar, a system for indoor positioning based on Received Signal Strength (RSS), which was the first time WIFI Signal was used for perception. In 2012, Chetty et al. [10] realized non-line-of sight perception of human movement by collecting WIFI signals and analyzing the Doppler frequency shift. WiVi [11], WiSee [12], and other systems realize gesture recognition based on WIFI signals without any sensors. In 2011, Halperin et al. [13] published the CSI Tool to extract Channel state information from commercial network CARDS, which greatly facilitates the acquisition of CSI information on commercial WFI devices, making it a new trend to use more granular CSI information for perception. Subsequently, human behavior perception technology based on WIFI signals developed rapidly, and a series of applications such as sleep detection, fall detection, gesture recognition, WIFI imaging, lip recognition, crowd detection, aerial touch, daily behavior detection, breath and heartbeat detection, gait recognition, emotion detection, human-computer interaction trajectory tracking appeared.

Recently, few surveys of the latest activity recognition methods have been presented, especially in the field of device-free. In this paper, we present a comprehensive survey about device-free activity recognition methods which differs from other surveys:

(i) As far as we know, this survey is the first one that systematically reviews the problem of device-free activity recognition based on WIFI and video.

(ii) We analyzed the principle in the depth of device-free activity recognition and made a comprehensive summary of state-of-the-art methods designed for device-free activity recognition system. In addition, we compare the existing methods in depth.

(iii) The future research directions are given by analyzing the disadvantages of the existing methods.

The remainder of this paper is organized as follows. Section 2 introduces the corresponding processes and fundamental principles of video-based and WIFI-based methods. Section 3 and Sect. 4 describe in detail video-based action recognition methods and WIFI-based action recognition methods, respectively. Section 5 introduces the future trend, and we concluded this paper in Sect. 6.

2 Categories and Principles

2.1 Categories

We divide device-free human action recognition methods into two categories: video-based and WIFI-based, as is shown in Fig. 1. Video-based action recognition can be summarized into the following four parts: inputting video, extracting action features, classifying actions, and outputting results. In this paper, we classified recognition methods by representation methods. First of all, we divide it into two parts: holistic representation and local representation, according to its focus on an entire human shape or a part of it. For the holistic representation, it includes space-time volume, optical flow, and deep neural networks. There are many methods based on deep networks, which can be further divided into four groups, including Spatio-temporal networks, multiple stream networks, generative models, and temporal coherency networks. Local representations can be divided into two parts: space-time features and space-time trajectories, according to the ways of extracting interesting points and describing the features around the interesting points. For the WIFI-based methods, we group them into two parts: Fine-grained methods and Coarse-grained methods, based on the level of effective human action imposed on the signals. For example, for the action of smoking [14], the movement of limbs of bodies is relatively large, resulting in the huge change of the magnitudes of CSI, so it is a coarse-grained method. For lip reading [15], it causes a minute change of the features of the signals, and it is a fine-grained method.

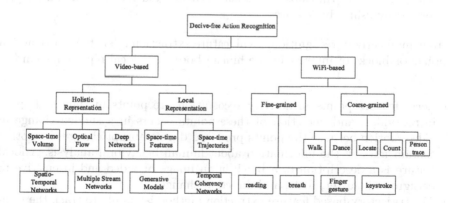

Fig. 1. Taxonomy of device-free human action recognition methods.

2.2   The Principles of Video-Based Action Recognition

According to what the action recognition process focuses on, entire human shape, or a part of it, it is divided into holistic representation and local representation. The holistic representation has the following methods.

(1) The Spatio-temporal method treats the input as a 3D (XYT) volume, the human behavior as a set of features in a 3D volume in the space-time dimension. The video volume is connected by the successive image frames along the time axis. The essence of space-time volume is that it compares the obscure activity record with the existing volume for identification.

(2) The optical flow method takes temporal information into consideration. It tracks the motion of pixels in the image by calculating the motion vector of them, to establish the optical flow field of the entire image. Then the instantaneous velocity and direction of moving objects can be observed and analyzed. If there is no moving target, the motion vector of all pixels will be continuously changing. If there is a moving object, there will be a relative motion between the target and the background. Because of the relative motion, the velocity vector of the moving object will be different from that of the background. With the difference, the moving object can be detected and calculated.

(3) The Deep learning method represents the category or feature of an attribute by combining low-level features to form a more abstract form of high-level data features. Deep learning algorithms enable the computer to automatically learn from samples to characterize the more essential features of these samples. First, the video image data is inputted into the deep convolutional neural network, and the information is transmitted through the neurons by the forward propagation method, and then the back propagation-based method is used. The method trains the neural network and optimizes the parameters of it to achieve great performance. The recognition model can automatically learn the features representing the actions from the video image data, and the subsequent classification and recognition can be performed by using the features.

In human activity recognition, local feature extraction refers to the extraction of points or blocks of interest in the human body. The local representation has two ways.

(1) Local feature points in activity recognition are points in time and space in the video, and detection of these points occurs in a sudden change in video motion because the points produced during abrupt changes in motion contain most of the information about human behavioral analysis. A local feature is a description of a block in an image or video and insensitive to background clutter, scale, and direction changes.

(2) The trajectory-based feature extraction method is mainly to track the position of the joint and thus perceive the human motion. The trajectory is established by joint points and points of interest. Different representations and comparing calculations coordinate the trajectories for action recognition.

2.3 The Principles of WIFI-Based Action Recognition

For the WIFI-based methods, human action recognition can be achieved based on WIFI for the fact that human bodies can affect nearby wireless signals, and WIFI signals can convey the information. Specifically, the signal sent by the sender (such as a router) will be blocked by a barrier. If the barrier was a static object, it would cause reflections, while dynamic objects like humans would cause scattering. Thus, human bodies can cause additional propagation paths, which can be represented by the Channel State Information (CSI), the time series of the Channel Frequency Responses (CFRs), describing the way a signal propagates from the transmitter to the receiver and able to be collected from the physical layer of existing WIFI devices. The CFR of a sub-carrier with frequency f at time t can be modeled as the sum of static CFR and dynamic CFR:

$$H\left(f,t\right) = e^{-j2\pi\Delta ft}\left(H_s(f) + H_d(f,t)\right) \tag{1}$$

where $H_s(f)$ is the sum of static CFRs and $H_d(f, t)$ is the sum of dynamic CFRs. With unique CSI signatures resulting from different signal scattering caused by different human actions, human action recognition can be achieved.

3 Video-Based Action Recognition

In recent years, HAR has attracted widespread attention in the field of computer vision, and many people are researching it. The reason is simply that human action recognition can be applied to numerous promising applications, such as security surveillance, video retrieval, and human-machine interaction, to name only a few.

The process of video-based human action recognition can be summed up into four parts: inputting videos, representing the actions, classifying the actions, and outputting the results. In this paper, we focus on the advanced researches and group them according to their methods of representation. First, we categorize them into two groups according to the fact that whether they use the shape and motion of the entire human body as the action descriptor or just parts of the human body. Then, we give them a more refined classification. For the reason that deep networks based methods are totally different, they can be further classified into four groups, Spatio-Temporal Network, Multiple Stream Network, Generative Models, and Temporal Coherency Networks.

3.1 Holistic Representation

Holistic Representation exploits the appearance and motion information of the whole human body as a representation, and it is easy to actualize for the reason that it does not need to detect and follow the tracks of any part of the body or joint. In this section, we review the recent progress in holistic representation method and classify them into three categories: Space-time Volume, Optical Flow, and Deep Networks.

Space-Time Volume. Space-time Volume based approaches employ the entire 3D volume as feature or template to match new action videos, which need to be recognized. Then the classification can be achieved. It mainly utilizes the outline of the human body to represent the body and movement. To get the outline, effort has been made to get rid of the noise and meaningless background information.

Qian et al. (2010) [16] presented a system framework to recognize activities. It firstly segmented motion targets by non-parameter background subtraction method and then the contour coding of the motion energy image (CCMEI) was extracted as a new type of global features. SVM multi-class classifier was used to classify feature points. Kim et al. (2010) [17] also extended MHI and defined the accumulated motion image (AMI), the average of image differences. Then the AMI was resized to a sub-image which was used to generate a rank matrix. Local windows, close to the query action spatially and temporally, were detected as candidates by computing the distances between the rank matrix of the query action video and that of all local windows using L1-norms. Silhouettes and skeletons were also taken into consideration for action recognition. Fang et al. (2010) [18] proposed HAR system based on the human silhouette, which considering both the spatial information and the motion trajectory. For this system, a novel TVTL framework was presented to combine spatial information with three kinds of temporal information, LTM, DTM, and TTM. Ziaeefard and Ebrahimnezhad (2010) [19] proposed cumulative skeletonized images to represent each video sequence and constructed a normalized-polar histogram based on it. By using two linear multi-class SVM to hierarchically classify, human actions can be recognized. The classification experienced a process from coarseness to meticulosity by using whole bins of the histogram and the special bins. Similarly, Vemulapalli [20] proposed a new skeletal representation. They used rotations and translations in 3-D space to model the body, lying in the Lie group. Then, human action could be represented as curves in this Lie group. The main drawback of space-time volume is that when multiple people are present in the picture, the recognition action is very difficult.

Optical Flow. Optical flow based approaches utilize optical flow to represent actions for its capability of reacting the information of actions, free of segmentation of the foreground and no need of background subtraction, compared with Space-time Volume based method.

Mahbub et al. [21] used optical flow and RANSAC to detect the motion of humans. The position of the person is first determined horizontally and vertically. And then, a small rectangular area where the person acted was indicated by means of RANSAC from optical flow and divided into multiple smaller blocks. Through the percentage of change in optical flow between frames within each block, actions can be represented and classified easily. Holte et al. [22] combined 3D optical flow into motion vector fields. For 3D optical flow, it was constructed from eight weighted 2D flow fields. For 3D motion vector fields, they were represented by 3D-MC and HMC. Then they were classified by normalized correlation.

The classification had the advantage that it considered the speed variations of different actors when acting the same action.

Deep Networks. Unlike the static image recognition which needs to learn about the static features in an image, action recognition needs to learn about dynamic features between frames and frames. Since video is much bigger than the image, the algorithm is more complex and time-consuming, which makes it difficult to work out an effective way to recognize human action. Different from the traditional methods which rely on manual and well-designed features, deep learning methods learning automatically by building deep learning networks. This part is to discuss deep networks that have been widely used in action recognition from videos. Furthermore, we divide these deep networks into the following four categories, namely, Spatio-temporal Networks, Multiple Stream Networks, Generative Models, and Temporal Coherency Networks. We will discuss these categories in detail and make comparisons and contrasts of these networks.

(1) Spatio-temporal Networks
Convolutional Neural Network (CNN) simulates the visual mechanism of human brain processing. It makes the most of the information in the image and reduces the search space of the network at the same time, using 'pooling' and 'weight-sharing' operations (Smaitha Herath et al.). By analyzing the structure and principle of CNN, we can see that the lower layers learn low-level features, while the upper layers learn high-level semantics features (Zeiler and Fergus, [5]), which makes convolutional networks work commonly as the generic feature extractors.

In order to achieve action recognition by using deep networks, Du et al. [23] introduced deep 3-D convolutional networks (3D ConvNets), and their experiment shows that 3D ConvNets can process spatiotemporal information better than 2D ConvNets. 3D ConvNets extract features from spatial and temporal dimensions at the same time, requiring an army of multi-view training data, which is costly and hard to get. Therefore, Rahmani et al. [24] proposed a method to generate such data rather than spend money and time collecting it. They synthesized a 3D human body model and fit it to captured real motion data. Then, massive training data was available with different poses from various viewpoints. And Sun et al. [25] proposed a factorized spatiotemporal convolutional network (FstCN), able to process 3D signals with much efficiency. Different from traditional 3D convolution kernel learning, it was composed of a process of learning 2D spatial kernels and learning 1D temporal kernels in the spatial and temporal convolutional layers relatively.

To make full use of temporal information, people investigated various fusion schemes. In the early fusion, Ji et al. (2013) [26] use the network, which is made up of a set of frames adjacent to each other. In the late fusion, Karpathy et al. [27] extend the connectivity of a CNN in the time domain by studying multiple methods to make full use of local spatiotemporal information. In their paper, they introduced slow fusion, trying to get more from temporal information. In slow fusion, the network receives consecutive images of a video through a set of layers and then processed the temporal information by fully connected layers. Ng et al. (2015) learned more about temporal pooling and suggested that it was much more efficient to use max-pooling in the temporal domain. Liu et al. [28] introduced Spatiotemporal-CNN, which could achieve action recognition indirectly through the transformation between two adjacent frames. Rahmani et al. [24] proposed a new representation. That is a group sparse Fourier Temporal Pyramid, which can solve the problem of depth noise and time misalignments.

Recently, it is shown that long-term RNN models can map inputs to corresponding outputs and both can be variable length. It can also process complex temporal dynamics. As its name suggests, RNN uses a feedback loop to model the dynamics. We usually feed the RNN block an external signal $x^t \in R^d$ and produce an output $z^t \in R^m$ based on its hidden-state $h^t \in R^r$ by

$$h^{(t)} = \sigma(W_x x^{(t)} + W_h h^{(t-1)}) \tag{2}$$

$$z^{(t)} = \sigma(W_z h^{(t)}) \tag{3}$$

Where $W_x \in R^{r \times d}$, $W_h \in R^{r \times r}$ and $W_z \in R^{m \times r}$. It is obvious that RNN is a realization of the LDS (Huang et al.). Since the training of RNN is not easy because of exploding gradient, LSTM constrains the state and outputs the RNN cell through gates.

(2) Multiple Stream Networks
Biologists and psychologists have done many experiments on visual perception. In the process of visual information processing, the human visual perception is not transmitted as it is but is processed in conjunction with input information and then output to other neurons. In general, different visual information is processed through the ventral and dorsal pathways. The ventral pathway is mainly responsible for receiving stimulation information. The generation of visual awareness requires the joint participation of visual awareness and the two pathways, ventral and dorsal. These two pathways complement each other, interdependent, and interact. Inspired by this, we can divide action recognition networks into two combined parts, one is used on appearance-based information, and the other is used on motion-related.

Simonyan et al. [29] introduced a multiple-stream convolutional neural network, named two-stream network, which used two parallel networks to recognize the action. In their multiple-stream network, the spatial stream network processes raw video frames while the optical flow fields are inputted into the temporal part. The two networks are combined with soft-max scores. Similarily, Feichtenhofer et al. [30] studied several ways to fuse multiple streams, both spatially and temporally. Their study shows that compared with the soft-max layer, the spatial and temporal network can be better fused at a convolution layer. They can be fused with fewer parameters and will not sacrifice performance.

Wang et al. [31] further optimized the two-stream method. Wang et al. introduced a trajectory-pooled deep convolutional descriptor (TDD), which using the Fisher vector to trace over convolutional feature maps of the two-stream network, and Wu et al. add an audio signal to the third stream and introduce a multi-stream frame.

(3) Deep Generative Models

Thinking about the ever-increasing videos available on the Internet, if we could find a way to learn the underlying distribution of data accurately and predict its future without labels for training, we could make better use of a large number of videos, especially in videos where annotating data is expensive. Compared with the Spatio-temporal networks, deep generative architecture does not require labels for training in nature. However, the unsupervised matter is beyond imagination, and we will review the famous examples of deep generative models in this part.

Inspired by the LDS model of Doretto et al. [32], Yan et al. (2014) [33] proposed a set of deep auto-encoders, Dynencoder, with one at the bottom and a few at the top. Dynencoder generates hidden states from the inputs via the bottom part and then encodes the dynamic of state transition overtime via the top part. Then Srivastava et al. [34] introduced the LSTM auto-encoder model, which uses a single or multiple encoder LSTMs to perform reconstructing the input sequence, predicting the future sequence and so on.

In order to conquer the difficulties in training models, Goodfellow et al. [35] proposed a new model named Generative Adversarial Nets (GANs). It trains two opposing networks simultaneously, one is a generator, and the other is a discriminator. The former aims to generate a picture, close to the real image, and the latter estimates the picture and determine whether it is generated or not. Mathieu et al. [36] trained a convolutional network and proposed three different and complementary feature learning methods in order to solve the problem of picture frame blur caused by Mean Squared Error loss function. One of the three methods is an adversarial training method, and it was used to complete the frame prediction purpose of unsupervised training.

(4) Temporal Coherency Networks

A temporal coherency is a form of weak supervision, and the relationship between spatial cues and time cues is strong since it is action. Here we would like to introduce some concepts that have been used by others. If the frames of a sequence are in the correct order, then we will call it coherent. If the input is the ordered and disordered sequences, considered as positive and negative samples respectively, then the deep learning model would learn the temporal coherency. Misra et al. [37] learn an unsupervised representation from the raw spatiotemporal signals in videos by using a CNN in order to recognize the action. In order to obtain classification, Wang et al. split the action into two phases: the state of the surroundings before the action happens and the state after the action. They introduced a Siamese Network that can transform human action on a high-level feature space as well.

Fernando et al. [38] suggest using rank pooling to capture the temporal evolution of a sequence for its efficiency. They presented hierarchical rank pooling to encode videos and capture the dynamic features for activity recognition.

3.2 Local Representation

Local Representation extracts interest points from videos and describes the feature information around the interest points. It often uses the shape and motion of parts of the human body as the action descriptor.

Space-Time Features. Approaches based on space-time features take the video as space-time volume data and utilize the response function to detect the position and the scale of space-time volume to extract response points. Jones et al. [39] used a Bag of Words model based on space-time interest points and described it with the gradient + PCA method. Then, they used ABRS-SVM to retrieve human actions. Sadek et al. [40] proposed an approach to recognizing human activity on the basis of keypoint detection. They described the local feature points through the temporal self-similarities, which was defined on the fuzzy log-polar histogram. Then, the SVM was used to recognize human action. Ikizler-Cinbis and Sclaro [41] combined features of people, objects, which were extracted densely, and the actions can be accurately identified with features of scene and objects serving as a complement to person features. They used a MIL-based framework to obtain the relationships between them. YM Lui et al. [42] also made efforts to find interest points. They used a tangent bundle to represent videos and then factorized the Spatio-temporal data to a set of tangent spaces by HOSVD. What is novel in their paper is that they characterized the action differences and classified them.

Space-Time Trajectories. Space-time trajectory methods emerged for that tracking joint positions can provide enough information for action recognition. The trajectories are generally obtained on the basis of interest points.

Wang et al. [43] introduced a method to extract dense trajectories. They tracked densely sampled points due to the displacement information achieved from an optical flow field. It also successfully overcame the problem of camera motion. Furthermore, they bettered the above approach to estimating camera motion [36] by SURF descriptors and optical flow field. Different from the approach Wang presented to tackling with camera motion, Jiang et al. [44] used both global and local reference points in order to characterize complex motion patterns and model the motion relationships.

3.3 Comparison of Video-Based Algorithms

Generally speaking, video-based human action recognition is usually archived by two steps, future representation and the understanding and recognition of actions. There are many challenges in HAR, such as the differences in data within the classes and between classes, the processing of data that get in different conditions. To conquer these challenges, in the early time, people use space-time volume [16–20,38,45,46] and optical flow [21,22] that we have introduced previously to modeling human body, and get quite good recognition rate in uniform background. However, the human body has a certain flexibility, and the recognition ability can be decreased on the data with a complex background. The local representation approaches, such as space-time futures methods [39–42] and space-time trajectories method [43,44,47] can process the data with complex background.

However, these traditional approaches, such as space-time volume method and optical flow method, or the local representation method, has high requirements for the video shooting condition. In recent years, with the emergence of deep learning, people start to apply these networks to human action recognition. Since it meets the mechanization of humans to know the world, these networks can preserve some structure, which makes it useful for recognition and analysis. What's more, deep learning networks [5,23–38,45,46,48–51] does not require any artificial intervention, it can be used to process the data sets directly. But most of these networks need a great deal of data and a long time training which requires optimization as soon as possible.

4 WIFI-Based Action Recognition

These video-based methods we had introduced previously had some disadvantages when it was used to achieve activity recognition. Lighting conditions and the presence of obstructions will affect the recognizing of human behavior. In some cases, the application of video may infringe people's privacy. Considering these disadvantages, people try to recognize actions by using the signals that get from WIFI. In this section, we will introduce the WIFI-based method briefly. According to the actions that we are recognizing, we divide WIFI-based methods into two parts, fine-grained and coarse-grained.

4.1 Fine-Grained

Fine-grained methods focus on the minute change of CSI to detect particular human actions, like talking and walking as follows.

Wang G et al. [15] designed WiHear to achieve lip-reading, which exploited partial multipath effects to detect fine-grained radio reflections from mouth movements and extract talking information from it. By analyzing it through its radiometric characteristics, lip-reading can be achieved. Chang lai Du et al. [52] also introduced a system to achieve lip-reading, WiTalk, with a distinct context-free character, which means that the CSI profiles needn't be reconstructed for a different user, location or multipath environment. Specifically, by means of signal processing techniques, WiTalk generated CSI spectrograms, which can be used to extract features by calculating the contours of it. With the DTW algorithm as a classification method, lip-reading can be achieved.

They used signal processing techniques to generate CSI spectrograms and extracted features from that, just like what Chang lai Du et al. [52] did. To better characterize the walking pattern, they removed imperfection in CSI spectrograms with autocorrelation on the contours of the torso reflection. For the promising application, keystroke, Ali K et al. [53] firstly proposed a system called WiKey. With the special movement of users' hands and fingers when they typed the key, the exclusive pattern of the CSI values can be generated. So, the keystroke of each key would have relative unique multipath signals, which could be utilized to recognize keystrokes. For the breath detection system, D Fan et al. [54] designed a respiratory rhythm-detection system, S-Breath system, which is noncontact and economically viable. The system consists of two-part: data extraction module and data processing module. It obtains 30 subcarriers by using S-band sensing, which can be described as:

$$H = [H(f_1), H(f_2), ..., H(f_N)]^T, i \in [1, 30] \tag{4}$$

Here, H can be seen as channel matrix various sensors. Every wireless channel can be described as follow, which shows the amplitude and phase of a subcarrier:

$$H(f_i) = \|H(f_i)\| \, e^{j \sin|\angle H(f_i)|} \tag{5}$$

$\|H(f_i)\|$ represented the amplitude and $\angle H(f_i)$ represented the phase of the subcarrier. And then, the system recorded the minute variations caused by breathing in the form of wireless data, which was expressed as a sequence:

$$H = [H_1, H_2, H_3, ..., H_k] \tag{6}$$

Where k was the total number of received data packets. By data processing like outlier removal and noise filtering, and breath rate estimation, respiratory rhythm detection could be achieved.

Gu et al. [55] presented a wireless channel data-driven sleep monitoring system leveraging commercial WIFI devices. The key idea behind Sleepy is that the energy characteristics of wireless channels follow a Gaussian mixture model (GMM) based on long-term cumulative channel data. Les S et al. [56] presented a new low-cost method for breathing and heart measurement using commercial WIFI devices. They exploited the amplitude of signal waves to represent breathing and heartbeat with the periodic and minute chest movements. Then, using the DTW algorithm to detect changes in signal pattern, breathing, and heart measurement can be achieved.

Li et al. [57] proposed WIFInger, the first attempt using wireless signals to realize the technology that inputting number text through WIFI devices. Their idea is from the key intuition that the movement of users' fingers having unique formation and direction while performing a certain gesture. Similarly, Tan et al.

[58] present a kind of fine-grained finger gesture recognition. It has the advantage that it uses a single WIFI device, which is low cost and portable. It examines the unique patterns that existed in CSI to identify the micromotion of the finger. What's more, in order to mitigate the influence of signal dynamics caused by the environment changes, in WIFIgner, they introduced an environmental noise removal mechanism.

4.2 Coarse-Grained

Zheng X et al. [14] originally presented a non-intrusive ubiquitous smoking detection system, named Smokey. For the fact that smoking is a rhythmic activity and contains a series of motions, they decomposed the smoking activity and extract information by using foreground detection. Wu X et al. [59] present a device-free passive human activity recognition system with Wi-Fi signals, which does not require any dedicated device and meets the scenarios of the signals through the wall. Xi W et al. [60] presented an approach to Crowd Counting without any devices. Based on the relationship between the changes of CSI and the changes of the crowd, they proposed a method called the Percentage of nonzero Elements (PEM). Then the Grey Verhulst model was used to count the number of people. Gu Y et al. [61] proposed a sleep monitoring system called Sleepy using commercial Wi-Fi devices. They designed a Gaussian Mixture Model (GMM) to distinguish the foreground of the background. That can make contributions to detect posture changes when people are asleep. He Li et al. [62] analyzed the CSI of multiple Aps, and they realized human activity recognition by applying a deep learning algorithm witch can process complex and large Wi-Fi CSI. With the correlation between CSI measurements on different channels, Gao Q et al. [63] transformed them into radio images and then extracted image features from radio images. They used a deep network to learn optimized deep image features and applied a machine learning approach to estimate the location and activity of humans.

Wang Y et al. [64] introduced a low-cost system, exploiting existing Wi-Fi points, no need for the extra device, and able to achieve location-oriented activity identification. They extract CSI from the complex web of Wi-Fi links, which makes it possible to realize action recognition efficiently. Xiao F et al. [65] presented a solution for exercise activity recognition, which was energy-efficient and based on Wi-Fi. They originally used CSI-waveform as an activity feature and designed several methods to eliminate noise. Arshad S et al. [66] is the first to gather information from all available subcarriers to achieve human activity detection. They incorporated variations in the subcarriers' phases and magnitudes and evaluated them with an adaptive Activity Detection Algorithm (ADA). That enabled them to achieve higher detection accuracy. Chang et al. [67] observe the similarity between CSI and texture, and they transformed the CSI into images so that they can pick up features with the methods that we used on images and then classify behavior via SVM classifiers. Wang et al. [68] designed a Human Activity Recognition and Monitoring system (CARM) based on CSI. The main innovation points of CARM are the two models, CSI-speed model, and CSI-activity model. The CSI-speed model shows the relationship between the changes in CSI power and the changes of human movement speeds. The CSI-activity model describes the relation between movement speeds of different human body parts and specific human activities. Zou et al. [69] proposed Tag-Free. They regarded the inherent radiometric properties of different objects as their labels, instead of artificial targets. In order to improve the robustness and efficiency of their model, they set a spatial safe zone and harness successive cancellation when realizing multiple object classification at the same time. Tian et al. [70] proposed a device-free gesture recognition system, named Wi-Catch. This system utilizes CSI to recognize the movement of hands. They proposed a novel data fusion-based interference elimination algorithm to reduce the interference caused by the reflected signals from stationary objects and the direct signals from transmitter and receiver, which makes it possible for Wi-Catch to detect weak signals reflected from human hands in the complex and multi-target integrated system. And Wi-Catch is the first system that can recognize the gesture of two hands by reconstructing the trajectories of hands. Kun et al. [71] proposed Widar2.0, it is the first human localization and tracking system based on Wi-Fi. The key idea of Widar2.0 is to use multi-dimensional signal parameters from one single link instead of using multiple links. They construct a multi-parameter joint estimation model to estimate AoA, ToF, DFS, and attenuation. Different from Tian et al., they eliminate random phase noises between packets by conjugate multiplication of CSI. What's more, they proposed a novel algorithm to get precise locations from wrong parameter estimates.

Duan et al. [72] designed an action recognition system for the driver. It uses Commercial-Off-The-Shelf (COTS) WIFI devices, using BP neural network to screen sensitive input data from the original CSI matrix. They also introduced posture sequences and driving context finite automate model. What's more, this is the first time to use CSI data in driver maneuver recognition. Guo et al. [73] proposed a fine-grained comprehensive view of human dynamics by using WIFI infrastructures. Their approach is convenient and costs less, and it can be realized without any participation of humans since it is device free. Their system can provide human dynamics monitoring after estimating the number of participants, human density, walking speed, and direction derivation. In this system, a semi-supervised learning method is used. In this way, their system does not need too much training. They also show that their system has the fine-grained capability to estimate how many people there are in the monitored area as well as get the walking speeds and directions of people so that we can get first-hand information of the monitored area and give suitable suggestions as soon as possible. Peng et al. [74] propose a WIFI signal, WIFInd. WIFInd is a simple and device-free method that can find driver's fatigue symptoms in the car without any camera. Its accuracy increases a lot since it applies Hilbert-Huang transform in motion detection mode. They analyze the driver's fatigue degree and its influences on wireless signals, in order to design the recognition features properly. For example, they use the following equation to conquer the problem of the instability of breath:

$$R = \frac{kT}{\sum_{i=1}^{k} N_j} \tag{7}$$

where k represents the total number of the sub-carriers, T represents the length of recognition windows and N_j represents the j_{th} sub-carrier's peak number.

They were the first to present a device-free fatigue detection system and in the system prejudge driver's state by the Coefficient of Variation (CV) of WIFI signals and then use the different strategies to detect the responding features. Lei et al. [75] propose a multi-runner step estimation system by using only one WIFI device, which called Wi-Run. Wi-Run uses Canonical Polyadic (CP) decomposition, which can separate running-related signals effectively, then they find the decomposed signal pairs for each runner by applying a stable signal matching algorithm. As for estimating steps of each runner, they use the peak detection method. Qian et al. [76] proposed a tracking system based on WIFI, named Widar. Widar can simultaneously estimate the moving velocity and locations of humans at the decimeter level. They build a geometrical model to quantify the relationships between CSI dynamics and human mobility. Based on that, they proposed techniques to identify PLCR components of human movements from noisy CSIs in order to get user's locations. Han et al. [77] proposed a device-free fall detection system that took the advantages of CSI, temporal stability, and frequency diversity, called WiFall. WiFall employed the time variability and special diversity of CSI to identify human activities. In order to achieve the fall detection, they reconstructed the radio propagation model and used SVM to detect falls. Qian et al. [78] used WIFI to extract information about motion-induced Doppler shifts and proposed a lightweight pipeline to detect, segment, and recognize motion. Based on that, they designed a contactless dance mat games. Zhao et al. [79] showed an approach to estimate human pose with occlusions such as walls. They applied a deep neural network approach to estimate 2D poses of human-based on the fact that wireless signals of WIFI frequencies can go through walls and reflect when hitting the human body. We all know that it is hard to annotate radio signals artificially. To conquer that, they used a state-of-the-art vision model to achieve cross-modal supervision.

4.3   Comparison of WIFI-Based Algorithms

For fine-grained methods, it is natural for a system to just detect and estimate single periodic and minute action like lip reading [15,52], breath [54,80], finger gestures [57,58] and keystroke [53]. WiKey recognizes keystrokes on the basis of unique CSI-waveform for each key, while WiHear [15] is based on the radio reflections from mouth movements. WIFInger identifies finger gestures with unique patterns in CSI. But all of them are context-related. Differently, WiTalk [52] is context-free, with no need to reconstruct CSI profiles facing different conditions. WiTalk [52] uses CSI spectrograms to extract features. It is also common for fine-grained methods to use DTW as a classification method, just as done in [15,52,80].

For cross-grained methods, it is used to recognize human body actions such as walking [64–66,77], dancing [78], locating [63], counting [62], personal tracing

[71] and so on. Just like the fine-grained methods, they extract features, pretreat the data and then classify them, most of the approaches we have introduced previously using many traditional methods, such as PCA, DWT, RSM, SVM, Bof-SIFT... While some of them apply deep learning methods, such as CNN [65,81], to process the data gotten from WIFI, which is much more convenient.

5   Future Trend

5.1   Self-deployed Vision-Based Action Recognition System

With the development of deep learning, the accuracy of the motion recognition algorithm based on vision has been greatly improved. However, there are still existing several problems as follows: (1) in the case of obstacle occlusion, the accuracy of human motion detection is low; (2) the speed of current motion detection is not high enough, and the real-time performance is low; (3) in order to improve the accuracy of motion recognition, we need to rely on a large number of data sets for training. Therefore, the future research direction of visual-based action recognition should be self-deployable visual perception framework. Users can add any action library at any time without prior training of data sets, which enhances the portability of the system.

5.2   Robustness of WIFI-Based Small Action Recognition Algorithm

CSI characterizes multipath propagation to a certain extent. By analyzing the amplitude and phase of CSI, we can get more fine wireless link states in the time domain and frequency domain, which makes human behavior perception based on CSI feasible. However, when the environment changes, the original CSI information collected often carries a lot of random noise and high-frequency noise. Therefore, the fine-grained sensing algorithm based on CSI has some drawbacks, such as low accuracy and poor robustness. In the future, the main research direction should be to study the robustness of fine-grained action-perception problem and reduce the impact of environmental changes on the system.

5.3   Action Recognition Method Combining WIFI and Vision

Behavior perception system based on computer vision technology has very high accuracy in the visual range environment, but such effect is not ideal under the circumstances of low image resolution, motion blurring, low brightness, serious occlusion, and incomplete target. In addition, there is the problem of exposing users' privacy. WIFI-based wireless sensing technology does not require light and has wider coverage and penetration, so it can work in many challenging scenarios. But WIFI wireless signal also has the disadvantage of environmental vulnerability. Environmental noise and equipment noise can easily affect signal stability. In view of their respective advantages and disadvantages, the future research direction should be to integrate the two methods and give full play to their respective advantages through effective fusion methods, so as to improve the accuracy and robustness of the system.

6   Conclusion

This paper is the first one that systematically reviews the problem of device-free activity recognition based on WIFI and video. Firstly, we analyzed the principle in the depth of device-free activity recognition. Furthermore, a comprehensive summary of state-of-the-art methods which are specially designed for a device-free activity recognition system. In addition, we compare the existing methods in depth. Finally, future research directions are given by analyzing the disadvantages of the existing methods.

References

1. Barr, P., Noble, J., Biddle, R.: Video game values: human-computer interaction and games. Interact. Comput. **19**(2), 180–195 (2007)
2. Foroughi, H., Aski, B.S., Pourreza, H.: Intelligent video surveillance for monitoring fall detection of elderly in home environments. In: 2008 11th International Conference on Computer and Information Technology, pp. 219–224. IEEE (2008)
3. Scheible, J., Ojala, T., Coulton, P.: MobiToss: a novel gesture based interface for creating and sharing mobile multimedia art on large public displays. In: Proceedings of the 16th ACM International Conference on Multimedia, pp. 957–960. ACM (2008)
4. Burton, A.M., Wilson, S., Cowan, M., Bruce, V.: Face recognition in poor-quality video: evidence from security surveillance. Psychol. Sci. **10**(3), 243–248 (1999)
5. Zeiler, M.D., Fergus, R.: Visualizing and understanding convolutional networks. In: Fleet, D., Pajdla, T., Schiele, B., Tuytelaars, T. (eds.) ECCV 2014. LNCS, vol. 8689, pp. 818–833. Springer, Cham (2014). https://doi.org/10.1007/978-3-319-10590-1_53
6. Newell, A., Yang, K., Deng, J.: Stacked hourglass networks for human pose estimation. In: Leibe, B., Matas, J., Sebe, N., Welling, M. (eds.) ECCV 2016. LNCS, vol. 9912, pp. 483–499. Springer, Cham (2016). https://doi.org/10.1007/978-3-319-46484-8_29
7. Insafutdinov, E., Pishchulin, L., Andres, B., Andriluka, M., Schiele, B.: DeeperCut: a deeper, stronger, and faster multi-person pose estimation model. In: Leibe, B., Matas, J., Sebe, N., Welling, M. (eds.) ECCV 2016. LNCS, vol. 9910, pp. 34–50. Springer, Cham (2016). https://doi.org/10.1007/978-3-319-46466-4_3
8. Cao, Z., Simon, T., Wei, S.E., Sheikh, Y.: Realtime multi-person 2D pose estimation using part affinity fields. In: Proceedings of the IEEE Conference on Computer Vision and Pattern Recognition, pp. 7291–7299 (2017)
9. Bahl, P., Padmanabhan, V.N.: Radar: an in-building RF-based user location and tracking system, vol. 2, pp. 775–784 (2000)
10. Chetty, K., Smith, G.E., Woodbridge, K.: Through-the-wall sensing of personnel using passive bistatic WIFI radar at standoff distances. IEEE Trans. Geosci. Remote Sens. **50**(4), 1218–1226 (2012)
11. Adib, F., Katabi, D.: See through walls with Wi-Fi!. In: ACM SIGCOMM Conference on SIGCOMM (2013)
12. Pu, Q., Gupta, S., Gollakota, S., Patel, S.N.: Whole-home gesture recognition using wireless signals, pp. 27–38 (2013)

13. Halperin, D., Hu, W., Sheth, A., Wetherall, D.: Tool release: gathering 802.11n traces with channel state information. ACM SIGCOMM Comput. Commun. Rev. **41**(1), 53 (2011)

14. Zheng, X., Wang, J., Shangguan, L., Zhou, Z., Liu, Y.: Smokey: ubiquitous smoking detection with commercial WIFI infrastructures. In: IEEE INFOCOM - The IEEE International Conference on Computer Communications (2016)

15. Wang, G., Zou, Y., Zhou, Z., Wu, K., Ni, L.M.: We can hear you with Wi-Fi!. In: International Conference on Mobile Computing & Networking (2014)

16. Qian, H., Mao, Y., Xiang, W., Wang, Z.: Recognition of human activities using SVM multi-class classifier. Pattern Recogn. Lett. **31**(2), 100–111 (2010)

17. Kim, W., Lee, J., Kim, M., Oh, D., Kim, C.: Human action recognition using ordinal measure of accumulated motion. Eurasip J. Adv. Signal Process. **2010**(1), 1–11 (2010)

18. Fang, C.-H., Chen, J.-C., Tseng, C.-C., Lien, J.-J.J.: Human action recognition using spatio-temporal classification. In: Zha, H., Taniguchi, R., Maybank, S. (eds.) ACCV 2009. LNCS, vol. 5995, pp. 98–109. Springer, Heidelberg (2010). https://doi.org/10.1007/978-3-642-12304-7_10

19. Ziaeefard, M., Ebrahimnezhad, H.: Hierarchical human action recognition by normalized-polar histogram. In: 2010 20th International Conference on Pattern Recognition, pp. 3720–3723. IEEE (2010)

20. Vemulapalli, R., Arrate, F., Chellappa, R.: Human action recognition by representing 3D human skeletons as points in a lie group. In: IEEE Conference on Computer Vision & Pattern Recognition (2014)

21. Mahbub, U., Imtiaz, H., Ahad, M.: An optical flow based approach for action recognition. In: International Conference on Computer & Information Technology (2012)

22. Holte, M.B., Moeslund, T.B., Nikolaidis, N., Pitas, I.: 3D human action recognition for multi-view camera systems. In: 2011 International Conference on 3D Imaging, Modeling, Processing, Visualization and Transmission, pp. 342–349. IEEE (2011)

23. Pham, C.H., Ducournau, A., Fablet, R., Rousseau, F.: Brain MRI super-resolution using deep 3D convolutional networks. In: IEEE International Symposium on Biomedical Imaging (2017)

24. Rahmani, H., Mian, A.: 3D action recognition from novel viewpoints. In: IEEE Computer Vision and Pattern Recognition (2016)

25. Lin, S., Jia, K., Yeung, D.Y., Shi, B.E.: Human action recognition using factorized spatio-temporal convolutional networks (FSTCN). In: IEEE International Conference on Computer Vision (2015)

26. Shuiwang, J., Ming, Y., Kai, Y.: 3D convolutional neural networks for human action recognition. IEEE Trans. Pattern Anal. Mach. Intell. **35**(1), 221–231 (2013)

27. Karpathy, A., Toderici, G., Shetty, S., Leung, T., Li, F.F.: Large-scale video classification with convolutional neural networks. In: Computer Vision & Pattern Recognition (2014)

28. Liu, C., Wei-Sheng, X.U., Qi-Di, W.U.: Spatiotemporal convolutional neural networks and its application in action recognition. Comput. Sci. (2015)

29. Kim, H., Uh, Y., Ko, S., Byun, H.: Weighing classes and streams: toward better methods for two-stream convolutional networks. Opt. Eng. **55**(5), 053108 (2016)

30. Feichtenhofer, C., Pinz, A., Zisserman, A.: Convolutional two-stream network fusion for video action recognition. In: Computer Vision & Pattern Recognition (2016)

31. Wu, Z., Jiang, Y.G., Xi, W., Hao, Y., Xue, X.: Multi-stream multi-class fusion of deep networks for video classification. In: ACM on Multimedia Conference (2016)

32. Doretto, G., Chiuso, A., Ying, N.W., Soatto, S.: Dynamic textures. Int. J. Comput. Vis. **51**(2), 91–109 (2003)

33. Yan, X., Chang, H., Shan, S., Chen, X.: Modeling video dynamics with deep dynencoder. In: Fleet, D., Pajdla, T., Schiele, B., Tuytelaars, T. (eds.) ECCV 2014. LNCS, vol. 8692, pp. 215–230. Springer, Cham (2014). https://doi.org/10.1007/978-3-319-10593-2_15

34. Srivastava, N., Mansimov, E., Salakhudinov, R.: Unsupervised learning of video representations using LSTMs. In: International Conference on Machine Learning (2015)

35. Goodfellow, I.J., et al.: Generative adversarial nets. In: International Conference on Neural Information Processing Systems (2014)

36. Duarte, M., Bonaventura, Z., Massot, M., Bourdon, A., Dumont, T.: A new numerical strategy with space-time adaptivity and error control for multi-scale streamer discharge simulations. J. Comput. Phys. **231**(3), 1002–1019 (2012)

37. Zhang, J., Han, Y., Tang, J., Hu, Q., Jiang, J.: Semi-supervised image-to-video adaptation for video action recognition. IEEE Trans. Cybern. **47**(4), 960–973 (2016)

38. Fernando, B., Anderson, P., Hutter, M., Gould, S.: Discriminative hierarchical rank pooling for activity recognition. In: Proceedings of the IEEE Conference on Computer Vision and Pattern Recognition, pp. 1924–1932 (2016)

39. Jones, S., Shao, L., Zhang, J., Liu, Y.: Relevance feedback for real-world human action retrieval. Pattern Recogn. Lett. **33**(4), 446–452 (2012)

40. Sadek, S., Al-Hamadi, A., Michaelis, B., Sayed, U.: An action recognition scheme using fuzzy log-polar histogram and temporal self-similarity. Eurasip J. Adv. Signal Process. **2011**(1), 540375 (2011)

41. Ikizler-Cinbis, N., Sclaroff, S.: Object, scene and actions: combining multiple features for human action recognition. In: Daniilidis, K., Maragos, P., Paragios, N. (eds.) ECCV 2010. LNCS, vol. 6311, pp. 494–507. Springer, Heidelberg (2010). https://doi.org/10.1007/978-3-642-15549-9_36

42. Lui, Y.M., Beveridge, J.R.: Tangent bundle for human action recognition. In: IEEE International Conference on Automatic Face & Gesture Recognition (2013)

43. Wang, H., Kläser, A., Schmid, C., Liu, C.L.: Action recognition by dense trajectories. In: Computer Vision & Pattern Recognition (2011)

44. Yu-Gang, J., Qi, D., Wei, L., Xiangyang, X., Chong-Wah, N.: Human action recognition in unconstrained videos by explicit motion modeling. IEEE Trans. Image Process. **2**(11), 3781–3795 (2015)

45. Cohen, N., Sharir, O., Shashua, A.: Deep SimNets. In: Computer Vision & Pattern Recognition (2016)

46. Wang, X., Farhadi, A., Gupta, A.: Actions transformations. In: IEEE Computer Vision & Pattern Recognition (2016)

47. Wang, H., Schmid, C.: Action recognition with improved trajectories. In: IEEE International Conference on Computer Vision (2014)

48. Donahue, J., et al.: Long-term recurrent convolutional networks for visual recognition and description (2015)

49. Wang, L., Yu, Q., Tang, X.: Action recognition with trajectory-pooled deep-convolutional descriptors. In: Computer Vision & Pattern Recognition (2015)

50. Wang, L., et al.: Temporal segment networks: towards good practices for deep action recognition. In: Leibe, B., Matas, J., Sebe, N., Welling, M. (eds.) ECCV 2016. LNCS, vol. 9912, pp. 20–36. Springer, Cham (2016). https://doi.org/10.1007/978-3-319-46484-8_2

51. Varior, R.R., Shuai, B., Lu, J., Xu, D., Wang, G.: A Siamese long short-term memory architecture for human re-identification. In: Leibe, B., Matas, J., Sebe, N., Welling, M. (eds.) ECCV 2016. LNCS, vol. 9911, pp. 135–153. Springer, Cham (2016). https://doi.org/10.1007/978-3-319-46478-7_9

52. Dan, W., Zhang, D., Xu, C., Hao, W., Xiang, L.: Device-free WIFI human sensing: from pattern-based to model-based approaches. IEEE Commun. Mag. 55(10), 91–97 (2017)

53. Ali, K., Liu, A.X., Wang, W., Shahzad, M.: Keystroke recognition using WIFI signals. In: International Conference on Mobile Computing & Networking (2015)

54. Dou, F., et al.: Breathing rhythm analysis in body centric networks. IEEE Access 6, 1 (2018)

55. Gu, Y., Zhang, Y., Li, J., Ji, Y., An, X., Ren, F.: Sleepy: wireless channel data driven sleep monitoring via commodity WIFI devices. IEEE Trans. Big Data 1 (2019)

56. Villamizar, M., Suarez, J., Villanueva, J., Borja, G., Rios, E.D.L.: Design and implementation of sleep monitoring system using electrooculographs signals. In: Health Care Exchanges (2014)

57. Hong, L., Wei, Y., Wang, J., Yang, X., Huang, L.: WIFInger: talk to your smart devices with finger-grained gesture. In: ACM International Joint Conference on Pervasive & Ubiquitous Computing (2016)

58. Tan, S., Yang, J.: WIFInger: leveraging commodity WIFI for fine-grained finger gesture recognition. In: ACM International Symposium on Mobile Ad Hoc Networking & Computing (2016)

59. Wu, X., Chu, Z., Yang, P., Xiang, C., Zheng, X., Huang, W.: TW-See: human activity recognition through the wall with commodity Wi-Fi devices. IEEE Trans. Veh. Technol. 68(1), 306–319 (2019)

60. Wei, X., Zhao, J., Li, X.Y., Zhao, K., Jiang, Z.: Electronic frog eye: counting crowd using WIFI. In: INFOCOM. IEEE (2015)

61. Yu, G., Zhan, J., Zhi, L., Jie, L., Ji, Y., Wang, X.: Sleepy: adaptive sleep monitoring from afar with commodity WIFI infrastructures. In: 2018 IEEE Wireless Communications and Networking Conference (WCNC) (2018)

62. He, L., Ota, K., Dong, M., Guo, M.: Learning human activities through Wi-Fi channel state information with multiple access points. IEEE Commun. Mag. 56(5), 124–129 (2018)

63. Gao, Q., et al.: CSI-based device-free wireless localization and activity recognition using radio image features. IEEE Trans. Veh. Technol. 66(11), 10346–10356 (2017)

64. Yan, W., Jian, L., Chen, Y., Gruteser, M., Liu, H.: E-eyes: device-free location-oriented activity identification using fine-grained WIFI signatures (2014)

65. Fu, X., Jing, C., Xiao, H.X., Gui, L., Sun, J.L., Wang, N.R.: SEARE: a system for exercise activity recognition and quality evaluation based on green sensing. IEEE Trans. Emerg. Top. Comput. 1 (2018)

66. Arshad, S., et al.: Wi-chase: a WIFI based human activity recognition system for sensorless environments. In: IEEE International Symposium on a World of Wireless (2017)

67. Chang, J.Y., Lee, K.Y., Lin, C.J., Hsu, W.: WIFI action recognition via vision-based methods. In: IEEE International Conference on Acoustics (2016)

68. Wang, W., Liu, A.X., Shahzad, M., Ling, K., Lu, S.: Device-free human activity recognition using commercial WIFI devices. IEEE J. Sel. Areas Commun. 35(5), 1118–1131 (2017)

69. Zou, Y., Wang, Y., Ye, S., Wu, K., Ni, L.M.: TagFree: passive object differentiation via physical layer radiometric signatures. In: IEEE International Conference on Pervasive Computing & Communications (2017)
70. Tian, Z., Wang, J., Yang, X., Mu, Z.: WiCatch: a Wi-Fi based hand gesture recognition system. IEEE Access 6(99), 16911–16923 (2018)
71. Qian, K., Wu, C., Zhang, Y., Zhang, G., Yang, Z., Liu, Y.: Widar2.0: passive human tracking with a single Wi-Fi link. In: Proceedings of the 16th Annual International Conference on Mobile Systems, Applications, and Services, pp. 350–361 (2018)
72. Duan, S., Yu, T., Jie, H.: WiDriver: driver activity recognition system based on WIFI CSI. Int. J. Wirel. Inf. Netw. 25(3), 1–11 (2018)
73. Guo, X., Liu, B., Shi, C., Liu, H., Chen, Y., Chuah, M.C.: WIFI-enabled smart human dynamics monitoring. In: Proceedings of the 15th ACM Conference on Embedded Network Sensor Systems, pp. 1–13 (2017)
74. Peng, H., Jia, W.: WiFind: driver fatigue detection with fine-grained Wi-Fi signal features. In: Globecom IEEE Global Communications Conference (2018)
75. Zhang, L., Liu, M., Lu, L., Gong, L.: Wi-run: multi-runner step estimation using commodity Wi-Fi. In: Annual IEEE International Conference on Sensing, Communication, and Networking, SECON (2018)
76. Qian, K., Wu, C., Zheng, Y., Yang, C., Liu, Y.: Decimeter level passive tracking with WIFI. In: Workshop on Hot Topics in Wireless (2016)
77. Wang, Y., Wu, K., Ni, L.M.: WiFall: device-free fall detection by wireless networks. IEEE Trans. Mob. Comput. 16(2), 581–594 (2016)
78. Qian, K., Wu, C., Zhou, Z., Yue, Z., Liu, Y.: Inferring motion direction using commodity Wi-Fi for interactive exergames (2017)
79. Zhao, M., et al.: Through-wall human pose estimation using radio signals. In: Proceedings of the IEEE Conference on Computer Vision and Pattern Recognition, pp. 7356–7365 (2018)
80. Wang, X., Chao, Y., Mao, S.: TensorBeat: tensor decomposition for monitoring multi-person breathing beats with commodity WIFI. ACM Trans. Intell. Syst. Technol. 9(1), 1–27 (2017)
81. Turaga, P., Chellappa, R., Subrahmanian, V.S., Udrea, O.: Machine recognition of human activities: a survey. IEEE Trans. Circuits Syst. Video Technol. 18(11), 1473–1488 (2008)

Analysis of Gait Symmetry Under Unilateral Load State

Shiyun Lv[1], Zhan Huan[1(✉)], Xingzhi Chang[2], Yuxi Huan[2], and Jiuzhen Liang[1]

[1] Changzhou University, Changzhou 213164, China
hzh@cczu.edu.cn
[2] Changzhou College of Information Technology, Changzhou 213164, China

Abstract. Weight-bearing is a common daily behavior. The analysis of gait during weight-bearing walking is helpful to reveal the health status and pathological characteristics of the human body. The purpose of this paper is to analyze the symmetry difference between shank and thigh segments under asymmetrical weight-bearing, and a regression rotation angle algorithm for a complete gait cycle is proposed. Based on multi-sensor data modeling, the gait symmetry is measured by the regression rotation angle radian under different weight-bearing modes. The time-series data of twenty healthy subjects under five weight-bearing modes were collected by changing the way they held weights and the degree of weight-bearing. After a series of preprocessing and cycle segmentation, a total of 18,000 effective gait cycles were obtained. The results on the experimental data set show that asymmetrical weight-bearing reduces the gait symmetry, and the weight held in the right hand has a higher gait symmetry than that held in the left hand. The gait symmetry is inversely proportional to the degree of weight-bearing. The algorithm in this paper makes full use of each sample point in the periodic segment of the subjects and makes comprehensive evaluation in combination with the discrete parameter method to obtain a more accurate symmetry conclusion.

Keywords: Asymmetrical weight-bearing · Gait · Multi-sensor · Symmetry

1 Introduction

Given the impact of weight-bearing on the lower limb gait of the human body, this paper analyzes gait symmetry under a unilateral load state by combining discrete parameters and the whole period curve assessment. This study has potential application value for health monitoring in biomedicine and kinematics and has important significance for understanding human behavior and gait [1–4].

Gait symmetry is one of the important features to characterize human gait [5], focusing on the analysis of symmetry variation and the evaluation methods for quantifying symmetry. Symmetry variation has achieved fruitful results in fields such as gait analysis and biomedical, but there are still some controversies. Symmetry variation aims to reveal the gait difference between left and right sides of the human body, for example, some scholars [6], proposed that the dominant functional difference of left and right

© Springer Nature Singapore Pte Ltd. 2020
Z. Hao et al. (Eds.): CWSN 2020, CCIS 1321, pp. 244–256, 2020.
https://doi.org/10.1007/978-981-33-4214-9_18

lower limbs during normal walking should be assumed as the embodiment of gait symmetry variation, and they believed that healthy human gait could also be found to be asymmetrical. The quantitative evaluation method of gait symmetry is mostly focused on clinical application and is still in the exploratory stage. Its basic idea is to analyze the gait parameters of the left and right sides of the human body quantitatively [7, 8] and to identify the similarity and difference between the two sides of the gait. For instance, Mahdi Abid et al. [9] studied the influence of different carrying modes and gait speeds on the symmetry index of step length parameters. Allen Hill et al. [10] studied the influence of arm swing amplitude on symmetrical indexes of step length, step width, and other parameters. Wafai et al. [11] explored the gait symmetry of healthy subjects and podiatrists based on gait parameters of plantar reaction forces.

In the existing research, plantar pressure data is often used to analyze the symmetry of gait, which method is to obtain plantar pressure while landing on the heel. The defect of this method is that it cannot obtain the plantar information in the swing stage and lacks a continuous and complete gait cycle. Hence, the analysis is limited to discrete gait parameters. However, when acquiring a human gait, inertial sensors [12–14] not only have advantages of real-time and continuity, but also can obtain the acceleration and angular velocity data in the process of human movement, and capture information on the complete gait of the left and right. In the existing research, the symmetry analysis of left and right gait mainly relies on the statistical data of discrete parameters, including variance analysis, principal component analysis, and deviation area analysis, etc., which has problems of low data utilization and large random error. For example, the amplitude range only compares the maximum and minimum values in the gait cycle but ignores the distribution of the whole cycle curve, which results in low data utilization. For another example, the mean square error is easily affected by the amplitude of the gait cycle curve, which results in a large random error.

The main contributions of this paper are as follows: first, a regression rotation angle algorithm for complete gait cycle evaluation symmetry is proposed, which makes full use of the information of each sample point, reduces the problems of low data utilization rate and large random error, and provides a new idea for symmetry evaluation. Second, based on the multi-sensor data modeling, the symmetry difference between shanks and thighs under different weight-bearing modes was compared and analyzed from the perspectives of discrete parameters and continuous periodic segments, which not only revealed the kinematics law of lower limb segments but also provided a reference for the weight-bearing study of the human body.

The rest organizational structure of this paper is as follows: Sect. 2 summarizes the current development status of asymmetrical weight-bearing at home and abroad; Sect. 3 introduces the regression rotation angle algorithm used to evaluate the symmetry of the left and right complete periodic curves; Sect. 4 explains the setup and scene of the experiment, analyzes the symmetry deviation of several important discrete gait parameters, and briefly describes the preprocessing of the experiment; Sect. 5 is discussion and analysis; summary and outlook are given in Sect. 6.

2 Related Work

The research on asymmetrical weight-bearing at home and abroad mostly analyzes dynamics, kinematics, and surface electromyography parameters to compare the impact of these parameters on the human body, which involves different gender and age, weight-bearing degree and weight-bearing modes, etc.

So far, researches on asymmetrical weight-bearing mostly have focused on a comprehensive analysis of multiple weight-bearing modes, such as a one-shoulder backpack, handbag, and cross-body bag. The analysis methods mainly compared the dynamic parameters of foot pressure and ground reaction force, as well as the kinematic parameters of step length, step width, step frequency, stride length, angle of landing, angle off the ground, percentage of supporting phase, etc. For example, Wontae et al. [15] studied the change of plantar pressure when standing and walking in a one-shoulder backpack and two-shoulder backpack, and found that there was no significant difference in the pressure of left and right foot bottoms during walking. Hyung et al. [16] studied the influence of weight-bearing degree on pelvic movement and believed that with the increase of weight-bearing degree, pelvic inclination angle had an increasing trend. Fowler et al. [17] studied the influence of asymmetrical weight-bearing on the spine and body posture and found that one-shoulder weight-bearing caused significant changes in the motion characteristics of the spine, and the trunk showed asymmetry during walking. Kellis et al. [18] analyzed the ground reaction force of non-loaded, handbag, and high-low position backpacks, and the results showed that the ground reaction force of handbag and low-position backpack increased significantly, while the high-position backpack did not change significantly. Son et al. [19] studied four weight-bearing modes, including walking with a weight in the left hand, right hand, left shoulder, and right shoulder, but his researches mainly focused on analyzing the effect on spatial and temporal parameters of healthy women in different weight-bearing modes. The research of Son et al. showed that there was no significant difference in parameters such as step length, stride length, step width, and support phase time.

Researches on weight-bearing mostly focused on two-shoulder backpack mode. For instance, Massimiliano Pau et al. [20] discussed the influence of two-shoulder backpack weight-bearing (5.2 kg, accounting for 15% of the body weight of more than half of the subjects) on children's sole pressure and other gait parameters. Castro et al. [21] measured the foot pressure and ground reaction force when walking at a slow speed (70 step/min) and a fast speed (120 step/min) in non-loaded and two-shoulder weight-bearing modes. Hotfiel et al. [22] studied the peak pressure of soles when subjects wearing weight-bearing vests of different weights. Two-shoulder backpack is a symmetrical weight-bearing, and there are few studies on asymmetrical weight-bearing. In addition, most of the studies focused on a single weight-bearing index and paid insufficient attention to the difference of lower limb segments and the whole gait. Results of some studies are still controversial due to the diversity of data acquisition ways [23–25] and data processing methods, which urgently requires researchers to have a deeper understanding of parameter changes and periodic changes in asymmetric weight-bearing.

3 Regression Rotation Angle Algorithm

Suppose that $\overrightarrow{L_{Kraw}}$ and $\overrightarrow{R_{Kraw}}$ represent the vector sets of a complete gait cycle on the left and right sides, respectively, which can be defined as:

$$\overrightarrow{L_{Kraw}} = \{L_K(1), L_K(2), \ldots, L_K(n)\} \tag{1}$$

$$\overrightarrow{R_{Kraw}} = \{R_K(1), R_K(2), \ldots, R_K(n)\} \tag{2}$$

Where, $\overrightarrow{L_{Kraw}}$ and $\overrightarrow{R_{Kraw}}$ represent the left and right gait data of the subject K, respectively, where $K \in \{1, \ldots, 20\}$. $L_K(i)$ and $R_K(i)$ represent the ith sample point of the left and right gait cycle of subject K, respectively, where $i \in \{1, \ldots, 101\}$. $\overrightarrow{L_{Ko}}(i)$ and $\overrightarrow{R_{Ko}}(i)$ are obtained after removing the mean, which can be calculated as follows:

$$\overrightarrow{L_{Ko}}(i) = \overrightarrow{L_{Kraw}}(i) - \left(\sum_{i=1}^{i=n} \overrightarrow{L_{Kraw}}(i)\right)_{ave} \tag{3}$$

$$\overrightarrow{R_{Ko}}(i) = \overrightarrow{R_{Kraw}}(i) - \left(\sum_{i=1}^{l=n} \overrightarrow{R_{Kraw}}(i)\right)_{ave} \tag{4}$$

Taking a single gait cycle of a certain subject in an experiment as an example, the linear regression model was constructed by taking the left gait data as the independent variable and the right gait data as the dependent variable:

$$Y(i) = \beta_0 + \beta_1 \overrightarrow{L_{Ko}}(i) + e(i) \tag{5}$$

Where, regression parameters β_1 and intercept β_0 represent offset and amplitude differences, respectively. Y is the value of the predicted right gait, and e is the residual term, which is the difference between the observed value $\overrightarrow{R_{Ko}}$ and the estimated regression value Y.

The information provided by the residuals is used to optimize the constructed regression model. Studentized residuals (r), the ratio of residuals to estimated standard deviations, are often used to test outliers. According to the variance property of the residual, $Var(e(i)) = \sigma^2(1 - h_{ii})$ can be obtained, where h_{ii} is a diagonal element of the hat matrix H. Studentized residuals (r) is defined as follows:

$$r(i) = \frac{e(i)}{\sigma\sqrt{1 - h_{ii}}} \tag{6}$$

If the left and right gait cycles are completely symmetric, then β_0 is 0, and the regression equation satisfies the proportional relationship. Assuming that the slope of the symmetry line is β_1', the rotation angle radian between the regression equation and the symmetric formula can be obtained according to the definition of the included angle between linear equations in geometric mathematics:

$$\theta_K = \arctan\left|\frac{\beta_1 - \beta_1'}{\beta_1' + \beta_1}\right| (rad) \tag{7}$$

Where, $0 < \theta_K < 1$. θ_K is used to measure the symmetry level of subject K in five gait modes. The closer the value of θ_K is to 0, the higher the symmetry of the left and right gait cycle is.

4 Experimental Method

In the following experiments, this paper will study the symmetry of the shank and thigh segments by analyzing the discrete gait parameters and the global periodic segment curve under the condition of unilateral weight-bearing. Assuming objects of different masses held in the left and right hands may alter the level of gait asymmetry. In this section, starting from the experimental settings and scenes, discrete gait parameters for evaluating symmetry, as well as the periodic segmentation process are analyzed [26, 27].

4.1 Experiment Settings

The flow diagram of the entire acquisition system is shown in Fig. 1. The system consists of a MySQL database container, ESP32, PC, MPU9250, and EMQTT container. The WiFi module included in ESP32 can make the system interconnect with each other and make the whole system connect with the network. Sports data collected by MPU9250 is published through the MQTT protocol based on ESP32's serial communication mode. The MQTT protocol is responsible for the data transmission among various components in this system, in which the EMQTT container is the message broker and is responsible for the connection and subscription of the client. The MySQL database container accepts the data collected by the ESP32 development board as the subscriber and inserts it into the table in real-time. Finally, PC imports the data from the MySQL database into the local area through TCP/IP communication protocol.

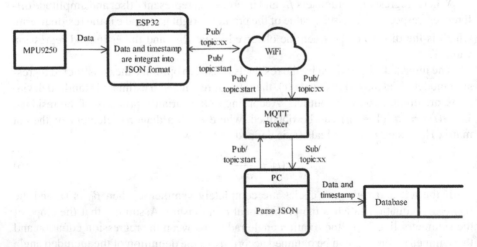

Fig. 1. System structures

Twenty healthy subjects, with a 23-year average age (age range 21–25 years), 1.71 m average height, and 75.6 kg average mass, from Changzhou University and Changzhou Institute of Information Technology participated in this study. There were no musculoskeletal injuries or gait disorders of these subjects, and they were accustomed to carrying heavy objects in the right hand, without left-handed people. Subjects were asked to walk at an autonomous pace on a 12-m long laboratory corridor and needed to wear an inertial sensor in the middle of each shank and thigh to collect gait data. Connected by Velcro, the X-axis was perpendicular to the horizontal direction and the Y-axis was perpendicular to the coronal direction.

This experiment consisted of five gait patterns: normal walking, walking with a 2.5 kg weight held in the right hand, walking with a 5 kg weight held in the right hand, walking with a 2.5 kg weight held in the left hand, and walking with a 5 kg weight held in the left hand, which could be recorded as G1, G2, G3, G4, and G5, respectively. Each experiment would be repeated 10 times. The laptop bag would be used as a carrier for carrying heavy objects. Subjects would perform hand-held exercises before the experiments. During each experiment, subjects were instructed to step forward and swing their arms naturally (when holding a heavy object on one side, they would naturally swing their arms on the side without weight). Subjects were allowed to rest for two minutes between experiments to prevent the effect of excessive fatigue on the accuracy of the experimental data. The sensor on the same side of the limb must always be on a vertical line to maintain data consistency. Subjects were required to avoid wearing shoes with heels or feet that did not meet their feet sizes, and they were required to wear the same shoes during all experiments.

4.2 Discrete Parameters for Evaluating Gait Symmetry

Seven important gait parameters are selected from the whole periodic curve, including the maximum acceleration Fz1 acquired when the foot is lifted to the highest point, the maximum acceleration Fz2 acquired when the foot is lifted to the ground from the highest point, and the minimum acceleration Fz3 acquired from the location of Fz1 to Fz2. The corresponding time point positions of the three accelerations are also achieved, which are recorded as Tz1, Tz2, and Tz3, respectively. Amplitude range Ar is also obtained as an important gait parameter. Coefficient of variation (CV) is used to estimate the variation of gait parameters in subjects' lower legs [28], and CV can be defined as follows:

$$CV = \frac{SD}{M} \times 100\% \tag{8}$$

Where SD and M represent the standard deviation and mean, respectively. When the absolute value of CV is less than or equal to 25%, the change of each gait parameter is regarded as an acceptable level. As can be seen from Table 1, the variability of the selected gait parameter is acceptable because the CV value of each parameter is less than 25%. The symmetry index (SI) is used to evaluate the symmetry deviation of these seven gait parameters, which is defined as:

$$SI = \frac{2(X_R - X_L)}{X_R + X_L} \times 100\% \tag{9}$$

Where, X_R and X_L are the right and left gait parameters, respectively. The deviation of gait symmetry can be considered as an acceptable level when the absolute value of SI is less than 10%. Results in Table 1 show that the symmetry range of seven important parameters in the periodic curve is within the acceptable level, and the symmetry degree

Table 1. CV and SI of left and right gait parameters.

Parameter	Left side (shank/thigh)		Right side (shank/thigh)		SI (%) (shank/thigh)
	CV (%)	Mean	CV (%)	Mean	
Fz1	[7.08–10.72]	[1.59–1.68]	[8.30–11.72]	[1.63–1.74]	[1.15–8.51]
	[11.24–13.31]	[1.62–1.69]	[11.09–12.76]	[1.69–1.76]	[0.65–8.32]
Fz2	[7.35–8.66]	[1.76–1.81]	[8.74–9.24]	[1.75–1.79]	[−3.40–0.99]
	[6.27–8.89]	[1.44–1.50]	[6.88–9.41]	[1.45–1.50]	[−0.66–4.29]
Fz3	[2.09–2.58]	[1.00–1.01]	[2.51–3.13]	[1.00–1.01]	[−4.6–3.1]
	[2.56–3.66]	[0.91–0.92]	[2.76–3.74]	[0.96–0.97]	[4.65–5.23]
Tz1	[17.82–22.08]	[27.06–28.42]	[17.81–19.61]	[27.63–30.37]	[−1.01–8.11]
	[14.95–17.29]	[26.44–27.56]	[15.61–18.64]	[26.92–28.41]	[0.01-6.78]
Tz2	[7.46–8.40]	[82.32–83.05]	[6.45–7.31]	[82.93–83.39]	[−0.01–3.11]
	[5.83–8.35]	[89.18–91.28]	[5.91–13.06]	[88.17–90.97]	[-8.37-0.24]
Tz3	[12.08–21.55]	[57.26–60.47]	[9.22–18.75]	[59.21–61.36]	[−2.82–6.24]
	[18.47–23.25]	[54.86–55.95]	[18.19–23.00]	[55.64–57.84]	[-0.26-8.30]
Ar	[12.32–15.50]	[1.23–1.30]	[10.89–17.21]	[1.20–1.27]	[−4.75–1.32]
	[22.24–24.41]	[1.00–1.12]	[20.98–24.85]	[1.04–1.15]	[−7.79–8.80]

of the curve on the left and right side of the initial prediction is relatively high. There are different symmetry index ranges on the shanks and thighs, and some parameters such as Fz2, Tz2, Ar on the shanks and Fz2, Fz3 on the thighs, have a small symmetry index range, so it can be considered that the five gait modes have smaller deviations in these features.

4.3 Gait Cycle Segmentation

The cycle segmentation [29] is required for the sake of extracting these discrete gait parameters and making a global assessment of the symmetry of the periodic curve. Before the cycle segmentation, it is necessary to preprocess the acceleration time series, including the calculation of signal amplitude, interpolation fitting, and resampling. The peak detection algorithm [30] is used to find the local minimum points in the signal sequence, and the number of sample points contained in each gait cycle is taken as the constraint to retrieve the heel landing event. The periodic sequences are resampling according to percentage [31, 32]. The median and amplitude range curves can be obtained as shown in Fig. 2, and each step cycle contains 101 sample points. Figure 2(a) and Fig. 2(b) are the curves of the left and right on the shanks, respectively, while Fig. 2(c) and Fig. 2(d) are the curves of the left and right on the thighs, respectively. To remove the high-frequency noise from the sensor and human body jitter [33], zero-phase forward and reverse third-order Butterworth low-pass filters are applied to the data, with a cut-off frequency of 5 Hz.

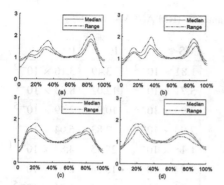

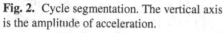

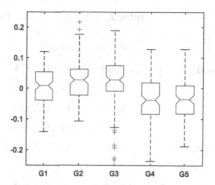

Fig. 2. Cycle segmentation. The vertical axis is the amplitude of acceleration.

Fig. 3. SI in five gait modes. The vertical axis is the value of SI.

5 Analysis and Discussion

Figure 3 is the symmetric exponential box diagram on subjects' shanks to preliminarily evaluate the symmetry deviation between weight-bearing modes and weight-bearing degree. When walking normally, SI value fluctuates around 0, and the symmetry of step length is the highest; When walking with a 2.5 kg and 5 kg weight held in the right hand, SI value is greater than 0; When walking with a 2.5 kg and 5 kg weight held in the left hand, SI value is less than 0. Statistical results show that the step length of the loaded side is longer than that of the non-loaded side, and with the increase of weight-bearing degree, SI value also shows a trend of direct proportional change.

Furthermore, the two-factor repeated measurement analysis of variance (RM ANOVA) is used to analyze the gait symmetry, and 18,000 steps in five gait modes are analyzed. The RM variance analysis is applied to the step length, and the step length follows the Gaussian distribution in different gait modes. The analysis results are shown in Table 2. In RM ANOVA, the F test is used to determine whether the relevant factors affect SI. The variance ratio of the two groups of SI values is used for analysis, and the P-value must be less than 5% to derive the influence of the factors studied on SI values. It is found in Table 2 that the weight-bearing mode and the weight-bearing degree have a significant impact on SI, and the weight-bearing degree has a greater impact on SI than the weight-bearing mode. When the weight-bearing mode factor interacts with the weight-bearing degree factor, the step length has a higher significance on the shank than when the weight-bearing mode factor and the weight-bearing degree factor acted alone.

The cycle similarity analysis of five gait modes is carried out before the gait cycle symmetry evaluation. Table 3 shows the Pearson Correlation Coefficient of the stride length period [34]. Results show that the similarity degree between the stride length of subjects is very high whether it is on the shanks or the thighs. It is proved again that it is not enough to evaluate the symmetry with discrete parameters. The correlation coefficient in Table 3 also shows that when walking normally, the similarity between the left and right gait is the highest. Once there is a unilateral weight-bearing, the periodic correlation of stride lengths on both sides of the body will be reduced. The gait correlation

Table 2. Repeated measurement analysis (RM ANOVA) results.

Factory	Position	Group	MS	F	P
mode	shank	G1, G2, G3	1.81×10^{-2}	3.49	3.16×10^{-2}
		G1, G4, G5	5.71×10^{-2}	12.02	8.93×10^{-6}
	thigh	G1, G2, G3	2.93×10^{-2}	10.9	2.59×10^{-5}
		G1, G4, G5	7.93×10^{-3}	2.83	6.04×10^{-2}
degree	shank	G1, G2, G4	1.15×10^{-1}	25.45	4.83×10^{-11}
		G1, G3, G5	9.94×10^{-2}	18.34	2.69×10^{-8}
	thigh	G1, G2, G4	2.89×10^{-2}	11.4	1.61×10^{-5}
		G1, G3, G5	1.15×10^{-2}	3.88	2.16×10^{-2}
Mode × degree	shank	G1, G2, G3, G4, G5	1.06×10^{-1}	20.35	1.05×10^{-15}
	thigh	G1, G2, G3, G4, G5	1.80×10^{-2}	6.14	7.65×10^{-5}

when holding a weight in the right hand is higher than that of holding a weight in the left hand.

Table 3. Pearson correlation coefficient.

Position	G1	G2	G3	G4	G5
shank	0.9720	0.9702	0.9661	0.9538	0.9584
thigh	0.9866	0.9859	0.9794	0.9606	0.9771

The regression rotation angle algorithm to evaluate the symmetry of the left and right complete period curves was applied to the gait data of five gait modes, and the radian of the regression curve and symmetry line was used as the global index to evaluate the symmetry of period. To test the effect of the model before and after the removal of outliers, a comparison diagram before and after the removal is given by taking G1 as an example. Figure 4(a) is the result before the removal and Fig. 4(b) is the result after the removal. It can be seen that there are some sporadic sample points before the outliers are removed, which may interfere with the regression of the model. After the outliers are removed, the change of regression rotation angle radian is closer to the ideal case.

Table 4 shows the regression rotation angle radians of eight subjects in five gait modes. From the five groups of experimental data in the table, it can be found that because everyone has different gait habits, it may lead to gaps in the analysis of experimental data. For example, subject S04 has the highest symmetry when holding a 2.5 kg weight in the left hand, while subject S03 has the worst symmetry when walking without a weight compared with walking with a weight on one side. However, the overall data suggest that the symmetry of the subjects' left and right gait is the best when walking normally. With the existence of asymmetrical weight-bearing, subjects have a lower symmetry level of

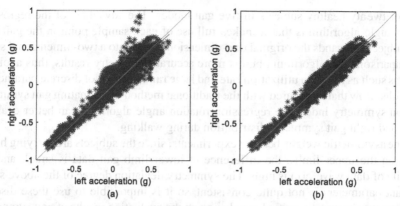

Fig. 4. Comparison before and after removing the outliers. The blue ∗ marks represent the sample points in each gait cycle, the horizontal axis represents the acceleration amplitude of the left gait, the vertical axis represents the acceleration amplitude of the right gait, the red line represents the regression curve, and the green line represents the symmetry line. (Color figure online)

the left and right gait. The study also finds that left and right gait symmetry is lower when heavy objects are held in the left hand than when heavy objects are held in the right, and the gait symmetry decreases with the increases of the unilateral weight-bearing degree.

Table 4. Regression rotation angle radians in five gait modes.

Group	θ_K (rad)								Mean	Std
	S01	S02	S03	S04	S05	S06	S07	S08		
G1	0.019	0.021	0.064	0.090	0.048	0.020	0.069	0.046	0.047	0.026
G2	0.038	0.027	0.059	0.071	0.051	0.028	0.086	0.140	0.063	0.038
G3	0.043	0.046	0.062	0.142	0.092	0.035	0.096	0.177	0.087	0.051
G4	0.045	0.027	0.060	0.053	0.053	0.018	0.053	0.201	0.064	0.057
G5	0.089	0.036	0.063	0.117	0.085	0.033	0.102	0.253	0.097	0.070

6 Conclusion and Prospect

In this study, the symmetry of lower limb gait is evaluated based on discrete gait parameters and complete periodic segment curves. Results show that the asymmetrical weight-bearing modes and weight-bearing degree change the symmetry level of the step length and the acceleration curve, which is of great significance for biomedical and kinematic health monitoring.

To investigate the symmetry of gait parameters and periodic curves of healthy adults under different weight-bearing modes and degrees, the experiment collects 18,000 gait cycles of twenty healthy subjects in five gait modes. The advantage of the regression rotation angle algorithm is that it makes full use of each sample point in the gait data of the subjects, expands the original one-dimensional data into a two-dimensional space for comparison. The algorithm obtains more accurate symmetry results, thus avoiding problems such as low data utilization rate and large random error of discrete parameters. The results show that, compared with the traditional method of evaluating gait symmetry based on symmetry index, the regression rotation angle algorithm can better evaluate the left and right gait symmetry distribution during walking.

In the asymmetric weight-bearing experiments, since the subjects are carrying heavy objects on the upper limbs, the difference of lower limb gait data is small, and the similarity of data waveform is high. The symmetry deviation degree of the above seven important parameters is not quite consistent, so it is impossible to use these discrete gait parameters to make a unified conclusion on the evaluation results of gait symmetry. Combined with the symmetry index and the regression rotation angle algorithm, it is found that the gait symmetry on both sides of subjects is the best when walking without a weight, and the asymmetrical weight-bearing will lead to the decrease of gait symmetry on both sides of subjects. Gait symmetry is lower when heavy objects are held in the left hand than when heavy objects are held in the right, and the gait symmetry decreases with the increase of the degree of unilateral weight-bearing. However, it is also found that not all subjects follow such standards because the gait of the human body is affected by interarticular interactions, internal muscle distribution, and sensory inputs like vision, which may affect the gait and the assessment of symmetry.

Future research directions: (1) the asymmetric weight-bearing data will be collected from left-handed subjects to compare the waveform characteristics and symmetry differences between two groups of subjects; (2) considering the small difference of asymmetric weight-bearing data in waveform, it is possible to find appropriate features [35] for effective action classification and personnel identification.

Acknowledgement(s). The authors would like to acknowledge the support of the national natural science foundation of China (No. 61772248) and the project name is Sensing Theory and Key Technologies of Big Behavioral Data for Wearable Computing.

References

1. Kirmizi, M., Simsek, I.E., Elvan, A., et al.: Gait speed and gait asymmetry in individuals with chronic idiopathic neck pain. Musculoskeletal Sci. Pract. **41**, 23–27 (2019)
2. Li, J.H., Tian, L., Wang, H., et al.: Segmentation and recognition of basic and transitional activities for continuous physical human activity. IEEE Access 1–1 (2019)
3. Clemens, S., Kim, K.J., Gailey, R., et al.: Inertial sensor-based measures of gait symmetry and repeatability in people with unilateral lower limb amputation. Clin. Biomech. **72**, 102–107 (2020)
4. Haji Ghassemi, N., Hannink, J., Martindale, C.F., et al.: Segmentation of gait sequences in sensor-based movement analysis: a comparison of methods in Parkinson's disease. Sensors **18**(1), 145 (2018)
5. Lin Yingjie, W., Jianning, L.L.: Research progress of the quantitative evaluation methods in human gait symmetry. Chin. J. Biomed. Eng. **38**(2), 222–232 (2019)

6. Viteckova, S., Kutilek, P., Svoboda, Z., et al.: Gait symmetry measures: a review of current and prospective methods. Biomed. Signal Process. Control **42**, 89–100 (2018)
7. Hardie, R., Haskew, R., Harris, J., et al.: The effects of bag style on muscle activity of the trapezius, erector spinae and latissimus dorsi during walking in female university students. J. Hum. Kinet. **45**(1), 39–47 (2015)
8. Zhao, G., Qu, F., Yang, C., et al.: Biomechanical effects of different ways of trunk load bearing on human walking. J. Phys. Educ. **2017**(2), 23 (2017)
9. Abid, M., Renaudin, V., Aoustin, Y., et al.: Walking gait step length asymmetry induced by handheld device. IEEE Trans. Neural Syst. Rehabil. Eng. **25**(11), 2075–2083 (2017)
10. Son, H.-H., Kim, E.-J.: Arm swing asymmetry and effect of auditory cues on amplitude in the patients with Parkinson's disease. J. Korea Acad.-Ind. Cooper. Soc. **14**(1), 344–350 (2013)
11. Linah, W., Aladin, Z., John, W., et al.: Identification of foot pathologies based on plantar pressure asymmetry. Sensors **15**(8), 20392–20408 (2015)
12. Rapp, W., Brauner, T., Weber, L., et al.: Improvement of walking speed and gait symmetry in older patients after hip arthroplasty: a prospective cohort study. BMC Musculoskeletal Disorders **16**(1), 291 (2015)
13. Iosa, M., Cereatti, A., Merlo, A., et al.: Assessment of waveform similarity in clinical gait data: the linear fit method. Biomed. Res. Int. **2014**, 1–7 (2014)
14. Park, K., Roemmich, R.T., Elrod, J.M., et al.: Effects of aging and Parkinson's disease on joint coupling, symmetry, complexity and variability of lower limb movements during gait. Clin. Biomech. **33**, 92–97 (2016)
15. Gong, W., Lee, S., Kim, B.: The comparison of pressure of the feet in stance and gait by the types of bags. J. Phys. Therapy Sci. **22**(3), 255–258 (2010)
16. Hyung, E.J., Lee, H.O., Kwon, Y.J.: Influence of load and carrying method on gait, specifically pelvic movement. J. Phys. Therapy Sci. **28**(7), 2059–2062 (2016)
17. Fowler, N.E., Rodacki, A.L.F., Rodacki, C.D.: Changes in stature and spine kinematics during a loaded walking task. Gait Posture **23**(2), 133–141 (2006)
18. Kellis, E., Arampatzi, F.: Effects of sex and mode of carrying schoolbags on ground reaction forces and temporal characteristics of gait. J. Pediatric Orthopaed. B **18**(5), 275–282 (2009)
19. Son, S.M., Noh, H.: Gait changes caused by the habits and methods of carrying a handbag. J. Phys. Therapy Sci. **25**(8), 969–971 (2013)
20. Pau, M., Mandaresu, S., Leban, B., et al.: Short-term effects of backpack carriage on plantar pressure and gait in schoolchildren. J. Electromyogr. Kinesiol. **25**(2), 406–412 (2015)
21. Castro, M.P., Figueiredo, M.C., Abreu, S., et al.: The influence of gait cadence on the ground reaction forces and plantar pressures during load carriage of young adults. Appl. Ergon. **49**, 41–46 (2015)
22. Hotfiel, T., Carl, H.D., Wendler, F., et al.: Plantar pressures increase with raising body weight: a standardised approach with paired sample using neutral shoes. J. Back Musculoskelet. Rehabil. **30**(3), 583–589 (2017)
23. Qiu, S., Liu, L., Zhao, H., et al.: MEMS inertial sensors based gait analysis for rehabilitation assessment via multi-sensor fusion. Micromachines **9**(9), 442 (2018)
24. Qiu, S., Liu, L., Wang, Z., et al.: Body sensor network-based gait quality assessment for clinical decision-support via multi-sensor fusion. IEEE Access **7**, 59884–59894 (2019)
25. Hsu, Y.L., Chung, P.C., Wang, W.H., et al.: Gait and balance analysis for patients with Alzheimer's disease using an inertial-sensor-based wearable instrument. IEEE J. Biomed. Health Inform. **18**(6), 1822–1830 (2014)
26. Mills, K., Hettinga, B.A., Pohl, M.B., et al.: Between-limb kinematic asymmetry during gait in unilateral and bilateral mild to moderate knee osteoarthritis. Arch. Phys. Med. Rehabil. **94**(11), 2241–2247 (2013)

27. Clemens, S., Kim, K.J., Gailey, R., et al.: Inertial sensor-based measures of gait symmetry and repeatability in people with unilateral lower limb amputation. Clin. Biomech. **72**, 102–107 (2020)
28. Wu, J., Wu, B.: The novel quantitative technique for assessment of gait symmetry using advanced statistical learning algorithm. Biomed. Res. Int. **2015**, 528971 (2015)
29. Zhao, H., Wang, Z., Qiu, S., et al.: Adaptive gait detection based on foot-mounted inertial sensors and multi-sensor fusion. Inf. Fusion **52**, 157–166 (2019)
30. Jiang, S., Wang, X., Kyrarini, M., et al.: A robust algorithm for gait cycle segmentation. In: 25th European Signal Processing Conference (EUSIPCO), pp. 31–35. IEEE (2017)
31. Ma, Y., Ashari, Z.E., Pedram, M., et al.: Cyclepro: a robust framework for domain-agnostic gait cycle detection. IEEE Sens. J. **19**(10), 3751–3762 (2019)
32. Gurchiek, R.D., Choquette, R.H., Beynnon, B.D., et al.: Remote gait analysis using wearable sensors detects asymmetric gait patterns in patients recovering from ACL reconstruction. In: 16th International Conference on Wearable and Implantable Body Sensor Networks (BSN), pp. 1–4. IEEE (2019)
33. Huan, Z., Chen, X., Lv, S., et al.: Gait recognition of acceleration sensor for smart phone based on multiple classifier fusion. Math. Probl. Eng. **2019**(12), 1–17 (2019)
34. Wang, L., Sun, Y., Li, Q., et al.: Estimation of step length and gait asymmetry using wearable inertial sensors. IEEE Sens. J. **18**(9), 3844–3851 (2018)
35. Nweke, H.F., Teh, Y.W., Mujtaba, G., et al.: Data fusion and multiple classifier systems for human activity detection and health monitoring: review and open research directions. Inf. Fusion **46**, 147–170 (2019)

The Mining of IP Landmarks for Internet Webcams

Yimo Ren[1], Hong Li[1], Hongsong Zhu[1], Limin Sun[1], Weizhong Wang[2(✉)],
and Yachao Li[3]

[1] Institute of Information Engineering, CAS, Beijing, China
{renyimo,lihong,zhuhongsong,sunlimin}@iie.ac.cn
[2] China Academy of Industrial Internet, Beijing, China
wangweizhong@china-aii.com
[3] Henan University Software College, Luoyang, China
chaoliya0928@163.com

Abstract. IP geolocation, which is important for the security of devices, heavily relies on the number of high-quality landmarks. As one kind of widely used Internet of Things (IoT) devices, Internet webcams are exposed to the Internet intentionally or unintentionally. While there are few researches on the methodology to extract landmarks for Internet webcams by now. In this paper, we proposed a framework GeoWAT to automatically generate landmarks from the watermarks of the webcams, which are accurate enough to improve some IP geolocation services. GeoWAT uses Optical Character Recognition (OCR) techniques to get text locations from the watermarks of public webcams on the Internet websites. Then GeoWAT queries the locations through online maps to get latitudes/longitudes of webcams as landmarks. We conducted experiments to evaluate the performance and effectiveness of GeoWAT in real world. Our results show that GeoWAT could automatically extract the locations of webcams with high precision and recall. Also, GeoWAT have got more accurate landmarks than other IP location services, such as IPIP, GeoLites2 and ipstack, on the webcams dataset we collected from the whole world.

Keywords: IP geolocation · Landmarks mining · Network measurement · Webcam watermarks

1 Introduction

IP geolocation is one kind of methods which pulls in high confidence locations of IPs to measure the real-world geographic locations of the whole network. Nowadays, IP geolocation is widely used in many fields, including online intrusion detection [1], location-based services [2], and content personalization [3]. The current researches on IP geolocation mainly rely on seeking more IPs with high confidence locations as geographic landmarks [4] to improve the algorithms of IP geolocation, such as GeoPing [5], CBG [6], TBG [7].

© Springer Nature Singapore Pte Ltd. 2020
Z. Hao et al. (Eds.): CWSN 2020, CCIS 1321, pp. 257–268, 2020.
https://doi.org/10.1007/978-981-33-4214-9_19

At present, researches are devoted to seek and select landmarks for the IP geolocation in many ways. Hao Liu [8] leveraged the locations which users are willing to share in location-sharing services to get accurate landmarks. Wang Jinxia [9] mined the geographic landmarks by using the closest-shortest rule to select high-confidence landmarks from the existing results. Although with many ways to find the landmarks in different fields, open-source landmarks are still insufficient and the quality needs to be improved simultaneously.

For advertising and sharing purposes, a lot of webcams upload living streams real time on the Internet with stable IP addresses. At the same time, some webcams have watermarks in their videos, which usually contain the date, location and other information. On many public websites, such as pictimo.com and te.ua, users can upload and share the content of their own webcams for interest, and others could download the videos legally and freely. Figure 1 shows an example of websites which contains the webcams all over the world. Webcams are widely used all over the world but there is a lack of researches to extract locations of webcams as landmarks. Therefore, more accurate locations of webcams need to be found to supply more landmarks.

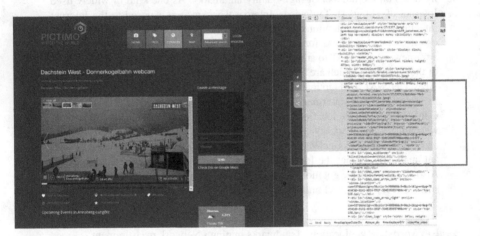

Fig. 1. pictimo.com is one of websites which contains many publicly shared cameras. The box shows the URL of an online camera.

There are many ways to get the locations of the webcams, Zakaria Laskar [10] used a deep learning approach to seek the locations of cameras based on looking for the most similar image in the database, whose locations are already known. Yun-peng Shi [11] proposed a strategy for improving camera location estimation in structure from motion. However, almost no watermark information is used to extract locations of webcams as landmarks.

Overall, our contributions are summarized as follows:

a) We first proposed a framework GeoWAT to extract accurate locations of webcams as geographic landmarks for IP geolocation based on their watermarks. And GeoWAT have got more accurate landmarks than other IP location services, such as IPIP, GeoLites2 and ipstack.

b) We extracted the locations of webcams, according to the combination of OCR technology and semantic analysis technology.

c) We extracted the locations of webcams around the world, and measured the distribution of webcams to explain the possible scope of GeoWAT.

2 Background

2.1 Public Webcams

Webcams have been increasingly connected to the Internet in the past decade. A webcam is one typical Internet of Things (IoT) device for monitoring physical surroundings, such as a plaza, a street, an industrial area, or a home theater. For the sake of remote access and control, webcam devices are visible and accessible through their IP addresses. In contrast to web services, webcam devices are fixed in physical places and remain relatively stable over time. Thus, online webcams have great potential to be used as promising landmarks but have not yet been explored.

In order to avoid the privacy and security risks caused by collecting webcams and their IPs, we only downloaded the webcams to construct our research dataset from the public websites based their robots.txt.

2.2 Watermarks

Digital watermark is a kind of related information embedded in carrier file by computer algorithm. It embeds some identification information (i.e. digital watermark) directly into the digital carrier. For video watermarks, the information embedded in video watermarks always includes invariance, which means some information embedded in the video, such as location, does not change frequently. Therefore, through the recognition and analysis of watermarks, the geographic landmarks with high confidence locations could be found and established.

2.3 Geolocation

IP geolocation is used to improve the positioning accuracy of IPs. It mainly consists of two parts:

a) The methods to find IPs with high confidence locations as geographic landmarks;
b) The methods to measure the connections, such as the network topology used in TBG algorithm, of geographic landmarks and other IPs to infer their positions.

To improve the performance of the IP geolocation in the networks, geographic landmarks should satisfy some requirements, which are: Firstly, the positions of IPs are relatively static and stable, and will not change much in a long time. Secondly, the positioning accuracy of geographic landmarks is at least higher than that of current ones to improve the performance of geolocation. Thirdly, there must be a large number of geographic landmarks extracted by each method in order to be worthy to improve the IP geolocation.

3   Methods

To automatically generate geographic landmarks from websites, firstly, we crawled images and other information of webcams from the public websites. Secondly, we built an automated model to detect and tag the watermarks of the webcams. Thirdly, we converted the watermark to texts by OCR and selected the real locations from all texts. Finally, we searched the latitude/longitude of the OCR results by some online map APIs (such as Google Map, Baidu Map, etc.). At the same time, we filtered noise and irrelevant content on each step to get high-quality geographic landmarks. To evaluate the quality of geographic landmarks, we inputted them into the CBG algorithm and compared with open sources landmarks. Figure 2 shows the architecture of GeoWAT.

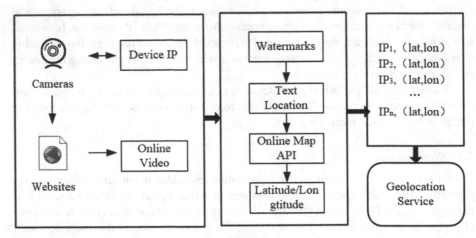

Fig. 2. The architecture of GeoWAT.

3.1 Web Crawler

Our web crawler is designed to periodically monitor a website to collect its webpages. Since different websites have different templates and HTML structures, we design a web crawler to scrape webpages from those sites. Given a website, we first utilize the web crawler to obtain all its pages through the breadth-first search. Specifically, we parse the website homepage to explore all its URL links, and iteratively parse the URL links to explore the next-layer pages, until no more links are found.

A problem here is that websites might change webpages or live webcams over time, e.g., new pages are added or old pages are removed. However, we believe that webcams are relatively stable for a long time period. The WCP periodically monitors websites/webpages by re-accessing those URL links to identify whether they are still available. In practice, the monitoring period for websites is one month, and the period for webpages is one week. Table 1 shows the regexes and keywords we used to extract useful information.

Table 1. The examples of regexes and keywords

Type	Regexes or keyword
IPv4	((25[0-5]|2[0-4][0-9]|[01]?[0-9][0-9]?) 3(25[0-5]|2[0-4][0-9]|[01]?[0-9][0-9]?) (/([0-2][0-9]|3[0-2]|[0-9]))?
Video/Image Formats	jpg, png, mjpg, cgi, …
Geographical Coordinate	longitude=.*? <lat>.*? <lon>.*?

3.2 Watermarks Detection

In order to save the time of overall process of geographic landmarks mining, we build an automated model to classify whether the image of the webcam has a watermark which contains location of the webcam. After detecting the watermarks of the webcams, we save the detected watermark results in the form of pictures.

For the task of text detection, it is natural to think of applying the method of image detection to select the text area in the image. Tian Zhi [12] proposed a novel Connectionist Text Proposal Network (CTPN) that accurately localizes text lines in natural image. The CTPN detects a text line in a sequence of fine-scale text proposals directly in convolutional feature maps. Figure 3 shows the inputs and the outputs of CTPN. If there are no watermarks on the images of cameras, none will be the output of CTPN.

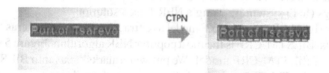

Fig. 3. The inputs and the outputs of CTPN.

We used a standard CTPN model to realize the watermarks detection of the webcams. To achieve a better performance, we pretrained the CTPN with dataset ICDAR 2015 [13]. ICDAR 2015 includes 1,500 images which were collected by using the Google Glass. And ICDAR 2015 is always used to train the model for object text detection, whose problem is like that of watermarks detection.

3.3 Watermarks Recognition

After getting the location of watermark embedded in the webcam, we build a text recognition model to convert watermark to texts. A common approach [14] to use the Convolutional Recurrent Neural Network (CRNN) model. With CNN features as input, bidirectional LSTM sequence processing greatly improves the efficiency of text recognition and the generalization ability of the model. The feature map is obtained by classification method, and then the result is translated by connectionist temporal classification (CTC) to get the output result. Figure 4 shows the inputs and the outputs of CRNN.

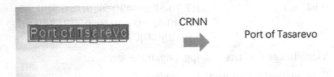

Fig. 4. The inputs and the outputs of CRNN.

Also, we used a standard CRNN model to realize the watermarks recognition of the webcams. To achieve a better performance, we pretrained the CRNN with dataset IIIT5k [15]. IIIT5k contains 3,000 cropped word test images collected from the Internet. Each image has been associated to a 50-words lexicon and a 1k-words lexicon.

3.4 Locations Extractor

When all the texts on the camera images are extracted, we need to further extract the location information from them. Generally speaking, the watermarks of cameras may include locations, dates, owner names, etc. Therefore, we established a locations extractor based on Named Entity Recognition (NER). NER is often used to extract some key information from natural language, such as persons, locations, dates, quantities, numbers, etc. Goyal [16] presents a survey of developments and progresses made in NER and Georgescu [17] enhances the process of diagnosing and detecting possible vulnerabilities within an Internet of Things (IoT) system by using a NER-based solution.

Therefore, we build a BiLSTM-CRF model to extract locations of cameras from their watermarks' texts. BiLSTM-CRF is the most popular NER algorithm. Figure 5 shows the typical structure of BiLSTM-CRF model. We put watermarks' texts into BiLSTM-CRF by words, and the BiLSTM-CRF judges whether a group of words are a name of possible location according to the relationship between the words. We pretrained BiLSTM-CRF to extract locations from the watermarks' texts based on Wikipedia [18]. If a word is the begin word of a location, it will be tagged as 'B-LOC', if a word is the inner word of the location, it will be tagged as 'I-LOC', if a word is not the word of location, it will be tagged as 'O'. For example, 'Port of Tasarevo 2018-01-01 12:00:00' will be tagged as 'B-LOC I-LOC I-LOC O O', which means 'Port of Tasarevo' is the possible location of the camera.

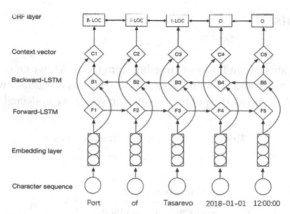

Fig. 5. BiLSTM-CRF Structure, B-LOC means the character is the begin of a location, I-LOC means the character is in the location, O means the character is not the part of the location.

3.5 Geolocation Coder

There are many online maps API, such as Google Map, Baidu Map, could help us get the latitude/longitude of the OCR results. Online maps provide the online information service, mostly about locations, for users by manual query, online communication, etc. A lot of applications use online maps to achieve a better performance. Aleksandar Pejic [19] uses Google Maps APIs to present prominent objects of tourists' destinations. Zamir A R [20] uses Google Maps APIs to calculate the similarity of two images to get accurate image localization. We query the online maps with the OCR results and call the process of getting the latitude/longitude from online map APIs as Geolocation Coder.

In a word, the example of GeoWAT to convert watermarks of webcams to high-quality landmarks, is as Fig. 6 shows.

Fig. 6. The example of GeoWAT.

4 Experiments

4.1 Dataset

To evaluate the quality of landmarks extracting from GeoWAT, we constructed a dataset which contains pictures and latitude/longitude of webcams on publics websites such as pictimo.com. Table 2 shows the public websites on which we collected the webcams.

Table 2. The public webcams websites

Websites	
pictimo.com	krvn.co
worldcam.eu	skjm.com
geocities.jp	reklboard.ru
webkams.com	webcams.bg
bbox.ch	ilm24.ee

We downloaded 7618 pictures from the public websites covering 90 countries all over the world to construct the dataset we used to evaluate GeoWAT. We put the number of webcams in each country on the world map, and used the depth of the color to show the size of the number. Figure 7 shows the distribution of webcams we collected all over the world.

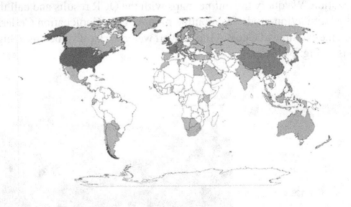

Fig. 7. World Webcams in Feb 2020, by Country.

And the top 10 countries with the largest number of webcams are as Table 3 shows.
As we can see from the Fig. 7 and Table 3, the public webcams are widely distributed all over the world and there are a large num of webcams in North America and Europe. Therefore, GeoWAT would well cover much more geographical areas and have visible effects on IP-based geolocation.

Table 3. The top 10 countries with the most webcams

Country	Webcams	Country	Webcams
United States	823	Italy	352
United Kingdom	620	Germany	294
France	542	Hungary	281
Japan	416	Iceland	254
China	410	Finland	202

4.2 Metrics

The quality of landmarks extracted from GeoWAT affected by those key factors: Watermarks Detection, Watermarks Recognition and Geolocation Coder. We use the precision and recall [21] to evaluate the performance of each step. The definitions are as follows:

$$Precision = \frac{TP}{TP + FP} \tag{1}$$

$$Recall = \frac{TP}{TP + FN} \tag{2}$$

where TP presents the number of the true positive, FP denotes the number of the false positive, and FN is the number of the false negative.

Watermarks Detection. For watermarks detection, we think that the images of webcams with watermarks are positive samples and the images without watermarks are negative samples. Therefore, the precision and recall of CTPN show the ability to detect the webcams with watermarks from all the webcams on the public websites. After evaluating the models, we can see that CTPN has 95% precision and 82% recall.

Watermarks Recognition. For watermarks recognition, we think that watermarks which have 75% words as same as corresponding results are positive samples, and the others are negative samples. Therefore, the precision and recall of CRNN show the ability to convert the watermarks to text location. After evaluating the models, we can see that CRNN has 87% precision and 79% recall.

Locations Extractor. For locations extractor, we think that locations of watermarks which have 75% words as same as corresponding results are positive samples, and the others are negative samples. Therefore, the precision and recall of BiLSTM-CRF show the ability to distinguish location information from others. After evaluating the models, we can see that BiLSTM-CRF has 88% precision and 81% recall.

After evaluating the models, then we removed some noise points, and we total extracted 2892 high-quality landmarks from the dataset as Sect. 4.1 shows.

4.3 Quality

As Sect. 2.3 shows, high-quality landmarks should have a large number and don't change frequently. Therefore, we calculate deviation distance and coverage of geographic landmarks extracting from GeoWAT.

Some cameras have corresponding location on the websites. After getting the inferred location from GeoWAT, we calculate the deviation distances between the corresponding location and inferred location to express the precision of geographic landmarks. We contacted the results of GeoWAT with IPIP, GeoLites2 and ipstack.

Figure 8.shows that nearly 83% of geographic landmarks extracted from GeoWAT have deviation distance less than 5 km compared with the real locations. And GeoWAT has achieved a better performance than IPIP, GeoLites2 and ipstack on the webcams dataset we collected. In a word, GeoWAT could locate the cameras with high precision according to their watermarks.

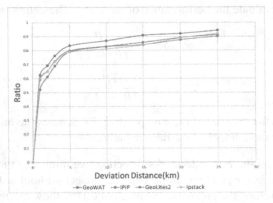

Fig. 8. The performance of landmarks in GeoWAT.

4.4 Analysis

With the accurate locations, landmarks from GeoWAT can be used as input to CBG for improving the locations of other IPs in the network. At the same time, because we can get the location of the webcams from their watermarks, even the users, entities, we suggest that public webcams must strictly deal with the watermarks, which can not only protect the copyright of the video images, but also not disclose too much privacy.

a) Personal cameras should not be connected to the public network as much as possible, even if they need to connect, purchase some cloud services, so that the IPs of cameras could change dynamically.
b) When people must use watermarks to tag their cameras, try to use symbols instead of texts, so that the privacy could not be disclosed too much.

5 Conclusion

IP geolocation heavily relies on the number of high-quality landmarks. In this paper, we proposed a framework GeoWAT to automatically generate landmarks from the watermarks of the webcams to provide IP-based geolocation services. GeoWAT uses OCR techniques and online maps API to get accurate locations from the webcams we collected on the public websites. We conducted experiments to evaluate the performance and effectiveness of GeoWAT and measured the existing webcams all over the world. Our results show that the OCR models of GeoWAT automatically detect webcams watermarks with 95% precision and 82% recall. Also, GeoWAT recognize webcams watermarks with 87% precision and 79% recall. Also, the deviation distance of GeoWAT is better than IPIP, Geolites2 and ipstack on the webcam dataset we collected all over the world with different levels. And nearly 83% of geographic landmarks extracted from GeoWAT have deviation distance less than 5 km compared with the real locations. Therefore, GeoWAT can get accurate locations of webcams though online maps using their watermarks. In a word, GeoWAT can generate stable and fine-grained landmarks, which are helping to achieve a better performance of IP geolocation from a new perspective.

However, due to the large number of websites which has public webcams, downloading all public webcams websites in the world would be a very heavy task. How to ensure that the webcams and the corresponding upload devices are in the same locations, even most webcams could connect to the Internet and upload the livestreams. At the same time, including this paper, it is suggested that the watermarks should be removed by the public webcams to prevent information leakage. Therefore, how to get a lot of public webcams automatedly and not to violate personal privacy will be an urgent problem to be solved in the next step.

References

1. Ulltveit-Moe, N., Oleshchuk, V.A., Køien, G.M.: Location-aware mobile intrusion detection with enhanced privacy in a 5G context. Wirel. Pers. Commun. 57(3), 317–338 (2011). https://doi.org/10.1007/s11277-010-0069-6
2. Choi, S.M.: Location-based information service method and mobile terminal therefor (2014)
3. Kim, E.: An automatic recommendation scheme of TV program contents for (IP) TV personalization. IEEE Trans. Broadcast. 57(3), 674–684 (2011)
4. Wang, Y.: Towards street-level client-independent IP geolocation. In: Proceedings of the 8th USENIX Conference on Networked Systems Design and Implementation, pp. 365–379. USENIX Association, Boston (2011)
5. Padamanabban, V.N.: Determining the geographic location of internet hosts. ACM SIGMETRICS Perform. Eval. Rev. 29(1) (2001)
6. Gueye, B.: Constraint-based geolocation of internet hosts. IEEE/ACM Trans. Netw. 14(6), 1063–6692 (2006)
7. Katz-Bassett, E.: Towards IP geolocation using delay and topology measurements. In: Proceedings of the 6th ACM SIGCOMM Conference on Internet Measurement, pp. 71–84. Association for Computing Machinery, Rio de Janeriro (2006)
8. Liu, H.: Mining checkins from location-sharing services for client-independent IP geolocation. In: IEEE INFOCOM 2014 - IEEE Conference on Computer Communications, pp. 619–627. IEEE, Toronto (2014)

9. Jinxia, W.: IP geolocation technology research based on network measurement. In: 2016 Sixth International Conference on Instrumentation & Measurement, Computer, Communication and Control, pp. 892–897. IEEE, Harbin (2016)

10. Laskar, Z.: Camera relocalization by computing pairwise relative poses using convolutional neural network. In: 2017 IEEE International Conference on Computer Vision Workshop (ICCVW). IEEE, Venice (2017)

11. Lerman, G.: Estimation of camera locations in highly corrupted scenarios: all about that base, no shape trouble. In: 2018 IEEE/CVF Conference on Computer Vision and Pattern Recognition. IEEE/CVF, Salt Lake City (2018)

12. Tian, Z., Huang, W., He, T., He, P., Qiao, Y.: Detecting text in natural image with connectionist text proposal network. In: Leibe, B., Matas, J., Sebe, N., Welling, M. (eds.) ECCV 2016. LNCS, vol. 9912, pp. 56–72. Springer, Cham (2016). https://doi.org/10.1007/978-3-319-464 84-8_4

13. Karatzas, D.: ICDAR 2015 competition on robust reading. In: Proceedings of the 2015 13th International Conference on Document Analysis and Recognition (ICDAR), pp. 1156–1160. IEEE Computer Society, USA (2015)

14. Shi, B.: An end-to-end trainable neural network for image-based sequence recognition and its application to scene text recognition. IEEE Trans. Pattern Anal. Mach. Intell. **39**, 2298–2304 (2017)

15. Mishra, A.: Scene text recognition using higher order language priors. In: BMVC - British Machine Vision Conference, BMVA, Surrey, United Kingdom (2012)

16. Archana, G.: Recent named entity recognition and classification techniques: a systematic review. Comput. Sci. Rev. **29**, 21–43 (2018)

17. Georgescu: Named-entity-recognition-based automated system for diagnosing cybersecurity situations in IoT networks. Sensors **19**(15), 3380(2019)

18. Dojchinovski, M., Kliegr, T.: Datasets and GATE evaluation framework for benchmarking Wikipedia-based NER systems. In: The International Conference on NLP and DBPEDIA. CEUR-WS.org (2013)

19. Pejic, A.: An expert system for tourists using Google Maps API. In: 7th International Symposium on Intelligent Systems and Informatics, pp. 317–322. IEEE, Subotica (2009)

20. Zamir, A.R., Shah, M.: Accurate image localization based on Google Maps street view. In: Daniilidis, K., Maragos, P., Paragios, N. (eds.) ECCV 2010. LNCS, vol. 6314, pp. 255–268. Springer, Heidelberg (2010). https://doi.org/10.1007/978-3-642-15561-1_19

21. Ting, K.M.: Precision and recall. In: Sammut, C., Webb, G.I. (eds.) Encyclopedia of Machine Learning. Springer, Boston (2011). https://doi.org/10.1007/978-0-387-30164-8_652

Multi-label Image Classification Optimization Model Based on Deep Learning

Xiaojuan Wang[1]([✉]), Jing Xu[2], Jie Hua[3], and Zhanjun Hao[2]

[1] College of Mathematics and Computer Science, Northwest Minzu University,
Lanzhou 730030, China
happywxj@163.com
[2] College of Computer Science and Engineering, Northwest Normal University,
Lanzhou 730070, China
31828555@qq.com, zhanjunhao@126.com
[3] Hebei Institute of Mechanical and Electrical Technology, Xingtai 054000, China
51860204@qq.com

Abstract. In order to meet the needs of diversified image information retrieval in the real world, to solve the "semantic gap" problem of image and natural language conversion, and to optimize the accuracy and efficiency of multi-label classification method, this paper proposes a deep learning and multi-label BR algorithm. An image classification method uses a residual neural network with better overall performance to extract image depth learning features, and takes the extraction result as an input, and generates a result vector through spatial regularization of the image space and the label, and the result is obtained. The elements are added as the final prediction result by directly using the residual network prediction result. The whole network is trained by the softmax loss function. Compared with other traditional models, the spatial relationship results of the labels provide a good regularization effect for multi-label image classification, which improves the accuracy on the NUS-WIDE dataset and its recall rate, etc.

Keywords: Multi-label · Deep convolution neural network · Image space · Image attention mechanism

1 Foreword

In recent years, with the continuous development of the Internet and the continuous introduction of multimedia technology, image data has exploded in people's daily lives with its advantages of being intuitive and easy to understand. How to process and utilize image data quickly and efficiently has become one of the most important tasks. The rise of machine learning and the heat of artificial intelligence, computer vision has also attracted more and more domestic and foreign scholars to study, multi-label image classification as an important branch of computer vision, also achieved very rapid in the past decade The development and many gratifying results.

Compared with multi-label image classification, single-label classification requires the least amount of information, and human cognition obtains the most information,

Z. Hao et al. (Eds.): CWSN 2020, CCIS 1321, pp. 269–285, 2020.
https://doi.org/10.1007/978-981-33-4214-9_20

while multi-label classification is between them. There are three main ideas for dealing with multi-label issues in dealing with label associations [1–3]:

The first one is ignoring the association between the label and the label, and treating each label as an independent attribute, constructing a two-classifier for each label to be classified, namely Binary Relevance (BR) algorithm.

The second one, take paired associations between the multi-labels into consider, such as the label sorting questions for relevant and irrelevant labels.

The last one, considering the multi-relationships of multi-labels, such as the affects that other any other labels might bring up. This is the best way, but it owes the highest model complexity.

There are also transformation data adaptation algorithms (commonly used to combine multiple categories into a single category, which will lead to the number of categories) and the transformation algorithm adapts the data (usually such as normal output q-dimensional data, where softmax regression is changed to sigmoid function, Finally, the output of f(.) greater than the threshold is output), and the multi-label classification network, label embedding, etc. are all effective.

However, these three ideas have their own shortcomings: the first idea ignores the association between tags, while the tags in the real world mostly have some kind of strong or similar association, such as for a decision tag is "Brazil" The image, which can be marked by the label "soccer", "rainforest", etc., has a higher probability than other images; the second idea only considers the association of a pair of tags, neglecting multiple associations between tags. The third considers all tag associations, but the algorithm is costly and the model complexity is high. All of the above problems may affect the efficiency or accuracy of the multi-label classification algorithm more or less. In recent years, image multi-label classification based on tag semantic relations has made great progress, but due to the particularity of image data structure, there is a relationship between its tag category and image space. Relatively small.

Deep convolutional neural networks (CNNs) have achieved great success in single-label image classification in recent years. Since the deep CNN model has strong recognition feature learning ability, the pre-trained model on the big data set can be easily transferred to other tasks, thereby improving the performance of the model. However, since images and tags do not all correspond, feature representations are not optimal for images with multiple tags. The variety and complexity of multi-label image content makes it difficult to learn effective feature representations and classifiers.

Therefore, this paper combines the BR idea and deep convolutional neural network associated with tag in multi-label, introduces the idea of attention mechanism, and realizes a better classification model than traditional algorithm (will be shown in Sect. 4.2).

2   Related Works

Image classification is an important task in image processing. In the field of traditional machine learning, the standard process of image recognition and classification is feature extraction, feature selection, and finally the feature vector is input into a suitable classifier to complete feature classification. However, it has been proved by experiments that the efficiency and accuracy of traditional machine learning methods on image classification problems are far less than those of neural networks.

In 2012, Alex Krizhevsky and others made a breakthrough in the network structure of AlexNet [4]. With the idea of deep learning, the three modules of the image were integrated into one, and the convolution of the five-layer convolutional layer and the three-layer fully connected layer was designed. The neural network structure extracts the image information in different directions layer by layer. The shallow convolution mainly acquires common features such as image edges, and the deep convolution obtains the specific distribution features of the specific data set. AlexNet won the 2012 ILSVRC (ImageNet Large-Scale Visual Identity Challenge) with a record low turnover rate of 15.4%, proving the superiority of neural networks (there was no concept of deep learning at the time) compared to traditional machine learning methods.

In 2013, Christian Szegedy and others improved on the basis of AlexNet and proposed ZF-net [5], and used visual means to show the world what is being done in each layer of the neural network, but ZF-net There is no structural breakthrough, only the details of the changes, accuracy and model efficiency has not been greatly improved.

In 2014, Simonyan K et al. proposed a deeper network model than AlexNet, VGG-net [6], and verified by experiments that the accuracy of the model is proportional to the depth of the network. Due to the introduction of this theory, more and more people tend to use deeper networks in the design of the model. In the subsequent experiments, it is found that the gradient disappears with the increase of the number of network layers.

In 2015, GoogleNet [7] came out. At this time, deep learning has undergone further refinement of ZF-net and VGG-net. In the depth of the network, the size of the convolution kernel, and the technical details of the gradient disappearance in back propagation. There has been a detailed discussion. Google has introduced the Inception unit based on these technologies, which breaks through the sequential arrangement of the computational units of the traditional deep neural network, namely the convolutional layer, the active layer, the pooled layer, and the next convolutional layer. The paradigm increases the ImageNet classification error rate to a high level of 6.7%.

In the trend that the network is getting deeper and the network structure is more and more complicated, the training of deep neural network is more and more difficult. In order to solve the problem of accurate and first saturation after training, Microsoft He Mingming and others will learn residuals in 2015. The concept introduces a deep learning framework, namely ResNet. The core idea is that when the neural network reaches saturation at a certain layer, the next layer is used to map a function of $f(x) = x$, which solves the problem of gradient disappearance to some extent.

In 2015, K. Xu, J. Ba and R. Kiros et al. first introduced the attention mechanism to the image classification problem [8]. It is considered that if the label 1 is marked on the input image, the image area associated with it should be given Higher attention value. Greatly improved the accuracy of image classification. However, this research has not been applied to the problem of multi-label image classification, and it cannot solve the image classification problem in real scenes.

In recent years, research progress on multi-label image classification has focused on the capture of semantic relationships between tags. This relationship or dependence can be solved by the probability graph model [9] proposed by X. Li, F. Zhao and Y.

Guo et al. in 2014, structured neural network or cyclic neural network (RNN). Although much progress has been made in the use of semantic relationships, existing methods are unable to capture the spatial relationships of tags because their spatial locations are not labeled for training.

It can be seen that with the development of computer vision, more complex convolutional neural networks have been proposed and played a huge role in the fields of target detection [10] and semantic segmentation [11, 12], but there are still many The part that is not perfect. Combining the advantages and disadvantages of the above model, this paper proposes a multi-label image classification optimization model, which solves the problem of using the residual learning on the gradient disappearance and complexity of the deep learning model. The results of association and regularization were trained using the sigmoid function, and better results were obtained.

3　Multi-label Image Classification Optimization Model

3.1　Label Prediction Based on Image Depth Learning Features (*fcnn*)

In this paper, the network used to extract image deep learning features adopts the idea of residual learning in ResNet101 [13], and uses the structure of the residual module of the residual learning network proposed by K. He et al. in 2016 [14]. On the one hand, by introducing residual learning, ResNet can theoretically approximate arbitrary models and results, which means that the deep learning network overcomes the shortcomings of the test results as the network deepens; on the other hand, combined with Identity-ResNet of Mapping theory shortens the training time of the original residual network.

The main design ideas of the model used are twofold: Plain Network and Residual Network. First of all, the idea of Plain Network mainly comes from VGG neural network. Since small convolution kernel is more efficient than large convolution kernel, 3×3 filters are generally selected in plain network. There are two designs when designing plain network. Details: 1) In order to output feature maps of the same size, the same number of filters are used in each layer. 2) In order to ensure that the calculation time complexity of each layer is the same, if the dimension of the feature map is reduced to 1/2, we will use twice the number of filters; secondly, the network is based on the common network. Adding an identity shortcut implementation requires superimposing the input and output feature maps, which means that the dimensions of the input and output are the same.

In the shortcut, in order to construct an identity map of f(yl) = yl, we regard the activation functions (ReLU and BN [15]) as "pre-activation of the weight layer" instead of the traditional "post-activation"; It can be seen from the research results in the literature [1] that the effect of pre-activated is the best (Fig. 1).

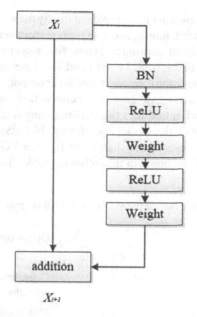

Fig. 1. Pre-activation process description

For a residual network ResNet-X (X is the number of layers of the network), it is mainly composed of two components: building block or bottleneck, as shown in the following figure:

There are two kinds of residual modules in ResNet-x. The difference is that the process in the process (H(x)) is different. This paper chooses the second module that performs more efficiently and takes less time, as shown in the figure below.

The module first uses the 1×1 convolution template for dimensionality reduction, 3×3 for convolution, and then uses 1×1 for dimensioning. Most importantly, after quoting this residual module, the model complexity of the 152-layer neural network ResNet-152 is much lower than that of VGG16 or 19.

In order to realize the problem of uniformity of the dimension of input and output, two main ideas are used: zero-complementing the position with insufficient dimension to achieve dimensional unification, and projecting and upgrading only in places where several dimensions are not uniform. Other places are still the way of identity.

In this experiment, the neural network input pixel is 224×224 image to be classified (or to be learned), and the algorithm of the algorithm is adapted to the BR algorithm in the processing of multi-label problem [16]—for each known possibility The included tags all have a corresponding two classifier. The neural network consists of 101 layers, which can be divided into seven parts according to the operation: the first part is a convolutional layer, 64 convolution kernels of size 7×7 are used, and the convolution operation is performed with a step size of 2. The product result is subjected to a max-pooling operation, and a preliminary image feature of 112×112 is output; the second part performs two operations, the first one is to use a 3×3 size convolution kernel and a stride. 2 Convolution operation and the same maximum pool connection, the result is input into three residual modules as shown in Fig. 3.3 (b), and finally the second part outputs 56×56 image feature vectors; the third, fourth, and fifth parts respectively It consists of 4, 23 and 3 residual modules. The residual learning and convolution operations are also performed. Finally, the feature vectors of 28×28, 14×14 and 7×7 are output respectively, where the input of each layer is The feature vector of one layer output; the last part is the 1000-d fully connected layer, and performs average-pool connection and softmax normalization operation. Since the network introduces two self-mapping relationships in design: f(x) (activation function) and h(x), the model complexity (FLOPS) of such a network with no parameters is 7.6×109, even lower than 16 or 19 layer VGG network.

The specific framework is shown in the following table (Table 1):

Table 1. Description of the structure of each layer of ResNet101

	Models			Operations	Output size
	Size	Number	Stride		
conv1	7×7	64	2	Convolution operation	112×112
conv2	3×3		2	Max-pooling	56×56
	$\begin{pmatrix} 1 \times 1,64 \\ 3 \times 3,64 \\ 1 \times 1,256 \end{pmatrix}$	3		Residual learning	
conv3	$\begin{pmatrix} 1 \times 1,128 \\ 3 \times 3,128 \\ 1 \times 1,1024 \end{pmatrix}$	4		Residual learning	28×28
conv4	$\begin{pmatrix} 1 \times 1,256 \\ 3 \times 3,256 \\ 1 \times 1,1024 \end{pmatrix}$	23		Residual learning	14×14
conv5	$\begin{pmatrix} 1 \times 1,512 \\ 3 \times 3,512 \\ 1 \times 1,2048 \end{pmatrix}$	3		Residual learning	7×7
Fully connected layer	1000-d			Average-pool + Softmax	$14 \times 14 \times 1024$

For an input image I, let all the known label sets in the Figure I be:

$$y = \left[y_1, y_2, \cdots, y_c\right]^T \tag{1}$$

Where C is the number of all known tags that may be included in the data set, T is a matrix transformation, and yl $(1 \leq l \leq C)$ is a binary variable. When $yl = 1$, the label l is in image I, and vice versa, then $yl = 0$.

Then the operation process of the neural network can be expressed as:

$$X = f_{cnn}(I; \theta_{cnn}), X \in R^{14 \times 14 \times 1024} \tag{2}$$

X represents the characteristic map of the output of the main network activation function "res4b22_relu" layer.

Based on the deep learning feature X of the input image, a preliminary prediction result is given by the main net(ResNet):

$$\hat{y}_{cls} = f_{cls}(X; \theta_{cls}), \hat{y}_{cls} \in R^{C} \tag{3}$$

The set of tag confidence values predicted by the primary network is:

$$\hat{y}_{cls} = \left[\hat{y}_{cls}, \cdots, \hat{y}_{cls}^{C} \right]^{T} \tag{4}$$

The forecasting process is shown below:
The measure of error is based on $\hat{y}_{cls}$ and the known label y (shown in Sect. 4.1).

3.2 Image Attention Mechanism (*fatt*)

In this paper, the feature vector X extracted based on deep neural network is taken as input. In the feature extraction process, a three-layer neural network is adopted, and the nonlinear ReLU function is used as the activation function. The first layer and the third layer are respectively composed convolution kernels which numbers are C and 512 and their size are both 1×1. And there are 512 convolution kernels in the second layer with the size of 3×3, and activation operations after layers 1 and 2. Then we can get the final attention as:

$$Z = f_{att}(X; \theta_{att}), Z \in R^{14 \times 14 \times C} \tag{5}$$

In which Z is the unnormalized label attention value of the function fatt(·) with parameters in the network as θatt. Then use the function softmax to normalize space Z, and then will get the attention map A like:

$$a_{i,j}^{l} = \frac{\exp\left(z_{i,j}^{l}\right)}{\sum_{i,j} \exp\left(z_{i,j}^{l}\right)}, A \in R^{14 \times 14 \times C} \tag{6}$$

$z_{i,j}^{l}$ and $a_{i,j}^{l}$ represent the attention values in the location (i, j) of label l that before normalization and after that.

Since the attention map of the correctly labeled label is not available, so the section fatt(.) can only be learned from the supervised image space. Let Xi, j $\in$ R1024 denote the visual feature vector of the image feature vector X at (i, j). In the original ResNet, the visual feature vector values at all spatial locations need to be averaged by the following formula before being used for classification.

$$x'_{i,j} = \frac{\sum\limits_{i,j} x_{i,j}}{7 \times 7} \tag{7}$$

We want to note that Al has a higher value for each label l in its label-related area, and has $\sum\limits_{i,j} a^l_{i,j} = 1$ for all l, used to use the attention map to weight the average visual characteristics of each label X:

$$v^l = \sum_{i,j} x_{i,j} a^l_{i,j}, v^l \in R^{1024} \tag{8}$$

The weighted average visual feature vector vl is more closely related to the image region corresponding to the label l than the original average visual feature shared by all tags. Each such feature vector is then used to learn a linear classifier to estimate the confidence of label l:

$$\hat{y}^l_{att} = W^l v^l + b^l \tag{9}$$

Wl and bl are parameters to the classification of label l. For all labels, there will be: $\hat{y}^l_{att} = [\hat{y}^1_{att}, \cdots, \hat{y}^C_{att}]^T$. Training is performed using only image level supervision y, and the parameters of the attention estimator are learned by minimizing the cross entropy loss between $\hat{y}_{att}$ and y.

In order to learn the attention map more effectively, we make:

$$\sum_{i,j} a^l_{i,j} = 1 \tag{10}$$

Then the formula (3–9) can be written as:

$$\hat{y}^l_{att} = \sum_{i,j} a^l_{i,j} \left(W^l x_{i,j} + b^l \right) \tag{11}$$

This equation can be seen as a linear classifier that applies a specific label at each corresponding position of the feature map X, and then spatially aggregates the label confidence based on the attention map. In our experiments, the linear classifier was used as a convolutional layer with the number of C cores of size 1×1 (see "conv1" in Fig. 2). The output of this layer is an attention map $S \in R14 \times 14 \times C$, in which its layer lth is Sl = Wl * X + b, and

* represents convolution operation. The label attention map A and the confidence map S are element-dependent multiplications, and then spatially aggregated to obtain the label confidence vector $\hat{y}_{att}$. This formula can generate an easy-to-implement network for learning label attention for generating attention-based confidence maps (in Sect. 3.4).

The above attention mechanism model is completed on the basis of the Encoder-Decoder structure. The Encoder is the main network in Sect. 3.1. With the Attention mechanism, the Decoder can select the required features in the input sequence and improve the performance of the Encoder-Decoder model.

For the sample in the data set, the above method is used for attention learning, and the final result is as shown in the following figure:

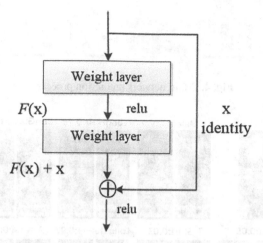

Fig. 2. Building-block of the residual network

3.3 Regularization and Spatial Association of Visual Attention Maps (*fsr*)

Regularization is the process of minimizing structural risk. Reference to the correct regularization method in the neural network can make the classification effect better. The regularization of the image space takes as input the $14 \times 14 \times C$ attention map (Fig. 3, 4, 5, and 6) obtained by weak supervised learning. The main operations include three-layer convolution operations. The specific frame diagram is as follows:

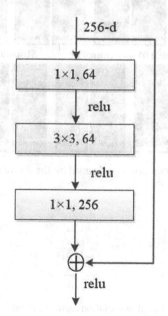

Fig. 3. Residual module used in this article

Fig. 4. Main network prediction process

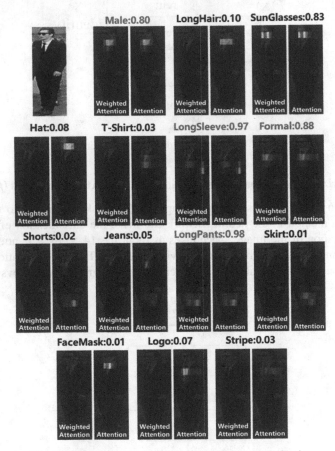

Fig. 5. The attention map learned by the above mechanism

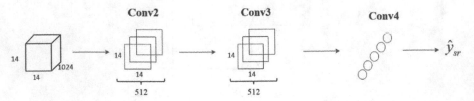

Fig. 6. Spatial association regularization structure

The first two layers set 512 filters of size $1 \times 1 \times C$, and finally produce 14×14 ($\times$ 512) output; The third layer groups the output of the previous layer, each of which is a group, which is divided into 512 groups and operate with 2048 filters of size $14 \times 14 \times 1$. Due to the inaccuracy of the true mark of the data set, the regularized image space learning from the weighted attention map $U \in R14 \times 14 \times C$ is selected:

$$U = \sigma(S) \circ A \tag{12}$$

In that:

$$\sigma(x) = \frac{1}{1 + e^{-x}} \tag{13}$$

is a sigmoid function used to convert the confidence value S into a number in the interval [0, 1]. Symbol "$\circ$" indicates that the array elements are multiplied in turn to get the weighted attention map U used to encode the attention and global visibility of each tag position confidence.

In the case of weighting the attention map U, a label regularization function is required to estimate the confidence of the label based on the label space information from U, so the resulting regularized prediction label confidence is:

$$\hat{y}_{sr} = f_{sr}(U; \theta_{sr}), \hat{y}_{sr} \in R^C \tag{14}$$

$\hat{y}_{sr} = \left[\hat{y}_{sr}^1, \hat{y}_{sr}^2, \cdots, y_{sr}^C \right]^T$ is the predictive label confidence through the label regularization function in that.

3.4 Cross-Entropy Loss Function Based on *Softmax*

Softmax regression can be seen as a generalization of logistic regression on classification problems. Let the classification label have c, the activation value of the image xi and the label j when fj(xi), then the posterior probability pij for the image xi and the label j are:

$$p_{ij} = \frac{e^{f_j(x_i)}}{\sum_{k=1}^{c} e^{f_k(x_i)}} \tag{15}$$

Then minimize the KL divergence of the model prediction label and the actual label (Kullback Leibler divergence, also known as relative entropy), which can be used to measure the difference between the two probability distributions - the theoretical distribution and the approximate distribution. For each label of each image, it can be assumed that each label is independent of each other, then these labels can form a label vector $y \in R1 \times C$, where yj = 1 means that the image marks the jth label. The opposite is the mark. The probability pij of the image xi and the label j can be obtained by the regularization operation on y:

$$\bar{p}_{ij} = \frac{y}{\|y\|_1} \tag{16}$$

Therefore, the overall cost function is minimized as:

$$J = -\frac{1}{m} \sum_{i=1}^{m} \sum_{j=1}^{c} \bar{p}_{ij} \log(p_{ij}) \tag{17}$$

3.5 Overall Network Structure and Training Method

The overall model architecture of this paper is below (Fig. 7):

As shown, the resulting label confidence is an aggregation of the primary network and SRN output:

$$\hat{y} = \alpha \hat{y}_{cls} + (1 - \alpha) \hat{y}_{sr} \tag{18}$$

Where α is a weighting factor. Although the weighting factor can be obtained through the training process, its performance is not significantly different from the value of 0.5. Therefore, in order to reduce the burden of training, we let $\alpha = 0.5$. The entire network is trained using the cross entropy loss function. The true value of the label is y, then:

$$F_{loss}(y, \hat{y}) = \sum_{l=1}^{C} y^l \log \sigma\left(\hat{y}^l\right) + \left(1 - \hat{y}^l\right) \log\left(1 - \sigma\left(\hat{y}^l\right)\right) \tag{19}$$

In the training, the pre-training results of 1000 classification tasks on the ImageNet data set are first used, and the main network is fine-tuned according to different target data sets. For both networks—fcnn(I;θcnn) and fcls(I;θcls) are trained using the cross entropy loss function, and then the cross entropy loss function is used to train fatt(I;θatt) and conv1; The fsr(U;θsr) is trained by adjusting the cross entropy loss function by adjusting all other sub-networks; finally, the whole network is jointly tuned with the overall loss function J.

The final model is implemented based on the Caffe library [17]. To avoid overfitting, a corresponding image enhancement strategy was used [18]. First adjust the input image to 256×256 size, and divide it into four corners and center of different sizes, where the width and height of the slice are randomly selected from the set $\{224,192,168,128\}$; finally, re-adjust the cropped The picture size is 224×224. The training was performed using a stochastic gradient descent algorithm with a batch size of 96, a momentum of 0.9, and a weight attenuation coefficient of 0.0005. The initial learning rate is set to 1×10^{-3}. When the loss reaches saturation, the initial learning rate is reduced to the original 0.1, and the iteration is stopped until $10-5$.

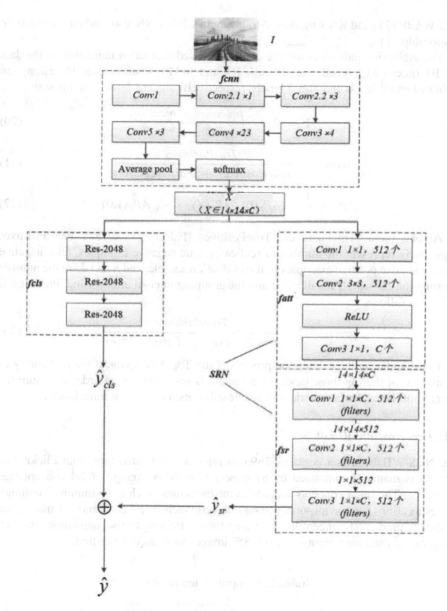

Fig. 7. Overall structure of the model

4　实验及结果

4.1　Evaluation Indicators and Comparison Methods

The experiment is based on the NUS-WIDE dataset [19]. To illustrate the effectiveness of the network, the experimental results compare the original ResNet101, CNN-RNN

[20], WARP [21] and KNN models. Among them CNN-RNN also studied the semantic relationship of tags.

The evaluation indicators use the commonly used evaluation indicators on the data set: F1 (micro-F1), recall rate (Recall, R), and mAP (MeanAverage Precision) are evaluated on all labels and Top-3 labels, respectively, and are defined as follows:

$$F1 = 2 \times \frac{precision \cdot recall}{precision + recall} \tag{20}$$

$$recall = \frac{TruePositives}{TruePositives + FalseNegatives} \tag{21}$$

$$mAP = \frac{1}{n} \cdot (AP_r(0), AP_r(d), \cdots, AP_r(1.0)) \tag{22}$$

Among them, TruePositives, TruePositives, FalseNegative, and FalsePositives respectively represent the number of real cases, true negative examples, false negative cases, and false positive examples in the evaluation sample, and n and d are the number of groups of the sample recall value and the grouping interval after sorting. Precision is defined as follows:

$$precision = \frac{TruePositives}{TruePositives + FalsePositives} \tag{23}$$

In particular, in the calculation process of the Top-3 indicator, if the probability of occurrence of the top three labels of a sample is less than 0.5, in order to ensure the integrity of the evaluation work, this article still uses it as the first three labels.

4.2 Experimental Result

The NUS-WIDE dataset contains 269,648 images and related tags from Flickr. The data set is manually annotated by 81 concepts, with an average of 2.4 concept tags per image. The main concepts include events/activities (such as swimming, running), scenes/locations (such as airports, oceans), objects (such as animals, cars). We trained our method to predict 81 concept labels. Using formal training/test segmentation, 161,789 images were used for training and 107,859 images were used for testing.

Table 2. Comparison test results

Models	All labels			Top-3	
	F1	R	mAP	F1	R
ResNet-101	72.1	69.1	59.8	61.7	69.1
CNN-RNN	–	–	–	55.2	61.7
WARP	–	–	–	53.9	60.5
KNN	–	–	–	47.6	53.4
Method of this paper	73.2	71.5	62.0	62.2	69.6

The experimental results of this data set are shown in the following table:

It can be seen from Table 2 that the model is superior to all existing models in terms of recall rate and the like. The CNN-RNN model shows that using the predictive label as the context (ResNet-101-semantic) also does not significantly improve the performance of the data set.

In order to explore the influence of the number of network layers on the classification of ResNet results, the 107-layer and 101-residue residual network used in this paper were compared in the image feature extraction, and the model comparison was made for the experimental results of all the labels and top-3 labels. The analysis and summary are illustrated in Table 3:

Table 3. Results of ResNet-X experiment

Models	All labels			Top-3	
	F1	R	mAP	F1	R
ResNet-101	72.1	69.1	59.8	61.7	69.1
ResNet-107	72.5	69.2	59.5	61.8	69.2

Experiments show that the performance of ResNet-107 is very close to that of ResNet-101 when adding more layers to match the size of our proposed SRN. This shows that the capacity of ResNet-101 in the data set NUS-WIDE is sufficient. Adding more parameters does not result in a significant increase in performance, but rather increases the cost of model training. In order to further reflect the contribution of the spatial and semantic relationship of the label to the classification performance improvement, we output the output of the fourth layer of neurons (Conv4) in the SRN part. The visualization results are shown in the following figure (Fig. 8):

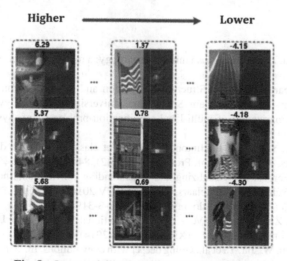

Fig. 8. Output of Conv4 on the NUS-WIDE data set

As can be seen from the figure, the output of SRN-Conv4 is mainly sensitive to the spatial and semantic association of image tags, and is very sensitive to the position changes of different semantic tags. Therefore, it can be further explained that the learned label space relationship provides a good regularization effect for multi-label image classification.

5   Conclusion

This topic mainly uses the BR framework in multi-label learning. The deep learning algorithm is used as the main network, and the visual attention mechanism and spatial association are introduced to improve the performance of the algorithm. The Python deep learning framework Caffe is used for programming. By comparing experiments with traditional classification algorithms (KNN), traditional deep learning algorithms (ResNet101, WARP) and semantic-based algorithms (CNN-RNN) in the same environment, each model is calculated for all labels and top3 according to the experimental results. The recall rate, F1 and mAP values of the label give the conclusion that the performance of the model is better.

However, since the algorithm is only tested for a typical data set, the performance of the model in terms of generalization is not known. In terms of model structure, only the combination of ResNet-101 and SRN framework has been tested, and the performance of other models combined with SRN has not been explored, that is, the performance of SRN framework itself has not been fully measured. Therefore, in the follow-up work, further exploration and research can be carried out for the above two aspects.

Funding. This research was funded by the National Natural Science Foundation of China under Grant No. 61762079, and No. 61662070, Innovation ability improvement project of colleges and universities in Gansu Province in 2019, Grant No: 2019B-024, the Fundamental Research Funds for the Central University of Northwest Minzu University, Grant No: 31920180050.

References

1. Li, S., Li, N., Li, Z.: Multi-tag data mining technology: a review. Comput. Sci. **40**(04), 14–21 (2013)
2. Chen, Z.: Research on Graph Structure Description and Several Learning Algorithms for Multi-label Classification Problem. South China University of Technology (2015)
3. Feng, X.: Summarization of multi-label classification problems. Inf. Syst. Eng. (03), 137 (2016)
4. Krizhevsky, A., Sutskever, I., Hinton, G.: ImageNet classification with deep convolutional neural networks. Adv. Neural Inf. Process. Syst. **25**(2), 84–90 (2012)
5. Zeiler, M.D., Fergus, R.: Visualizing and understanding convolutional networks. In: Fleet, D., Pajdla, T., Schiele, B., Tuytelaars, T. (eds.) ECCV 2014. LNCS, vol. 8689, pp. 818–833. Springer, Cham (2014). https://doi.org/10.1007/978-3-319-10590-1_53
6. Simonyan, K., Zisserman, A.: Very Deep Convolutional Networks for Large-Scale Image Recognition. Computer Science. arXiv:1049.1556 (2014)
7. Szegedy, C., Liu, W., Jia, Y., et al.: Going deeper with convolutions. In: 2015 IEEE Conference on Computer Vision and Pattern Recognition (CVPR), Boston, MA, USA, pp. 1–12 (2015)

8. Xu, K., et al.: Show, attend and tell: neural image caption generation with visual attention. In: ICML, vol. 2, no. 3 (2015)

9. Li, X., Zhao, F., Guo, Y.: Multi-label image classification with a probabilistic label enhancement model. In: Proceedings of the Uncertainty in Artificial Intelligence, vol. 1, no. 2 (2014)

10. Liu, G., Liu, S., Wu, J., Luo, W.: Machine vision target detection algorithm based on deep learning and its application in bill detection. China Test **45**(05), 1–9 (2019)

11. Wang, Y., Zhang, H., Huang, H.: A survey of image semantic segmentation algorithms based on deep learning. Appl. Electron. Tech. **45**(06), 23–27+36 (2019)

12. Li, Y.: Multispectral image and multi-label scene classification based on convolutional neural network. Electron. Des. Eng. **26**(23), 25–29 (2018)

13. He, K., Zhang, X., Ren, S., Sun, J.: Deep residual learning for image recognition. arXiv preprint arXiv:1512.03385 (2015)

14. He, K., Zhang, X., Ren, S., Sun, J.: Identity mappings in deep residual networks. In: Leibe, B., Matas, J., Sebe, N., Welling, M. (eds.) ECCV 2016. LNCS, vol. 9908, pp. 630–645. Springer, Cham (2016). https://doi.org/10.1007/978-3-319-46493-0_38

15. Ioffe, S., Szegedy, C.: Batch normalization: accelerating deep network training by reducing internal covariate shift. In: ICML (2015)

16. Montañes, E., Senge, R., Barranquero, J., et al.: Dependent binary relevance models for multi-label classification. Pattern Recogn. **47**(3), 1494–1508 (2014)

17. Jia, Y., et al.: Convolutional architecture for fast feature embedding. arXiv pre-print arXiv: 1408.5093 (2014)

18. Wang, L., Xiong, Y., Wang, Z., Qiao, Y.: Towards good practices for very deep two-stream ConvNets. CoRR, abs/1507.02159 (2015)

19. Chua, T.-S., Tang, J., Hong, R., Li, H., Luo, Z., Zheng, Y.: NUS-WIDE: a real-world web image database from National University of Singapore. In: Proceedings of the ACM International Conference on Image and Video Retrieval (2009)

20. Wang, J., Yang, Y., Mao, J., Huang, Z., Huang, C., Xu, W.: CNN-RNN: a unified framework for multi-label image classification. In: CVPR (2016)

21. Gong, Y., Jia, Y., Leung, T., Toshev, A., Ioffe, S.: Deep convolutional ranking for multilabel image annotation. In: ICLR (2014)

Author Index

Printed in the United States
By Bookmasters